OVERSIZE 303.6 P944p

Preventing violence

Preventing
Violence

Preventing
Violence

RESEARCH AND EVIDENCE-BASED
INTERVENTION STRATEGIES

Edited by JOHN R. LUTZKER

American Psychological Association • Washington, DC

Chapters 1, 5, 8, 12, and 13 were authored or coauthored by employees of the United States government as part of official duty and are considered to be in the public domain.

Published by
American Psychological Association
750 First Street, NE
Washington, DC 20002
www.apa.org

To order
APA Order Department
P.O. Box 92984
Washington, DC 20090-2984
Tel: (800) 374-2721
Direct: (202) 336-5510
Fax: (202) 336-5502
TDD/TTY: (202) 336-6123
Online: www.apa.org/books/
E-mail: order@apa.org

In the U.K., Europe, Africa, and the Middle East, copies may be ordered from
American Psychological Association
3 Henrietta Street
Covent Garden, London
WC2E 8LU England

Typeset in Goudy by World Composition Services, Inc., Sterling, VA

Printer: United Book Press, Baltimore, MD
Cover Designer: Naylor Design, Washington, DC
Technical/Production Editor: Harriet Kaplan

The opinions and statements published are the responsibility of the authors, and such opinions and statements do not necessarily represent the policies of the American Psychological Association.

Any views expressed in chapters 1, 5, 8, 12, and 13 do not necessarily represent the views of the United States government, and the authors' participation in the work is not meant to serve as an official endorsement

Library of Congress Cataloging-in-Publication Data
Preventing violence : research and evidence-based intervention strategies / edited by John R. Lutzker.
    p. cm.
  Includes bibliographical references and index.
  ISBN 1-59147-342-X
  1. Violence. 2. Family violence. 3. Violence—Prevention. I. Lutzker, John R., 1947- . II. American Psychological Association.
  HM1116.P738 2006
  303.6—dc22   2005015470

British Library Cataloguing-in-Publication Data
A CIP record is available from the British Library.

Printed in the United States of America
First Edition

To Jack and Zoe. May violence never touch their lives.

CONTENTS

CONTRIBUTORS

Ileana Arias, National Center for Injury Prevention and Control, Centers for Disease Control and Prevention, Atlanta, GA

Carl C. Bell, Community Mental Health Council, Chicago, IL

Eloise J. Berry, New Jersey Child Abuse, Research, Education and Services Institute, Stratford

Morris A. Blount Jr., Community Mental Health Council, Chicago, IL

Elissa J. Brown, St. John's University, Jamaica, NY

Rebecca J. Bulotsky-Shearer, Office of Research and Evaluation, School District of Philadelphia, PA

Leon D. Caldwell, University of Nebraska—Lincoln

Suzanne Camou, Virginia Commonwealth University, Richmond

Mark Chaffin, University of Oklahoma Health Sciences Center, Oklahoma City

Phaedra S. Corso, National Center for Injury Prevention and Control, Centers for Disease Control and Prevention, Atlanta, GA

Linda L. Dahlberg, National Center for Injury Prevention and Control, Centers for Disease Control and Prevention, Atlanta, GA

Esther Deblinger, New Jersey Child Abuse, Research, Education and Services Institute, Stratford

John W. Fantuzzo, University of Pennsylvania, Philadelphia

Albert D. Farrell, Virginia Commonwealth University, Richmond

Arthur M. Horne, The University of Georgia, Athens

Robin M. Ikeda, National Center for Injury Prevention and Control, Centers for Disease Control and Prevention, Atlanta, GA

Maureen C. Kenny, Florida International University, Miami

John R. Lutzker, National Center for Injury Prevention and Control, Centers for Disease Control and Prevention, Atlanta, GA

Christine M. McWayne, New York University, New York

K. Daniel O'Leary, State University of New York at Stony Brook

Pamela Orpinas, The University of Georgia, Athens

Le'Roy E. Reese, National Center for Injury Prevention and Control, Centers for Disease Control and Prevention, Atlanta, GA

Jerome Richardson, Cook County Department of Public Health, Oak Park, IL

Melissa K. Runyon, New Jersey Child Abuse, Research, Education and Services Institute, Stratford

Susan Schmidt, University of Oklahoma Health Sciences Center, Oklahoma City

Thomas R. Simon, National Center for Injury Prevention and Control, Centers for Disease Control and Prevention, Atlanta, GA

Cris M. Sullivan, Michigan State University, East Lansing

Elizabeth M. Vera, Loyola University Chicago

Erica M. Woodin, State University of New York at Stony Brook

Jennifer M. Wyatt, National Center for Injury Prevention and Control, Centers for Disease Control and Prevention, Atlanta, GA

PREFACE

Virtually any civilized human being would undoubtedly agree that violence is a serious problem for society and for individuals touched by it. Less consensus would likely be apparent when people are asked if violence is preventable. To many, violence may seem an unavoidable problem given the nature and circumstances of many humans. Is it possible to end all violence? Realistically, probably not. Is it possible to drastically reduce violence? Absolutely. How? There are many ways that violence can be reduced. They are broad in scope and require policy changes by governments; solid economic conditions; support for violence prevention, social change, and attitude and behavior change; community support; and a host of other sociological, environmental, political, and even biobehavioral efforts.

The purpose of this book is to focus on one significant, hopeful, and effective mechanism for examining and trying to reduce violence, that being the application of the public health model to violence prevention. In chapter 1, the authors detail the public health model and provide a brief rationale for why the model is so useful in violence prevention as well as a rationale for the forms of violence covered in this volume: child maltreatment, youth violence, intimate partner violence, and self-inflicted violence (suicide). The argument made in favor of the public health model is that is is focused on prevention and steeped in science in its examination of etiology and surveillance, the development and evaluation of effective interventions and prevention programs, the replication and dissemination of effective programs, and the ability to educate and inform the public about public health problems such as violence.

Another basic tenet of this volume is that violence prevention must be examined within, guided by, and implemented within the context of carefully conceived and executed science. Much attention today is given to the need for evidence-based intervention and prevention programs. Each chapter in this book offers evidence and suggestions for improvements in the empirical base for violence prevention research.

In chapter 1, Lutzker and Wyatt provide an overview of the book, a rationale for how the book is organized, and an overview of the data on the prevalence of the forms of violence covered. Part I of the book covers child maltreatment. In chapter 2, Runyon, Kenny, Berry, Deblinger, and Brown examine the etiology and surveillance of child maltreatment. In chapter 3, Chaffin and Schmidt review evidence-based interventions. In chapter 4, Fantuzzo, Bulotsky-Shearer, and McWayne describe a model for targeting relevant competencies for child maltreatment victims.

The second section of Part I covers youth violence in three chapters. Dahlberg and Simon review developmental pathways, risks, and implications for prevention in chapter 5. School-based interventions are covered by Farrell and Camou in chapter 6; bullying is the topic of chapter 7 by Orpinas and Horne.

Part II covers intimate partner violence, suicide, crosscutting issues, and cultural-competence etiology. Intimate partner violence surveillance is covered in chapter 8 by Arias and Ikeda and interventions to address intimate partner violence in chapter 9 by Sullivan. Suicide is reviewed in chapter 10, a single comprehensive chapter by Bell, Richardson, and Blount, because there are fewer empirically based intervention programs for this problem. Crosscutting issues, especially between child maltreatment and intimate partner violence, are examined in chapter 11 by O'Leary and Woodin. The role of culture and the need to address it in violence prevention are addressed in chapter 12 by Reese, Vera, and Caldwell. Finally, in chapter 13, Lutzker, Wyatt, and Corso analyze common issues addressed in this book and provide commentary on the role of economic evaluation in violence prevention research.

This book can be used as a resource for professionals, students, agencies, and policymakers. It can also serve as a primary or secondary text in courses related to violence prevention within a variety of academic disciplines, given the interdisciplinary nature of violence prevention.

ACKNOWLEDGMENTS

Thanks to Alex Crosby, Lynda Doll, Linda Koenig, Courtney Pippen, Le'Roy Reese, Emilie P. Smith, and Daniel J. Whitaker, each of whom provided some consultation in the development of this book. I particularly express gratitude to Jennifer M. Wyatt, who in addition to coauthoring two chapters with me provided considerable assistance with the preparation of the book. James A. Mercy provided a number of helpful editorial comments and reviews along with other suggestions. Finally, Susan Reynolds at the American Psychological Association has been endlessly helpful, gracious, and patient in the conception and development of this volume.

Preventing Violence

1

INTRODUCTION

JOHN R. LUTZKER AND JENNIFER M. WYATT

Violence is a major public health problem in the United States and elsewhere. The number of violent deaths and violence-related injuries remains alarming. Though more prevalent in certain racial and ethnic groups and lower socioeconomic status individuals, the effects of violence impact all people in some way, directly or indirectly. There are serious health, social, economic, and personal sequelae from violence (Krug, Dahlberg, Mercy, Zwi, & Lozano, 2002). This book provides an overview of how the public health model is applied to violence prevention. Data are presented on the incidence and prevalence of child maltreatment (CM), youth violence, intimate partner violence (IPV), and suicide. Within each of these areas, there are chapters covering interventions. We will introduce the volume in this chapter and provide necessary background information.

Recent mortality data indicate a rate of 17.99 fatal injuries from violence per 100,000 people (51,326 individuals) and a rate of 758 per 100,000 for nonfatal violence-related injuries treated in emergency departments

This chapter was authored by employees of the United States government as part of official duty and is considered to be in the public domain. Any views expressed herein do not necessarily represent the views of the United States government, and the authors' participation in the work is not meant to serve as an official endorsement.

($N = 2,163,373$; Centers for Disease Control and Prevention [CDC], 2003b). In 2002, data collected through the National Child Abuse and Neglect Data System indicated that 2.6 million reports of suspected CM were made to child protective services (CPS), and 1,400 children died as a result of abuse or neglect (U.S. Department of Health and Human Services, Administration on Children, Youth and Families, 2004). Almost 66,000 juvenile arrests for violent crimes were made in 2000, and nearly one third of these arrests were of youths under 15 years old (U.S. Department of Justice, 2001). Over 1,200 women (a third of all female murder victims) were killed by an intimate partner in 2001 (Rennison, 2003). The National Violence Against Women Survey has found that among women who were physically assaulted by a partner, 42% sustained injuries, and 28% of those injured received medical attention (CDC, 2003a). Among women who were sexually assaulted by an intimate partner, 36% sustained injuries, and 31% of those injured received medical treatment (CDC, 2003a). Further, there were over 29,000 incidents of fatal self-directed violence (i.e., suicide) in 2000, and over 250,000 nonfatal self-inflicted injuries were treated in emergency departments (CDC, 2002).

Violence has been defined by the World Health Organization (WHO) as

> the intentional use of physical force or power, threatened or actual, against oneself, another person, or against a group or community, that either results in or has a high likelihood of resulting in injury, death, psychological harm, maldevelopment, or deprivation. (Krug et al., 2002, p. 5)

In this volume, the authors examine four types of violence related to the WHO definition: CM, youth violence, IPV, and suicidal behaviors. These areas correspond to those funded within the Division of Violence Prevention in the National Center for Injury Prevention and Control at the CDC. The four-step public health model depicted graphically in Figure 1.1 provides the basis for the CDC's scientific approach to a wide array of diseases, disorders, and injuries. It also offers an ideal vehicle for addressing the prevention of violence-related outcomes; thus, it serves as the framework for the succession of chapters within each content area. Steps 1 and 2 (defining the problem and identifying risk and protective factors) involve the descriptive and etiological research on a public health problem. Thus, each topical section of this book contains one or more chapters that pertain to definitional issues, surveillance mechanisms, incidence and prevalence data, and risk and protective factors that have been identified for that type of violence. Discussions of risk and protective factors also include attention to the relevant mediating and moderating variables that can alter the course of development by those at risk of violent perpetration or victimization.

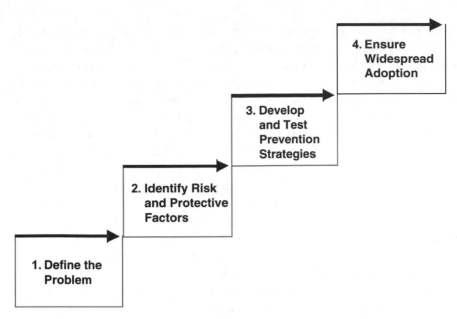

Figure 1.1. The public health approach to prevention.

For example, in sections on child physical abuse and neglect, Runyon, Kenny, Berry, Deblinger, and Brown (see chap. 2, this volume) discuss parental mental health and substance abuse, poverty and correlates of poverty, and other violence in the home or in the parents' history as factors that increase the likelihood of the occurrence of maltreatment and exacerbate the effects of CM on a child's socioemotional or physical growth trajectory.

Step 3 of the public health model uses knowledge gained through surveillance and etiological research to develop and test prevention strategies and programs. In doing so, researchers must consider questions of optimal times, settings, modes, and levels of interventions for actual or potential victims and perpetrators—the answers to which often differ for groups defined by variables such as age, gender, socioeconomic status, personal history, and race or ethnicity. In addition, during this phase of public health research, valuable knowledge is accumulated through studies of efficacy (program success as measured under controlled research conditions) and effectiveness (program success in more naturalistic settings). For example, in youth violence prevention, this would mean a range of activities from developing a school-based youth violence prevention program teaching a number of problem-solving and conflict-diffusing skills to evaluating an extant community-based program aimed at preventing youth violence through extracurricular engagement of youth.

Ensuring widespread adoption, Step 4 of the public health model, represents a focus on the adaptation and application of tested prevention strategies for use by broader constituencies in "real-world" settings. An example of these activities would include using the results of an effective program aimed at preventing IPV, modifying the intervention on the basis of those results (if necessary), and disseminating the program for use by state and local health departments. Or, this step could involve using the media to prevent youth suicide through a targeted campaign. The overarching goal of this step is to increase the utility of proven programs by those outside the research community while still maintaining the integrity of the strategies that have withstood scientific rigor to show positive results.

Part and parcel of the public health model is good science. The basic goals of science (e.g., standards for outcome measurement and study design and the procedures of proposing, testing, replicating, and modifying hypotheses) are applicable to the model and to the focus of this book. Behavioral phenomena, such as the areas of violence covered here, should be measured by direct or indirect observation rather than by relying solely on self-reports, especially when the outcomes of interest deal with perpetration of violence. These phenomena should be measured with valid and reliable measures that can then be used to predict and, we hope, change behavior. The science must be robust and described in a manner sufficient for replication. Dissemination and replication must be informed by evidence-based research and should in turn inform future research efforts. Thus, work described and suggested in this volume is largely based on these premises.

CHILD MALTREATMENT

In the United States, nearly 900,000 children are known victims of CM annually (U.S. Department of Health and Human Services, Administration on Children, Youth and Families, 2004). This figure is based on data collected nationally from CPS records. These data represent a conservative estimate of the incidence of CM because they only count the number of cases that were reported, investigated, and substantiated. Because CM often goes undetected, the true incidence of CM is difficult to determine.

CM was only recognized professionally in 1962 (Kempe, Silverman, Steele, Droegemueller, & Silver, 1962). Initial etiological theories suggested intrapsychic reasons that would lead a parent to perpetrate CM. It did not take long, however, for experts to recognize a host of other factors (such as socioeconomic status, social isolation, cultural norms about physical punishment and violence, and characteristics of the child) likely contribute to CM. Thus, the dominant perspective over the past several years could be called social–ecological.

In chapter 2 of this volume, Runyon and colleagues detail the etiology and surveillance of CM. Clear from their discussion is the need for uniform definitions in CM so that data are more valid. Another serious problem with the validity of CM data is that many of the data are gleaned from reports from CPS. It is not clear, for a variety of reasons, that CPS caseworkers make the most informed decisions as to when to indicate or substantiate CM in any given family. Reasons for indicating or substantiating CM often go beyond the immediate circumstances of the child or family and may vary because of personal history of a caseworker; training issues; previous experience with a family; caseload issues; the current political climate in a region, city, county, or child welfare office; and a host of other variables. This speaks also to the need for standardized definitions of CM, highly structured training and monitoring of caseworkers, and manageable workloads for caseworkers. As noted by Runyon and colleagues, the etiology of CM requires multifaceted research. To date there is limited information on the potential biological role played in poor parenting along with other personal variables of parents. A host of situational factors and some child factors may contribute to CM, and there is insufficient evidence about child and parent protective factors on which to base preventive interventions.

Chaffin and Schmidt (see chap. 3, this volume) discuss promising interventions for child physical and sexual abuse and caveats associated with results from evaluations of such programs. In addition, they point out that one of the greatest needs in the field of CM prevention is the translation from research on to widespread implementation of evidence-based programs. In chapter 4 of this volume, Fantuzzo, Bulotsky-Shearer, and Wayne offer a model on which to base a comprehensive, communitywide system for the prevention of CM. Together, these two chapters provide not only an overview of CM interventions but also a vision for the future of more successful prevention efforts.

YOUTH VIOLENCE

According to the Federal Bureau of Investigations, 16% of those arrested for violent crimes in 2000 were under age 18, and a third of those were under age 15 (Snyder, 2002). Although violent behavior tends to peak in adolescence, 20% to 45% of seriously violent teenage offenders continue to engage in violent behavior well into adulthood (see chap. 5, this volume).

The bulk of the empirical work in youth violence prevention has been conducted in school-based programs. There have been some good empirical efforts with large-scale projects in this area. Prevention and intervention have been addressed through universal projects that may include all youth in sample schools, selective programs that are intended for high-risk youth in sample schools, and targeted interventions for youth already exhibiting violent behavior. Behaviors and attitudes have been positively affected by many of these efforts. Still in need of investigation are broader dissemination of such efforts and examination of implementation issues as it becomes more difficult for schools and teachers to be asked to incorporate more than basic education (the "three Rs") into their curricula.

Though the majority of empirical work in youth violence prevention has occurred in schools and though there are many community efforts to prevent youth violence, many fewer of these efforts have been systematically evaluated. With shrinking resources and changing priorities, it would seem all the more important to conduct efficacy and effectiveness evaluations to ensure that only effective and cost-effective programs are disseminated. It will also be worthwhile to examine comprehensive, broad-based community-level social–ecological approaches with schools, communities, and individuals. Dahlberg and Simon (see chap. 5, this volume) argue the importance of addressing multiple social ecologies (e.g., the youth, their peers, and their parents) in preventing or reducing youth violence, highlighting two successful programs (the Seattle Social Development Project and Multi-systemic Therapy).

INTIMATE PARTNER VIOLENCE

Data from the National Crime Victimization Survey indicate that during 2001, 20% of violent crimes against women were committed by intimate partners, for a total of 588,490 IPV victimizations (Rennison, 2003). Because these self-report data are dependent on the respondents' perceptions of whether IPV is a crime, they are generally considered to be underestimates of the incidence of IPV. Surveys designed specifically to assess violence (rather than crime more generally) report higher rates of IPV and are more likely to capture victimization rates accurately (see chap. 8, this volume). The National Violence Against Women Survey (CDC, 2003a) estimated that each year 1,309,061 women are physically assaulted by an intimate partner, and 201,394 women are sexually assaulted by an intimate partner (CDC, 2003a).

Interventions to address IPV have primarily been conducted through three general modalities: community-based services for victims, interventions for perpetrators, and coordinating councils (see chap. 9, this volume). Unfortunately, systematic and rigorous outcome evaluations of IPV interventions have not been the mode. Further, crosscutting work between IPV and CM interventions for victims and perpetrators has been quite limited. Numerous community, theoretical, empirical, practical, logistic, funding, and advocacy issues have created or fostered some of the gaps in empirical and crosscutting work in IPV. Some of the barriers and potential solutions are presented in this volume.

SUICIDE PREVENTION

Comprehensive violence prevention efforts should include self-directed violence in addition to violence directed toward others. In 2000, there were 29,350 fatal suicides and an estimated 264,108 nonfatal suicidal behaviors (CDC, 2003b). The costs of suicide can be measured not only with hospitalization costs immediately associated with nonfatal suicidal behaviors but also with mental health and hospitalization costs in the months prior to and following a suicide attempt (Corso & Haileyesus, 2004) and with years of potential life lost for those who die by their own hand.

Although etiological data in suicide are quite rich, research in suicide prevention has been limited. Aside from obvious research obstacles (e.g., low frequency of the target behavioral outcome in small samples and the dearth of proxy measures with adequate sensitivity and specificity to predict who will engage in self-harm behaviors and who will not), there simply has not been much of a focus on evidence-based analyses of programs and outcomes. There is a great need to conduct research at the primary prevention level, particularly for youth, but primary prevention should be applied with older samples as well.

CROSSCUTTING THE VIOLENCE AGENDAS

The need for crosscutting work in violence prevention appeared in the 2002 *Injury Research Agenda* published by the National Center for Injury Prevention and Control (NCIPC; 2002). Beginning in December 2000, NCIPC staff collaborated with and sought input from various groups to guide the development of a set of research priorities in areas of violence and unintentional injuries. The first draft was guided by input from researchers, practitioners, and policymakers as well as by NCIPC staff. Next, topical workgroups composed of experts in specific fields were convened to prioritize and refine the agenda. In the final steps, public comment and expert feedback were solicited. The resulting document was intended to guide injury research and programs, and included specific sections on IPV, CM, suicidal behavior, and youth violence.

A clear theme among the recommendations for research in violence prevention was the need for crosscutting efforts. The pathways from CM to other areas of violence covered in the present volume are becoming increasingly clear. Victims of CM are at higher risk for perpetrating youth violence as they grow older, for perpetrating violence against women, and for attempting suicide than children who have not suffered the victimization of CM (Berliner & Elliott, 2002; Ehrensaft et al., 2003; Kolko, 2002). As elaborated by O'Leary and Woodin in chapter 11 of this volume, researchers, service providers, and advocates in CM and IPV have held separate agendas and, for the most part, have not conducted their research, service, or advocacy informed by their counterparts in other arenas. Yet it seems clear that to conduct truly effective research, service, and advocacy in CM and IPV, one area should inform the other, and collaborative efforts will likely lead to more effective outcomes. This logic naturally extends to youth violence and suicide prevention. In addition to research collaborations across violence topics, researchers should also engage in partnerships with the community to more effectively inform research, service, and advocacy efforts. Though Fantuzzo and colleagues (see chap. 4, this volume) detail this argument only with respect to CM prevention, such partnerships are equally necessary in youth violence, suicide, and IPV prevention.

All work in violence prevention must be sensitive to the role and function of culture, as suggested in chapter 12 of this volume by Reese, Vera, and Caldwell. This issue is especially relevant in ethnic minority communities because of the prevalence of violence in them and the limited success of interventions and prevention programs to date in those communities. These authors point out that awareness of the place of cultural variables in addressing violence in a community is insufficient if successful efforts in prevention and intervention are to be made. Cultural values and norms must be appropriately considered and addressed to create effective assessments and programs. They also note that cultural relevance can be treated in the same manner as any other component of a program should be. For example, cultural relevance needs to be validated before implementing a program, and outcomes should be addressed in part through examinations of whether the cultural relevance played a role in the outcome. Doing so can ultimately improve the likelihood of favorable outcomes in violence prevention in ethnic minority communities.

THE DEVELOPMENTAL STATUS OF VIOLENCE PREVENTION RESEARCH

There are more chapters in this volume devoted to prevention of CM and youth violence than there are devoted to prevention of IPV and suicide. The chapters of the book devoted to CM and youth violence have been included in Part I: Evidence-Based Research: Child Maltreatment and Youth Violence; whereas the chapters devoted to IPV and suicide are included in Part II: Developing Research Arenas: Intimate Partner Violence and Suicide. This is because CM and youth violence interventions have a more robust evidence base at this stage than the areas of IPV and suicide. The majority of youth violence prevention has been conducted in schools; this is reflected in two chapters devoted to the issue. The etiology of suicide has been extensively researched, but there is little suicide prevention research. This is in no way to diminish or dilute the needed efforts in the developmental arenas; however, the work is simply not as developed, particularly in evidence-based intervention research on these topics. Youth violence prevention and CM prevention research and service have received research funds and legislative actions longer than intimate partner and suicide prevention efforts. For example, the Child Abuse Prevention and Treatment Act was first legislated in 1974; whereas the Violence against Women Act was first legislated in 1994.

That there is a more stable knowledge base in CM and youth violence prevention and that scientific intervention efforts are being developed in IPV and suicide speaks all the more for the need for crosscutting efforts in all four of these arenas. The developing arenas can glean much information from the evidence bases in CM and youth violence prevention. The developing areas can also gain from the experience of the evidence-based arenas, especially from the increasing validation of the pathways from CM and the correlated prevalence of IPV with other forms of family violence. It seems eminently logical that a melding of research agendas in these areas would serve to benefit each.

TERMINOLOGY

Although the title of this volume, *Preventing Violence: Research and Evidence-Based Intervention Strategies*, seems clear, each word could cause discussions among researchers, practitioners, advocates, policymakers, and survivors about the "correct" definitions. Hence, several chapters in this volume contain entire sections devoted to the definitional issues that limit our ability to draw conclusions from different surveillance and evaluation efforts. Recognizing the validity and potential volatility of this issue, we have created a "primer" on the language used in this book by its multiple contributors. Our intent here is neither to define nor redefine the terminology of the field. Rather, we have created a common lexicon for readers.

With respect to violence, decades have been spent by those in the field debating the most valid and accurate means by which to operationalize each of the different forms of violence. The conventions used here are intended to help inform, not further divide, the field. General definitions such as these are not precise enough for specific research, intervention, or policy purposes.

Violence Prevention Definitions

Aggression is a relatively general term used to label all behaviors intended to physically or psychologically harm another, whether or not through the use of physical force. A subset of aggressive behaviors is referred to as *violence*, wherein threatened or actual physical force is intentionally used to harm another. The four types of violence serving as the topical foci for this volume are child maltreatment, youth violence, intimate partner violence, and suicide.

Child maltreatment (abbreviated here as "CM") is often subdivided into (a) child physical abuse, in which real or threatened physical harm or injury results from a caregiver's nonaccidental actions; (b) child sexual abuse, in which the child is exposed to or involved in sexual behavior or images inappropriate to his or her developmental level; and (c) child neglect, in which the caregiver fails to provide for a child's physical, emotional, medical, mental health, or educational needs.

Intimate partner violence (abbreviated here as "IPV") generally refers to physical, psychological, or sexual violence between adults in an intimate relationship and is the term most used in this volume for this type of adult-to-adult violence. *Domestic violence* is a subset of IPV that only includes violence occurring between married and cohabiting individuals. Some terms also refer to different levels of severity, intensity, or duration of IPV. For example, *partner aggression* refers to one partner intending to physically or psychologically harm the other, whereas *battering* is used to describe a more chronic succession of aggression and violence in which the batterer also engages in the practices of fear, isolation, or intimidation of the victim.

Youth violence involves a youth exhibiting violent behavior toward another youth or an adult. *Bullying* is one type of youth violence typified by a more powerful youth committing repeated acts of physical, verbal, relational, sexual, or racial or cultural aggression or violence against a less powerful youth.

Suicide is used to describe acts of self-directed violence, which can be nonfatal (sometimes referred to as *attempted suicide*) or fatal (sometimes referred to as *completed suicide*).

The word *prevention* is no less of a professional minefield than the word *violence*. For the most part, prevention is used here in the general sense, as in the prevention of violent behavior in the future, regardless of whether the individual engaged in violent behavior in the past. *Primary prevention* specifies actions to avoid the first occurrence of violence. When in combination with or in contrast to *prevention, intervention* and *treatment* specify actions to avoid the recurrence of violent behaviors. When *interven-*

tion is used alone as a noun (e.g., "although the intervention does focus on parent–child interaction"), it is similar in meaning to *program* and means the actual activities provided for the target population.

There is also a vocabulary for describing the target population of an intervention. Prevention strategies can be *universal* or *targeted* with respect to population, and targeted strategies may be either *selective* or *indicated*. Universal prevention strategies are those offered or administered to the general population (usually within a geographically defined region); whereas targeted prevention strategies are offered or administered to a subset of the general population. Within targeted prevention strategies, selective interventions are designed for individuals or groups considered to be at higher risk for the undesirable outcome, and indicated interventions are designed for individuals or groups who have already engaged in the undesirable outcome.

Our primer here is intended to allow a common lexicon for this volume. That said, the reader will note that these terms are best understood within the context of their use in each chapter, in part because of the unique definitional interpretations of each contributing author.

IS VIOLENCE PREVENTABLE?

The goal of this book is to offer clear hope that violence, a very serious public health problem, is preventable. Compared with most other fields of basic and applied science, the field of violence prevention is still in a nascent stage. However, there is ample testimony in this volume that a scientific groundwork is being laid for increasingly improved surveillance and more informed etiology that has and will lead to interventions for violence that are promising, efficacious, or effective. As will also become apparent, there are gaps in these areas and a need for much closer cross-fertilization in CM, youth violence, IPV, and suicide. In chapter 11 of this volume, O'Leary and Woodin provide an excellent framework for how such cross-fertilization can occur. Each of the topical areas of violence covered in this volume will also benefit from improvements made in any of these arenas and from keeping a close eye on relevant work in the biobehavioral aspects of violence and psychosocial research in aggression. Finally, researchers in the field will also make strides as they understand better how to bridge the gap between research and service. That is, as etiology, surveillance, prevention and intervention strategies are refined, much more research is needed in implementation and dissemination research in violence prevention.

REFERENCES

Berliner, L., & Elliott, D. M. (2002). Sexual abuse of children. In J. E. B. Myers, L. Berliner, J. Briere, C. T. Hendrix, C. Jenny, & T. A. Reid (Eds.), *The APSAC handbook on child maltreatment* (2nd ed., pp. 55–78). Thousand Oaks, CA: Sage.

Centers for Disease Control and Prevention. (2002). Nonfatal self-inflicted injuries treated in hospital emergency departments—United States, 2000. *Morbidity and Mortality Weekly Report, 51,* 436–438.

Centers for Disease Control and Prevention. (2003a). *Costs of intimate partner violence against women in the United States.* Atlanta, GA: National Center for Injury Prevention and Control, Centers for Disease Control and Prevention.

Centers for Disease Control and Prevention. (2003b). *Web-based injury statistics query and reporting system (WISQARS).* National Center for Injury Prevention and Control, Centers for Disease Control and Prevention. Retrieved October 22, 2003, from http://www.cdc.gov/ncipc/wisqars

Child Abuse Prevention and Treatment Act, as amended, 42 U.S.C. § 5101 et seq. (1974).

Corso, P., & Haileyesus, T. (2004, October). *Defining episodic costs of injuries: The case of suicide attempts.* Poster session presented at the Annual Meeting of the Society for Medical Decision Making, Atlanta, GA.

Ehrensaft, M. K., Cohen, P., Brown, J., Smailes, E., Chen, H., & Johnson, J. G. (2003). Intergenerational transmission of partner violence: A 20-year prospective study. *Journal of Consulting and Clinical Psychology, 71,* 741–753.

Kempe, C. H., Silverman, F. N., Steele, B. F., Droegemueller, W., & Silver, H. K. (1962). The battered child syndrome. *Journal of the American Medical Association, 181,* 17–24.

Kolko, D. J. (2002). Child physical abuse. In J. E. B. Myers, L. Berliner, J. Briere, C. T. Hendrix, C. Jenny, & T. A. Reid (Eds.), *The APSAC handbook on child maltreatment* (2nd ed., pp. 21–54). Thousand Oaks, CA: Sage.

Krug, E. G., Dahlberg, L. L., Mercy, J. A., Zwi, A. B., & Lozano, R. (Eds.). (2002). *World report on violence and health.* Geneva, Switzerland: World Health Organization.

National Center for Injury Prevention and Control. (2002). *Injury research agenda.* Atlanta, GA: Centers for Disease Control and Prevention.

Rennison, C. M. (2003). *Intimate partner violence, 1993–2001* (NCJ 197838). Washington, DC: U.S. Department of Justice, Bureau of Justice Statistics.

Snyder, H. N. (2002). *Juvenile arrests 2000* (NCJ 191729). Washington, DC: U.S. Department of Justice, Office of Juvenile Justice and Delinquency Prevention.

U.S. Department of Health and Human Services, Administration on Children, Youth and Families. (2004). *Child maltreatment 2002.* Washington, DC: U.S. Government Printing Office.

U.S. Department of Justice. (2001). *Crime in the United States—2000* (Federal Bureau of Investigation, Uniform Crime Reports). Washington, DC: U.S. Government Printing Office.

Violence Against Women Act, 42 U.S.C. § 13981 (1994).

I

EVIDENCE-BASED RESEARCH: CHILD MALTREATMENT AND YOUTH VIOLENCE

SECTION INTRODUCTION:
CHILD MALTREATMENT PREVENTION

Research in child maltreatment to date is both relatively advanced and in need of considerable expansion and improvement. The advancements are noteworthy: Numerous data have been collected over the past 40 or more years on the extent of the problem; there is more concrete evidence than ever before as to some of the risk and protective factors; there are some demonstrably efficacious and effective prevention and intervention programs; and there are efforts to disseminate effective programs. On the other hand, as indicated in chapter 2 in this section, the definitional problems in child maltreatment are sufficient to question the validity of all incidence and prevalence data, all risk and protective factor data are correlations and have not yet been tied closely enough to prevention and intervention programs to be able to best inform such programs, only a relative handful of evidence-based programs are efficacious and effective, and most programs that have been widely disseminated have not been evaluated or have been poorly evaluated. Thus, there is considerable need for major advancements in child maltreatment research covering surveillance, etiology, evaluation of applied programs, and examinations of broad dissemination of effective programs.

In chapter 2, Runyon and colleagues spell out the high incidence and prevalence data in child maltreatment and note why these data may represent serious underreporting. They also note that child neglect remains the modal reason for indicating a family for child maltreatment. Complicating the overall definition and surveillance problems in child maltreatment is the fact that kinds of maltreatment may overlap in many families.

When one examines the risk factor data, it becomes apparent that the modal factors relate more closely to broader social–ecological issues than individual family characteristics. Thus, for example, poverty is the single biggest predictor of neglect, yet few programs specifically target poverty for prevention and intervention, and often if there is a program aimed at battling poverty, there may be no assessment of that program's effect on child neglect.

In chapter 2, the authors provide a full discussion of the negative sequelae of child maltreatment. These sequelae range from short term to lifetime and create serious psychological burdens along with physical health consequences for victims. There are also considerable social and economic costs to society. In addition to covering risk factors and outcomes of physical child abuse and neglect, in chapter 2, the authors examine prevalence, outcomes, and risk factors for sexual abuse. Recent scandals regarding the clergy have opened the public's eyes to the problem of sexual abuse. Because the sequelae of sexual abuse are seriously deleterious, it is hoped that increased attention and outrage by the public will lead to increased funding for research aimed at identifying and preventing the sexual abuse of children.

Peers as perpetrators of child maltreatment have often been overlooked. Although chapter 7 in the section on youth violence prevention is devoted entirely to the subject of bullying, Runyon and colleagues also give attention to this topic in chapter 2 because bullying is a form of child maltreatment that also has serious side effects for victims and for society.

Important recommendations emerge from chapter 2. The authors stress the need for longitudinal studies that can far better inform researchers in child maltreatment about outcomes from the problem. The need to further explore protective factors is well stated. The more information that can be gleaned on protective factors, the more prevention programs and interventions can be tailored to try to "vaccinate" children and their families who may lack such factors. For example, if the data continue to show the importance of frequent utterances and talking to very young children by their parents (Hart & Risley, 1995), programs should examine how to translate this information into behavioral skill-building strategies that encourage parents at risk to speak more often and more affectionately to their children.

In chapter 3, Chaffin and Schmidt move the discussion of child maltreatment from etiology and surveillance to evidence-based interventions. The authors are quick to point out how few efficacy and effectiveness evaluations have been conducted on the multitude of child maltreatment prevention and intervention programs. They cover in detail five behavioral skill–based models that have had evaluations. Additionally, they examine programs for child victims of sexual abuse and cognitive–behavioral interventions for perpetrators of child sex abuse. It is clear that there is a need for more programs aimed at victim treatment and at changing perpetrator behavior and that such programs are in need of stronger evaluation research. The authors review home-visiting programs and conclude that overall results of these programs have been disappointing. Recently, however, the Centers for Disease Control and Prevention has concluded that home-visiting programs do offer promise in the prevention of child maltreatment (Task Force on Community Preventive Services, 2003). Finally, in chapter 3, the authors review the limited evaluation literature on sex abuse prevention programs. Many professionals working in child maltreatment prevention believe that these programs offer the best hope of reducing the incidence of child maltreatment, especially sex abuse. Unfortunately, thorough evaluations of these programs have been too few; more are in order.

In chapter 4, Fantuzzo, Bulotsky-Shearer, and McWayne focus on a wellness model for victims of child maltreatment. For some time, Fantuzzo and colleagues have stressed and addressed the critical importance of community involvement in all aspects of community-based research in child maltreatment. They have pointed to the need for having community members active in the selection of assessment measures and in the implementation of programs. This theme is stressed again in chapter 4, in which there is additional discussion of work done by this group on helping high-risk children transition to school by making use of known protective factors. Socially skilled children were used as social facilitators for low-interactive children who were victims of child maltreatment. This intervention model helped greatly in the successful transition to school for the child victims.

Cultural sensitivity and responsiveness are mentioned in each chapter. Increasing attention has appropriately been given to the need for cultural awareness and relevant responses in all human service programs. Child maltreatment is no exception. Fantuzzo and colleagues provide models for involving inner-city communities in all levels of planning applied research. Considerable research is possible and needed on cultural norms that may serve as protective or risk factors regarding child maltreatment. Such information can also be used in the development and evaluation of prevention and intervention programs. As applied researchers in recent years have attempted to examine fidelity processes, that is, the degree to which intervention protocols are implemented in the manner that they were prescribed, so too should programs look at how well staff are trained and whether they are successful in implementing the cultural components of programs.

Since 1962, much progress has been made in the legal, legislative, assessment, surveillance, etiology, and intervention arenas. More thorough science is clearly needed in this young century to make a dent in the incidence of child maltreatment. Needed are tighter definitions, evaluation of laws, validated training in risk assessment and decision making, quantitative evaluations of extant programs, and development and evaluation of universal and selected prevention programs.

REFERENCES

Hart, B., & Risley, T. R. (1995). *Meaningful differences in the everyday experience of young American children.* Baltimore: Brookes Publishing.

Task Force on Community Preventive Services. (2003). First reports evaluating the effectiveness of strategies for preventing violence: Early childhood home visitation. *Morbidity and Mortality Weekly Report, 52*(RR-14), 1–9.

2

ETIOLOGY AND SURVEILLANCE IN CHILD MALTREATMENT

MELISSA K. RUNYON, MAUREEN C. KENNY, ELOISE J. BERRY,
ESTHER DEBLINGER, AND ELISSA J. BROWN

Child maltreatment is a highly prevalent public health problem that has short- and long-term negative consequences for child victims and their families. Child physical abuse (CPA), child sexual abuse (CSA), and child neglect have been acknowledged as forms of child maltreatment for some time. However, peer abuse or bullying has only just begun to be recognized as a serious form of maltreatment. Recent child abuse statistics indicate that approximately 2.6 million reports of possible maltreatment are made to child protective service agencies each year (U.S. Department of Health and Human Services [USDHHS], 2004). In 2002 alone, 896,000 cases of child abuse and neglect were substantiated across 50 states. According to the National Child Abuse and Neglect Data System, approximately 81% of these cases involved abuse and neglect by a parent (USDHHS, 2004). Of the perpetrators, 60% were women; 40% were men. Of these cases, 60% were related to neglect (523,704 cases), 19% to physical abuse (166,920 cases), and 10% to sexual abuse (88,656 cases). Although data compiled by state child protective services do not include statistics on peer abuse—which of course is not committed by a caregiver—recent data indicate that 8% of students reported that they had been bullied in school in the past

6 months compared with 5% in 1999 (U.S. Department of Education, 2002).

Unfortunately, these startling statistics are most likely underestimated given that many cases go unreported. And when they are reported, they may not be investigated, as evidenced by reports that only 26% of the cases of seriously injured and moderately injured children were investigated by child protective service agencies (Sedlak & Broadhurst, 1996). In cases of CSA, national surveys of the children themselves indicate that the rates may be about 10 times higher than the reports made by professionals working with children (Finkelhor & Dziuba-Leatherman, 1994; Gallup Organization, 1995). It is important to note that many children experience more than one form of victimization (Finkelhor & Dziuba-Leatherman, 1994; USDHHS, 2002).

Nonetheless, these devastating statistics highlight the need to develop and empirically test effective prevention and intervention models to target these widespread issues that negatively impact children and families as well as society. A lack of uniformity among state legal definitions as well as subjective judgments about what constitutes maltreatment have contributed to the complex and contradictory data that are reported regarding the prevalence rates and socioemotional consequences of maltreatment. However, the National Incidence Study of Child Abuse and Neglect—3 (NIS–3; Sedlak & Broadhurst, 1996) broadened the definitions of CPA, CSA, and neglect by collecting data from professionals in the community in an effort to capture child abuse incidents that may not have been reported to state child protective service agencies. In this chapter, we present the broad definitions that are generally used by professionals in the field for these types of maltreatment. Research findings are summarized related to risk factors, etiology, psychosocial impact on children, and protective factors for each type of maltreatment. These factors are of the utmost importance because they inform the development of effective prevention models.

NEGLECT

Definition and Prevalence of Neglect

Although neglect constitutes a majority of the reports made to state child protection agencies (USDHHS, 2004), it has been ignored in the intervention and research arenas relative to physical and sexual abuse. There is a paucity of research on neglect, with available data emphasizing primarily the observable physical effects. However, many types of neglect leave no discernable marks or bruises (Erickson & Egeland, 2002) and do not necessarily result in an immediate observable impact on the child's functioning, which further complicates the task of identifying children who have been neglected.

Defining neglect is a complex task, with little consensus among the experts. Unlike other forms of child maltreatment, neglect is defined by the absence of specific events. In general, it is a failure to provide care (passive), rather than an overt act (active; Erickson & Egeland, 2002). There are currently five major subtypes of neglect (Erickson & Egeland, 2002). Failure to provide adequate food, clothing, and shelter represents *physical neglect*, which is defined as a failure to provide for a child's physical needs. *Emotional neglect* is defined as a failure to provide for a child's emotional needs. In extreme cases, this can lead to nonorganic *failure to thrive* (stunted growth and physical illness or abnormalities) that can even result in death. Children who suffer from failure to thrive do not develop appropriately from an emotional, cognitive, or physical standpoint related to a lack of stimulation in their environment or inadequate food and nutrition (Miller-Perrin & Perrin, 1999). *Medical neglect* is defined as a failure to provide or comply with prescribed medical treatment for a child such as immunizations, surgery, or medications. Although it is not a widely accepted or investigated form of neglect, mental health neglect involves a failure to provide or comply with recommended corrective or therapeutic procedures in cases of serious emotional or behavioral disorders. Last, *educational neglect* is defined as a failure to comply with state requirements for school attendance.

In the identification of neglect, Miller-Perrin and Perrin (1999) advocated considering issues such as frequency and duration of neglectful acts and severity of consequences. Single neglectful events may occur in many families; thus, neglect may need to be defined on the basis of the chronicity of the behavior. The same behavior (e.g., lack of parental supervision) can be more dangerous in some situations and can result in more severe consequences for the child compared with other situations.

According to national data for 2002 (USDHHS, 2004), a rate of 7.2 victims per 1,000 children in the United States experienced neglect. In a prospective study by Chaffin, Kelleher, and Hollenberg (1996) that examined data from Waves I and II of the National Institute for Mental Health's Epidemiologic Catchment Area survey, 7,103 parents who did not report neglect were followed over time. From Wave I to Wave II, 84 parents (1.2%) endorsed at least one neglectful act.

Studies have noted a high rate of reoccurrence for neglect when compared with physical or sexual abuse (Marshall & English, 1999; Zuravin & DePanfilis, 1996). Marshall and English (1999) reported a 53% higher chance of multiple recurrent referrals when physical neglect is the primary allegation. This is similar to other reports of a 27% chance of reoccurrence of maltreatment for children who had been neglected (USDHHS, 2004).

Risk Factors and Conceptual Model

The association between neglect and multiple demographic, perpetrator, and child-related risk factors has been examined. Among the most commonly identified is poverty (see Slack, Holl, McDaniel, Yoo, & Bolger, 2004). Living in areas of localized high unemployment is likely to put families at risk for neglect (Gillham et al., 1998). On the basis of official reporting statistics from the American Association for Protecting Children, Miller-Perrin and Perrin (1999) reported that neglect appears to be related to ethnicity, with rates being highest for African American and Hispanic children. Similar findings were reported in a 17-year longitudinal study examining a nationally representative sample conducted by Brown, Cohen, Johnson, and Salzinger (1998). Because ethnicity is also related to socioeconomic status, which has been identified as one of the greatest correlates, the relationship between ethnicity and neglect remains unclear. However, results from this longitudinal investigation do support the association between neglect and low maternal education, parental age, and marital status, with young single parents being at increased risk (Brown et al., 1998).

Compared with abusive parents, those who neglect their children are more likely to experience difficulties (Bath & Haapala, 1993) such as anger control problems, low self-esteem, parental psychopathology, and parental sociopathy (Brown et al., 1998). Other factors associated with neglect include violence in the marital relationship and lack of a social support network (Dubowitz, 1999), parental alcohol abuse (Bath & Haapala, 1993; Dube, Anda, Felitti, Croft, et al., 2001), parental unemployment (Dubowitz, 1999; Gillham et al., 1998), and a history of child abuse in mothers (Weston et al., 1993; Zuravin & DiBlaso, 1992). With respect to parenting variables, a nationally representative sample revealed that low parental involvement and low parental warmth are associated with neglect (Brown et al., 1998). Family-of-origin factors associated with neglect included early separation from mother and maternal alienation. Child variables, including anxiety and withdrawal, a low verbal IQ, premature birth, and low birth weight, also seemed to be associated with an increased risk for child neglect (Zuravin & DiBlaso, 1992).

Impact of Neglect on Children

On the basis of our current knowledge base, neglect may have the most far-reaching implications for children's psychological and physical outcomes when compared with other forms of abuse (Azar, Povilaitis, Lauretti, & Pouquette, 1998). These consequences range from short- to long-term psychosocial difficulties and even death. However, there is a lack of research that directly examines the unique effects of child neglect on children's functioning (Miller-Perrin & Perrin, 1999). Available data from a number of studies have described neglected children as having anxious attachments; lacking enthusiasm; and being easily frustrated, angry, and noncompliant but also as being highly dependent on their mothers for help (see Erickson & Egeland, 2002). Observations indicate that young children (ages 3.5–6 years) display poor impulse control, rigidity, a lack of creativity, and general adjustment problems in school. Children who were neglected, compared with those who suffered physical abuse, were found to be more emotionally withdrawn and inattentive (Erickson & Egeland, 1996). Other findings have shown that child victims of neglect seem to lack self-confidence, concentration, and social skills necessary for them to succeed in school and interpersonal relationships (Erickson & Egeland, 2002) and are socially withdrawn (Hildyard & Wolfe, 2002). These children also exhibit an array of internalizing and externalizing problems, such as apathy and withdrawal, low self-esteem, conduct disorder, and physical and verbal aggression (Hildyard & Wolfe, 2002; Miller-Perrin & Perrin, 1999).

Law and Conway (1992) reviewed a number of studies that support effects of neglect on children's language development with associated delays ranging from 6 to 9 months. These delays include greater difficulty in verbal comprehension, articulation, and cognitive development. Relative to physically abused children, neglected children demonstrated more severe cognitive and academic deficits (Hildyard & Wolfe, 2002); consistently scored lower on standardized math, language, and reading tests than their peers (Kurtz, Gaudin, Wodarski, & Howing, 1993); and were ranked low by their teachers in peer acceptance and overall emotional health (Erickson & Egeland, 2002).

Mediating Factors

The effects of neglect on children are not inevitable or invariant (Gaudin, 1999), and these effects may be mediated by protective factors (Gaudin, 1999). The outcome for a child victim of neglect may be dependent on the interaction of a variety of potential influences (Erickson & Egeland, 1995). For example, Kurtz et al. (1993) examined a sample of children who had been neglected; they found no deficits in adaptive functioning. They hypothesized that these children may gain the personal care and communication skills they need for survival from other support persons, despite parents' not providing adequate care for them. Other studies have reported that mothers of children with failure to thrive who are given support, care, and knowledge of feeding and nurturing may decrease the long-term impact of neglect on children (Zuravin & DiBlaso, 1992), which emphasizes the need to have a supportive parent actively involved in the treatment of the child (Weston et al., 1993).

Definitions and Prevalence of Child Physical Abuse

Given the lack of uniformity among state legal CPA definitions, the NIS–3 (Sedlak & Broadhurst, 1996) broadened the definition of CPA and categorized physical punishment administered by caregivers as physical abuse if either the harm (sustained injury) or endangerment (at risk for injury) standard was met as a result of being hit by a hand or an object, kicked, thrown, shaken, burned, stabbed, or choked. Also, *child physical abuse* has commonly been defined as the nonaccidental (not necessarily intentional) injury of a child under the age of 18 by a parent or caregiver (Kemp, 1998). Nonaccidental injuries include, but are not limited to, beating, shaking, burning, immersion in scalding water, broken bones, internal injuries, human bites, cuts, and bruises. Others have added the caveat that CPA occurs whenever the parent or caregiver willfully injures, causes, or allows the child to be injured or maimed or when considerable force is used (Kemp, 1998). According to Kemp (1998), CPA should include injury, risk of injury, and fear of injury by the child.

Surveys using these broad definitions for CPA have yielded different rates. The NIS–3 reported an incidence rate of approximately 9 per 1,000 children (Sedlak & Broadhurst, 1996). A national telephone survey conducted by Finkelhor and Dziuba-Leatherman (1994) with a sample of 2,000 children ages 10 through 16 revealed that 5.2% reported having been assaulted by a family member during the previous year, and approximately 20% of these were assaulted by a parent (resulting in a rate of 0.9%). Other studies have yielded much higher incidence rates of CPA, such as a rate of 49 per 1,000 children (The Gallup Organization, 1995), which is more than 5 times the rate reported in the NIS–3. In a prospective study by Chaffin et al. (1996) examining data from Waves I and II of the National Institute of Mental Health's Epidemiologic Catchment Area survey, 7,103 parents who did not report CPA were followed over time. From Wave I to Wave II, 63 parents (0.9%) endorsed at least one item representing CPA.

Risk Factors and Conceptual Model

Multiple factors, including perpetrator, victim, and family variables, associated with an increased risk for a child to experience CPA have been examined. Although only some of those factors have been summarized here, a complete review of the literature has been conducted by Black, Heyman, and Smith Slep (2001). With respect to perpetrator characteristics, anecdotal reports and statistics based on reports to child protective services have suggested that a young single woman with a low socioeconomic status from an ethnic minority population may be at risk for engaging in CPA. However, studies examining nationally representative samples have not demonstrated a significant relationship between severe child–parent physical abuse and age of perpetrator (Chaffin et al., 1996; Wolfner & Gelles, 1993), marital status (Chaffin et al., 1996; Connelly & Straus, 1992), parent gender (Chaffin et al., 1996; Connelly & Straus, 1992), and socioeconomic status (Chaffin et al., 1996; Connelly & Straus, 1992; Wolfner & Gelles, 1993). Results examining the relationship between CPA and ethnic group have varied (Chaffin et al., 1996; Connelly & Straus, 1992; Straus, Hamby, Finkelhor, Moore, & Runyan, 1998). These contradictory results are most likely related to reporting biases as well as biases in child protective service investigations of lower income minority groups. It is notable that age of perpetrator (Straus, 1994) and gender (Straus, 1994; Wolfner & Gelles, 1993) were associated with minor parent–child aggression that does not meet state and legal definitions for CPA but has been defined as corporal punishment (Straus, 1994). Substance abuse and depression have also been associated with CPA, with depression being the stronger risk factor (Chaffin et al., 1996). Specifically, depressed parents were 3.45 times more likely to engage in CPA when compared with nondepressed parents.

In his examination of the NIS–3 data, Sedlak (1997) identified child-related variables that may increase a child's risk for CPA. He found that the relationship between a child's age and CPA varies depending on ethnic group and family structure. Specifically, older children were at the greatest risk for CPA in Black and Hispanic populations if both parents were living in the home. Male and female children were equally at risk for being physically abused (Sedlak, 1997). On the basis of data collected in the National Survey of Child Maltreatment and Parenting, Sedlack (1997) reported that children ages 3 to 6 were at greater risk than older children for minor physical victimization (e.g., spanking and shoving), but children of all ages were at equal risk for severe physical victimization.

Some studies have demonstrated a positive correlation between severe CPA and number of children in the home, but results were inconsistent across independent samples (Chaffin et al., 1996; Connelly & Straus, 1992; Wolfner & Gelles, 1993). With respect to family of origin, fathers and mothers who were physically abused during adolescence are at 1.76 and 2.64 times greater risk, respectively, for abusing their children compared with those who did not experience CPA (Ross, 1996).

Over the past 3 decades, several theoretical models have been proposed to conceptualize the development and maintenance of abusive parent–child interactions in families. These include a parental psychopathology model (Spinetta & Rigler, 1972), a developmental–ecological model (Belsky, 1993), as well as comprehensive ecobehavioral approaches (see Lutzker, Van Hasselt, Bigelow, Greene, & Kessler, 1998). A detailed description of individual theoretical models can be found in a number of good reviews (Hansen, Sedlar, & Warner-Rogers, 1999; Kolko, 2002). However, for the purposes of this chapter, a cognitive–behavioral model integrating elements from several conceptual models is used to conceptualize coercive parent–child interactions, because cognitive–behavioral treatment (CBT) approaches have gained the most empirical support to date (see Corcoran, 2000; Kolko, 1996).

According to Patterson's (1982) social learning model, parents use familiar parenting strategies, which may involve coercive and violent disciplining techniques, to control their children's behavior. When the target behavior initially stops, the parent's coercive behavior is reinforced. To expand on the behavioral model, others have proposed models that include parental cognitions and appraisals as a variable that mediates the relationship between children's behavior problems and the use of coercive parenting strategies (see Dadds, Mullins, McAllister, & Atkinson, 2002; Milner, 2003). When children fail to meet their parents' unrealistic expectations, preexisting schema based on past and present experiences as well as external stressors may result in parents' negative interpretations of their children's behavior that have been associated with an increase in parental anger (Averill, 1978; Bandura, 1977) and the use of punishment in child-rearing situations (Grusec, Dix, & Mills, 1982). Thus, as the parents' anger increases, they may revert to coercive parenting behavior. Because parents who engage in coercive practices tend to lack anger regulation skills (see Hansen & MacMillan, 1990), general parenting knowledge, and parental problem-solving abilities (see Azar, 1989), the coercive behavior is maintained when the parental anger subsides and the child complies. It may then be necessary for parents to use more coercion (e.g., yelling, threatening, spanking, and beating) over time to gain their child's compliance as the child begins to habituate to the previous strategy (see Urquiza & McNeil, 1996). This cycle can result in a chronic and escalating pattern of parent–child conflict.

Impact of Physical Abuse on Children

Research has identified a wide range of emotional, psychological, behavioral, and interpersonal difficulties, ranging from mild to severe, that are exhibited by children who have experienced CPA. On the basis of child victim reports, common emotional responses include anger, hostility, guilt, shame, anxiety, and depression (e.g., Famularo, Kinscherff, & Fenton, 1992; Pelcovitz et al., 1994). Studies have also provided support for the association between posttraumatic stress disorder (PTSD) and CPA (Ackerman, Newton, McPherson, Jones, & Dykman, 1998), with rates of PTSD ranging from 7% to 36% (Ackerman et al., 1998; Deblinger, McLeer, Atkins, Ralphe, & Foa, 1989). Additionally, some of the most frequent behaviors reported for children who experience CPA are aggressive behavior, poor social problem-solving and communication skills, and lower levels of empathy and sensitivity toward others (e.g., Dodge, Pettit, & Bates, 1994; Salzinger, Feldman, Hammer, & Rosario, 1993). When compared with their nonabused peers, victims of CPA alienate themselves from their peers (Salzinger et al., 1993), given their tendency to interpret interactions with peers as hostile (Dodge, Pettit, & Bates, 1990) and to respond in a retaliatory manner. These negative behaviors may escalate across the life span, as evidenced by documented relationships between CPA and criminal behavior in adolescents (Herrenkohl, Egolf, & Herrenkohl, 1997) and adults (Widom, 1989), abusive or coercive behaviors in dating relationships (Wolfe, Wekerle, Reitzel-Jaffe, & Lefebvre, 1998), an increased risk of being battered by a partner during adulthood (see Kanner, Bulik, & Sullivan, 1993), and an increased risk for adult survivors to abuse their own children (Crouch, Milner, & Thomson, 2001). These studies suggest that CPA not only has an immediate negative psychological impact on children but also may lead to psychosocial difficulties that persist into adulthood and potentially impact the victims' adult relationships as well as the next generation of children. In addition to the socioemotional and behavioral impact of CPA, associated medical and physical injuries have been identified that may be associated with long-term brain impairment, intellectual deficits, learning disabilities, language and comprehension deficits, and poor academic performance (see Kolko, 2002).

Mediating Factors

A number of protective factors have been identified that may buffer children from the negative effects of CPA and that can explain the variability in symptom development in child victims. With respect to CPA populations, a study involving 585 families with 5-year-old children demonstrated that peer acceptance and friendships moderated the association between family adversity and externalizing behavior problems (Criss, Pettit, Bates, Dodge, & Lapp, 2002). These effects were not qualified by gender, ethnicity, child temperament, or social information processing.

With regard to child-specific traits, Brown and Kolko (1999) reported that abuse-specific attributions were related to abuse-specific fears such as going to court or being taken away from home; whereas internal attributions were related to depression and anxiety in child victims of CPA. Depression in children who have been physically abused has also been associated with negative general attributions (Runyon & Kenny, 2002). Another study by Toth, Cicchetti, and Kim (2002) identified general attributional style as a moderator of externalizing behavior problems. Children's perceptions of parents were related to internalizing and externalizing behaviors, such that children who had less positive perceptions of their parents had more behavior problems. These studies support the notion that children's perceptions about the abuse, themselves, others, and the world mediate the development of postabuse symptomatology.

To address the multifaceted issues related to child physical abuse, researchers and clinicians have begun to examine the utility of structured CBT that focuses not only on the offending parent but on the child victim as well (Kolko, 1996; Kolko & Swenson, 2002; Runyon, Deblinger, Ryan, & Thakkar-Kolar, 2004). A randomized controlled trial (Kolko, 1996) found that the CBT and family therapy conditions, compared with routine community care, were associated with relative improvements in parent reports of child externalizing behavior problems, parental distress, abuse risk, and family conflict and cohesion as well as child reports of internalizing symptoms. However, CBT was most effective relative to the other two conditions for reducing parental anger and the use of physical punishment (Kolko, 1996). Other researchers have directly examined the added benefit of including the child in the parents' treatment (Runyon et al., 2004). This combined parent–child CBT model (Runyon et al., 2004) incorporates elements from empirically supported CBT models for child maltreatment (Deblinger & Heflin, 1996; Donohue, Miller, Van Hasselt, & Hersen, 1998; Kolko, 1996; Kolko & Swenson, 2002; Runyon, Basilio, Van Hasselt, & Hersen, 1998) and has three primary goals: (a) to reduce the recurrence of CPA by helping parents learn nonviolent disciplining and anger control strategies, assisting them in altering faulty beliefs about who is responsible for the abuse, and challenging unrealistic expectations and misattributions about the causality of their children's behavior; (b) to decrease children's emotional distress by assisting them in processing their abusive experiences and developing adaptive coping skills; and (c) to increase positive parent–child interactions that are necessary for beneficial developmental outcomes for children.

CHILD SEXUAL ABUSE

Definition and Prevalence of Child Sexual Abuse

The term *child sexual abuse* may be broadly defined as the exploitation, involvement, or exposure of children to age-inappropriate sexual behavior by older or "more powerful" peers or adults for purposes of sexual gratification. Although all states have laws against child molestation (Meyers, 1992), each state has its own individual definition of CSA for purposes of child protection and law enforcement. Abusive sexual acts imposed on children may include, but are not limited to, penile penetration of the vagina or anus, oral genital contact, simulated intercourse, and direct genital touching as well as noncontact sexual acts such as exposure and voyeurism. In many instances, potential child victims are engaged in a process of *grooming*, in which the offender slowly gains the child's trust while gradually introducing the child to increasingly invasive sexual behaviors (Berliner & Conte, 1990). Offenders also may use physical force, verbal threats, bribes, gentle coaxing, or playfulness to both engage children in inappropriate sexual interactions and encourage the maintenance of secrecy (Conte, Wolfe, & Smith, 1989). Research has, in fact, documented that the vast majority of children remain silent about their abuse regardless of whether the abuse was a single incident or repetitive episodes over the course of many years (Paine & Hansen, 2002).

Numerous studies have been conducted producing varying incidence and prevalence rates depending on the definitions of CSA and the methodologies used to collect information. Still, the overall findings reveal disturbingly high rates of CSA in the general population. The national incidence rate of CSA in the NIS–3 was 4.4 per 1,000 children (Sedlak & Broadhurst, 1996). Retrospective reports from adults have revealed even higher rates. Telephone and mail surveys on a national probability sample of adults indicated that about 30% of women and 15% of men reported a contact sexual offense by age 18 (Finkelhor, 1994). Weighted average estimates based on a series of studies reviewed by Fergusson and Mullen (1999) indicated that approximately 10.4% of child molesters are immediate family members (i.e., parents, stepparents, or siblings). An estimated 47.8%, the largest category of child molesters, appear to be acquaintances known to the child as family friends, neighbors, boyfriends, girlfriends, and so forth. The remaining offenders include other relatives outside the immediate family and strangers.

Risk Factors and Conceptual Model

Although CSA impacts children across all educational, socioeconomic, racial, and ethnic groups (Wyatt & Peters, 1986), there are factors that may place some children at higher risk for experiencing such abuse. Girls are at higher risk for sexual abuse than boys, particularly with respect to intrafamilial abuse. In addition, boys and girls may be at increased risk if they have lived without a natural parent, experienced significant family conflict (Finkelhor, 1993), or exhibited behavioral or developmental disabilities (Sullivan & Knutson, 2000). Unfortunately, the limitations of the studies that have identified these risk factors as well as the overinclusive nature of the characteristics preclude any effective means of identifying potential victims of CSA.

Similarly, research suggests that there is little value in attempting to identify a characteristic sex offender personality profile. In fact, child molesters appear to present a wide variety of personality styles and psychopathological disorders. They do not typically limit their abuse to certain types of victims, and they may engage in other paraphilic or criminal behaviors. It should also be noted that sex offenders often begin to engage in sexually abusive behavior patterns in their teenage years, and there appears to be no upper age limit for offenders; sex offenses may be committed against children by individuals well into their senior years.

Our understanding of the etiology of CSA remains limited, although it is a long-standing problem that cuts across most if not all cultures around the world. Although there is evidence that a certain percentage of sex offenders have a history of CSA, the majority of child molesters do not report such a history. The popular belief that most sex offenders are reenacting their own childhood experience of sexual abuse is not supported by research. In fact, only a small percentage of child molesters appear to have a history of sexual abuse, although this is a higher rate than in the general population. Thus, such a history may underlie sexually abusive behaviors in some cases, particularly in combination with other factors such as lack of parental support, no specialized treatment, and other traumatic experiences. However, it appears that the majority of sex offenses cannot be explained by reenactment theories. The most widely held theories explaining CSA suggest a variety of mechanisms leading offenders to engage children in sexual acts. These include (a) the identification with children on an emotional level; (b) sexual attraction to children; (c) the inability to form meaningful intimate relationships with adults; and (d) the lack of sensitivity to or respect for social norms as a result of factors such as mental retardation, senility, and substance abuse (Araji & Finkelhor, 1985).

Impact of Sexual Abuse on Children

The psychosocial impact of CSA on its victims varies widely. Although some children suffer full-blown PTSD, major depression, sexual behavior problems, and other severe and sometimes long-lasting psychiatric difficulties, other children appear to be asymptomatic, particularly in the immediate aftermath of a disclosure and investigation (Kendall-Tackett, Williams, & Finkelhor, 1993). However, it should be noted that children who exhibit seemingly resilient initial responses may deteriorate over time (Calam, Horne, Glasgow, & Cox, 1998; Gomes-Schwartz, Horowitz, Cardarelli, & Sauzier, 1990).

In fact, numerous studies have documented the negative long-term effects of CSA (Beitchman et al., 1992). For example, a study of sexual and physical victimization experiences in childhood and adulthood documented that after controlling for relevant background variables, CSA was the most powerful predictor of later psychiatric difficulties (Briere, Woo, McRae, Foltz, & Sitzman, 1997). Additionally, there is mounting evidence suggesting that CSA increases one's risk for suffering sexual dysfunctions, substance abuse difficulties, suicidal behaviors, and revictimization experiences in adulthood (Arata, 2000; Briere & Runtz, 1990; Dube, Anda, Felitti, Chapman, et al., 2001).

Mediating Factors

In general, the great variability in psychological adjustment following sexual abuse has led to numerous studies conducted in an effort to identify potential protective factors. The findings of studies examining abuse characteristics as possible mediating influences have been somewhat inconsistent. However, the following abuse factors have been associated repeatedly with increased postabuse symptomatology: (a) abuse involving physical force, (b) abuse involving more invasive sexual contact (e.g., intercourse), and (c) abuse perpetrated by fathers or stepfathers (Beitchman et al., 1992; Browne & Finkelhor, 1986). Although these factors may be useful in gauging a child's risk of developing symptoms, they are not immutable characteristics of abuse and have limited value as direct targets of intervention. On the other hand, studies examining the psychosocial responses of victims and their nonoffending parents have offered findings that may have more direct implications for treatment. The findings of several studies suggest that survivors whose coping responses are characterized by avoidance, denial, or self-blame tend to exhibit more negative psychological outcomes (Johnson & Kenkel, 1991; Leitenberg, Greenwald, & Cado, 1992). Similarly, researchers have found that negative parental responses appear to be associated with higher symptom rates in children who have suffered sexual abuse (Kendall-Tackett et al., 1993), and not surprisingly, more positive, supportive parental reactions are associated with lower symptom rates (Everson, Hunter, Runyan, Edelson, & Coulter, 1989). Although supportive parental reactions have been defined differently across studies, they generally include believing the allegations, taking steps to protect the child, and responding appropriately to the child's disclosures and difficulties.

These findings seem to highlight the value of involving and assisting nonoffending parents in their efforts to respond to their children's therapeutic needs while also emphasizing the importance of directly helping children to develop effective coping responses. In fact, a series of randomized controlled trials has documented the benefits of cognitive–behavioral approaches in individual and group formats that incorporate parent and child interventions (Cohen, Deblinger, Mannarino, & Steer, 2004; Cohen & Mannarino, 1996, 1998; Deblinger, Lippmann, & Steer, 1996; Deblinger,

Stauffer, & Steer, 2001; King et al., 2000). In general, the treatment outcome research in this field, though limited, is providing increasing evidence supporting the value of structured, trauma-focused approaches that involve the nonoffending parent in helping children recover from the experience of sexual abuse (Deblinger & Heflin, 1996).

PEER ABUSE

Definition and Prevalence of Peer Abuse (Bullying)

Peer abuse, or bullying, is often overlooked as a serious form of childhood maltreatment. Given that peer abuse has just begun to be recognized as a form of child maltreatment, we are providing a brief overview in this chapter. For a more detailed discussion, see chapter 7 in this volume by Orpinas and Horne. By definition, a child or student is bullied or victimized "when he or she is exposed, repeatedly and over time, to negative actions on the part of one or more other students" (Olweus, 1993, p. 9). Bullying includes a wide range of behaviors from very mild (e.g., verbal taunts) to extreme (e.g., aggressive behaviors leading to physical injury and even death; Bosworth, Espelage, & Simon, 1999). Different types of bullying have been identified: physical (contact or noncontact from fighting to posturing), verbal, sexual (direct or indirect bullying based on sexual issues such as sexual orientation or bodily development), and racial or cultural (direct or indirect bullying based on racial, ethnic, or other cultural issues).

The prevalence of reports of bullying by students in one school term differs, ranging from a low of 15% to 20% in some countries to a high of 70% in others (Nansel et al., 2001). Using a nationally representative sample of 15,686 students in Grades 6 through 10 in public, Catholic, and private schools, Nansel et al. (2001) found that of the total sample, 29.9% reported some type of involvement in moderate or frequent bullying as a bully (13.0%), as a target of bullying (10.6%), or both (6.3%).

Risk Factors and Conceptual Model

Research examining risk factors for peer abuse or bullying is limited. However, it seems that a person may be a target, a bully, or a bystander at anytime. With little variation between urban, suburban, town, and rural areas, bullying is prevalent by age 7 or 8 and peaks in middle school (sixth–eighth grades; Nansel et al., 2001). On the basis of U.S. Department of Education statistics on bullying for 2001, boys were more likely than girls to be bullied (9% and 7%, respectively; DeVoe et al., 2002). However, boys and girls appear to be at equal risk to bully others, with boys having a propensity for physical bullying and girls using indirect or relational bullying.

Bullying is a complex issue that has been conceptualized by an ecological perspective (Bronfrenbrenner, 1977; Fried & Fried, 1996) examining the contributions of individual traits, family context, school environment, community characteristics, and culture in explaining how a child may become a target or a bully. In regard to individual traits, children may be more likely to experience peer abuse or bullying if they are physically smaller and weaker (especially for boys) than their peers. In general, victims of peer abuse are anxious, insecure, have difficulty asserting themselves, and often relate better to adults than to peers (Olweus, 1993). However, there is a subgroup of provocative victims or targets who may display a combination of anxious and aggressive behaviors and attempt to bully weaker students (Olweus, 1993).

Children who bully are more likely to be physically stronger than their peers and have a tendency to be impulsive, become easily angered, display little empathy toward targets, and be aggressive in other relationships (e.g., with teachers, parents, and siblings; Olweus, 1993). Contrary to popular belief, bullies tend to have high self-esteem and report ease in making friends (Nansel et al., 2001; Olweus, 1993). These behaviors may be supported by a permissive caregiver who models aggressive behavior; a school environment that lacks a bullying policy or does not enforce it; and community, societal, and cultural attitudes that glamorize violence as a strategy for resolving conflict (Olweus, 1993). Also, children must contend with the traditional view of bullying as a part of growing up, which trivializes it and ignores negative short- and long-term consequences.

Impact of Peer Abuse on Children

The deleterious effects of bullying impact the target, the bully, the larger school environment, and society. In a ground-breaking U.S. study on bullying, Nansel et al. (2001) found that perpetrating and experiencing bullying were associated with poorer psychosocial adjustment. These consequences can be far reaching, from lower school attendance and student achievement to increased incidences of violence and juvenile crime. Children who are bullied, when compared with those who are not, have reported greater avoidance of school (16.7%), classes (31.0%), and extracurricular activities (33.2%; Addington, Ruddy, Miller, & DeVoe, 2002). Bullying has been found to be related to negative reports on school climate, suggesting a decrease in children's perception of safety.

Children, especially girls (Grills & Ollendick, 2002), who are being bullied are more likely than those who are not to report being anxious, having trouble sleeping, feeling unhappy or sad, having stomachaches, having headaches, and wetting the bed (Weir, 2001). Poorer relationships with classmates and increased loneliness have been associated with both being bullied and with coincident bullying and being bullied (Nansel et al., 2001). In a sample of Norwegian eighth graders, bullies and targets had higher scores on measures of suicidal thoughts, and targets had significantly higher scores on depressive thoughts, with girls scoring significantly higher than boys on whether they were classified as bullies, targets, or neutral (Roland, 2002).

Little research has been conducted to examine the long-term effects of bullying; however, what has been done shows that negative effects may last into adulthood (Nansel et al., 2001). For instance, targets of bullying have reported higher levels of depression and poorer self-esteem at the age of 23 years, despite the fact that as adults they were no more harassed or socially isolated than other adults. However, the perpetrators were more likely to have criminal records (Olweus, 1993, 1994).

Mediating Factors

Recent national school tragedies alert us to the serious role bullying can play in the lives of children. Several protective factors mediate the impact of the experience of bullying. Children who report that they have at least one friend are far less likely to be victimized compared with those who are completely rejected by others (Hodges & Perry, 1999; Pellegrini, Bartini, & Brooks, 1999). Also, caring and supportive adults who develop open lines of communication with children and model nonaggressive ways to resolve conflicts can positively impact the issue of bullying (Garbarino & deLara, 2002). Espelage, Bosworth, and Simon (2001) found that beliefs supportive of violence and misconduct, fewer positive adult influences, and more negative peer influences were associated with the greater likelihood of bullying over time for a group of middle school students. Finally, responsive systems (with policies that give latitude to special situations) that provide opportunities for the reinforcement of prosocial behaviors increase the likelihood that school climate will be perceived as more positive (Beane, 1998). These responsive systems that also have extensive adult involvement along with individualized interventions for targets and perpetrators of bullying have been shown to be the most effective interventions for peer abuse (Olweus, 1993).

SUMMARY AND RECOMMENDATIONS

As outlined in this chapter, several factors complicate the task of collecting accurate statistics regarding rates of child maltreatment. Despite the devastating rates reported, child abuse continues to be underidentified and underreported by professionals. First, legal definitions are vastly different from state to state and are somewhat limited in scope. Large-scale multisite surveys involving nationally representative samples should use uniform and broad definitions to accurately reflect the number of children who experience maltreatment. Furthermore, retrospective accounts using lifetime prevalence rates make it difficult to identify potential risk or causal factors and the onset of abuse and neglect. To address these issues, more prospective longitudinal studies should be conducted. These studies should follow families over time and document the occurrence and impact of maltreatment while also identifying potential risk factors and correlates.

In addition, perhaps the focus should be shifted or at least expanded to further explore protective factors, because the identification of these factors is critical to the development of prevention models. This work is in its infancy with regard to CSA and CPA but has been all but ignored with respect to neglect and bullying. When neglect has been explored, it has routinely been combined with CPA, and these two types of maltreatment should clearly be treated as distinct entities.

To ensure better identification and reporting, child maltreatment should not only be considered a specialty area but should also be a mandatory topic of training for all professionals working with children. That is, all medical, mental health, child protection, and school personnel should be exposed to a mandatory child abuse curriculum at various levels of training (e.g., graduate school, internship and residency, and postgraduate continuing education). Many states have adopted such policies for mandatory domestic violence training but have overlooked the importance of training in child maltreatment.

Furthermore, cultural sensitivity training specific to child maltreatment based on data from social norms should be offered to child protective service workers and school personnel as well as other professionals to reduce the likelihood of reporting biases. Research has suggested that referral patterns to child protective services are biased, with maltreatment being more frequently correctly and incorrectly identified in poor African American children compared with White middle-class families (Newberger, Reed, Daniel, Hyde, & Kotelchuk, 1977). On the basis of data from nationally representative samples (Chaffin et al., 1996; Sedlak & Broadhurst, 1996), maltreatment indeed cuts across all ethnic and socioeconomic groups, with the exception of neglect, which is highly correlated with poverty. Therefore, we need to ensure that data from all of these groups are being accurately assessed and reported.

To intervene effectively, perhaps professionals should take a proactive rather than reactive approach. Professionals may not identify or report abuse until it rises to a level of great seriousness. If professionals are more willing to make reports when they recognize the precursors of child maltreatment, then families may receive support services before the maltreatment escalates. Although these reports may not meet requirements for substantiation by child protection standards, child protection, as a human service agency, could assist families even if investigations are closed or not initiated in the first place. In such cases, families would be supported rather than judged and consequently referred to available intervention services that may reduce the likelihood of future abuse reports that are substantiated.

REFERENCES

Ackerman, P. T., Newton, J. E. O., McPherson, W. B., Jones, J. G., & Dykman, R. A. (1998). Prevalence of posttraumatic stress disorder and other psychiatric diagnoses in three groups of abused children (sexual, physical, and both). *Child Abuse and Neglect, 22,* 759–774.

Addington, L. A., Ruddy, S. A., Miller, A. K., & DeVoe, J. F. (2002). *Are America's schools safe? Students speak out: 1999 school crime supplement.* Washington, DC: National Center for Education Statistics.

Araji, S., & Finkelhor, D. (1985). Explanations of pedophilia: Review of empirical research. *Bulletin of the American Academy of Psychiatry and the Law, 13,* 17–37.

Arata, C. M. (2000). From child victim to adult victim: A model for predicting sexual revictimization. *Child Maltreatment, 5,* 28–38.

Averill, J. R. (1978). Anger. In H. E. Howe & R. A. Dienstbier (Eds.), *Nebraska Symposium on Motivation* (pp. 1–80). Lincoln: University of Nebraska Press.

Azar, S. T. (1989). Training parents of abused children. In C. E. Schaefer & J. M. Briesmeister (Eds.), *Handbook of parent training: Parents as co-therapists for children's behavior problems* (pp. 414–441). New York: Wiley.

Azar, S. T., Povilaitis, T. Y., Lauretti, A. F., & Pouquette, C. L. (1998). The current status of etiological theories in intrafamilial child maltreatment. In J. R. Lutzker (Ed.), *Handbook of child abuse research and treatment* (pp. 3–30). New York: Plenum Press.

Bandura, A. (1977). *Social learning theory.* Englewood Cliffs, NJ: Prentice-Hall.

Bath, H. I., & Haapala, D. A. (1993). Intensive family preservation services with abused and neglected children: An examination of group differences. *Child Abuse and Neglect, 17,* 213–225.

Beane, A. (1998). The trauma of peer victimization. In T. M. Miller (Ed.), *Children of trauma: Stressful life events and their effects on children and adolescents* (pp. 205–218). Madison, CT: International Universities Press.

Beitchman, J. H., Zucker, K. J., Hood, J. E., daCosta, G. A., Akman, D., & Cassavia, E. (1992). A review of the long-term effects of child sexual abuse. *Child Abuse and Neglect, 16,* 101–118.

Belsky, J. (1993). Etiology of child maltreatment: A developmental–ecological analysis. *Psychological Bulletin, 114*, 413–434.

Berliner, L., & Conte, J. R. (1990). The process of victimization: The victims' perspective. *Child Abuse and Neglect, 14*, 29–40.

Black, D. A., Heyman, R. E., & Smith Slep, A. M. (2001). Risk factors for child physical abuse. *Aggression and Violent Behavior, 6*, 121–188.

Bosworth, K., Espelage, D. L., & Simon, T. (1999). Factors associated with bullying behavior in middle school students. *Journal of Early Adolescence, 19*, 341–362.

Briere, J., & Runtz, M. (1990). Differential adult symptomatology associated with three types of child abuse histories. *Child Abuse and Neglect, 14*, 357–364.

Briere, J., Woo, R., McRae, B., Foltz, J., & Sitzman, R. (1997). Lifetime victimization history, demographics, and clinical status in female psychiatric emergency room patients. *Journal of Nervous and Mental Disease, 185*, 95–101.

Bronfenbrenner, U. (1977). Toward an experimental ecology of human development. *American Psychologist, 32*, 513–531.

Brown, J., Cohen, P., Johnson, J. G., & Salzinger, S. (1998). A longitudinal analysis of risk factors for child maltreatment: Findings of a 17-year prospective study of officially recorded and self-reported child abuse and neglect. *Child Abuse and Neglect, 22*, 1065–1078.

Brown, E. J., & Kolko, D. J. (1999). Child victims' attributions about being physically abused: An examination of factors associated with symptom severity. *Journal of Abnormal Child Psychology, 27*, 311–322.

Browne, A., & Finkelhor, D. (1986). Impact of child sexual abuse: A review of the research. *Psychological Bulletin, 99*, 66–77.

Calam, R., Horne, L., Glasgow, D., & Cox, A. (1998). Psychological disturbance and child sexual abuse: A follow-up study. *Child Abuse and Neglect, 22*, 901–913.

Chaffin, M., Kelleher, K., & Hollenberg, J. (1996). Onset of physical abuse and neglect: Psychiatric, substance abuse, and social risk factors from prospective community data. *Child Abuse and Neglect, 20*, 191–203.

Cohen, J. A., Deblinger, E., Mannarino, A. P., & Steer, R. A. (2004). A multisite, randomized controlled trial for sexually abused children with PTSD symptoms. *Journal of the American Academy of Child and Adolescent Psychiatry, 43*, 393–402.

Cohen, J. A., & Mannarino, A. P. (1996). A treatment outcome study for sexually abused preschool children: Initial findings. *Journal of the American Academy of Child and Adolescent Psychiatry, 35*, 42–50.

Cohen, J. A., & Mannarino, A. P. (1998). Interventions for sexually abused children: Initial treatment findings. *Child Maltreatment, 3*, 17–26.

Connelly, C. D., & Straus, M. A. (1992). Mother's age and risk for physical abuse. *Child Abuse and Neglect, 16*, 709–718.

Conte, J. R., Wolfe, S., & Smith, T. (1989). What sexual offenders tell us about prevention strategies. *Child Abuse and Neglect, 13*, 293–301.

Corcoran, J. (2000). Family interventions with child physical abuse and neglect: A critical review. *Children and Youth Services Review, 22*, 563–591.

Criss, M. M., Pettit, G. S., Bates, J. E., Dodge, K. A., & Lapp, A. L. (2002) Family adversity, positive peer relationships, and children's externalizing behavior: A longitudinal perspective on risk and resilience. *Child Development, 73,* 1220–1237.

Crouch, J. L., Milner, J. S., & Thomson, C. (2001). Childhood physical abuse, early social support, and risk for maltreatment: Current social support as a mediator of risk for child physical abuse. *Child Abuse and Neglect, 25,* 93–107.

Dadds, M. R., Mullins, M. J., McAllister, R. A., & Atkinson, E. R. (2002). Attributions, affect, and behavior in abuse-risk mothers: A laboratory study. *Child Abuse and Neglect, 27,* 21–45.

Deblinger, E., & Heflin, A. (1996). *Treating sexually abused children and their non-offending parents: A cognitive–behavioral approach.* Thousand Oaks, CA: Sage.

Deblinger, E., Lippmann, J., & Steer, R. (1996). Sexually abused children suffering posttraumatic stress symptoms: Initial treatment outcome findings. *Child Maltreatment, 1,* 310–321.

Deblinger, E., McLeer, S. V., Atkins, M. S., Ralphe, D., & Foa, E. (1989). Posttraumatic stress in sexually abused, physically abused, and non-abused children. *Child Abuse and Neglect, 13,* 403–408.

Deblinger, E., Stauffer, L. B., & Steer, R. (2001). Comparative efficacies of supportive and cognitive–behavioral group therapies for young children who have been sexually abused and their non-offending mothers. *Child Maltreatment, 6,* 332–343.

DeVoe, J. F., Peter, K., Kaufman, P., Ruddy, S. A., Miller, A. K., Planty, M., et al. (2002). *Indicators of school crime and safety: Nonfatal student victimization. Student reports.* Washington, DC: National Center for Education Statistics.

Dodge, K. A., Pettit, G. S., & Bates, J. E. (1990, December 21). Mechanisms in the cycle of violence. *Science, 250,* 1678–1683.

Dodge, K. A., Pettit, G. S., & Bates, J. E. (1994). Effects of physical maltreatment on the development of peer relations. *Development and Psychopathology, 6,* 43–55.

Donohue, B., Miller, E., Van Hasselt, V. B., & Hersen, M. (1998). Ecological treatment of child abuse. In V. B. Van Hasselt & M. Hersen (Eds.), *Sourcebook of psychological treatment manuals for children and adolescents* (pp. 203–278). Hillsdale, NJ: Erlbaum.

Dube, S. R., Anda, R. F, Felitti, V. J., Chapman, D. P., Williamson, D. F., & Giles, W. H. (2001). Childhood abuse, household dysfunction, and the risk of attempted suicide throughout the life span: Findings from the Adverse Childhood Experiences Study. *Journal of the American Medical Association, 286,* 3089–3096.

Dube, S. R., Anda, R. F., Felitti, V. J., Croft, J. B., Edwards, V. J., & Giles, W. H. (2001). Growing up with parental alcohol abuse: Exposure to childhood abuse, neglect, and household dysfunction. *Child Abuse and Neglect, 25,* 1627–1640.

Dubowitz, H. (Ed.). (1999). *Neglected children: Research, practice and policy.* Thousand Oaks, CA: Sage.

Erickson, M. F., & Egeland, B. (1995). Throwing a spotlight on the developmental outcomes for children: Findings of a seventeen year follow up study. In E. Wattenberg (Ed.), *Children in the shadows: The fate of children in neglecting families* (pp. 113–126). Minneapolis: University of Minnesota Press.

Erickson, M. F., & Egeland, B. (1996). Child neglect. In J. Briere, L. Berliner, J. Bulkey, C. Jenny, & T. Reid. (Eds.), *The APSAC handbook on child maltreatment* (pp. 4–20). Thousand Oaks, CA: Sage.

Erickson, M. F., & Egeland, B. (2002). Child neglect. In J. E. B. Myers, L. Berliner, J. Briere, C. T. Hendrix, C. Jenny, & T. Reid (Eds.), *The APSAC handbook on child maltreatment* (2nd ed., pp. 3–20). Thousand Oaks, CA: Sage.

Espelage, D. L., Bosworth, K., & Simon, T. (2001). Short-term stability and change of bullying in middle school students: An examination of potential demographic, psychosocial, and environmental influences. *Violence and Victims, 16,* 411–426.

Everson, M. D., Hunter, W. M., Runyan, D. K., Edelson, G. A., & Coulter, M. L. (1989). Maternal support following disclosure of incest. *American Journal of Orthopsychiatry 59,* 197–207.

Famularo, R., Kinscherff, R., & Fenton, T. (1992). Psychiatric diagnoses of maltreated children: Preliminary findings. *Journal of the American Academy of Child and Adolescent Psychiatry, 31,* 863–867.

Fergusson, D. M., & Mullen, P. E. (1999). *Childhood sexual abuse: An evidence-based perspective.* Thousand Oaks, CA: Sage.

Finkelhor, D. (1993). Epidemiological factors in the clinical identification of child sexual abuse. *Child Abuse and Neglect, 17,* 67–70.

Finkelhor, D. (1994). Current information on the scope and nature of child sexual abuse. *Future of Children, 4,* 31–53.

Finkelhor, D., & Dziuba-Leatherman, J. (1994). Children as victims of violence: A national survey. *Pediatrics, 94,* 413–420.

Fried, S., & Fried, P. (1996). *Bullies and victims: Helping your child through the schoolyard battlefield.* New York: Evans.

The Gallup Organization. (1995). *Gallup nationwide poll.* Washington, DC: U.S. Government Printing Office.

Garbarino, J., & deLara, E. (2002). *And words can hurt forever: How to protect adolescents from bullying harassment and emotional violence.* New York: Free Press.

Gaudin, J. (1999). Child neglect: Short-term and long-term outcomes. In H. Dubowitz (Ed.), *Neglected children: Research, practice and policy* (pp. 89–108). Thousand Oaks, CA: Sage.

Gillham, B., Tanner, G., Cheyne, B., Freeman, I., Rooney, M., & Lambie, A. (1998). Unemployment rates, single parent density, and indices of child poverty: Their relationship to different categories of child abuse and neglect. *Child Abuse and Neglect, 22,* 79–90.

Gomes-Schwartz, B., Horowitz, J. M., Cardarelli, A. P., & Sauzier, M. (1990). The aftermath of child sexual abuse: 18 months later. In B. Gomes-Schwartz, J. M.

Horowitz, & A. P. Cardarelli (Eds.), *Child sexual abuse: The initial effects* (pp. 132–152). Newbury Park, CA: Sage.

Grills, A. E., & Ollendick, T. H. (2002). Peer victimization, global self-worth, and anxiety in middle school children. *Journal of Clinical Child and Adolescent Psychology, 31,* 59–68.

Grusec, J. E., Dix, T., & Mills, R. (1982). The effects of type, severity, and victims of children's transgressions on maternal discipline. *Canadian Journal of Behavioral Science, 14,* 276–289.

Hansen, D. J., & MacMillan, V. M. (1990). Behavioral assessment of child-abusive and neglectful families. *Behavior Modification, 14,* 255–278.

Hansen, D. J., Sedlar, G., & Warner-Rogers, J. E. (1999). Child physical abuse. In R. T. Ammerman & M. Hersen (Eds.), *Assessment of family violence: A clinical and legal sourcebook* (2nd ed., pp. 127–156). New York: Wiley.

Herrenkohl, R. C., Egolf, B. P., & Herrenkohl, E. C. (1997). Preschool antecedents of adolescent assaultive behavior: A longitudinal study. *American Journal of Orthopsychiatry, 67,* 422–432.

Hildyard, K. L., & Wolfe, D. A. (2002). Child neglect: Developmental issues and outcomes. *Child Abuse and Neglect, 26,* 679–695.

Hodges, E. V. E., & Perry, D. G. (1999). Personal and interpersonal antecedents and consequences of victimization by peers. *Journal of Personality and Social Psychology, 76,* 677–685.

Johnson, B. K., & Kenkel, M. B. (1991). Stress, coping, and adjustment in female adolescent incest victims. *Child Abuse and Neglect, 15,* 293–305.

Kanner, A., Bulik, C. M., & Sullivan, P. F. (1993). Abuse in adult relationships of bulimic women. *Journal of Interpersonal Violence, 8,* 52–63.

Kemp, A. (1998). *Abuse in the family: An introduction.* Pacific Grove, CA: Brooks/Cole.

Kendall-Tackett, K. A., Williams, L. M., & Finkelhor, D. (1993). Impact of sexual abuse on children: A review and synthesis of recent empirical studies. *Psychological Bulletin, 113,* 164–180.

King, N. J., Tonge, B. J., Mullen, P., Myerson, N., Heyne, D., Rollings, S., et al. (2000). Treating sexually abused children with post-traumatic stress symptoms: A randomized trial. *Journal of the American Academy of Child and Adolescent Psychiatry, 39,* 1347–1355.

Kolko, D. J. (1996). Individual cognitive–behavioral treatment and family therapy for physically abused children and their offending parents: A comparison of clinical outcomes. *Child Maltreatment, 1,* 322–342.

Kolko, D. J. (2002). Child physical abuse. In J. E. B. Myers, L. Berliner, J. Briere, C. T. Hendrix, C. Jenny, & T. A. Reid (Eds.), *The APSAC handbook on child maltreatment* (2nd ed., pp. 21–54). Thousand Oaks, CA: Sage.

Kolko, D. J., & Swenson, C. (2002). *Assessing and treating physically abused children and their families: A cognitive–behavioral approach.* Thousand Oaks, CA: Sage.

Kurtz, P. D., Gaudin, J. M., Wodarski, J. S., & Howing, P. T. (1993). Maltreatment and the school-aged child: School performance consequences. *Child Abuse and Neglect, 17,* 581–589.

Law, J., & Conway, J. (1992). Effect of abuse and neglect on the development of children's speech and language. *Developmental Medicine and Child Neurology, 34,* 943–948.

Leitenberg, H., Greenwald, E., & Cado, S. (1992). A retrospective study of long-term methods of coping with having been sexually abused during childhood. *Child Abuse and Neglect 16,* 399–407.

Lutzker, J. R., Van Hasselt, V. B., Bigelow, K. M., Greene, B. F., & Kessler, M. L. (1998). Child abuse and neglect: Behavioral research, treatment, and theory. *Aggression and Violent Behavior, 3,* 181–196.

Marshall, D. B., & English, D. J. (1999). Survival analysis of risk factors for recidivism in child abuse and neglect. *Child Maltreatment, 4,* 287–296.

Meyers, J. E. B. (1992). *Legal issues in child abuse and neglect.* Newbury Park, CA: Sage.

Miller-Perrin, C., & Perrin, R. D. (1999). *Child maltreatment: An introduction.* Thousand Oaks, CA: Sage.

Milner, J. S. (2003). Social information processing in high-risk and physically abusive parents. *Child Abuse and Neglect, 27,* 7–20.

Nansel, T. R., Overpeck, M., Pilla, R. S., Ruan, W. J., Simons-Morton, S., & Scheidt, P. (2001). Bullying behaviors among U.S. youth: Prevalence and association with psychosocial adjustment. *Journal of the American Medical Association, 285,* 2094–2100.

Newberger, E. H., Reed, R. B., Daniel, J. H., Hyde, J. N., & Kotelchuck, M. (1977). Pediatric social illness: Toward an etiologic classification. *Pediatrics, 60,* 178–185.

Olweus, D. (1993). *Bullying at school: What we know and what we can do.* Cambridge, MA: Blackwell Publishers.

Olweus, D. (1994). Bullying at school: Long-term outcomes for the victims and an effective school-based intervention program. In L. R. Huesmann (Ed.), *Aggressive behavior: Current perspectives* (pp. 97–130). New York: Plenum Press.

Paine, M. L., & Hansen, D. J. (2002). Factors influencing children to self-disclose sexual abuse. *Clinical Psychology Review, 22,* 271–295.

Patterson, G. R. (1982). *Coercive family process.* Eugene, OR: Castalia.

Pelcovitz, D., Kaplan, S., Goldenberg, B., Mandel, F., Lehane, J., & Guarrera, J. (1994). Post-traumatic stress disorder in physically abused adolescents. *Journal of the American Academy of the Child and Adolescent Psychiatry, 33,* 305–312.

Pellegrini, A. D., Bartini, M., & Brooks, F. (1999). School bullies, victims, and aggressive victims: Factors relating to group affiliation and victimization in early adolescence. *Journal of Educational Psychology, 91,* 216–224.

Roland, E. (2002). Bullying, depressive symptoms, and suicidal thoughts. *Educational Research, 44,* 55–67.

Ross, S. M. (1996). Risk of physical abuse to children of spouse abusing parents. *Child Abuse and Neglect, 20,* 589–598.

Runyon, M., Basilio, I., Van Hasselt, V. B., & Hersen, M. (1998). Child witnesses of interparental violence: A manual for child and family treatment. In V. B. Van Hasselt & M. Hersen (Eds.), *Sourcebook of psychological treatment manuals for children and adolescents* (pp. 203–278). Hillsdale, NJ: Erlbaum.

Runyon, M. K., Deblinger, E., Ryan, E. E., & Thakkar-Kolar, R.(2004). An overview of child physical abuse: Developing an integrated parent–child cognitive–behavioral treatment approach. *Trauma, Violence, & Abuse, 5,* 65–85.

Runyon, M. K., & Kenny, M. (2002). Relationship of attributional style, depression, and post-trauma distress among children who suffered physical or sexual abuse. *Child Maltreatment, 7,* 254–264

Salzinger, S., Feldman, R. S., Hammer, M., & Rosario, M. (1993). The effects of physical abuse on children's social relationships. *Child Development, 64,* 169–187.

Sedlak, A. J. (1997). Risk factors for the occurrence of child abuse and neglect. *Journal of Aggression, Maltreatment, and Trauma, 1,* 149–187.

Sedlak, A. J., & Broadhurst, D. D. (1996). *Executive summary of the Third National Incidence Study of Child Abuse and Neglect.* Washington, DC: U.S. Government Printing Office.

Slack, K. S., Holl, J. L., McDaniel, M., Yoo, J., & Bolger, K. (2004). Understanding the risks of child neglect: An exploration of poverty and parenting characteristics. *Child Maltreatment, 9,* 395–408.

Spinetta, J. J., & Rigler, D. (1972). The child abusing parent: A psychological review. *Psychological Bulletin, 77,* 296–304.

Straus, M. A. (1994). *Beating the devil out of them: Corporal punishment in American families.* New York: Lexington Books.

Straus, M. A., Hamby, S. L., Finkelhor, D., Moore, D. W., & Runyan, D. (1998). Identification of child maltreatment with the Parent–Child Conflict Tactics Scales: Development and psychometric data for a national sample of American parents. *Child Abuse and Neglect, 22,* 249–270.

Sullivan, P. M., & Knutson, J. F. (2000). Maltreatment and disabilities: A population-based epidemiological study. *Child Abuse and Neglect, 24,* 1257–1273.

Toth, S. L., Cicchetti, D., & Kim, J. (2002). Relations among children's perceptions of maternal behavior, attributional styles, and behavioral symptomatology in maltreated children. *Journal of Abnormal Child Psychology, 30,* 487–501.

Urquiza, A. J., & McNeil, C. B. (1996). Parent–child interaction therapy: An intensive dyadic intervention for physically abusive families. *Child Maltreatment, 1,* 134–144.

U.S. Department of Education. (2002). *Indicators of school crime and safety: Nonfatal student victimization. Student reports.* Washington, DC: National Center for Education Studies.

U.S. Department of Health and Human Services. (2002). *National Center on Child Abuse and Neglect, Child Maltreatment, 2000: Reports from the States for the National Child Abuse and Neglect Data Systems*. Washington, DC: U.S. Government Printing Office.

U.S. Department of Health and Human Services. (2004). *National Center on Child Abuse and Neglect, Child Maltreatment, 2002: Reports from the States for the National Child Abuse and Neglect Data Systems*. Washington, DC: U.S. Government Printing Office.

Weir, E. (2001). The health impact of bullying. *Canadian Medical Association Journal, 165*, 1249.

Weston, J., Colloton, M., Halsey, S., Covington, S., Gilbert, J., Sorrentino-Kelly, L., & Renoud, S. (1993). A legacy of violence in non-organic failure to thrive. *Child Abuse and Neglect, 17*, 709–714.

Widom, C. S. (1989). Child abuse, neglect, and violent criminal behavior. *Criminology, 27*, 251–271.

Wolfe, D. A., Wekerle, C., Reitzel-Jaffe, D., & Lefebvre, L. (1998). Factors associated with abusive relationships among maltreated and nonmaltreated youth. *Development and Psychopathology, 10*, 61–85.

Wolfner, G. D., & Gelles, R. J. (1993). A profile of violence toward children: A national study. *Child Abuse and Neglect, 17*, 197–212.

Wyatt, G. E., & Peters, S. D. (1986). Methodological considerations in research on the prevalence of child sexual abuse. *Child Abuse and Neglect, 10*, 241–251.

Zuravin, S., & DePanfilis, D. (1996). *Child maltreatment recurrences among families served by child protective services. Final report to the National Center on Child Abuse and Neglect*. Washington, DC: U.S. Government Printing Office.

Zuravin, S., & DiBlaso, F. (1992). Child-neglecting adolescent mothers: How do they differ from their nonmaltreating counterparts? *Journal of Interpersonal Violence, 7*, 471–489.

3

AN EVIDENCE-BASED PERSPECTIVE ON INTERVENTIONS TO STOP OR PREVENT CHILD ABUSE

MARK CHAFFIN AND SUSAN SCHMIDT

In this chapter, we focus on treatment and prevention interventions targeted at one particular facet of violence—that directed against children by their parents or caretakers. Not all forms of child maltreatment involve violence. For example, although environmental, supervisory, or other forms of child neglect are by far the most prevalent types of child maltreatment (U.S. Department of Health and Human Services [USDHHS], 2001), none involve violent behavior. Conversely, not all forms of violence directed against children are child abuse. For example, violence committed by peers is often not thought of as child abuse. Children's overall risk for violent victimization and the extent to which that violence is committed by parents or caretakers versus peers or other persons varies considerably with the age of the child. Children are at the greatest risk for violence in their younger (preschool) and older (later adolescent) childhood years. However, the sources of violence are different during these two peak risk periods. Young children who are victims of violence are more often victimized by parents or caretakers, whereas adolescents who are victims of violence are more often victimized by peers or others outside their family (Finkelhor & Dzuiba-

Leatherman, 1994). The public sector agencies that respond to violence against children also vary according the child's relationship to the person committing the violence, that person's age, and the child's age. Many forms of violence against children are not handled by the law enforcement or criminal justice systems. Violence committed by parents is often routed solely through the child welfare system; peer-on-peer violence may be handled by school authorities or by parents (Finkelhor, Wolak, & Berliner, 2001). The type and severity of parent-to-child violence also determines which public sectors may become involved. For example, criminal justice system involvement, in addition to child welfare system involvement, is more likely in cases of intrafamilial sexual abuse than in cases of intrafamilial physical abuse and may be more likely in severe or fatal forms of physical abuse than in more routine forms of physical abuse (Whitcomb, 1991).

Parent-to-child violence is often subdivided into two major forms, physical abuse and sexual abuse. Physical abuse and sexual abuse are quite different phenomena across many dimensions, including epidemiology, motivating factors, and demographics. Of the two, physical abuse is far more prevalent among child welfare cases (USDHHS, 2001), although sexual abuse has received a larger percentage of professional attention over the past 20 years (Behl, Conyngham, & May, 2003). Women (mothers or stepmothers), who are most often the primary caretakers for children, are the largest group of physical abusers. The abused child may be of either gender. Men, on the other hand, commit the vast majority of sexual abuse, and girls are victimized more often than boys (USDHHS, 2001). Physical abuse is more closely tied to socioeconomic stresses such as poverty and is often comorbid with child neglect. Sexual abuse cuts more evenly across socioeconomic groups. Physical abuse is typically an exaggerated extension of a common parenting practice: corporal punishment (which is how it is typically viewed by physically abusive parents). Sexual abuse, on the other hand, is a deviant behavior that is distinct from normal parenting practices. Physically abusive parents limit their abusive behavior almost exclusively to their own children or wards. It is virtually never a predatory behavior in the sense that parents typically do not seek out or recruit children to physically abuse. Sexual abusers, on the other hand, may target children both inside and outside the family (Abel et al., 1987). Finally, the nature of the violence involved differs. Physical abuse is inherently assaultive. Although sexual abuse also may be explicitly violent and assaultive, it also may be seductive or even lack physical contact (e.g., parental solicitation of sex acts or exposure). However, we can still categorize "nonviolent" sexual abuse of children as a form of violence and abuse on the basis of its inherently exploitative and potentially harmful aspects (Ondersma, Chaffin, Berliner, Cordon, & Goodman, 2001). Despite these distinctions between physical and sexual abuse, there is considerable comorbidity in the sense that the presence of either increases risk for the other, and both may be embedded within a broader nexus of family violence and adversity (Molnar, Buka, & Kessler, 2001; for a discussion, see Slep & Heyman, 2001). In particular, child abuse often overlaps with intimate partner violence or domestic violence (Edleson, 1999; Hartley, 2002), and there are many shared characteristics or potential risk factors between child abuse and partner violence (Shipman, Rossman, & West, 1999). Rates of physical and sexual child abuse have declined considerably over the past few decades, paralleling overall reductions in crime, domestic assault, and other forms of violence (Jones & Finkelhor, 2003).

TREATMENT INTERVENTIONS

This section summarizes outcome research for selected interventions. These are grouped by the maltreatment category within which the intervention has most often been tested.

Child Physical Abuse

With a few important exceptions, interventions designed to treat or prevent child physical abuse have not been evaluated for efficacy. This is not to suggest that they have not been studied. Gains in parenting information, reductions in parenting stress, changes in self-reported attitudes, or similar results have been widely reported. However, because of the research designs of most of these studies, it has not been possible to rule out expectancy effects, spontaneous improvement, or other possible sources of these findings, nor is it possible to know whether these changes will ultimately translate into reductions in future child abuse. Few physical abuse treatment interventions have ever been subjected to randomized-trial outcome research, and among those, most have measured soft outcomes such as presumed risk factors rather than hard outcomes such as future violent or abusive behavior. At present, no physical abuse treatment interventions have research evidence sufficient to meet standard criteria as being "well supported." The customary criteria for a well-supported treatment include demonstrated efficacy for the intended bottom-line outcome in at least two well-designed randomized controlled trials compared either with no treatment or with a standard treatment and conducted by at least two different research groups. In the case of physical abuse, a bottom-line outcome would involve measuring the occurrence (or recurrence) of parent-to-child physical violence. Some evidence suggests that improvements on soft outcomes, such as risk instruments, may not correspond to actual changes in risk for the bottom-line behavior (Chaffin & Valle, 2003). Although no treatments designed to stop physical abuse are empirically well supported, there are some that have sufficient empirical underpinnings to be considered promising.

We discuss five treatments that have sufficient research evidence to be considered promising from an evidence-based perspective: an adapted version of Eyberg's Parent–Child Interaction Therapy (PCIT), an adapted version of Henggeler's Multisystemic Therapy (MST), Kolko's cognitive–behavioral therapy (CBT) and family therapy (FT) approaches for parents, and Lutzker's Project 12-Ways and SafeCare models. We also review a number of standard interventions with less evidence, such as didactic parenting education or support groups, anger management groups, and family preservation models, and then we review these promising models.

Group Parenting Classes or Parent Support Groups

One of the most common intervention approaches to the treatment of parents who physically abuse is psychoeducational parenting classes or parent support groups that involve teaching parents nonviolent child behavior management (Wolfe & Wekerle, 1993). Often, these parenting programs are conducted in a clinic-based group format where parents are presented with materials, and there is group discussion about parenting practices. Studies evaluating these forms of parent training have reported that parents increase their knowledge of alternatives to physical punishment and knowledge of normal child development (Alexander & Parsons, 1973; Barkley, Guevremont, Anastopoulos, & Fletcher, 1992; Golub, Espinosa, Damon, & Card, 1987; Hughes & Wilson, 1988). These improvements have been shown to generalize when sessions are conducted in the home (Wolfe, Sandler, & Kaufman, 1981). However, it is less clear whether these benefits translate into actual reductions in future parent-to-child physical violence or that any reductions in violent behavior are actually due to the treatment given, because there have not been controlled randomized trials evaluating this outcome. Perhaps the most widely used parent support group model for physically abusive parents, Parents Anonymous, has never been rigorously evaluated.

Anger Management Groups

A second common group treatment approach for parents who physically abuse involves anger management therapy, typically in a group setting (Acton & During, 1992; Nurius, Lovell, & Edgar, 1988; Whiteman, Fanshel, & Grundy, 1987). Again, some uncontrolled studies suggest improvement over time for clients in these programs, but it remains unclear whether these improvements are due to the intervention and whether they translate into actual reductions in parent-to-child violent behavior.

Family Preservation and Reunification Models

Family preservation and reunification models have been implemented in most states. Although there is considerable variability across programs, most share an in-home service model based on crisis intervention, social support, and case management principles. Initial evaluations of these models examined their effectiveness in preventing out-of-home placements. It is our opinion that preventing placement is more of a service philosophy or method than an outcome and that the programs must also be evaluated for their effectiveness in stopping or preventing parent-to-child violence. Several evaluations of in-home intensive family preservation programs, whether they are ad hoc models designed by grassroots agencies or are more standardized (e.g., the Homebuilders model, the Family Connections model), have found these programs to be of little benefit, regardless of dose or intensity of services, for stopping maltreatment (Chaffin, Bonner, & Hill, 2001; Littell, 1997). For example, in perhaps the largest and best controlled study to date—a large multisite randomized trial comparing the well-regarded Homebuilders model with standard child welfare services—no reductions in future maltreatment reports were found (USDHHS, 2001). Recent randomized trials of the Family Connections model have yield similarly disappointing results (MacMillian et al., 2005).

Parent–Child Interaction Therapy

PCIT is a dyadic, live-coached behavioral parent-training protocol originally developed to treat young children with behavior disorders. The intervention involves training parents to criteria on specific behavioral parenting skills using live coaching of skills in dyadic parent–child sessions. PCIT teaches a limited number of specific relationship-enhancing and discipline skills, such as use of labeled praise and reflection and a specific time-out protocol for compliance training. Controlled studies have shown that PCIT is highly effective in decreasing child behavior problems, that treatment effects generalize to nontreated siblings and to other environmental settings, and that improvements are maintained over time (Eisenstadt, Eyberg, McNeil, Newcomb, & Funderburk, 1993; McNeil, Eyberg, Eisenstadt, Newcomb, & Funderburk, 1991).

Given that many of the parenting skills PCIT teaches for reducing child behavior problems are also thought to be relevant for reducing parent-to-child violent behavior, researchers have adapted the method as a promising approach for physically abusive parents and their children (Urquiza & McNeil, 1996). A single randomized trial with physically abusive parents compared outcomes for PCIT with those for a standard group-based parenting program. Parents receiving PCIT had far fewer future physical abuse reports than parents receiving the standard group parenting program, and the relatively greater benefit of the PCIT intervention appeared to be related to greater reductions of negative parent behaviors in parent–child interactions (Chaffin et al., 2004).

Cognitive–Behavioral Therapy and Family Therapy Approaches

One small randomized study has compared CBT and FT interventions with routine community services for physically abusive parents and their children. In this study, CBT addressed views on violence and physical punishment, parents' attributional style and expectations, self-management, and child behavior management skills, whereas FT focused on parent–child interactions and teaching parent–child problem-solving routines (Kolko, 1996a, 1996b). On the basis of children's reports, families in the FT condition had less parent-to-child violence than families in either of the other conditions, and in general, families receiving CBT or FT did better than families receiving routine community services across measures.

Project 12-Ways and Project SafeCare

Project 12-Ways (Lutzker, Frame, & Rice, 1982) is based on an ecological–behavioral intervention model for physical abuse and neglect. Project SafeCare is a streamlined version of the model, adapting only the most commonly used Project 12-Ways behavioral intervention modules (Lutzker & Bigelow, 2002). Project 12-Ways was designed for multiproblem families involved in the child protective services system for neglect, physical abuse, or both, and most studies of the model have evaluated its effects on maltreatment globally rather than on physical abuse in particular. The model focuses on specific behavioral skills that are trained to criteria, and all services are provided in the home (i.e., the family's social ecology). These models have a number of single-subject studies supporting their effectiveness as well as some quasi-experimental studies measuring abuse outcomes and randomized trials measuring softer outcomes. Families served by Project 12-Ways and Project SafeCare have been found to be less likely to have a child maltreatment recurrence than an arguably less severe quasi-experimental comparison group, and they are less likely to have children removed than comparison families receiving other child welfare services (Gershater-Molko, Lutzker, & Wesch, 2002; Lutzker & Rice, 1987; Wesch & Lutzker, 1991).

Multisystemic Therapy

MST is a high-intensity, low-caseload, time-limited, family- and community-based treatment program that includes home-based delivery of services and applies empirically best supported interventions to all systems (individual, dyadic, family, school, community, etc.) and that can be applied to physical abuse (Swenson, 2000). One small-scale randomized controlled trial with maltreating parents showed that MST was more effective than standard parent training for restructuring parent–child interactions (Brunk, Henggeler, & Whelan, 1987), although it is not clear that this translated into actual reductions in parent-to-child violence. A larger randomized controlled trial with physically abusive families including children ages 10 through 17 has just been completed comparing MST with a standard parenting group and community services. Preliminary results suggest better child placement outcomes for families receiving MST, and additional analyses are currently underway (C. C. Swenson, personal communication, February 16, 2005).

Child Sexual Abuse

Interventions designed to stop parent–child sexual abuse differ considerably from those designed to stop parent–child physical abuse, in line with the many differences in etiology and nature of the two problems. Parent–child sexual abuse is not conceptualized as a parent–child interaction problem. The nature of the parent's problem may vary from deviant sexual interest patterns to impulsivity or psychopathic tendencies or some combination, but regardless, it is conceptualized as the abusive parent's problem, not a problem originating in the parent–child relationship, and it may not always be limited to victimizing children within the immediate family (Abel et al., 1987). Consequently, most interventions are targeted at the individual abusive parent, and involvement of others in the family is more on a collateral basis than a central approach to intervention. Treatment of adult sex abuse perpetrators is customarily much more likely to be delivered under court or probation supervision and is far more invasive, restrictive, and authoritarian than treatment for physical abusers.

There is far less variability in the types of interventions delivered, with almost all modern sex offender interventions relying on specialized cognitive–behavioral sex-offender-specific (CBSOS) models, including relapse prevention components and close authoritative monitoring of offender behavior. The nature of the available research evidence on the effectiveness of modern sexual abuser treatment is different as well. There are a large number of treatment outcome studies, and almost all report data on hard behavioral outcomes (i.e., sex offense re-reports or recidivism). However, in almost all outcome studies, there are problems with comparison conditions, and there is only one contemporary true randomized trial in the literature. In addition, it is clear that sex offenders against children are a heterogeneous group that is also quite heterogeneous with respect to reoffense risk (Hanson & Thornton, 1999). This means that the outcomes for sex offenders against children in general might not be accurate for particular child sex offender subgroups. At present, there is no consistently applied system for defining subgroups in the treatment outcome literature, so we review broad outcomes, bearing in mind that outcomes specifically for within-family sexual abusers may be different. In general, "incest only" sexual abusers have lower recurrence rates than many other groups.

Cognitive–Behavioral Sex-Offender-Specific Interventions

Marshall, Fernandez, Hudson, and Ward (1998) reviewed data from over 30 sex offender treatment programs in different settings and for different offender populations worldwide. They concluded that despite the diversity of settings and clients, most programs operate from a cognitive–behavioral perspective and include relapse prevention (Pithers, 1990) as the connective theme running throughout the various treatment components. Most programs begin with the requirement that participants acknowledge at least some portion of their offense (e.g., Gordon & Hover, 1998). Some type of formal psychosexual assessment is usually conducted and frequently includes actuarial risk assessment tools (e.g., Moro, 1998). CBSOS intervention is a multicomponent approach. It commonly includes components intended to increase victim empathy, change distorted thinking patterns such as justifications and minimizations, improve social skills, teach self-control, and develop lifelong self-management strategies. Treatment also may include behavioral interventions to reduce deviant sexual arousal. Relapse prevention is a treatment model that is commonly implemented throughout the other treatment components. Relapse prevention is based on several core assumptions, including the assumptions that risk for sexual offenses against children is long term and cannot be entirely eliminated, that offenses are planned in advance, and that triggers or warning signs for offending can be identified and then used to develop a plan to reduce the likelihood of recidivism. Patients develop detailed plans for avoiding behavioral relapse and managing potentially risky situations and urges. Some programs include periodic polygraph interrogations as part of case monitoring, although the validity of the polygraph for these purposes and its impact on outcomes remains untested.

Surgical and Pharmacological Interventions

Surgical and pharmacological interventions are occasionally used with small select subgroups of adult sex offenders. Physical castration is almost never used in the United States. A less invasive procedure for reducing sex drive is to administer one of several pharmacological agents. Early efforts at "chemical castration" relied on estrogens. However, these caused extensive side effects and were replaced with antiandrogens, including medroxy-progesterone acetate and cyproterone acetate (Balon, 1998). These medications have been shown to reduce sex drive and sexual fantasy among selected offenders, but noncompliance with the drugs as a result of their side effects may be a problem (Balon, 1998). Luteinizing hormone-releasing hormone agonists such as leuprolide have been tried but not completely evaluated. A recent class of drugs to be used with sex offenders includes the antidepressants sertraline, clomipramine, and fluoxetine. In most reported cases, subjects had comorbid mood disorders, and these medications were intended both to reduce deviant sex drive and to improve depressed mood. A potential advantage of these drugs is that their side effects are far less serious, and therefore noncompliance may be less of a problem. Pharmacotherapy is almost always used in combination with CBSOS therapy and is limited to use with the small subgroup of sex offenders who have an unusually strong and uncontrollable sexual interest in children (Marshall & Eccles, 1991).

Treatment Effectiveness

Does treatment of adult sex offenders against children work? Determining treatment outcomes is complicated by difficulties in constructing adequate comparison groups and by the diversity of offenders. Pharmacological interventions have not been tested outside of a few uncontrolled open-label or single-case studies. To date, there has been only one randomized trial of contemporary CBSOS treatment (Marquez, Wiederanders, Day, Nelson, & van Ommeren, 2005). The study was sizable, well designed, and used highly regarded modern treatment approaches, but the 8-year follow-up results found no treatment-related reduction in sex crime recidivism. Among the numerous quasi-experimental studies, the pattern of outcomes is variable and complex and may not yet lend itself to a clear synopsis. Overall, the results of the quasi-experimental studies suggest a moderate, but positive, effect. A recent meta-analytic study combining the data from 43 studies and 9,454 subjects found that sex offender treatment was associated with a moderate reduction in detected sexual recidivism from 16.8% to 12.3% over an average of 46 months of follow-up (Hanson et al., 2002). However, it must be borne in mind that this larger body of quasi-experimental studies is methodologically inferior to the Marquez et al. (2005) trial, which found no treatment effects. The upshot of this is that the effectiveness of adult sex offender treatment, both CBSOS therapy and pharmacological therapy, currently must be considered unproven. The relevance of these findings for parent-to-child sexual abusers is further complicated by the fact that abusers who are exclusively parent–child sexual abusers, have no other sex offenses or other criminal convictions, are married, are older, and have abused female children exclusively tend to have low recidivism rates (Hanson & Thornton, 1999). In fact, the recidivism rates for this group are so low that sexual abuse recidivism may not be the sole appropriate standard for evaluating treatment benefit, and evaluations of effectiveness may include other aspects of parenting as well as abstinence from sexually abusive behavior.

CHILD ABUSE PREVENTION PROGRAMS

In one of the more influential child abuse research articles of the past quarter century, Cohn and Daro (1987) reported on the limited effectiveness of a collection of federally funded abuse treatment programs. Basing their opinion on the disappointing results, they suggested that treatment was often too late to make a difference and recommended shifting priorities toward primary prevention efforts to reduce child abuse and neglect. Substantial resources remain devoted to intervention with identified cases through state child protective service agencies, but in the past decade, programs designed to prevent abuse and neglect have flourished. Prevention programs have many diverse approaches, and as we have noted throughout this chapter, there are considerable distinctions between physical abuse prevention and sexual abuse prevention interventions.

Physical Abuse Prevention: Home Visitation and Parenting Programs

The enthusiasm during the past decade for physical abuse and neglect prevention programs based on home-visiting models would be difficult to overstate. In 1993, the U.S. Advisory Board on Child Abuse and Neglect reiterated its opinion that "no other single intervention has the promise for preventing child abuse that home visitation has" (U.S. Department of Health and Human Services, U.S. Advisory Board on Child Abuse and Neglect, 1993, p. 7). Such programs have received millions of dollars of public and private child abuse prevention funding in recent years. It is estimated that up to 550,000 children per year receive home-visiting prevention services (Gomby, Culross, & Behrman, 1999). Although home visitation prevention programs have been widely implemented, the term *home visitation* refers only to the location where primary service delivery occurs and may say little about the content or quality of the service or who delivers it. Home visitors may be volunteers, paraprofessionals, or degreed professionals, depending on the service model. Programs may offer a set curriculum in which the home visitor delivers most of the services, or the program may provide mostly case management and referral services along with social support. Programs may be universal (i.e., offering services to all new parents in a designated high-risk area) or targeted (i.e., offering services to parents individually screened as being at risk) and may range from moderate term (e.g., less than a year) to long term (e.g., several years) in duration.

Many home-visitation programs have been large-scale statewide or nationwide efforts buoyed by national organizations promoting a particular model or approach. Some of the higher profile home visit models include the Nurse–Family Partnership Program (Olds et al., 1998), Healthy Families America, and the Hawaii Healthy Start model. Preventing child abuse and neglect is not the only goal for any of the major home-visitation prevention programs. However, abuse prevention is a benchmark goal, and substantial program funding has derived from this expected outcome.

As is often the case, large-scale implementation of perinatal home visitation programs was predicated on favorable but methodologically limited preliminary results from early projects. As more rigorous random-assignment evaluations of larger scale replications have ensued, it has become clear that child abuse prevention outcomes fall well short of what was hoped. Over the past 25 years, 12 true randomized trials evaluating perinatal home-visiting prevention programs and directly measuring child maltreatment outcomes have been conducted. Only one has yielded a significant positive finding (for a summary, see Chaffin, 2005). Other reviews have arrived at similar conclusions (Gomby et al., 1999). No reductions in future child maltreatment reports have been found in large-scale controlled studies of Hawaii's Healthy Start Program (Bugental et al., 2002; Duggan et al., 1999), Healthy Families America (Daro & Harding, 1999), and Parents as Teachers (Wagner & Clayton, 1999). A particularly comprehensive, intensive, and expensive home visitation demonstration project, the Comprehensive Child Development Program, was found to be associated with virtually no benefits (St. Pierre & Layzer, 1999). Despite these poor findings from true randomized trials directly measuring maltreatment outcomes, these models continue to be touted as "research supported" on the basis of logic models, single-group or quasi-experimental studies, or meta-analytic studies relying on soft or "proxy" outcomes.

The notable and positive exception to this disappointing trend is the Nurse–Family Partnership. Established in 1977 as a research–demonstration project in Elmira, New York, the intervention was designed to improve pregnancy outcomes, child health and development, and family economic self-sufficiency in low-income first-time mothers and their families (Olds et al., 1999). It is important to note that child maltreatment prevention is only one of a range of intended outcomes for the model. In fact, it might be argued that maltreatment prevention is one of the less central outcomes for which the model was designed. Although the intervention does focus on parent–child interaction during later phase participant involvement, the majority of the intervention is focused on improving pregnancy, delivery, early child health outcomes, and maternal life course benefits such as delaying subsequent pregnancy.

Olds et al. (1998) have reported results from two randomized trials (Elmira, New York, and Memphis, Tennessee). In the Elmira trial, mothers who received nurse home visiting did not have significantly fewer maltreatment reports in early follow-ups but did have fewer reports at the 15-year follow-up. Low overall base rates for maltreatment outcomes in the Memphis trial precluded testing the effectiveness of the model, so it remains unclear whether the Elmira findings can be replicated. Because of the staff qualifications required for nurse home visitors and the duration of the intervention, the model is expensive to implement, and it might be more cost-effective when focused on select subpopulations (i.e., very low income, single, young, less educated first-time mothers).

In addition to home visitation models, a number of other physical abuse prevention approaches have been implemented. These include family support programs, parenting classes, informational programs, case management programs, mutual aid programs, parent–infant nurturing programs, and programs for teen mothers. These are often smaller community-based efforts. Most are unevaluated, and virtually none have been rigorously evaluated. One recent statewide evaluation found that parents receiving services in these programs were no less likely to have a future valid child maltreatment report than were program dropouts or recipients of one-time services or recipients of concrete-needs services only, controlling for initial levels of risk (Chaffin et al., 2001).

Most physical abuse prevention models have relied on an intervention approach and involve services delivered to individuals. Public health approaches, similar to the broad social campaigns directed against cigarette smoking or alcohol consumption during pregnancy, may offer another perspective on physical abuse prevention. Because public health approaches may focus on achieving broad cultural changes in attitudes and behavior, controlled-trial evaluation paradigms may not be applicable to these programs. It does appear that rates of physical and sexual abuse move in concert with other broad social indicators (Jones & Finkelhor, 2003), suggesting that public health approaches to promoting broad social changes may be promising.

Sexual Abuse Prevention Programs

Historically, almost all sexual abuse prevention programs began as small grassroots efforts rather than as the large-scale national-level models described for physical abuse prevention. Child sexual abuse prevention programs are markedly different from the types of home-visiting and parenting programs intended to prevent physical abuse and neglect. Physical abuse and neglect prevention programs target parents and are designed to prevent maltreatment perpetration and reduce broad risk factors. With few exceptions, sexual abuse prevention programs target potential victims (i.e., children) rather than potential abusers. These programs are designed to prevent maltreatment victimization and target children's behavior in response to efforts to initiate sexual abuse. Many sexual abuse prevention programs are school based. Most are designed to teach young children about sexual abuse, teach personal safety and abuse avoidance skills (e.g., saying no), and encourage children to report abuse. This approach to sexual abuse prevention has been questioned on several grounds (Reppucci & Haugaard, 1989), including the assumption that children are capable of preventing their own sexual abuse by saying no. Concerns that sexual abuse victimization programs may make children unduly fearful or suspicious have not been supported for a majority of children participating in the programs but have been reported to occur with some children in response to some prevention materials (Daro, 1994; Finkelhor, Asdigian, & Dziuba-Leatherman, 1995b).

To date, none of the many packaged sexual victimization prevention curricula have been evaluated in a randomized trial to determine if they actually prevent sexual victimization. Most evaluations of these programs have been uncontrolled. Moreover, most evaluations have measured only knowledge acquisition as the outcome and not whether the intervention actually prevented future sexual abuse. The two quasi-experimental studies measuring future sexual abuse outcomes have reported mixed results. Gibson and Leitenberg (2000) found that college students who reported receiving sexual abuse prevention information also reported less sexual victimization. Results of a national survey of children found that children who participated in comprehensive sexual abuse victimization prevention programs at school retained some of the knowledge, reported using some of the safety strategies, and were more likely to tell if abuse had occurred. Unfortunately, the results suggested that children who participated in the programs were not less likely to experience sexual abuse and, in fact, were slightly more likely to be injured in the course of a sexual assault (Finkelhor et al., 1995a, 1995b). Both of these studies were retrospective and quasi-experimental, and consequently we cannot confidently know if sexual abuse victimization prevention programs are helpful, harmful, or inert.

There are few prevention models focused on potential or undetected abusers, and none have had controlled outcome studies. STOP IT NOW! is one of the few programs actively attempting to reduce sexual abuse by targeting adults, including at-large undetected sex offenders (Chasan-Taber & Tabachnick, 1999). Originators of this novel campaign reviewed the strategies of other successful public health initiatives and surveyed adults in a specific geographic region, including adult male sex offenders. On the basis of this information, three strategies were developed to intervene in sexually abusive behavior, including public education and a toll-free hotline where offenders and potential offenders can confidentially call for help. Proponents of public health approaches to sexual offense prevention (e.g., Laws, 1996, 1999) have argued that any reduction in sexual abuse is a step in the right direction even if complete abstinence for all sex offenders is not obtained and even if not all sex offenders are caught and subjected to criminal sanctions. Laws's controversial theory of harm reduction argues that services should be made readily available to potential and at-large undetected offenders without requiring legal involvement up front, similar to the policy currently used to treat users of illegal drugs. Policy attempts to augment criminal justice approaches with public health models will doubtless be controversial, and at present there are no rigorous data available to judge their effectiveness.

SUMMARY AND FUTURE DIRECTIONS: BUILDING AN EVIDENCE-BASED APPROACH TO CHILD ABUSE INTERVENTION AND PREVENTION

The study of treatment and prevention of parent-to-child violence is only beginning to develop the knowledge needed to evolve into an evidence-based field. As we have pointed out at various points in this chapter, no treatment or prevention intervention currently meets the most basic scientific criteria to be considered a well-supported evidence-based intervention, either for parent-to-child physical violence or parent-to-child sexual violence. This is true both for prevention and intervention programs. Some interventions have been heavily evaluated and found repeatedly to be ineffective in the most rigorous evaluation studies (e.g., the Healthy Start prevention model and its derivatives, crisis intervention and support, and case-management-based family preservation interventions). Adult sex offender treatment has a large and significant body of support in less rigorous studies, but the lone rigorous randomized trial has demonstrated no ultimate benefits, suggesting considerable caution in drawing conclusions about effectiveness. Many of the most widely practiced interventions simply have very little outcome data at all, rigorous or not (e.g., parenting groups, anger management groups, Parents Anonymous, and sexual abuse prevention programs).

Some treatment interventions do appear promising from an evidence-based perspective. For example, PCIT for physically abusive parents and Kolko's CBT model have at least one randomized controlled trial. The 12-Ways and SafeCare in-home models have a strong body of evidence using single-case experimental and quasi-experimental designs supporting their efficacy but less limited randomized trial testing. Most of the randomized trials of these promising treatment models have been conducted in the past few years. Also, among prevention approaches, the Nurse–Family Partnership model appears to be a promising prevention intervention, with support in one large randomized study with lengthy follow-up. Additional controlled trials of four of these promising models (PCIT, MST, Nurse–Family Partnership, and SafeCare) are currently underway, and depending on findings, these could emerge as well-supported models in the near future. As additional controlled-trial data emerge, we might expect to gain a far more confident evidence-based picture of what works to stop and prevent parent-to-child violence.

However, in a field that has historically been driven by advocacy more than by data, it remains to be seen how well field practitioners will assimilate emerging evidence-based interventions. Many of the interventions with emerging data supporting their effectiveness for stopping or preventing future parent-to-child violence are based on behavioral intervention models (e.g., PCIT and SafeCare), a perspective in which few field practitioners are trained and which may be uncomfortable or aversive for some practitioners. Other promising models, such as MST, require considerable time, effort, and resources to deliver.

Considerable loyalty exists and probably will continue to exist for unproven models. Some models, although demonstrated in the most rigorous studies to be ineffective for preventing child abuse, are supported by large national organizations and by dissemination and implementation networks (e.g., Healthy Families), and other large national dissemination and implementation networks promote models that have never been rigorously tested (e.g., Parents Anonymous). On the other hand are models with randomized trial support (e.g., PCIT or Kolko's CBT model) but no comparable dissemination and implementation infrastructure. Successful treatment or prevention efforts require both effective models and strong dissemination and implementation support systems. The main challenge we currently face involves merging the two.

REFERENCES

Abel, G. G., Becker, J. V., Mittelman, M. S., Cunningham-Rathner, J., Rouleau, J. L., & Murphy, W. D. (1987). Self-report sex crimes of nonincarcerated paraphiliacs. *Journal of Interpersonal Violence, 2*, 3–25.

Acton, R. G., & During, S. M. (1992). Preliminary results of aggression management training for aggressive parents. *Journal of Interpersonal Violence, 7*, 410–417.

Alexander, J. P., & Parsons, B. V. (1973). Short-term behavioral intervention with delinquent families: Impact on family process and recidivism. *Journal of Abnormal Psychology, 81*, 219–225.

Balon, R. (1998). Pharmacological treatment of paraphilias with a focus on antidepressants. *Journal of Sex and Marital Therapy, 24*, 241–254.

Barkley, R. A., Guevremont, D. C., Anastopoulos, A. D., & Fletcher, K. (1992). A comparison of three family therapy programs for treating family conflicts in adolescents with attention-deficit/hyperactivity disorder. *Journal of Consulting and Clinical Psychology, 60*, 450–462.

Behl, L. E., Conyngham, H. A., & May, P. F. (2003). Trends in child maltreatment literature. *Child Abuse and Neglect, 27*, 215–229.

Brunk, M., Henggeler, S. W., & Whelan, J. P. (1987). Comparison of multisystemic therapy and parent training in the brief treatment of child abuse and neglect. *Journal of Consulting and Clinical Psychology, 55,* 171–178.

Bugental, D. B., Ellerson, P. C., Lin, E. K., Rainey, B., Kokotovic, A., & O'Hara, N. (2002). A cognitive approach to child abuse prevention. *Journal of Family Psychology, 16,* 243–258

Chaffin, M. (2005). "Is it time to rethink Healthy Start/Healthy Families?": Response to letters. *Child Abuse and Neglect, 29,* 241–249.

Chaffin, M., Bonner, B., & Hill, R. (2001). Family preservation and family support programs: Child maltreatment outcomes across client risk levels and program types. *Child Abuse and Neglect, 25,* 1269–1290.

Chaffin, M., Silovsky, J., Funderburk, B., Valle, L. A., Brestan, E. V., Balachova, T., et al. (2004). Parent–child interaction therapy with physically abusive parents: Efficacy for reducing future abuse reports. *Journal of Consulting and Clinical Psychology, 72,* 491–499.

Chaffin, M., & Valle, L. (2003). Dynamic predictive validity of the Child Abuse Potential Inventory. *Child Abuse and Neglect, 27,* 463–482.

Chasan-Taber, L., & Tabachnick, J. (1999). Evaluation of a child sexual abuse prevention program. *Sexual Abuse: Journal of Research and Treatment, 11,* 279–292.

Cohn, A. C., & Daro, D. (1987). Is treatment too late? What ten years of evaluative research tell us. *Child Abuse and Neglect, 11,* 433–442.

Daro, D. (1994). Prevention of child sexual abuse. *Future of Children, 4,* 198–223.

Daro, D., & Harding, K. (1999). Healthy Families America: Using research to enhance practice. *Future of Children, 9,* 152–176.

Duggan, A. K., McFarlane, E. C., Windham, A. M., Rohde, C. A., Salkever, D. S., Fuddy, L., et al. (1999). Evaluation of Hawaii's Healthy Start Program. *Future of Children, 9,* 66–90.

Edleson, J. L. (1999). The overlap between child maltreatment and woman battering. *Violence Against Women, 5,* 134–154.

Eisenstadt, T. H., Eyberg, S., McNeil, C. B., Newcomb, K., & Funderburk, B. W. (1993). Parent–child interaction therapy with behavior problem children: Relative effectiveness of two stages and overall treatment outcome. *Journal of Clinical Child Psychology, 22,* 42–51.

Finkelhor, D., Asdigian, N., & Dziuba-Leatherman, J. (1995a). The effectiveness of victimization prevention instruction: An evaluation of children's responses to actual threats and assaults. *Child Abuse and Neglect, 19,* 141–153.

Finkelhor, D., Asdigian, N., & Dziuba-Leatherman, J. (1995b). Victimization prevention programs for children: A follow-up. *American Journal of Public Health, 85,* 1684–1689.

Finkelhor, D., & Dzuiba-Leatherman, J. (1994). Victimization of children. *American Psychologist, 49,* 173–183.

Finkelhor, D., Wolak, J., & Berliner, L. (2001). Police reporting and professional help seeking for child crime victims: A review. *Child Maltreatment, 6*, 17–30.

Gershater-Molko, R. M, Lutzker, J. R, & Wesch, D. (2002). Using recidivism data to evaluate Project SafeCare: Teaching bonding, safety, and health care skills to parents. *Child Maltreatment, 7*, 277–285.

Gibson, L. E., & Leitenberg, H. (2000). Child sexual abuse prevention programs: Do they decrease the occurrence of child sexual abuse? *Child Abuse and Neglect, 24*, 1115–1125.

Golub, J. S., Espinosa, M., Damon, L., & Card, J. (1987). A videotape parent education program for abusive parents. *Child Abuse and Neglect, 11*, 255–265.

Gomby, D. S., Culross, P. L., & Behrman, R. E. (1999). Home visiting: Recent program evaluations—Analysis and recommendations. *Future of Children, 9*, 4–26.

Gordon, A., & Hover, G. (1998). The Twin Rivers sex offender treatment program. In W. L. Marshall, Y. M. Fernandez, S. M. Hudson, & T. Ward (Eds.), *Sourcebook of treatment programs for sexual offenders* (pp. 3–15). New York: Plenum Press.

Hanson, R. K., Gordon, A., Harris, A. J. R., Marquez, J. K., Murphy, W., Quinsey, V. L., & Seto, M. C. (2002). First report of the collaborative outcome data project on the effect of psychological treatment for sex offenders. *Sexual Abuse: A Journal of Research and Treatment, 14*, 169–194.

Hanson, R. K., & Thornton, D. (1999). Static-99: *Improving actuarial risk assessments for sex offenders* (Users Report 99-02). Ottawa, Ontario: Department of the Solicitor General of Canada.

Hartley, C. C. (2002). The co-occurrence of child maltreatment and domestic violence: Examining both neglect and child physical abuse. *Child Maltreatment, 7*, 349–358.

Hughes, R. C., & Wilson, P. H. (1988). Behavioral parent training: Contingency management versus communication skills training with or without the participation of the child. *Child and Family Behavior Therapy, 10*, 11–23.

Jones, L. M., & Finkelhor, D. (2003). Putting together evidence on declining trends in sexual abuse: A complex puzzle. *Child Abuse and Neglect, 27*, 133–135

Kolko, D. J. (1996a). Clinical monitoring of treatment course in child physical abuse: Psychometric characteristics and treatment comparisons. *Child Abuse and Neglect, 20*, 23–43.

Kolko, D. J. (1996b). Individual cognitive–behavioral treatment and family therapy for physically abused children and their offending parents: A comparison of clinical outcomes. *Child Maltreatment, 1*, 322–342.

Laws, D. R. (1996). Relapse prevention or harm reduction? *Sexual Abuse: A Journal of Research and Treatment, 8*, 243–247.

Laws, D. R. (1999). Harm reduction or harm facilitation? A reply to Maletzky. *Sexual Abuse: A Journal of Research and Treatment, 11*, 233–241.

Littell, J. H. (1997). Effects of the duration, intensity, and breadth of family preservation services: A new analysis of data from the Illinois Family First Experiment. *Children and Youth Services Review, 19,* 17–39.

Lutzker, J. R., & Bigelow, K. M. (2002). *Reducing child maltreatment: A guidebook for parent services.* New York: Guilford Press.

Lutzker, J. R., Frame, J. R., & Rice, J. M. (1982). Project 12-Ways: An ecobehavioral approach to the treatment and prevention of child abuse and neglect. *Education and Treatment of Children, 5,* 141–155.

Lutzker, J. R., & Rice, J. M. (1987). Using recidivism data to evaluate Project 12-Ways: An ecobehavioral approach to the treatment and prevention of child abuse and neglect. *Journal of Family Violence, 2,* 283–289.

MacMillian, H. L., Thomas, B. H., Jamieson, E., Walsh, C. A., Boyle, M. H., Shannon, H. S., & Gafni, A. (2005). Effectiveness of home visitation by public-health nurses in prevention of the recurrence of child physical abuse and neglect: A randomized controlled trial. *The Lancet, 365,* 1786–1793.

Marquez, J. K., Wiederanders, M., Day, D. M., Nelson, C., & van Ommeren, A. (2005). Effects of a relapse prevention program on sexual recidivism: Final results from California's Sex Offender Treatment and Evaluation Project (SOTEP). *Sexual Abuse: A Journal of Research and Treatment, 17,* 79–107.

Marshall, W. L., & Eccles, A. (1991). Issues in clinical practice with sex offenders. *Journal of Interpersonal Violence, 6,* 68–93.

Marshall, W. L., Fernandez, Y. M., Hudson, S. M., & Ward, T. (1998). *Sourcebook of treatment programs for sexual offenders.* New York: Plenum Press.

McNeil, C. B., Eyberg, S., Eisenstadt, T. H., Newcomb, K., & Funderburk, B. W. (1991). Parent–child interaction therapy with behavior problem children: Generalization of treatment effects to the school setting. *Journal of Clinical Child Psychology, 20,* 140–151.

Molnar, B. E., Buka, S. L, & Kessler, R. C. (2001). Child sexual abuse and subsequent psychopathology: Results from the National Comorbidity Survey. *American Journal of Public Health, 91,* 753–760.

Moro, P. E. (1998). Treatment for Hispanic sexual offenders. In W. L. Marshall, Y. M. Fernandez, S. M. Hudson, & T. Ward (Eds.), *Sourcebook of treatment programs for sexual offenders* (pp. 445–456). New York: Plenum Press.

Nurius, P. S., Lovell, M., & Edgar, M. (1988). Self-appraisals of abusive parents: A contextual approach to study and treatment. *Journal of Interpersonal Violence, 3,* 458–467.

Olds, D. L., Henderson, C. R., Jr., Cole, R., Eckenrode, J., Kitzman, H., Luckey, D., et al. (1998). Long-term effects of nurse home visitation on children's criminal and antisocial behavior: 15-year follow-up of a randomized controlled trial. *Journal of the American Medical Association, 280,* 1238–1244.

Olds, D. L., Henderson, C. R., Jr., Kitzman, H. J., Eckenrode, J. J., Cole, R. E., & Tatelbaum, R. C. (1999). Prenatal and infancy home visitation by nurses: Recent findings. *Future of Children, 9,* 44–65.

Ondersma, S. J., Chaffin, M., Berliner, L., Cordon, I., & Goodman, G. S. (2001). Sex with children is abuse: Comment on Rind, Tromovitch, and Bauserman (1998). *Psychological Bulletin, 127,* 707–714.

Pithers, W. D. (1990). Relapse prevention with sexual aggressors: A method for maintaining therapeutic gain and enhancing external supervision. In W. L. Marshall & D. R. Laws (Eds.), *Handbook of sexual assault: Issues, theories, and treatment of the offender* (pp. 343–361). New York: Plenum Press.

Reppucci, N. D., & Haugaard, J. (1989). Prevention of child sexual abuse: Myth or reality. *American Psychologist, 44,* 1266–1275.

Shipman, K. L., Rossman, B. B., & West, J. C. (1999). Co-occurrence of spousal violence and child abuse: Conceptual implications. *Child Maltreatment, 4,* 93–102.

Slep, A. M., & Heyman, R. E. (2001). Where do we go from here? Moving toward an integrated approach to family violence. *Aggression and Violent Behavior, 6,* 353–356.

St. Pierre, R. G., & Layzer, J. I. (1999). Using home visits for multiple purposes: The comprehensive child development program. *Future of Children, 9,* 134–151.

Swenson, C. C. (2000, October). Community-based treatment of child physical abuse: Costs and outcomes. In M. Rowland (Chair), *MST Research: University Affiliated Projects.* Symposium conducted at the First International MST Conference, Savannah, GA.

Urquiza, A. J., & McNeil, C. B. (1996). Parent–child interaction therapy: An intensive dyadic intervention for physically abusive families. *Child Maltreatment, 1,* 132–141.

U.S. Department of Health and Human Services. (2001). *Evaluation of family preservation and reunification programs: Interim report.* Washington, DC: Author.

U.S. Department of Health and Human Services, U.S. Advisory Board on Child Abuse and Neglect. (1993). *The continuing child protection emergency: A challenge to the nation.* Washington, DC: U.S. Government Printing Office.

Wagner, M. M., & Clayton, S. L. (1999). The Parents as Teachers Program: Results from two demonstrations. *Future of Children, 9,* 91–115.

Wesch, D., & Lutzker, J. R. (1991). A comprehensive evaluation of Project 12-Ways: An ecobehavioral program for treating and preventing child abuse and neglect. *Journal of Family Violence, 6,* 17–35.

Whitcomb, D. (1991). Improving the investigation and prosecution of child sexual-abuse cases: Research findings, questions, and implications for public policy. In D. Knudsen & J. L. Miller (Eds.), *Abused and battered: Social and legal responses of family violence. Social institutions and social change* (pp. 181–190). Hawthorne, NY: Aldine de Gruyter.

Whiteman, M., Fanshel, D., & Grundy, J. F. (1987, November/December). Cognitive–behavioral interventions aimed at anger of parents at risk of child abuse. *Social Work, 32,* 469–474.

Wolfe, D. A., Sandler, J., & Kaufman, K. (1981). A competency based parent-training program for child abusers. *Journal of Consulting and Clinical Psychology*, 49, 633–640.

Wolfe, D. A., & Wekerle, C. (1993). Treatment strategies for child physical abuse and neglect: A critical progress report. *Clinical Psychology Review*, 13, 473–500.

4

THE PURSUIT OF WELLNESS FOR VICTIMS OF CHILD MALTREATMENT: A MODEL FOR TARGETING RELEVANT COMPETENCIES, CONTEXTS, AND CONTRIBUTORS

JOHN W. FANTUZZO, REBECCA J. BULOTSKY-SHEARER,
AND CHRISTINE M. McWAYNE

Child maltreatment is a national social problem that disproportionately threatens the development of our most vulnerable groups of children. According to the most recent national statistics (U.S. Department of Health and Human Services [USDHHS], Administration on Children, Youth and Families, 2004), nearly 900,000 children were victims of abuse and neglect in the United States in 2002. Overall, out of every 1,000 children, 12.3 were abused or neglected. A closer look at these data indicates that children in their most formative stages of development, 0 to 3 and 4 to 7 years old (Shonkoff & Phillips, 2000), have the highest likelihoods of victimization, with rates of 15.7 and 13.3 per 1,000, respectively. Moreover, the youngest age group (children 0–3) is more likely than any other to experience a recurrence of maltreatment (USDHHS, 2004).

An inspection of family demographic data from the National Incidence Study of Child Abuse and Neglect—3 (Sedlak & Broadhurst, 1996) reveals a significant relationship between other known risk factors for adverse child development and child maltreatment. Children from families with annual incomes below $15,000 were over 22 times more likely to be victimized than children from families with higher incomes, and children of single parents had a greater than 70% risk of being victimized than children living with both parents (Sedlak & Broadhurst, 1996). The association between maltreatment and poverty is most distressing for early childhood advocates, because children 0 to 5 years old have the highest prevalence rates of poverty compared with other age groups. Two out of every five young children in the United States are living in low-income families (National Center for Children in Poverty, 2005).

The challenge of responding to the needs of these vulnerable young children is particularly daunting for mental health scientist–practitioners. Young low-income and ethnic minority children are disproportionately underserved by traditional mental health service delivery systems (National Institute of Mental Health [NIMH], 1998). Inadequate access to developmentally and culturally sensitive services and lack of an adequate research database to inform services greatly impedes the ability to implement effective interventions on behalf of vulnerable children. Recently, the U.S. surgeon general (USDHHS, 1999) called attention to the significant disconnect between service providers and mental health scientists in addressing the needs of vulnerable children. He issued three major mandates to address these problems: (a) reduce stigma and increase sensitivity at points of entry and assessment, (b) expand supply and cultivate natural resources, and (c) establish real connections among disciplines and between research and practice (USDHHS, 1999).

These comprehensive mandates create a common purpose to advance inquiry and intervention efforts; they also represent an incredibly tall order for mental health scientist–practitioners. The mandates are necessary to focus psychologists' attention, but they are insufficient to produce significant results. What scientist–practitioners need are heuristic models to guide the design of culturally responsive and ecologically valid assessment and intervention methods for the most vulnerable groups of young children. The purpose of this chapter is to present a model that is both responsive to the mandates and capable of producing effective methods. The value and utility of this model is illustrated by a sequence of research studies that were designed as applications of the model to address the needs of victims of child maltreatment.

A CONCEPTUAL APPROACH TO GUIDE INQUIRY

Our conceptual model consists of three distinctive elements. It is child centered, partnership based, and population focused. These elements guide a mental health research agenda to serve the needs of urban low-income children who are victims of maltreatment. Each element contributes to the formation of a strategic community agenda to develop effective interventions using strategic natural resources. These dimensions of the model comprehensively address the "what and why," "how and with whom," and "where and when" of rigorous and relevant inquiry.

What and Why: The Child-Centered Element

Our model reflects a broad developmental–ecological systems perspective (Bronfenbrenner & Morris, 1998). It emphasizes a "whole child" theory that informs the collection of high-quality information about children's development. A whole-child perspective stresses the value of salient child competencies, contexts, contributors, and various courses or pathways of development. Competencies of the whole child, not disorders, are core to this developmental perspective. This perspective seeks to understand human development in terms of changes in the multiple domains of child functioning over time. Development is understood by looking at the central tasks that children are expected to perform as a function of their age and culture. These tasks require children to use their physiological, language, cognitive, emotional, and social competencies to meet major developmental challenges. Studying what constitutes competent, normal performance in these areas of functioning for diverse groups of children and considering how this development occurs along various pathways (courses) across time is the major focus of this approach.

In this approach, context plays an important role in determining the course of development. Context is the larger sphere in which development takes place. Interaction with context affects how and when children manifest psychological competencies. Context includes spheres of influence that create the expectations for performance and hence impact the child throughout development. Various influences can alter the course of development, creating different pathways for children attempting to adapt within their context. These systems or spheres of influence can in various ways enhance or impede development. Overall, multiple influences and multiple areas of functioning combine to shape the course of a child's development, resulting in adaptive or maladaptive patterns of child behavior (Cicchetti, 1993; Sroufe, 1997).

Embedded in these natural spheres of influence are important persons who are major contributors to child development (i.e., family members, peers, teachers, and community leaders). Forming partnerships with these key natural contributors is essential to promoting beneficial systemwide change for children. Recognizing the key contexts and key contributors to children's development informs the collection of high-quality information about children's competencies and ultimately leads to establishing beneficial connections to enhance development at multiple system levels.

How and With Whom: The Partnership-Based Element

Our model focuses on the process of forming partnerships with important natural contributors to maximize the healthy development of vulnerable children. Partnership is a genuine two-way exchange of information with stakeholders at multiple system levels that leads to the coconstruction and coimplementation of effective assessment and intervention strategies. What is essential here is to understand how to establish partnerships to foster beneficial change for children, families, and systems. In other words, what basic steps are necessary to transform salient contributors to child development into effective collaborators?

It is important to establish a dialogue with relevant contributors that fosters an understanding of the nature of the problem, factors influencing the problem, and interventions that can address the problem. It is particularly critical for researchers to recognize community stakeholders' theories of change and recommendations for addressing the problem. As has been pointed out in a number of recent reports, intervention research has often failed to serve low-income minority populations (see also Reese, Vera, & Caldwell, chap. 12, this volume). Researchers often unwittingly create stigma by being culturally unresponsive to this population's needs (USDHHS, 1999). Particularly with low-income minority populations in which there is a great disparity between the cultures of the researchers and the participants, therefore, researchers should be open to alternative approaches that are responsive to the needs of the participants (Lamb Parker, Greenfield, Fantuzzo, Clark, & Coolahan, 2000; Sherrod, 1999).

The first step in reducing stigma and distrust by the participant community is to "partner with resistance" (Fantuzzo & Mohr, 2000, p. 347). Instead of researchers just obtaining permission to collect information or conduct an intervention, they first must create a two-way dialogue with all members of the participant community. In our model, the first step to establishing a partnership base for research with low-income minority participants is to connect with the voice of the "no" members of the research participant community. Historically, there have been a disproportionate number of "no"s from research participants representing low-income or minority groups (Fantuzzo & Mohr, 2000). Their "no"s are shown through various overt and covert distancing actions that threaten the validity of the research findings (e.g., low participation rates, incomplete protocols, attrition rates, and lack of fidelity in following intervention protocol (NIMH, 1998).

Forming partnerships with the individuals behind these "no" voices means that researchers must temporarily suspend their initial research agenda and be open to eliciting and understanding the points of resistance of participant communities. Understanding reasonable causes (points of resistance) for potential participants' mistrust and tension about research in their community can guide the coconstruction of a more relevant and culturally responsive research agenda (Lamb Parker et al., 2000; Sigel, 1997). Recognition of and respect for specific points of resistance in a context that fosters discussion of concerns can create a rich two-way exchange of information. These exchanges can provide valuable information from the participant community about barriers and resources that are unknown to the researcher. This dialogue can form a basis for establishing common commitments to address problems and provide an opportunity to create a common language about the purpose of the research and the necessity of some research methods to achieve that purpose. For example, researchers need to create a shared understanding of why many items on a parent or teacher behavior rating scale are necessary to capture important dimensions of child development and targets for classroom intervention (e.g., competence motivation, interactive peer play, and self-regulation).

This context is also essential for identifying major gaps or questions regarding objectionable research methods. Recognition of gaps can potentially add another set of objectives to the original agenda, allowing partners to build additional research capacity. Coconstruction of a new research agenda or intervention makes the partnership between researcher and participant community more genuine (Fantuzzo & Mohr, 2000). Natural helpers in the community can work with researchers to share their unique knowledge and experiences and propose more relevant research objectives or methods. Involving these partners in the design and implementation of research strategies maximizes their contributions to the process, and their participation ensures the validity of the research activity (Lamb Parker et al., 2000). Shared commitments to children's health and development form the basis for the coconstruction of a shared plan of action; in other words, genuine partnership = shared commitments + shared ideas + shared actions.

Where or When: The Population-Focused Element

Often, mental health research with vulnerable children involves studying children in specialized intervention and treatment settings (e.g., clinics and school programs). The difficulty with studying children who show up (or who are compelled to show up) at specialized clinics is that the researchers do not know how representative these children are of the group of children exposed to the problem in the larger community. These samples of convenience, therefore, are not sufficient for a full understanding of the problem and possible solutions. To address this issue, researchers' first step is to understand the scope and impact of the problem in the child population (at various system levels, such as city, district, and school).

A public health approach provides researchers with the most comprehensive framework to investigate major threats to the development of child competencies (Teutsch, 1994). This approach highlights three principles that guide inquiry: (a) definition and substantiation of the communitywide problem, (b) representativeness of the problem in the community, and (c) collaboration among community practitioners and scientists (Teutch, 1994). These principles interact to guide the establishment of scientifically sound methods for collecting information and identifying strategic agencies in the community to investigate the problem and to develop and test interventions.

It is critical here to identify useful existing databases that are most representative of the group of children who are being studied. There has been increasing national recognition of the importance of administrative data to improve public service system responsiveness to vulnerable children and families with multiple interrelated needs (Reidy, George, & Lee, 1998). Administrative records (linked longitudinally by individual child) can be a powerful dynamic research and evaluation tool that captures important variables related to children's experiences across time (e.g., sequence, duration, and movement within service systems) and across service systems (service settings and programs; Reidy et al., 1998). Integrating such data enhances program capacity to examine service provision and create new initiatives to meet the needs of children and families. Researchers need to explore existing administrative databases in the community that are directly relevant to the problem under study. Building partnerships with authorized community investigators who maintain these databases can provide researchers with population-focused information to stimulate interagency discussion and corporate actions.

Our model is thus child centered, partnership based, and population focused. It guides programmatic research from the broadest population-focused level to the most specific level of testing the effectiveness of a particular classroom-based intervention. It should be noted that at each level, the scientist–practitioner is establishing successively a variety of essential partnerships to advance inquiry. At the larger system levels, partnerships are formed with leaders across relevant agencies. The scientist–practitioner also forms partnerships with the administrators of the strategic agency and, within the agency, with relevant practitioners and families.

APPLICATIONS OF THE MODEL TO CREATE COMMUNITYWIDE INTERVENTION

The following sections highlight empirical research that applies our model to the complex task of developing a community response to meet the needs of maltreated children. We demonstrate an intervention agenda that is based on communitywide partnerships aimed at enhancing the effectiveness of strategic change agencies.

Large-Scale Population-Focused Research

A research agenda guided by a child-centered perspective focuses on promoting children's early development and growth. Such an agenda examines early risk and protective factors within multiple contexts that influence children's development. The goal of this agenda is to minimize factors that impede development and maximize children's exposure to early protective factors that can promote healthy development and learning.

A primary developmental challenge for young children is being successful as they enter school (Entwisle & Alexander, 1993; Rimm-Kaufman & Pianta, 2000). When children enter school for the first time, they experience demands and expectations for performance that are different from those at home. Primary grade classrooms demand more intentional and focused academic learning as well as a high level of social and emotional competence (Love, Logue, Trudeau, & Thayer, 1992; Rimm-Kaufman & Pianta, 2000). Children's success in early years of formal schooling strongly predicts positive academic and social outcomes in later grades (Entwisle & Alexander, 1993). From a developmental ecological perspective, making a successful transition from home to school is critical for young children, and researchers must examine the multiple contexts that promote a successful transition (Rimm-Kaufman & Pianta, 2000). Understanding this developmentally appropriate transitional point is critical to identifying the factors that may play a protective role in mitigating early risks and positively influencing children's future school trajectory (Rimm-Kaufman & Pianta, 2000).

Unfortunately, children who have difficulty navigating the transition to the school context are at risk for continued educational difficulties, socially and academically (Entwisle & Alexander, 1993). Children who have been victims of maltreatment are more at risk for such difficulties in their transition to school (Cicchetti & Toth, 1997). For example, they are at greater risk for difficulties interacting with peers and teachers; are less likely to demonstrate a "secure readiness to learn" (Aber, Allen, Carlson, & Cicchetti, 1989); and are more likely than their nonmaltreated peers to perform poorly on standardized tests, to obtain lower grades, and to repeat a grade (Eckenrode, Laird, & Doris, 1993).

In the following two sections, we present large-scale population-focused research for developing a community agenda to meet the needs of maltreated children, focusing on their transition to school. The purpose of these studies was to create community dialogue and generate high-quality information to form partnerships, generate hypotheses, and build capacity for intervention.

Study 1: Population-Based Study of Risk for School Adjustment Problems

The first study involved investigation of a number of hypothesized risks to children's successful transition to school. The purpose was to integrate relevant administrative databases in a large urban center to conduct a population-based study of the impact of health and caretaking risk factors, including child maltreatment, on the school adjustment of first-grade students (Weiss & Fantuzzo, 2001). Specifically, we examined the relative impact of early childhood risk factors on children's first-grade academic performance, school behavior, grade retention, and attendance.

First, we linked records across major municipal agencies for an entire cohort of first-grade students ($N = 19,000$) attending public school in the city during one academic year. Participating agencies included the Department of Public Health, the Department of Human Services (DHS), and the city's school district. Information regarding children's early experiences was traced from the computerized records of these agencies to create an integrated record of experiences from birth to first grade for each child. Data for health-related risk factors (e.g., low birth weight and lead poisoning) were obtained from birth certificate records and lead-screening information. Caretaking risk factors (birth to a single parent, birth to a teenage parent, child maltreatment, and out-of-home placement) were collected from birth certificate and DHS records. First-grade school outcome data were collected from the school district.

A multivariate approach consistent with a child-centered developmental–ecological model was used to account for multiple risks. Multiple logistic regression was used to determine the likelihood of outcomes. This method tests models that simultaneously account for multiple influences such as poverty, child maltreatment, and single parenthood, thus allowing investigators to determine the unique contribution of each of the hypothesized risk factors on children's first-grade outcomes. In this study (Weiss & Fantuzzo, 2001), each of the early health and caretaking risk (explanatory) variables were entered into several logistic regression models to predict school adjustment outcomes. Children's school adjustment was measured by four outcome variables: (a) academic performance attained from teacher performance assessments in the areas of language arts and mathematics reported for each report card period; (b) school behavior attained from teacher evaluations, also reported for each report card period; (c) grade retention; and (d) school attendance.

Controlling for other risk variables in the model, children with a history of maltreatment were at significantly increased risk for poor school adjustment. The multivariate logistic regression findings indicated that three risk factors uniquely contributed to children's school adjustment problems: maltreatment, poverty, and single parenthood.

Study 2: Population-Focused Study of a Mutable Protective Factor

Although we were able use the available information from administrative databases in Study 1 to examine hypothesized risk factors to children's school adjustment, we had not yet developed the capacity to study hypothesized protective influences for these vulnerable children. Findings from Study 1 called for the need to learn more about how different types of preschool experiences buffer children from the negative impact of known risk factors. The next step was to initiate a communitywide study of the protective influence of early childhood experiences to promote school success.

We shared recent national studies from the empirical knowledge base with our community partners to support a population-focused investigation of formal early childhood experiences (Barnett, 1998; National Institute of Child Health and Human Development [NICHD] Early Child Care Research Network, 2002). The literature shows that high-quality early childhood educational experiences significantly influence the achievement and academic success of children living in poverty (Barnett, 1998). An additional major study supported by the NICHD documented significant relationships between the quality of early formal child-care experiences and children's social–emotional, cognitive, and language development and school performance (NICHD Early Child Care Research Network, 2002).

With the literature's support, rich dialogue ensued, and it became evident that the school district (which served the public education needs of over 200,000 children in the city) needed to develop the capacity to examine children's early childhood learning experiences before kindergarten entry. With the school district's Office of Kindergarten, we created a method to study this important protective factor, which had not been studied previously in this city.

We discovered that kindergarten teachers were required by contract to devote the first week of school (before the children started kindergarten) to parent–teacher conferences. We worked with the kindergarten administration and parent leadership to create a standardized, structured interview that could be implemented by teachers across the school district's kindergarten classrooms during these initial parent–teacher conferences. The interview was modeled after surveys conducted by the National Association for the Education of Young Children and asked parents about the nature and extent of their child's experiences prior to entering kindergarten. The interview method was piloted in partnership and was found to be reliable and reasonable to administer.

Using this interview method, we conducted a second population-focused study with a representative sample of kindergarten children ($N = 7,000$). For analysis, the types of children's early child-care experiences drawn from the survey were organized into three categories: formal, informal, and parent-only care. Formal care included center-based care, including Head Start and comprehensive day-care centers run by the school district. Informal care included family day care, in-home care, and relative care. Parent-only care included children with no other formal or informal care reported. This sample of students was followed into their first year of kindergarten to examine the protective influence of early childhood learning experiences. At three points during the kindergarten year, teachers assessed children's academic performance. Assessments were collected in the areas of early language arts, early mathematics, motor skills, personal knowledge (i.e., personal information about one's address, birthday, family, or city), and work habits. These assessments were standardized to allow for evaluation across time and subject area. In partnership with the school district, children's attendance across the year was also collected. To determine the influence of early childhood experiences on early kindergarten success, analysis of variance, repeated-measures analysis of variance, and multiple logistic regression were used. These multivariate methods comported with our developmental–ecological model, accounting for multiple influences on children's success.

Controlling for poverty, we found that early formal child-care experiences were significantly more protective than any other early child-care experiences for children's kindergarten success (Fantuzzo, 2002). During the first assessment period, children with formal care experiences were more likely to demonstrate higher assessment scores at the beginning of the kindergarten year in language arts, mathematics, social studies, and motor skills compared with children with either informal or parent-only care. At the first assessment period, this group of children was also more likely to have better attendance than peers without the same kind of formal early childhood educational experiences. This effect held up throughout the entire kindergarten school year.

Further, the school readiness advantages of center-based experiences did not diminish across the school year. Repeated measures analysis of variance indicated that children with center-based experience consistently maintained superior scores across the three evaluation points in kindergarten (Fantuzzo, 2002). Thus, the advantage of formal early child-care experiences (such as Head Start or other center-based care) held up across the year, consistently placing this group of children in the more academically successful group through the end of the year.

Finally, we examined the influence of the largest formal program in the city serving low-income preschool children—Head Start—on vulnerable children's kindergarten success. We specifically targeted Head Start because it was a strategic agency serving children experiencing a disproportionate level of risk (children were disproportionately from households headed by single women living in poverty). We found that Head Start was associated with better outcomes for vulnerable children. Children who attended Head Start showed higher assessment scores than matched comparison children with no Head Start experience at the beginning of the kindergarten year in language arts, mathematics, social studies, and motor skills. This advantage held up across the three evaluation points during the kindergarten school year. Findings from this population-focused study underscore the important protective influence of early formal educational experiences on children's kindergarten success.

Head Start as a Strategic Context for Capacity-Building Research

Head Start is the largest federally funded early intervention program for children living in poverty (Zigler & Styfco, 2004). Communitywide data resulting from the partnership projects described above provided valuable information that identified Head Start as a strategic service agency that could serve as a base for building high-quality assessment and intervention capacity for maltreated children. Head Start is guided by a developmental–ecological perspective that uses a whole-child model of service delivery (Zigler & Styfco, 2004). Given the diversity of low-income families that Head Start serves, the program strives to be culturally sensitive and responsive. To this end, a significant percentage of staff also comes from the local communities that Head Start serves. Head Start centers, therefore, provide an excellent natural laboratory with committed natural helpers to study children's competencies, the ill effects of exposure to risks, and promising interventions.

Our next task in applying our model was to document for our community partners the strategic nature of Head Start in relation to the problem of child maltreatment. With the cooperation of Head Start and child protective services, we integrated databases and mapped out regions in the city that contained the highest density of young maltreated children (ages 0–5 years). We determined that 20% of the Head Start centers were located in neighborhoods with the greatest concentration of maltreated preschool children. We then identified a representative sample of 250 Head Start children drawn from the Head Start population of 5,000 to conduct a prevalence assessment. We found that 20% of the Head Start children in this sample were identified with a verified history of DHS child protective services contact. This rate was compared with the national statistics for the general population, which indicate that approximately 13 out of 1,000 preschool children nationally are victims of child maltreatment (USDHHS, 2002). In addition to child maltreatment, prevalence rates were high for other known risk factors: 29% had mothers with less than high school education, 22% were born to teenage mothers, 86% had single parents, 13% had substantiated crime in the household, 11% had low birth weight, and 23% had high lead levels (>10 micrograms per deciliter).

With this information, we formed a sequence of inquiry with our partners to build assessment and intervention capacity. First, we wanted to maintain a strength-based approach to studying the problem of maltreatment and therefore needed valid measures of children's competencies in context. Next, we needed to understand the impact of maltreatment on children's competencies and the impact of Head Start on both maltreated and nonmaltreated children's competencies. Last, we needed to develop ecologically valid interventions to respond to the problem of maltreatment for Head Start children.

Building Strength-Based Assessment

In partnership with Head Start staff and parents, we assessed the appropriateness of existing measures of preschool children's competencies. We needed multidimensional measures that produced valid constructs for a diverse Head Start population. Several preschool measures of classroom behavior were reviewed and empirically tested with Head Start children. Some measures came under scrutiny by parents and teachers and were rejected outright because individual items focused on children's deficiencies rather than on their strengths (e.g., the Child Behavior Checklist and the Conflict Tactics Scale). Other measures were tested and found not valid for this population (Fantuzzo, McDermott, Manz, Hampton, & Burdick, 1996). After extensive discussions with our partners, we decided to coconstruct new measures of children's competencies and rigorously test their validity across diverse groups of Head Start children and across natural respondents (Gaskins, 1994; Rogers, 1998).

We developed partnerships to build capacity for high-quality measurement of children's strengths in the natural Head Start context, focusing on key competencies that have been identified in the literature as protective factors for school success. We conducted empirical studies to establish high-quality measurement of two relevant child competencies—peer play interactions and approaches to learning (Light & Littleton, 1999; McDermott, Green, Francis, & Stott, 2000). These competencies are relevant in that they both have been found to be related to successful outcomes and amenable to intervention.

The Penn Interactive Peer Play Scale (PIPPS) was developed by Head Start teachers, parents, and researchers to measure children's ability to engage positively with peers during play (McWayne, Sekino, Fantuzzo, & Hampton, 2002). The PIPPS is a multidimensional scale that differentiates Head Start children who successfully establish and maintain positive peer play relationships from those who are less successful with peers during play. The PIPPS provides an assessment of three types of peer play behaviors in the home, neighborhood, and school settings: Play Interaction, Play Disruption, and Play Disconnection. *Play Interaction* refers to creative, cooperative, and helpful behaviors that facilitate successful peer play interactions. *Play Disruption* captures a child's aggressive and disruptive play behaviors; whereas *Play Disconnection* refers to withdrawn and avoidant behaviors that impede active participation in play. Numerous studies have validated the PIPPS for use with a Head Start population (see McWayne et al., 2002). Strong associations between the PIPPS play dimensions and other developmentally salient constructs have been demonstrated. For example, classroom peer play interactions were found to be related concurrently to children's communication ability, receptive and expressive vocabulary, and emotion regulation and autonomy (see McWayne et al., 2002). The PIPPS dimensions were also found to predict psychological adjustment and developmental status. For example, early assessments of positive engagement in play were associated with lower levels of aggressive, shy, and withdrawn adjustment problems at the end of the preschool year. Furthermore, students who successfully interacted with peers early in the year were observed to show greater cognitive, social, and motor abilities at the end of the preschool year. Conversely, disruptive and disconnected peer play behaviors were associated with negative emotional and behavioral adjustment outcomes.

Preschool children's approaches to learning were identified as another important competency. They involve foundational learning behaviors such as persistence, competence motivation, flexibility, and attentiveness. These learning behaviors are distinct from cognitive ability or intelligence because they are uniquely teachable and account for substantial aspects of school performance untapped by ability measures (Barnett, Bauer, Ehrhardt, Lentz, & Stollar, 1996). The construct of children's approaches to learning was assessed using the Preschool Learning Behaviors Scale (PLBS; McDermott et al., 2000), a teacher-report measure validated for use with a Head Start population (Fantuzzo, Perry, & McDermott, 2004). The instrument yields three reliable learning behavior dimensions: Competence Motivation, Attention/Persistence, and Attitude Toward Learning. Competence Motivation reflects children's willingness to take on tasks and their determination to complete activities successfully. The Attention/Persistence dimension refers to the degree to which children pay attention and are able to follow tasks through to completion. Last, the Attitude Toward Learning dimension focuses on such concepts as children's willingness to be helped, desire to please the teacher, and ability to cope when frustrated. These learning behavior dimensions were found to relate significantly to teacher and parent ratings of Head Start children's behavior. Positive multivariate relationships were found between the PLBS dimensions and interactive peer play competencies at home and at school. Conversely, negative relationships were found between the PLBS dimensions and classroom problem behaviors (e.g., inattentiveness, conduct problems, and hyperactivity; Fantuzzo et al., 2004).

Impact of Maltreatment on Head Start Children's Competencies

We next sought to understand how maltreatment impacts the development of preschool competencies using our validated constructs (Fantuzzo & Cicchetti, 2000). We obtained a geographically and ethnically representative sample of children from Head Start centers. To examine maltreatment in the context of multiple risks and selected competencies, an interagency, integrated database was constructed and included information from child protective service reports (i.e., substantiated investigations) and public health, police department, and Head Start records.

We again used a multivariate approach for examining the relationships between sets of child competencies and risk variables. Specifically, multiple logistic regression modeling was used to examine the unique risk that child maltreatment poses for the development of peer play and learning behavior competencies (from the PIPPS and PLBS), controlling for other known risk factors (e.g., crime in the household, teen mother, low birth weight, and high lead level).

Child maltreatment was the most significant explanatory variable. For all three dimensions of peer play, children who were maltreated were much more likely to experience problems negotiating within the play context at school, controlling for the effects of the other risk variables in the model. For example, Head Start children who experienced maltreatment were three times more likely to have a disproportionate number of disruptive peer play experiences than children who were not maltreated and four times more likely to have disconnected peer play experiences than their nonmaltreated peers (Fantuzzo, 2002).

Similarly, children's learning behaviors were more significantly impacted by maltreatment than any other risk variables placed in our model.

Children who were maltreated were twice as likely to demonstrate low competence motivation as their nonmaltreated Head Start peers and three times more likely to have difficulty with adults and peers during learning activities.

Impact of Head Start on Maltreated Children's Competencies

In addition to the valuable information obtained concerning the impact of maltreatment on children's competencies, we needed to investigate the hypothesized protective effects of exposure to the strategic service agency across time for maltreated children. We asked the following questions: Does the Head Start experience result in significant gains for maltreated children across time? How does the trajectory of maltreated children compare with a group of nonmaltreated Head Start children?

We examined several children's competencies to answer these questions. One example concerns the peer play competencies of a representative sample of Head Start children. These children were assessed at the beginning and at the end of the Head Start year (Fantuzzo & Cicchetti, 2000). In this study, children with a history of maltreatment were matched with a sample of children with no verifiable history of maltreatment (i.e., on the basis of a careful examination of child protective services' data) on the basis of age, sex, ethnicity, Head Start classroom, and residence. Scores on the PIPPS were collected for these children in the participating centers during the months of October and May. Head Start professionals and research assistants were blind to children's maltreatment status.

An analysis of variance was conducted to examine peer play competencies of children in the two groups across time. For each peer play dimension, a main effect for time and group was found. For nonmaltreated and maltreated children, interactive peer play behaviors significantly increased across the academic year. However, nonvictims were consistently rated as more interactive during play activities than their maltreated peers.

In terms of play difficulties, ratings of disconnected play experiences for both groups of children significantly decreased over the year. Victims again were rated as more disconnected during peer play than their nonmaltreated counterparts at both points. Ratings of disruptive play experiences for both groups of children also decreased over the year. As expected, victims were rated as displaying more aggressive and disruptive play behaviors than nonvictims. However, a significant Time × Group interaction effect was found, showing that decreases in disruptive play experiences were significantly greater for maltreated children than for children who were not maltreated (Fantuzzo & Cicchetti, 2000).

Overall, these findings suggested that Head Start is associated with a beneficial effect for maltreated and nonmaltreated preschool children without any special programming. However, we found that maltreated children continued to be less likely to demonstrate adaptive peer play behaviors than their nonmaltreated peers, even after a year of Head Start. This gap between the peer social competencies of children who were victims and those who were not signaled the need to develop interventions in partnership with Head Start to enhance the agency's impact and to intentionally close the gap.

Multilevel Systems Intervention

Previous intervention research has been focused on the development of very specific time- and resource-intensive interventions that are typically demonstrated as effective by researchers but often not adopted by practitioners for routine use because they lack ecological validity (Henke, Chen, & Goldman, 1999). We believe effective interventionists must consider the context and available resources before intervening. Our model of intervention engages key contributors within and outside of Head Start to enhance Head Start's beneficial impact for maltreated children. Central to this approach is determining what resources are available in the classroom, program, and community to support intensive intervention efforts. Our efforts are guided by an ecological–transactional framework (Cicchetti & Toth, 1997), which defies a traditional medical model of childhood psychopathology promulgating one specific treatment for a problem. Instead, an ecological–transactional model postulates that factors at multiple system levels exert influences on individual development. Intensive intervention for maltreated children, therefore, calls for the cultivation of natural and relevant resources at these various levels to close the gap between the competencies of maltreated and nonmaltreated children. In accord with this perspective, we targeted various levels of Head Start children's environment: (a) classroom, (b) program, and (c) community.

A Classroom-Level Intervention

The first objective was to develop and test an intensive classroom-based intervention to close the gap between maltreated and nonmaltreated Head Start children's peer play competencies. This intervention was designed to use classroom peer play as a natural context for enhancing the social competency of preschool child victims. In keeping with the principles of our approach, this strategy was based on empirical research and was designed in partnership with teachers and parents to maximize the benefit of natural Head Start resources (see Fantuzzo, Weiss, & Coolahan, 1998). This intervention specifically targeted resilient and relevant contributors in this natural Head Start context.

We worked with Head Start classroom teachers to cultivate resources within the classroom for children having great difficulty engaging in productive peer interactions during free-play sessions. The intervention involved three natural contributors: teachers, socially competent peers (i.e., as measured by the PIPPS), and parent volunteers who were identified by staff as nurturing and supportive. Teachers were involved in the process of engineering space in their classrooms for the intervention play corner; socially skilled children served as direct treatment agents (play facilitators); and socially skilled parent volunteers served as indirect treatment agents by supporting positive interactions within the classroom. Parents were trained to support the peer play facilitators' attempts to draw the target child into play by prompting and praising the facilitators' efforts at the beginning and end of play sessions. The typical classroom session included the following steps. First, the parent volunteer entered the classroom and set up a portion of the classroom play area for the play sessions. Next, the parent talked individually with the skilled peer in preparation for the 20-minute play session. During play sessions, the parent helper observed from outside the play corner, noting specific collaborative behaviors. At the session's end, the parent helper made supportive comments to both children about their play, reinforcing them for specific collaborative behaviors observed (see Fantuzzo & Hampton, 2000).

Multisite randomized field tests were conducted to evaluate the effectiveness of this intervention with children demonstrating poor interactive peer play skills, including children with and without a history of abuse or neglect (Fantuzzo et al., 1996). Findings supported the effectiveness of the classroom-based peer-mediated intervention for children with social difficulties. Posttest assessments indicated significant gains in prosocial classroom peer interactions for the treatment group. These gains were comparable for maltreated and nonmaltreated children as seen by a main effect for group (treatment, control) and no main effect for maltreatment or Group × Maltreatment interaction. Therefore, regardless of maltreatment history, children who were randomly assigned to the treatment condition showed significantly higher levels of positive interactive play behavior and significantly lower levels of solitary play behavior at posttest than children assigned to the control condition. These findings demonstrate that a coconstructed intervention implemented in a natural classroom context and using the skills of natural contributors can close the gap for child victims of maltreatment.

A Program-Level Intervention

Given our successful demonstration of a classroom peer-mediated intervention incorporating exemplary teachers, socially competent peers, and exceptional parent volunteers, our task was to address the issue of generalizability to less resilient classrooms. Our systems perspective makes clear that early childhood classrooms vary greatly in quality and thus in the ability to sustain such an intensive intervention. Therefore, our next step was to collaborate with the Head Start administration to study the quality of classrooms across their program. We reviewed with program administrators, supervisors, and teachers a variety of measures used to assess the quality of early childhood classroom environments. As a result of these discussions, the Early Childhood Environment Rating Scale—Revised Edition (ECERS–R; Harms, Clifford, & Cryer, 1998) was selected as the assessment instrument.

The ECERS–R is used to assess the quality of the group learning environment for children ages 2.5 to 5 years. This 43-item observational tool measures the developmental appropriateness of classroom practices across seven dimensions: Space and Furnishings, Program Routines, Language and Reasoning, Activities, Interactions of Children and Staff, Program Structure, and Provision for the Needs of Parents and Staff. Items are rated on a 7-point scale with descriptors for 1 (*inadequate*), 3 (*minimal*), 5 (*good*), and 7 (*excellent*). These seven subscales together provide a descriptive look at the global quality of the individual classroom environment. The ECERS–R instrument has been shown to have good reliability and validity (Harms et al., 1998). More important, studies using the ECERS–R have shown relationships between classroom quality and children's competencies (Harms et al., 1998). Therefore, the ECERS–R is an excellent tool to use in identifying the strengths as well as possible areas for improvement of a particular classroom environment.

We selected 84 classrooms to be geographically representative of the program, and ECERS–R assessments of classroom environments were conducted by doctoral students trained to reliability. Analyses of the ECERS–R ratings provided an overall picture of classrooms across the program to be in the good to excellent range (78% of classrooms). However, classroom ratings within each classroom and across the program showed great variability. For example, 44% of classrooms scored in the excellent range for the Language and Reasoning subscale, whereas only 2% of classrooms scored in this same range for the Learning Materials and Activities subscale. The variability of scores suggests there are different profiles of classrooms within the program.

The information from this ECERS–R evaluation has fostered two studies currently underway. The first study is examining the effectiveness of a programwide intervention to raise the quality of all the classrooms in the Head Start program. The second study involves working with teachers to determine the minimal levels of classroom quality, including ECERS levels, teacher training, and program resources that are necessary to sustain an intensive, developmentally appropriate intervention for maltreated children, such as the intervention demonstrated in the above classroom studies.

A Community-Level Intervention

The third level of intervention involves a communitywide effort to foster support for Head Start centers serving as strategic agencies for vulnerable children. Just as Head Start classrooms demonstrated great variability, central-city neighborhoods vary in their capacity to support Head Start and other beneficial community programs. Therefore, it becomes even more important that community agencies collaborate with one another and share resources to enhance Head Start's effectiveness. At this step, we went back to our original set of cooperating municipal agencies that allowed us to integrate data for population study. We demonstrated how ad hoc across-agency data integration projects produced valuable information to enhance efforts to help vulnerable children (see the studies discussed above). We discussed with them various proposals and fundraising strategies to build and maintain a longitudinal, archival database to inform communitywide policy planning and allocation of resources. These efforts led to the development of a formal partnership effort.

A formal task force was established including faculty from the University of Pennsylvania and city commissioners to develop a Web-based, aggregate, integrated database for children and youth. Under the leadership of Dennis Culhane at the University of Pennsylvania's Cartographic Modeling Lab, three municipal agencies joined us to develop this integrated data system. These agencies include the school district, the Department of Human Services, and the Department of Public Health (including the Office of Mental Health and Community Behavioral Health). The system is based on the integration of aggregate administrative records for such variables as school attendance, child welfare, and child mortality. The data are aggregated to multiple planning geographies and made available with reporting, charting, and mapping tools through a secure Web site. This tool is the first of its kind in the nation at the municipal level and has demonstrated the power of an integrated database. This project has informed policy, planning, and program evaluation for agencies serving over a quarter of a million children. For a presentation of the relevant archival databases used, see Project Presentations (Neighborhood Information Systems and Philadelphia Services Utilization Monitoring System at the Web site for the Cartographic Modeling Lab, found through the University of Pennsylvania's online directory (http://cml.upenn.edu/). Studies are now underway to examine these neighborhood variables in relation to program quality and child readiness outcomes.

CONCLUSION

This chapter has presented an approach designed to generate the information necessary for a comprehensive, communitywide service agenda for young child victims of maltreatment. This approach has three distinct elements: It is (a) child centered, (b) partnership based, and (c) population focused. With a substantial partnership foundation and a child-centered perspective, we initiated a series of studies to determine how child maltreatment uniquely threatens children's mastery of basic school readiness competencies. A population focus allowed us to identify the availability of existing administrative data on a host of hypothesized risk factors, including child maltreatment, and then use these data to test risk models. This broad macropopulation focus enabled us to stimulate community dialogue about relevant protective factors for vulnerable children and to identify Head Start as a strategic service agency. Here, strategic agency is defined by its location in the community where the greatest density of vulnerable children live and by its capacity to serve as a natural setting for the development and testing of effective interventions. After research partnerships were established with Head Start, we studied how risk and protective factors affected the emergence of school readiness competencies and how partnerships with natural helpers could inform ecologically valid interventions. These research partnerships provided us with a base for initiating an intervention development process at multiple system levels. At each system level, the same basic strategy was applied: (a) Identify natural resources to enhance inquiry and to create intervention, (b) study impact using methods constructed in partnership, (c) consider the resources at more distal system levels (i.e., program and community) that are necessary to sustain quality intervention at more proximal system levels (i.e., classroom and family), (d) initiate intervention development and evaluation activity, and (e) bring evaluation information back to key partners to guide next steps.

This approach reflects the need to be responsive to national mandates for more appropriate and comprehensive child mental health service delivery systems for young victims of maltreatment (USDHHS, 1999). By focusing on children's competencies (instead of child or family deficiencies) and seeking a priori genuine partnerships at multiple system levels, we reduce stigma and increase the likelihood of more culturally responsive intervention. Collaborations that lead to productive applied research with strategic community agencies such as Head Start provide us with unique opportunities to build agency capacity and expand the supply of services to vulnerable young children. Finally, working with municipal leaders to integrate administrative data to address the needs of child victims of maltreatment fosters evidence-based interdisciplinary information and resource sharing. Like many known risks that threaten young children in the United States, child abuse and neglect is a massive and complex social problem; it therefore requires scientist–practitioners to develop and test models that are sufficient in scope and rigor to "occupy the space." Our model, and the data that support it, provides one such approach—a work in progress offered to meet this challenge.

REFERENCES

Aber, J. L., Allen, J. P., Carlson, V., & Cicchetti, D. (1989). The effects of maltreatment on development during early childhood: Recent studies and their theoretical, clinical, and policy implications. In D. Cicchetti & V. Carlson (Eds.), *Child maltreatment: Theory and research on the causes and consequences of child abuse and neglect* (pp. 579–619). New York: Cambridge University Press.

Barnett, D. W., Bauer, A. M., Ehrhardt, K. E., Lentz, F. E., & Stollar, S. A. (1996). Keystone targets for changes: Planning for widespread positive consequences. *School Psychology Quarterly, 11,* 95–117

Barnett, W. S. (1998). Long-term cognitive and academic effects of early childhood education on children in poverty. *Preventive Medicine, 27,* 204–207.

Bronfenbrenner, U., & Morris, P. (1998). The ecology of developmental processes. In W. Damon & R. Lerner (Eds.), *Handbook of child psychology* (Vol. 1, pp. 993–1028). New York: Wiley.

Cicchetti, D. (1993). Developmental psychopathology: Reactions, reflections, projections. *Developmental Review, 13,* 471–502.

Cicchetti, D., & Toth, S. L. (1997). Transactional ecological systems in developmental psychopathology. In S. S. Luthar, J. A. Burack, D. Cicchetti, & J. R. Weisz (Eds.), *Developmental psychopathology: Perspectives on adjustment, risk, and disorder* (pp. 317–349). New York: Cambridge University Press.

Eckenrode, J., Laird, M., & Doris, J. (1993). School performance and disciplinary problems among abused and neglected children. *Developmental Psychology, 29,* 53–62.

Entwisle, D., & Alexander, K. (1993) Entry into school: The beginning school transition and educational stratification in the United States. *Annual Review of Sociology, 19,* 401–423

Fantuzzo, J. (2002, September). *Evidence-based Head Start intervention: A fresh start.* Paper presented at the Philadelphia Head Start Conference, Philadelphia.

Fantuzzo, J., & Cicchetti, D. (2000, June). The impact of community and family violence on school readiness outcomes for Head Start children: An investigation of risk and resilience. In E. Kresh (Chair), *Findings from ACYF/Head Start–University Partnership Grants: 1996 Cohort.* Poster symposium presented at the Fifth Head Start National Research Conference, Washington, DC.

Fantuzzo, J., & Hampton, V. (2000). Penn Interactive Peer Play scale: A parent and teacher rating system for young children. In K. Gitlin-Weiner, A. Sandgrund, &

C. Schaefer (Eds.), *Play diagnosis and assessment* (pp. 599–620). New York: Wiley.

Fantuzzo, J., McDermott, P., Manz, P., Hampton, G., & Burdick, N. (1996). The Pictorial Scale of Perceived Competence for Young Children: Does it work with low-income urban children? *Child Development, 67,* 1071–1084.

Fantuzzo, J., & Mohr, W. (2000). Prevalence and effects of child exposure to domestic violence. *The Future of Children, 9,* 21–32.

Fantuzzo, J., Perry, M. A., & McDermott, P. (2004). Preschool approaches to learning and their relationship to other relevant classroom competencies for low-income children. *School Psychology Quarterly, 19,* 212–230.

Fantuzzo, J., Sutton-Smith, B., Atkins, M., Meyers, R., Stevenson, H., Coolahan, K., et al. (1996). Community-based resilient peer treatment of withdrawn maltreated preschool children. *Journal of Consulting and Clinical Psychology, 64,* 1377–1386.

Fantuzzo, J., Weiss, A., & Coolahan, K. (1998). Community-based partnership-directed research: Actualizing community strengths to treat child victims of physical abuse and neglect. In J. R. Lutzker (Ed.), *Child abuse: A handbook of theory, research, and treatment* (pp. 213–238). New York: Pergamon Press.

Gaskins, S. (1994). Integrating interpretive and quantitative methods in socialization research. *Merrill-Palmer Quarterly, 40,* 313–333.

Harms, T., Clifford, R. M., & Cryer, D. (1998). *Early Childhood Environment Rating Scale* (Rev. ed.). New York: Teachers College Press.

Henke, R. R., Chen, X., & Goldman, G. (1999). *What happens in classrooms? Instructional practices in elementary and secondary schools, 1994–1995.* Washington, DC: U.S. Department of Education, National Center for Education Statistics.

Lamb Parker, F., Greenfield, D. B., Fantuzzo, J. F., Clark, C., & Coolahan, K. C. (2000). Shared decision making in early childhood research: Foundation for successful community–university partnerships. *NHSA Dialog, 3,* 234–257.

Light, P., & Littleton, K. (1999). *Social processes in children's learning.* Cambridge, England: Cambridge University Press.

Love, J. M., Logue, M. E., Trudeau, J. V., & Thayer, K. (1992). *Transitions to kindergarten in American schools.* Portsmouth, NH: U.S. Department of Education.

McDermott, P. A., Green, L. F., Francis, J. M., & Stott, D. H. (2000). *Preschool Learning Behaviors Scale.* Philadelphia: Edumetric & Clinical Science.

McWayne, C., Sekino, Y., Fantuzzo, J., & Hampton, G. (2002). *Penn Interactive Peer Play Scale (PIPPS): Teacher and parent rating scales for preschool and kindergarten children.* Philadelphia: University of Pennsylvania.

National Center for Children in Poverty. (2005). *Basic facts about low-income children in the United States (February 2005).* New York: National Center for Children in Poverty, Mailman School of Public Health, Columbia University.

National Institute of Child Health and Human Development Early Child Care Research Network. (2002). Child-care structure→process→outcome: Direct and indirect effects of child-care quality on young children's development. *Psychological Science, 13,* 199–206.

National Institute of Mental Health. (1998). *Bridging science and service: A report by the National Advisory Mental Health Council's Clinical Treatment and Services Research Workgroup.* Bethesda, MD: Author.

Reidy, M., George, R., & Lee, B. J. (1998). Developing an integrated administrative database. In M. Little & D. Gordon (Eds.), *Exploring research methods in social policy research* (pp. 185–210). Aldershot, England: Ashgate Publishing.

Rimm-Kaufman, S. E., & Pianta, R. C. (2000). An ecological perspective on the transition to kindergarten: A theoretical framework to guide empirical research. *Journal of Applied Developmental Psychology, 21,* 491–511.

Rogers, M. (1998). Psychoeducational assessment of culturally and linguistically diverse children and youth. In H. Booney Vance (Ed.), *Psychological assessment of children* (2nd ed., pp. 355–384). New York: Wiley.

Sedlak, A., & Broadhurst, A., (1996). *National Incidence Study of Child Abuse and Neglect—3.* Washington, DC: Westat.

Sherrod, L. R. (1999). A commentary on "Head Start and mental health: An argument for early screening and intervention" by Edward G. Feil. *National Head Start Association Dialogue, 2,* 412–415.

Shonkoff, J. P., & Phillips, D. A. (Eds.). (2000). *From neurons to neighborhoods: The science of early childhood development.* Washington, DC: National Academy Press.

Sigel, I. E. (1997). Practice and research: A problem in developing communication and cooperation. In I. E. Sigel & A. K. Renninger (Vol. Eds.), *Handbook of child psychology: Vol. 4. Child psychology in practice* (5th ed., pp. 1113–1132). New York: Wiley.

Sroufe, L. A. (1997). Psychopathology as an outcome of development. *Development and Psychopathology, 9,* 251–268.

Teutsch, S. M. (1994). Considerations in planning a surveillance system. In S. M. Teutsch & R. E. Churchill (Eds.), *Principles and practice of public health surveillance* (pp. 31–82). New York: Oxford University Press.

U.S. Department of Health and Human Services. (1999). *Mental health: A report of the surgeon general.* Rockville, MD: Author.

U.S. Department of Health and Human Services, Administration on Children, Youth and Families. (2004). *Child maltreatment 2002.* Washington, DC: U.S. Government Printing Office.

Weiss, A., & Fantuzzo, J. W. (2001). Multivariate impact of health and caretaking risk factors on the school adjustment of first graders. *Journal of Community Psychology, 29,* 141–160.

Zigler, E., & Styfco, S. J. (2004). Moving Head Start to the states: One experiment too many. *Applied Developmental Science, 8,* 51–55.

SECTION INTRODUCTION:
YOUTH VIOLENCE PREVENTION

Though youth can be a wonderful time of life, an unfortunate reality is that perpetration of violence and victimization among youths are very high for that age group. Distressing though this information may be, it also seems logical that with this age group, an enhanced possibility for prevention might exist. Thus, in this section, chapters are devoted to the developmental pathways in youth violence; school-based programs aimed at prevention and intervention; and the challenges, sequelae, and prevention of bullying.

In chapter 5, Dahlberg and Simon cover the developmental pathways of violent and delinquent behavior, risk factors, and the implications of this knowledge for designing interventions. The authors address the concern over life-course-persistent offenders and the factors that may predict and drive such behavior. The earlier that such characteristics can be identified in the developmental sequence, perhaps the better the chances of preventing a lifetime of offending. That children with the highest levels of aggression in kindergarten are known to be more prone to lifetime offending also suggests that many difficult-to-control risk factors may be operating with these children. Also of concern is that the vast majority of data have been collected on boys, though the incidence of violence by girls is increasing.

Thus, similar information will need to be gleaned with girls. In chapter 5, the authors detail the comorbid factors, such as hyperactivity and impulsivity, that may act as moderators or mediators of aggressive behavior with these children.

The data are relatively clear about the adverse role played by associating with delinquent peers. This suggests the need for parental monitoring and opportunities to allow children more positive associations through community organizations, such as engagement in organized after school programs. There is also increasing information about the potentially dangerous outcomes for children who are socially rejected. This has important implications for assessment and intervention strategies.

"Weak" family environments, characterized by single parent families, poor parental supervision, or parental substance abuse, increase risk for youth violence. Such families need early intervention ranging from parent training to helping improve the social–ecological circumstances that mitigate violent family and community violence. Poor academic achievement is also highly correlated with youth violence. In chapter 5, Dahlberg and Simon address a number of school factors that may add to risk, such as ability grouping. Putting academically challenged children, many of whom are also behaviorally disruptive, together in the same setting may create a breeding ground for escalating challenging behaviors for students at risk.

It is clear that disadvantaged neighborhoods foster youth violence in a number of ways, such as limited resources for parents and children for positive social development and situations that make parental monitoring difficult. Though it is challenging, there are modifications that can be made in neighborhoods to reduce youth violence risk factors. In chapter 5, the authors also suggest mechanisms from selective (high-risk) to universal (whole-population) prevention that offer opportunities for change and systematic evaluation of such efforts.

School-based interventions aimed at preventing youth violence are reviewed in chapter 6 by Farrell and Camou. They note how schools represent ideal natural settings for prevention. Though seriously violent incidents in schools themselves are statistically rare, the authors note that schools can potentially breed violent behaviors that may be displayed outside of the school setting.

Four dimensions used to classify prevention strategies form the basis for the discussion in chapter 6: social systems, individuals, developmental stages, and goals of programs. Though elementary schools have very little serious violence, they are ideal settings for primary prevention efforts. However, it is important to create violence prevention curricula that are developmentally appropriate. Often programs may represent ambitious attempts to change children's attitudes, knowledge, and behavior, but if developmental factors are not considered, such programs will be necessarily ineffective. For example, if a curriculum is clearly above the developmental level of the first and second graders for whom it might be intended, the children will not understand or benefit from such a program. Similarly, fifth graders might understand a program but not value it if they feel it is too juvenile.

The middle school population has been a ground for considerable evaluation of youth violence prevention programs. Farrell and Camou cover some of the most salient features of some of the better evaluated middle school programs. High school programs have in recent years focused on dating violence prevention. This age group represents an excellent opportunity for primary and minimal secondary prevention of subsequent intimate partner violence and its related sequelae. For example, the SafeDates Program (Foshee et al., 2004) was implemented with 9th- through 12th-graders, and data collected 4 years postintervention showed a significant intervention effect for reductions in physical violence, serious physical violence, and sexual violence.

Farrell and Camou also address the sad fact that most efforts at school-based youth violence prevention are not sufficiently evaluated or that when some of these programs have been evaluated, they have been found not only to be ineffective but possibly harmful. Such outcomes speak to the need not only for carefully evaluated programs but also for programs that have undergone replicated efficacy trials prior to effectiveness testing. Then, after effectiveness demonstrations, programs must be "tweaked" so that they can be disseminated without diluting their positive effects. An especially poignant issue addressed in chapter 6 is the need for programs that teach specific skills and endeavor to make sure that such skills are generalizable. In addition, programs should be based on well-tested theory.

Farrell and Camou cover other well-addressed methodological concerns such as including process fidelity measures in research aimed at school-based violence prevention, ensuring the collection of follow-up data, planning research of sufficient power, and conducting component evaluations. These are solid recommendations for research in most applied settings and are certainly applicable to school-based violence prevention programs.

Bullying has been identified as being responsible for several negative sequelae in child victims, including subsequent violence. In chapter 7, Orpinas and Horne address this problem that is of increasing concern. They examine the definition of bullying, the scope of the problem and its modal age group, the serious consequences from bullying, and attempts to reduce bullying in schools. One of their suggestions for reducing bullying in schools is the development of bullying prevention teams that include district plans for preventing the problem. They also address the critical need for support for such programs by teachers and other school personnel and present some evidence of the effectiveness of such programs. They suggest that student education in the form of skill-based training should go hand in hand with school programs.

Thus, the Youth Violence Prevention section of this book addresses the etiology and surveillance issues in youth violence, school-based violence prevention programs, and the particular problem of bullying. Community-based programs aimed at youth violence prevention are not addressed in this section, because these efforts are more nascent than school-based programs and thus have had fewer robust effectiveness trials. Clearly, parents and the community are important components of a comprehensive effort to prevent youth violence, and there is a need for more and better evaluations of all programs. Reducing the rates of youth violence will undoubtedly have positive effects on the rest of society in terms of economic costs and the reduction of adult-perpetrated violence over time. As with child maltreatment, programs aimed at youth violence prevention must be culturally sensitive and relevant. That is, a youth violence program will only be effective if the youths are receptive to it. Any program that fails to address cultural issues will necessarily leave many potential recipients behind.

REFERENCE

Foshee, V. K., Bauman, S., Ennett, G., Linder, T., Benefield, T., & Suchindran, C. (2004). Assessing the long-term effects of the SafeDates Program and a booster in preventing and reducing adolescent dating violence victimization and perpetration. *American Journal of Public Health, 94,* 619–624.

5

PREDICTING AND PREVENTING YOUTH VIOLENCE: DEVELOPMENTAL PATHWAYS AND RISK

LINDA L. DAHLBERG AND THOMAS R. SIMON

In 2002, a total of 18,022 homicides occurred in the United States, for an annual age-adjusted rate of 6.2 per 100,000 population (Kochanek, Murphy, Anderson, & Scott, 2004). Young people are disproportionately represented as victims and perpetrators of homicide. In 2002, 35% of all victims of homicide were younger than 25 years of age (Centers for Disease Control and Prevention, 2005). The majority of these victims (81%) were boys and young men. Young people are also overrepresented in arrest rates for murder, nonnegligent manslaughter, robbery, forcible rape, and other crimes. In 2003, 44% of all persons arrested for violent crimes and 57.4% of all persons arrested for property crimes were under 25 years of age (U.S. Department of Justice, 2004). Nearly 80% of those arrested for either a violent or property crime in the United States were male.

This chapter was authored by employees of the United States government as part of official duty and is considered to be in the public domain. Any views expressed herein do not necessarily represent the views of the United States government, and the authors' participation in the work is not meant to serve as an official endorsement.

The relationship between age and crime is well known and has been documented throughout history. Although different types of offenses tend to peak at different ages, violent and delinquent behavior typically increase during the teenage and early years of adulthood and taper off with advancing age (U.S. Department of Justice, 2003). There also appears to be little specialization in the types of offenses committed by young people, and they generally commit a variety of violent and nonviolent offenses (Farrington & Loeber, 2000; U.S. Department of Justice, 2004).

In recent years, researchers have begun to explore whether violent and delinquent behavior in adolescence is part of a general pattern of antisocial and aggressive behavior that emerges during childhood or whether it is the result of certain personal, situational, and environmental factors that occur in adolescence and young adulthood. Some children, for example, exhibit stubborn, defiant, and disobedient behavior at very young ages and progress to mild and eventually more severe forms of aggressive and delinquent behavior by adolescence and young adulthood. Other children either do not exhibit serious problem behavior until they reach adolescence or seem to outgrow aggressive behavior by the time they enter elementary school. Any number of psychological, social, and environmental factors could be related to the continuity or change in violent and delinquent behavior over the life course. A question of great interest to researchers is the extent to which patterns of aggressive and antisocial behavior in childhood are predictive of violent and delinquent behavior at later ages. From the perspective of violence prevention, researchers are also interested in knowing which factors increase or buffer the risk for violent and delinquent behaviors at different ages. Understanding continuity or change in behavior during different developmental periods, for instance, is key to identifying appropriate points for intervention.

The purpose of this chapter is threefold: (a) to describe the developmental pathways of aggressive, violent, and delinquent behavior; (b) to describe the factors that increase the risk for violent and delinquent behavior at different ages and across developmental periods; and (c) to discuss the implications of the different patterns of behavior and risk for designing preventive interventions.

DEVELOPMENTAL PATHWAYS

Previous research indicates that there may be different developmental pathways that can lead to serious violence and delinquency during adolescence and young adulthood and that the age of onset for these behaviors may vary considerably (Loeber et al., 1993; Loeber, Wei, Stouthamer-Loeber,

Huizinga, & Thornberry, 1999; Tolan & Gorman-Smith, 1998; Tolan, Gorman-Smith, & Loeber, 2000). Loeber et al. (1993, 1999) have identified three pathways to problem behavior: an authority conflict pathway, a covert pathway, and an overt pathway. The authority conflict pathway consists of a sequence of stubborn, defiant, and disobedient behavior in early childhood and shows a progression to other authority avoidance behaviors by adolescence such as truancy, running away, and staying out late. The covert pathway consists of minor covert behaviors such as lying and shoplifting, shows a progression to moderate behaviors such as vandalizing property and setting fires, and eventually progresses to more serious delinquent behaviors such as burglary. The overt pathway begins with forms of aggression such as bullying and shows a progression to physical fighting and more serious forms of violence by adolescence and adulthood. Each of these pathways begins with milder behaviors and progresses to more serious behaviors. Together, the pathways indicate a range of problem behaviors and variability with respect to the age of onset.

Children who follow a developmental pathway toward serious violence and delinquency have been referred to as *life-course-persistent offenders* (Moffitt, 1993). Across the life span, depending on circumstances and available opportunities, such children exhibit changing manifestations of antisocial behavior. These offenders share a number of characteristics that set them apart from other offenders—including an early onset of offending, active offending during adolescence, persistence of crime and violence during adulthood, and an escalation of the seriousness of offending (Howell & Hawkins, 1998; Krohn, Thornberry, Rivera, & LeBlanc, 2001). Between 20% and 45% of boys who are serious violent offenders at 16 to 17 years of age are said to be on a *life-course-persistent developmental pathway* (D'Unger, Land, McCall, & Nagin, 1998; Stattin & Magnusson, 1996; U.S. Department of Health and Human Services [USDHHS], 2001).

A number of longitudinal studies have found evidence of life-course-persistent offending (Farrington, 2003; Huesmann, Eron, Lefkowitz, & Walder, 1984; Krohn et al., 2001; Moffitt, Caspi, Dickson, Silva, & Stanton, 1996; Olweus, 1979; Stattin & Magnusson, 1989). In one study spanning 22 years, children who exhibited aggressive behavior at age 8 were more likely to score higher on aggression on the basis of the Minnesota Multiphasic Personality Inventory at age 30, to report higher levels of physical aggression and spouse abuse as adults, to have more criminal convictions as adults, and to engage in more serious criminal acts. The children of these subjects also tended to exhibit aggressive behavior (Huesmann et al., 1984). A prospective study of boys spanning a period of 40 years also showed a significant continuity in aggression and violence from childhood to adulthood (Farrington, 2003). Boys with a history of early aggression were more likely as adults to commit violence toward spouses and intimate partners; to engage in other high-risk behaviors such as drinking, driving drunk, and using drugs; and to have more criminal and noncriminal convictions.

Longitudinal research on more than 4,000 youths from three cities (Rochester, Denver, and Pittsburgh) also shows a pattern of offending that begins at relatively early ages and, for a small proportion of youths, persists over time. Data from the Rochester Youth Development Study indicate that among those who began committing violent offenses before age 9, nearly 40% became chronic violent offenders by the age of 16 (i.e., committing violent offenses with high frequency) compared with 30% who began committing violent offenses between the ages of 10 and 12 and 23% who began at age 13 or older (Thornberry, Huizinga, & Loeber, 1995). Among those who initiated violent offending before age 10, 30% continued offending into early adulthood (ages 19–22) compared with 16% who began committing violent offenses between the ages of 11 and 12 and 11% who began at age 13 or 14 (Krohn et al., 2001).

Life-course-persistent offenders, however, represent a small proportion of the overall offender population. A much larger proportion of the offender population engages in violent and delinquent behavior for a more limited period of time. Some have characterized this group as *adolescence-limited offenders* (Moffitt, 1993), in part because they begin committing violent or delinquent offenses at a later age (e.g., 13 and older) and have a shorter offending career than life-course-persistent offenders (Loeber & Farrington, 2001). For example, results from the National Youth Survey (which is based on a national probability sample of youths ages 11–17 years in 1976 who were followed until ages 27–33) suggest a limited period of offending during the adolescent years. Although a small percentage of youths exhibited a continuity of violence into and through early adulthood, the majority of youths were involved in delinquent or violent activities for approximately 1 to 3 years (Williams, Guerra, & Elliott, 1997).

Research on offending also has shown that it tends to be varied and intermittent as opposed to continuous. For example, data from the Denver Youth Survey for one 5-year period indicate that among serious violent offenders (i.e., those whose acts resulted in serious injury requiring medical treatment), the majority were involved in violent offending for only 1 year or not at all; 22% were involved in serious violent offending for 2 contiguous years during the 5-year period; and 12% engaged in serious violent offending for 3 or more contiguous years. Among the multiple-year offenders (i.e., those youths whose violent offending lasted more than 3 years), over half were not active every year (Thornberry et al., 1995).

The extent to which these patterns are characteristic of both boys and girls is less clear. Most of the major longitudinal research on delinquent and violent offending has focused on the offending patterns of boys. Studies examining the offending patterns of girls are mixed with respect to the continuity of violence. Girls exhibiting an early history of high aggression in the Columbia County Study in New York, for example, scored significantly higher on aggression, punishment, and criminality 22 years later compared with those in the low- or medium-aggression groups, though the differences were less significant than for boys. (Huesmann et al., 1984). Findings from the Orebro project in Sweden do not show a relationship between early aggression and later violent offenses for girls (Stattin & Magnusson, 1989), whereas those from a follow-up study of children from the Woodlawn neighborhood in Chicago found consistent patterns for both boys and girls (McCord & Ensminger, 1995). A six-site cross-national study found a clear linkage between childhood physical aggression and violent and delinquent offending in adolescence for boys but not for girls (Broidy et al., 2003). Longitudinal research on other cohorts of youths has indicated a later onset of aggressive and delinquent behavior among girls than boys and a peak occurring at younger ages (Elliott, 1994). A small proportion of girls with late onset, however, continue offending into early adulthood.

It is not clear the extent to which patterns of aggression and antisocial behavior evident in the first 5 years of life are predictive of later patterns of aggression and antisocial behavior. Many of the longitudinal studies showing life-course-persistent offending have followed children as early as 5 years of age (although more typically from the ages of 7–13), with parent, self-report, school, and arrest data collected at various times until young adulthood. Some researchers have selected birth cohorts and followed subjects in arrest records (Denno, 1990; Tracy & Kempf-Leonard, 1996), but few investigators have collected data from multiple sources on children from birth until adulthood.

Information on patterns of aggression and antisocial behavior among young children comes primarily from studies of child development. Research on young children using observational techniques and parental reports suggests that most children are aggressive during the first few years of life (Coie & Dodge, 1997; Loeber & Hay, 1994; Tremblay, 2000). In infancy, physical discomfort and the need for attention are among the most frequent determinants of aggressive behavior. By the 3rd and 4th years of life, the most frequent determinants for aggressive behavior are peer conflicts and conflicts over material possessions (Coie & Dodge, 1997). It is not unusual for children to push and shove siblings or peers, to grab toys away from others, or occasionally even to bite or kick other children to get what they want. These types of aggressive behaviors tend to subside as children develop speech capabilities to express needs and handle conflicts (Loeber & Hay, 1994). However, although physical aggression tends to decrease normatively between 2 and 4 years of age, verbal aggression tends to increase during this period (Coie & Dodge, 1997).

Noncompliant or disobedient behavior is also a common problem in young children. Estimates of noncompliance among population-based samples of children, as reported by parents, range from 25% to 65% (Kalb & Loeber, 2003). The percentage of parents reporting frequent or severe noncompliance is much lower (1%–9%). Similar to aggressive behavior, noncompliant or disobedient behavior subsides as children prepare for elementary school (Kalb & Loeber, 2003). The usual developmental course is to shed these problems by 8 years of age (Coie & Dodge, 1997). In short, most children learn not to be aggressive and to respond appropriately to the demands of authority figures.

If there are different developmental pathways leading to violence and delinquency, then which factors explain why some children outgrow aggressive, disobedient, and oppositional behavior early in life whereas others continue to exhibit aggressive and problem behavior throughout childhood and on into adolescence and adulthood? Are there, for instance, a constellation of individual, familial, situational, and environmental factors that distinguish children who deviate from the norm and for whom there is an increased risk for violent and delinquent behavior at different ages and continuously across developmental periods?

PREDICTORS OF VIOLENT AND DELINQUENT OFFENDING

There is a large body of research on the factors that increase the probability of violent and delinquent behavior, and comprehensive reviews of this literature are available elsewhere (Coie & Dodge, 1997; Farrington, 1998; Hawkins et al., 1998; Loeber & Hay, 1997; USDHHS, 2001). This body of research suggests that there are a variety of factors—some residing in the individual and others in the social environment—that increase the likelihood of violent and delinquent behavior. However, it is worth noting that previous research has not always clearly distinguished the factors that are specifically associated with violent behavior from those factors associated with nonviolent behavior. Given the versatility in offending, there may be significant overlap in the factors that predict violent or delinquent behavior, but there may also be some important differences.

Apart from assuming that the factors predictive of violent behavior are similar to those predicting delinquent behavior, few researchers have tried to disentangle the factors that are associated with life-course-persistent offending from those factors associated with offending over a more limited period of time (e.g., during adolescence). There is some evidence that the factors associated with the onset of offending (either during childhood or adolescence) may be different from those associated with persistent offending (Chung, Hawkins, Gilchrist, Hill, & Nagin, 2002; Farrington, 2003; Kosterman, Graham, Hawkins, Catalano, & Herrenkohl, 2001; Loeber, Keenan, & Zhang, 1997; White, Bates, & Buyske, 2001). There is also recognition that even with stability in violent and delinquent behavior over time (Brame, Mulvey, & Piquero, 2001), there are also large within-individual differences in offending (Laub & Lauritsen, 1993). Moreover, the factors that are predictive of differences between individuals may be different than those within individuals (Farrington, Loeber, Yin, & Anderson, 2002; Johnson, Hoffmann, Su, & Gerstein, 1997). Biological factors may also play a role in the development and persistence of violent and delinquent behavior (Coie & Dodge, 1997; Raine, Farrington, Brennan, & Mednick, 1997). These are important considerations when reviewing the available evidence linking different factors to patterns of violent and delinquent offending over the life course.

Individual Factors

Violent and delinquent behavior has been linked to a number of behavioral factors in childhood, including attention problems, hyperactivity, poor behavioral control (e.g., impulsiveness), and disruptive and oppositional behavior (af Klinteberg, 1997; Farrington, 1998, 2003; Hawkins et al., 1998; Lipsey & Derzon, 1998; Nagin & Tremblay, 1999, 2001). For example, in the meta-analysis conducted by Lipsey and Derzon (1998), factors such as hyperactivity, daring behavior, impulsiveness, and attention problems measured at 6 to 11 years of age were among the important predictors for violent and serious delinquent behavior between 15 and 25 years of age. In the Pittsburgh Youth Study, persistent serious violent offenders were nearly three times as likely to qualify for a disruptive behavior disorder diagnosis as nondelinquents (Stouthamer-Loeber & Loeber, 2002). Moreover, between 21% and 28% of all eventual persistent serious offenders qualified for a disruptive behavior disorder diagnosis by the age of 13.5 years (Stouthamer-Loeber & Loeber, 2002).

There is some evidence that factors such as hyperactivity, oppositional behavior, and poor behavioral control may be particularly related to persistent violent offending (as opposed to persistent nonviolent offending). In the Dunedin, New Zealand, Multidisciplinary Health and Development Study, boys with convictions for violence up to the age of 18 years were significantly more likely to have had poor scores in behavioral control between ages 3 and 5 years compared with boys with no convictions or convictions for nonviolent offenses (Henry, Caspi, Moffitt, & Silva, 1996). In a longitudinal study of boys followed repeatedly from ages 6 to 15, Nagin and Tremblay (2001) found that children with the highest levels of physical aggression in kindergarten were the most prone to follow a path of chronic violence. The two most powerful predictors in the high-aggression trajectory were high levels of hyperactivity and opposition at age 6, individually accounting for about a threefold increased risk and together about a ninefold increased risk.

Other research, however, suggests that hyperactivity may primarily be associated with entry into a particular pathway and not necessarily associated with advancement to more serious violent and delinquent behavior (Loeber et al., 1997). For example, in their study of developmental pathways toward serious delinquency, Loeber et al. (1997) found attention-deficit/hyperactivity disorder (ADHD) to be higher among persisters than among those who were experimenters (i.e., those whose problem behavior was more temporary) and lowest among those with no disruptive symptoms. There were, however, few differences in ADHD between persisters in the early stages of a developmental pathway and persisters in later stages of a developmental pathway. Evidence from other studies suggests that hyperactivity is predictive of later delinquency only when it co-occurs with physical aggression or oppositional behavior (Lahey, McBurnett, & Loeber, 2000; Nagin & Tremblay, 1999). Of all the behavioral factors, early physical aggression is the most significant predictor of involvement in violent and delinquent behavior before the age of 13 (Loeber & Farrington, 2001). Longitudinal evidence also indicates that youths who become involved in violent or delinquent behavior prior to the age of 13 (especially those with an arrest) are also more likely to become persistent chronic offenders by the age of 18 (Patterson, Forgatch, Yoerger, & Stoolmiller, 1998).

Other characteristics that may separate youths with stable patterns of violent and delinquent behavior from other youths are related to personality traits, belief systems, and social–cognitive processes. Youths who have highly aggressive attitudes, have high levels of distrust and estrangement from others, lack empathy and guilt, and are sensation seekers are more likely to be involved in violent and delinquent behavior (Kosterman et al., 2001; LeBlanc & Lanctot, 1998; Loeber, Farrington, Stouthamer-Loeber, Moffitt, & Caspi, 1998). These types of personality traits and belief systems may also separate those with life-course-persistent offending patterns from others. In the Dunedin study, boys who exhibited antisocial behavior continuously from ages 3 to 18 years (about 7% of the total sample) also endorsed extremely aggressive attitudes; were hostile, alienated, suspicious, and cynical; and felt callous and cold toward other people (Moffitt et al., 1996). By age 26, they continued to be elevated on a number of psychopathic personality traits (Moffitt, Caspi, Harrington, & Milne, 2002). Youths with a later onset of problem behavior and who were involved in violent and delinquent behavior for a more limited period of time, by comparison, had more typical personality structures, desired more close relationships with friends and family, and had less aggressive attitudes (Moffitt et al., 1996).

In terms of social–cognitive processes, research has shown that children and adolescents with social–cognitive impairment often have difficulty interpreting social situations, make social decisions quickly, and perceive the actions or intentions of others as hostile (Coie & Dodge, 1997). When confronted with aggressive responses from others, highly aggressive youths tend to have difficulty arriving at nonaggressive solutions, endorse retaliatory aggression, and believe that aggression reduces aversive treatment by others. Social–cognitive deficits have been linked to aggressive behavior in childhood and adolescence (Dodge et al., 2003; Hudley, 1994; Lochman & Dodge, 1994; Slaby & Guerra, 1988), but they have not been studied in relation to persistent violent and delinquent offending over the life course. This is mostly the result of an absence of such measures in the major longitudinal studies of youth violence. More serious manifestations of social–cognitive impairment may appear in adolescence or early adulthood, but it seems unlikely that social–cognitive deficits would appear for the first time in these developmental periods. In this regard, social–cognitive deficits are likely to be a more important marker for early-onset as opposed to later onset offending.

Peer Factors

Research on delinquency has shown that associating with delinquent peers increases the risk of serious delinquency and involvement in criminal activity severalfold (Huizinga, Weiher, Espiritu, & Esbensen, 2003; Thornberry et al., 1995). In the longitudinal studies reviewed by Lipsey and Derzon (1998), social ties and involvement with antisocial peers were the strongest predictors for later offending among the 12-to-14 age group—ranking higher than other individual and family factors. Youths at risk on these predictors had 3 to 20 times the probability of engaging in subsequent violent or serious delinquency of those not at risk on these predictors. An important question is the extent to which associations with deviant peers are a cause of violent and delinquent behavior or a mediating factor in both the development and persistence of violent and delinquent behavior.

There is evidence to suggest that peer influences play an important role across developmental periods and are related to the onset of offending among some youths and the escalation of offending among other youths (Chung et al., 2002; Elliott & Menard, 1996; Keenan, Loeber, Zhang, Stouthamer-Loeber, & Van Kammen, 1995; Thornberry, 1998). Research on adolescents without a prior history of problem behavior shows a relationship between exposure to deviant peers and the initiation of offending (Elliott & Menard, 1996; Keenan et al., 1995). For example, Elliott and Menard (1996) examined the temporal transitions between exposure to deviant peers and delinquent behavior using data from the National Youth Study. They found that exposure to deviant peers more often preceded delinquency than the reverse. Keenan et al. (1995) reported similar findings related to the initiation of offending among a sample of youths in Grades 4 and 7, whose behavior and exposure to deviant peers was measured at half-year intervals over five successive assessment periods. Boys without a history of involvement in disruptive behavior, when exposed to peers engaging in authority conflict, either covert or overt behaviors, were 1.5 to 2.2 times more likely to subsequently engage in the same behavior as boys who had not been exposed to deviant peers.

Among youths with a history of offending, the exposure to deviant peers has an impact on the frequency and severity of offending during adolescence (Chung et al., 2002; McCord & Conway, 2002; Thornberry, 1998). For example, among youths already delinquent by age 13, Chung et al. (2002) found associating with antisocial peers to be among the primary predictors distinguishing youths whose delinquent behavior escalated from those whose problem behavior desisted. Other research has shown that offending with others increases the likelihood of serious offending (e.g., index crimes), regardless of age at first offense (McCord & Conway, 2002).

Gangs are probably the best example of how exposure to deviant peers can lead to more frequent and severe offending. Gang members have significantly higher rates of violent and delinquent offending than nongang members, especially serious violent offending (Battin, Hill, Abbott, Cata-lano, & Hawkins, 1998; Huizinga et al., 2003; Thornberry, Krohn, Lizotte, Smith, & Tobin, 2003). In the Rochester Youth Development Study, gang members made up 30% of the sample but were responsible for 86% of the serious acts of delinquency and 68% of the violent acts (Thornberry, 1998). In Denver, gang members constituted 14% of the total sample but were responsible for 79% of the acts of serious violence (excluding gang fights; Huizinga et al., 2003). Longitudinal studies have shown much higher rates of offending during the period of active membership, with lower rates both preceding and following gang membership (Hill et al., 1996; Huizinga et al., 2003; Thornberry et al., 2003). Active membership in a gang also seems to increase involvement in violent and delinquent behavior over and above prior offending behavior and associations with delinquent peers (Battin et al., 1998; Battin-Pearson, Thornberry, Hawkins, & Krohn, 1998). In the Rochester study, across all eight waves of data, gang members reported committing violent offenses at significantly higher rates than nongang members who associated with highly delinquent peers, even after controlling for family poverty, parental supervision, associations with delinquent peers, previous involvement in violent behavior, commitment to school, and negative life events (Battin-Pearson et al., 1998; Thornberry, 1998).

Deviant peer associations have generally not been measured in childhood, making it more difficult to ascertain their role in the development of early aggressive and other problem behavior. Social rejection by peers, on the other hand, is a factor that may lead aggressive and disruptive children to gravitate toward more deviant peer groups by adolescence (Coie, 1990; Coie & Miller-Johnson, 2001). Although the factor of social rejection was not specifically studied in the Cambridge Study in Delinquent Development, Farrington (2003) found that convicted delinquents compared with nondelinquents were unpopular with peers by age 10 (on the basis of peer ratings) but had more delinquent friends by age 14. Dishion, Patterson, Stoolmiller, and Skinner (1991) found an association between peer rejection by age 10 and involvement with antisocial peers 2 years later.

Social rejection by peers, which is partly a function of aggression and the social–cognitive deficits and biases that accompany aggression, has also been linked to later antisocial behavior. In a recent study, Dodge et al. (2003) found an association between social rejection by peers in early elementary school and later antisocial behavior, even after controlling for previous antisocial behavior. The effect held only for those children who were initially above the median in aggressive behavior, and it held equally well for boys and girls. A large proportion of the effect was mediated by biases and deficits in social information processing. According to Dodge et al. (2003, p. 390), initial problems in processing social information leads children to be rejected by their peers. The experience of social rejection, in turn, alters the way children attend to social cues and solve social problems. Socially rejected children become hypervigilant in attending to hostile cues and tend to generate aggressive responses. Over time, the aggressive and rejected child seeks out others who are similar (Bagwell, Coie, Terry, & Lochman, 2000).

Although peer relationships may have some of their earliest influences in childhood and greatest influences in terms of the initiation and escalation of offending during adolescence, they play less of a role with age. Reiss and Farrington (1991) found that most juvenile and young adult offenses were committed with others, but the incidence of co-offending declined steadily with age. McCord and Conway (2002) analyzed the offending patterns of 400 youths randomly selected from police tapes in Philadelphia and followed up in court records. They divided the sample into three groups on the basis of the age at first recorded offense: early starters (those whose first offense was committed before age 13), late starters (those whose first offense occurred after age 16), and modal offenders (those whose first offense occurred between 13 and 15 years of age; 32.5% of the sample). Overall, 66% of the offenses committed prior to age 13 were committed with others. They also found that the probability of offending alone (as opposed to with others) increased as a function of age at first offense. Fewer than 5% of the early starters committed all crimes alone compared with 15% among modal offenders and 30% among late starters.

Peers play an important role across developmental periods, but they are only one of several influences that need to be considered in understanding the onset and persistence of offending over the life course. Factors related to family, school, and community contexts also have the potential to alter a youth's developmental course and later life chances, opportunities, and outcomes.

Family Factors

A number of family characteristics increase the probability of involvement in violent and delinquent behavior. Apart from demographic characteristics such as large family size, low income, and growing up in a single-parent household (Farrington, 1998; Wasserman & Seracini, 2001), youths at risk for violence tend to come from weak family environments. A *weak* family environment is one that can include constellations of poor family management and parenting practices, deficiencies in communication and problem solving, family conflict and violence, parental problem behaviors such as alcohol and drug use, and involvement in criminal activities. Although each of these factors has been linked to violent and delinquent offending, findings from several longitudinal studies are less clear in terms of the relative importance of some of these factors in predicting early- versus late-onset offending or persistent offending into adulthood.

Poor family management includes the failure of a parent to set clear expectations for a child, poor monitoring and supervision, a lack of involvement in the child's activities, and harsh or inconsistent discipline. In the longitudinal studies reviewed by Lipsey and Derzon (1998), these types of parenting practice were more important as predictors of later violence and delinquency in the 12-to-14 age group than in the 6-to-11 age group. The differences in effect size between the two age groups, however, were small ($r = .19$ vs. $r = .15$). Herrenkohl et al. (2000) found that a condition of poor family management practices at ages 14 to 16 was more predictive of self-reported violence at age 18 than at age 10. However, in the Cambridge study, poor parenting (especially the combination of punitive punishment with poor supervision and authoritarian child-rearing attitudes) at ages 8 to 10 was among the most important predictors of later violent and delinquent behavior (Farrington, 2003).

Poor parental supervision and monitoring are likely to be more proximal factors in offending during adolescence than during late childhood, which probably explains their stronger association with violence and delinquency in the adolescent period than in the childhood period. A stronger association with the adolescent period, however, does not imply that it is associated only with late-onset offending. For those with an early onset of offending (i.e., before age 13), poor supervision and monitoring may mean the difference in adolescence between escalation in offending and desistence (Chung et al., 2002). When coupled with other poor parenting practices in childhood, such as harsh discipline and authoritarian child-rearing attitudes, it may also set the stage for long-term persistent offending. Moffitt and Caspi (2001), for example, found that youths with an early onset of offending had childhoods characterized by poor parenting. Similar findings have been reported elsewhere (Wasserman & Seracini, 2001).

Parental problem behavior such as alcohol or drug use or involvement in criminal activities may further erode parenting skills and complicate parental efforts to discipline and exercise effective monitoring or supervision. Data from the Pittsburgh Youth Study show a strong association between family criminality and delinquency, with convicted fathers having the most impact on the delinquency of youths (Farrington, Jolliffe, Loeber, Stouthamer-Loeber, & Kalb, 2001). Evidence from longitudinal studies that have followed youths from childhood until the age of 45 also shows a strong relationship between parental criminality and persistent offending well into adulthood (Farrington, Barnes, & Lambert, 1996; Farrington & West, 1993; McCord, 1977). In the Cambridge study, having a convicted parent before the age of 10 was one of the best predictors of convictions for violent and delinquent behavior up to the age of 40 (Farrington, 2003). Exposure to a delinquent sibling, especially one close in age, also has a strong impact on both early offending and persistent offending into adulthood (Reiss & Farrington, 1991).

Family criminality is predictive of persistent offending, but it is only one marker of family dysfunction. It is also present in a relatively small proportion of families (Farrington et al., 1996, 2001). Other forms of violence in the family, such as intimate partner violence, child maltreatment, and a general family climate of conflict and hostility, provide significant exposure. Findings from one longitudinal study showed a dose–response relationship between exposure to family violence and involvement in violent behavior (Thornberry, 1994; Thornberry et al., 1995). Whereas 38% of youths from nonviolent families reported involvement in violent behavior, the rate increased to 60% for youths exposed to one form of family violence, 73% for youths exposed to two forms of family violence, and 78% for youths exposed to three forms of family violence.

It is difficult, however, to separate the proportion of risk that is due to witnessing intimate partner violence from that associated with experiencing abuse or the other negative consequences associated with family violence. Children growing up in homes where there is intimate partner violence are at higher risk of emotional, mental health, and behavioral problems (Edleson,

1999; Wolfe, Crooks, Lee, McIntyre-Smith, & Jaffe, 2003). They are also at greater risk for child maltreatment (Edleson, 1999). Children with an abuse history show higher levels of physical aggression, ADHD, social–cognitive problems, and absenteeism from school (Lansford et al., 2002; Shields & Cicchetti, 1998; Toth, Cicchetti, & Kim, 2002)—all factors that are associated with violent and delinquent behavior. Chronically maltreated children are also more likely to be rejected by their peers across multiple years from childhood to adolescence, mostly as a function of their physically aggressive behavior (Bolger & Patterson, 2001). Women who are victims of partner violence, on the other hand, are more likely to experience a number of physical and mental health consequences that, in and of themselves, compromise parenting and make them less available to their children emotionally and otherwise (Levendosky & Graham-Bermann, 2001). Families reporting domestic violence also show higher levels of poverty, fewer years of parental education, and higher levels of social isolation and are more likely to be headed by a woman (Wasserman & Seracini, 2001).

All of the above factors play an important role in the early onset and persistence of violent and delinquent behavior. They also help to explain why children with abuse histories are more likely to exhibit aggression in school and community settings (Lynch & Cicchetti, 1998; Shields & Cicchetti, 1998), to engage in serious delinquent and violent behavior as adolescents (Kelly, Thornberry, & Smith, 1997; Maxfield & Widom, 1996; Stouthamer-Loeber, Wei, Homish, & Loeber, 2002), and to be arrested for a violent crime as an adult (Maxfield & Widom, 1996; Widom, 1989).

School Factors

Children who are products of weak family environments also have difficulty adjusting to school. There appear to be mutual relationships among a weak family environment, involvement in delinquent peer groups, and school failure. Involvement in delinquency, for example, tends to reduce levels of attachment to parents (Jang & Smith, 1997) and attachment to school (Thornberry, Lizotte, Krohn, Farnsworth, & Jang, 1991). Poor academic performance, low commitment to school, and school failure, on the other hand, are related both to the onset, escalation, and seriousness of offending in adolescence and to persistent offending into adulthood (Ayers et al., 1999; Farrington, 2003; Kosterman et al., 2001; Maguin & Loeber, 1996; Moffitt et al., 1996).

School settings in general may contribute to disruptive behavior and persistent patterns of offending. A number of characteristics of the school environment may engender more aggression and negative peer influences. These include undisciplined classrooms; lax enforcement of school rules and policies; tight physical space; and conformity to behavioral routines that seem to produce feelings of anger, resentment, and rejection in some students (National Research Council, 1993). Certain school practices have also been implicated in fostering negative peer group interactions and the problems most likely to result from these interactions. Ability grouping (or *tracking*), for example, tends to place academically poor students and those with disruptive behavioral patterns together in classes. Ability grouping has not been shown to improve learning among low-achieving students, and indeed, has been associated with many negative social consequences (Dornbusch, Glasgow, & Lin, 1996; Oakes, 1990). Students in low tracks are more negative toward school, have lower educational aspirations, and are at a much greater risk of dropping out of school—factors that increase the risk of becoming involved in violent and delinquent behavior. Suspension and expulsion, routine policies for students involved in physical fighting, weapon carrying, and substance use (Gottfredson & Gottfredson, 2001; Small et al., 2001), also make problem behavior more likely by reducing supervision and creating opportunities for risk-taking behaviors.

Community Factors

It is not possible to fully understand the developmental trajectories of violent and delinquent behavior without taking into account the myriad social and economic influences that operate in communities. Crime and violence are high in neighborhoods with concentrated disadvantage (Morenoff, Sampson, & Raudenbush, 2001; Peterson, Krivo, & Vélez, 2001). In addition to having high concentrations of poor and unemployed people, these areas are characterized by high levels of residential instability, crowded housing, drug-distribution networks, and low community participation and collective efficacy (Reiss & Roth, 1993; Sampson, Raudenbush, & Earls, 1997). These areas also tend to have high rates of school dropouts, high rates of substance abuse and teenage pregnancy, and a disproportionate number of households headed by women (Proctor & Dalaker, 2003; Reiss & Roth, 1993).

Apart from their demographic characteristics, disadvantaged neighborhoods differ from affluent neighborhoods in a number of ways. These neighborhoods have diminished private economic activity. They are limited in the types of public and social services that are available to residents, and they tend to have more limited recreation and developmental programs for youths as well as fewer civic and voluntary associations (National Research Council, 1993). Disadvantaged neighborhoods also tend to be characterized by disorganization or a lack of neighborhood cohesion. Neighborhoods that are disorganized lack effective social controls (Elliott et al., 1996; Sampson et al., 1997; Sampson, Morenoff, & Earls, 1999). Factors such as high levels of residential instability along with fewer institutional resources make it difficult for individuals to establish common values and norms and to develop informal ties and support networks (Elliott et al., 1996; Sampson et al., 1997; Sampson, Morenoff, & Gannon-Rowley, 2002). People living in such neighborhoods often experience social isolation and exhibit lower levels of trust and attachment to the community (Sampson et al., 1997). High levels of social disorganization also limit the ability and willingness of community residents to supervise and control children and adolescents (Laub & Lauritsen, 1998; Sampson et al., 1999, 2002).

The net effect of these social processes and conditions is diminished opportunity for the youngest residents. Young people growing up in disadvantaged neighborhoods have fewer positive role models to offset the negative influences in the environment. It is also difficult for families, most often single mothers, to reduce children's level of exposure to the unhealthy lifestyles that characterize these communities or to reduce the level of exposure to violence in these communities. Over the long term, children growing up in these communities are at greater risk of abandoning educational goals, of becoming teenage parents, and of becoming involved in delinquent peer groups, and they are more likely to adopt lifestyles and behaviors that put them at risk for violent victimization and perpetration. The cumulative disadvantage diminishes their later life chances and opportunities.

IMPLICATIONS FOR PREVENTION

The development of effective violence prevention programs depends on the ability of etiologic research to identify factors that either contribute to or decrease the probability of violence. Researchers and prevention program developers use information about these factors to determine who should receive which types of prevention programs and to guide the content of prevention efforts so as to enhance protective influences and minimize risks.

Although existing etiologic research does not permit a confident determination of a particular child's developmental trajectory on the basis of an assessment of that child's risk factors, the information available on developmental pathways and predictors of violent and delinquent offending provides valuable knowledge for designing preventive interventions. Youths who begin offending at an early age are 2 to 3 times more likely to become serious, violent, and chronic offenders than youths who begin offending during their teenage years (Loeber & Farrington, 2001). Many of the risks for serious, violent, and chronic offending are present in early childhood, indicating a need for early intervention. Because the age of onset for aggressive, violent, and delinquent behavior may vary considerably and encompass a fairly broad age range, there is also a need for prevention efforts across developmental periods. By intervening early and providing a variety of approaches across developmental periods, violence prevention strategies can accommodate youths with an early onset of offending as well as those who may be at risk for late-onset offending.

In addition to the timing of prevention efforts, it is also important to think about the target groups for prevention activities and the intensity of approach required to alter behavioral patterns. Violence prevention activities can be directed to the entire population of youth without regard to risk (e.g., universal intervention), focused specifically on youths who have one or more established risk factors for violence (e.g., selective intervention), or designed specifically for youths who have engaged in or are engaging in violent and delinquent behavior (e.g., indicated intervention). Selective and indicated populations, by definition, face more barriers and require more intensive approaches. There are many more deficits to overcome with young people who are at risk for violent and delinquent offending or already engaging in these high-risk behaviors. Well-designed universal, selective, and indicated prevention programs, however, have the potential to foster prosocial behavior and change developmental trajectories (Mihalic, Irwin, Elliott, Fagan, & Hansen, 2001; USDHHS, 2001).

As noted here and elsewhere, risk and protective factors for youth violence operate at multiple levels of social influence (Loeber & Farrington, 2001; Resnick, Ireland, & Borowsky, 2004; USDHHS, 2001). Prevention programs therefore can benefit from considering how best to address individual-level factors while taking into account the factors within families, peer groups, schools, or communities that contribute to violence-related behavior. Prevention approaches that address multiple domains of influence on behavior are more likely to have a greater impact than those that focus on a single risk factor (Williams et al., 1997).

There are several examples of developmentally appropriate violence prevention strategies that incorporate multiple domains of social influence with demonstrated effectiveness (i.e., strategies that have produced sustained effects on violence or serious delinquency in studies using experimental or quasi-experimental designs; Mihalic et al., 2001; USDHHS, 2001). The Seattle Social Development Project, for instance, is an example of a universal prevention program. This program is designed to enhance prosocial behavior, interpersonal problem solving, and academic success and to help youths avoid substance use by providing elementary school children with classroom behavior management and skills training as well as training to their parents (Hawkins et al., 1992). By focusing on the issues of behavioral control and parent training within the general population of elementary school children, the program addresses well-established, developmentally appropriate risk factors for subsequent involvement in violence.

An example of a selective prevention approach is home visitation by nurses (Olds, 2002). This approach has been shown to reduce violence-related behavior among 15-year-olds by providing visits by trained nurses from shortly before they are born until they are 2 years of age (Olds et al., 1998). The program is designed to offer low-income women the care, information, and support they need to improve their health, pregnancy outcomes, and child care. The program also enhances the family's network of social support and works with the mother to complete schooling and improve her employability. By focusing on low-income single mothers and addressing critical family-related factors such as appropriate and reasonable discipline, family attachment, and maternal education, the program's strategies are consistent with what is known about early and long-term risk and protective factors for violent and delinquent behavior.

An example of an effective, indicated prevention program is Multisystemic Therapy (Henggeler, Clingempeel, Brondino, & Pickrel, 2002). This intensive, systemic approach works with children in the juvenile justice system to address issues at the individual, family, peer, school, and neighborhood levels using family therapy, parent training, and cognitive–behavior therapy with the child. Etiologic research strongly indicates the high degree of co-occurrence of multiple problem behaviors (e.g., substance abuse and suicidal behavior) with psychological, social, academic, and criminal problems experienced by youth. This research base provides a strong rationale for using comprehensive and intensive interventions when attempting to address the often complex needs of youths who have exhibited violent and delinquent behavior.

The evidence base for a variety of individual, parent, family, and school-based approaches is growing (Hahn, Bilukha, Mercy, & Pearson-Clarke, 2005; Mihalic et al., 2001; Thornton, Craft, Dahlberg, Lynch, & Baer, 2000; USDHHS, 2001). Unfortunately, much less is known about effective approaches for reducing gang violence and the conditions that give rise to violence in communities. Tackling the often complex social and economic conditions of communities and the social processes and behavior that are tied to such conditions is difficult, but it is a necessary ingredient for true change and progress.

CONCLUSION

Much has been learned over the past decade about the developmental pathways toward serious violent and delinquent behavior and about the types of prevention approaches required to change adverse developmental trajectories. Even so, a few important gaps remain. Longitudinal studies of violent and delinquent offending have revealed much about the offending patterns of boys. Less is known about the offending patterns of girls, although efforts to remedy this gap are currently underway (e.g., Fergusson & Horwood, 2002; Hipwell et al., 2002). The knowledge base for boys is expansive, but even here, there remains a need for more information on which risk factors have differential effects on the escalation, persistence, and termination of offending at different ages.

Much more information is also needed about protective factors (National Center for Injury Prevention and Control, 2002). Protective factors are not simply the inverse of risk factors. Rather, they are factors that decrease, buffer, or moderate the effect of risk. Just as risk factors vary in terms of their influence on behavior, with some having larger effect sizes than others, protective factors may also vary in the extent to which they exert influence, and they may do so across different developmental periods (Resnick et al., 2004; Stouthamer-Loeber, Loeber, Wei, Farrington, & Wikström, 2002). Understanding how protective factors operate within different domains of influence is potentially as important to violence prevention efforts as research on risk factors (USDHHS, 2001).

Finally, we need a much better understanding of how social and economic factors might be effectively modified to reduce violence through the development and evaluation of community-level interventions and continued commitment to rigorously evaluating and disseminating other prevention approaches (National Center for Injury Prevention and Control, 2002). Building the knowledge base across all domains of influence and putting into practice those approaches with demonstrated and replicated effectiveness is key to creating peaceful and healthier communities.

REFERENCES

af Klinteberg, B. (1997). Hyperactive behavior and aggressiveness as early risk indicators for violence: Variable and person approaches. *Studies on Crime and Crime Prevention, 6,* 21–34.

Ayers, C. D., Williams, J. H., Hawkins, J. D., Peterson, P. L., Catalano, R. F., & Abbott, R. D. (1999). Assessing correlates of onset, escalation, deescalation, and desistence of delinquent behavior. *Journal of Quantitative Criminology, 15,* 277–306.

Bagwell, C. L., Coie, J. D., Terry, R. A., & Lochman, J. E. (2000). Peer clique participation and social status in preadolescence. *Merrill-Palmer Quarterly, 46,* 280–305.

Battin, S. R., Hill, K. G., Abbott, R. D., Catalano, R. F., & Hawkins, J. D. (1998). The contribution of gang membership to delinquency beyond delinquent friends. *Criminology, 36,* 93–115.

Battin-Pearson, S. R., Thornberry, T. P., Hawkins, J. D., & Krohn, M. D. (1998, October). Gang membership, delinquent peers, and delinquent behavior. *Juvenile Justice Bulletin* (NCJ 171119). Washington, DC: U.S. Department of Justice, Office of Juvenile Justice and Delinquency Prevention.

Bolger, K. E., & Patterson, C. J. (2001). Developmental pathways from child maltreatment to peer rejection. *Child Development, 72,* 549–568.

Brame, R., Mulvey, E. P., & Piquero, A. R. (2001). On the development of different kinds of criminal activity. *Sociological Methods and Research, 29,* 319–341.

Broidy, L. M., Nagin, D. S., Tremblay, R. E., Bates, J. E., Brame, B., Dodge, K. A., et al. (2003). Developmental trajectories of childhood disruptive behaviors and adolescent delinquency: A six-site, cross-national study. *Developmental Psychology, 39,* 222–245.

Centers for Disease Control and Prevention. (2005). *Web-based Injury Statistics Query and Reporting System—WISQARS.* Retrieved February 18, 2005, from http://www.cdc.gov/ncipc/wisqars/default.htm

Chung, I. J., Hawkins, J. D., Gilchrist, L. D., Hill, K. G., & Nagin, D. S. (2002). Identifying and predicting offending trajectories among poor children. *Social Science Review, 76,* 663–685.

Coie, J. D. (1990). Towards a theory of peer rejection. In S. R. Asher & J. D. Coie (Eds.), *Peer rejection in childhood* (pp. 365–401). Cambridge, England: Cambridge University Press.

Coie, J. D., & Dodge, K. A. (1997). Aggressive and antisocial behavior. In W. Damon (Series Ed.) & N. Eisenberg (Vol. Ed.), *Handbook of child psychology: Vol. 3. Social, emotional, and personality development* (5th ed., pp. 779–862). New York: Wiley.

Coie, J. D., & Miller-Johnson, S. (2001). Peer factors and interventions. In R. Loeber & D. P. Farrington (Eds.), *Child delinquents: Development, intervention, and service needs* (pp. 191–209). Thousand Oaks, CA: Sage.

Denno, D. W. (1990). *Biology and violence: From birth to adulthood.* Cambridge, England: Cambridge University Press.

Dishion, T. J., Patterson, G. R., Stoolmiller, M., & Skinner, M. L. (1991). Family, school, and behavioral antecedents to early adolescent involvement with antisocial peers. *Developmental Psychology, 27,* 172–180.

Dodge, K. A., Lansford, J. E., Salzer Burks, V., Bates, J. E., Pettit, G. S., Fontaine, R., & Price, J. M. (2003). Peer rejection and social information-processing factors in the development of aggressive behavior problems in children. *Child Development, 74,* 374–393.

Dornbusch, S. M., Glasgow, K. L., & Lin, I. (1996). The social structure of schooling. *Annual Review of Psychology, 47,* 401–429.

D'Unger, A. V., Land, K. C., McCall, P. L., & Nagin, D. S. (1998). How many latent classes of delinquent/criminal careers? Results from a mixed Poisson regression analysis. *American Sociological Review, 103,* 1593–1620.

Edleson, J. L. (1999). Children's witnessing of adult domestic violence. *Journal of Interpersonal Violence, 14,* 839–870.

Elliott, D. S. (1994). Serious violent offenders: Onset, developmental course, and termination: The American Society of Criminology 1993 Presidential Address. *Criminology, 32,* 1–21.

Elliott, D. S., & Menard, S. (1996). Delinquent friends and delinquent behavior: Temporal and developmental patterns. In J. D. Hawkins (Ed.), *Delinquency and crime: Current theories* (pp. 28–67). Cambridge, England: Cambridge University Press.

Elliott, D. S., Wilson, W. J., Huizinga, D., Sampson, R. J., Elliott, A., & Ranklin, B. (1996). The effects of neighborhood disadvantage on adolescent development. *Journal of Research in Crime and Delinquency, 33,* 389–426.

Farrington, D. P. (1998). Predictors, causes and correlates of male youth violence. In M. Tonry & M. H. Moore (Eds.), *Youth violence. Crime and justice: A review of research* (Vol. 24, pp. 421–475). Chicago: University of Chicago Press.

Farrington, D. P. (2003). Key results from the first forty years of the Cambridge Study in Delinquent Development. In T. P. Thornberry & M. D. Krohn (Eds.), *Taking stock of delinquency: An overview of findings from contemporary longitudinal studies* (pp. 137–183). New York: Kluwer Academic/Plenum Publishers.

Farrington, D. P., Barnes, G. C., & Lambert, S. (1996). The concentration of offending in families. *Legal and Criminological Psychology, 1,* 47–63.

Farrington, D. P., Jolliffe, D., Loeber, R., Stouthamer-Loeber, M., & Kalb, L. M. (2001). The concentration of offenders in families, and family criminality in the prediction of boys' delinquency. *Journal of Adolescence, 24,* 579–596.

Farrington, D. P., & Loeber, R. (2000). Epidemiology of juvenile violence. *Child and Adolescent Psychiatric Clinics of North America, 9,* 733–748.

Farrington, D. P., Loeber, R., Yin, Y., & Anderson, S. J. (2002). Are within-individual causes of delinquency the same as between-individual causes? *Criminal Behavior and Mental Health, 12,* 53–68.

Farrington, D. P., & West, D. J. (1993). Criminal, penal and life histories of chronic offenders: Risk and protective factors and early identification. *Criminal Behavior and Mental Health, 3,* 492–523.

Fergusson, D. M., & Horwood, L. J. (2002). Male and female offending trajectories. *Development and Psychopathology, 14,* 159–177.

Gottfredson, G. D., & Gottfredson, D. C. (2001). What schools do to prevent problem behavior and promote safe environments. *Journal of Educational and Psychological Consultation, 12,* 313–344.

Hahn, R. A., Bilukha, O., Mercy, J. A., & Pearson-Clarke, T. (Eds.). (2005). Interventions to reduce injury and death from violence: Systematic reviews of evidence. Recommendations from the Task Force on Community Preventive Services, and expert commentary. *American Journal of Preventive Medicine, 28*(2, Suppl. 1), 1–92.

Hawkins, J. D., Catalano, R. F., Morrison, D. M., O'Donnell, J., Abbott, R. D., & Day, L. E. (1992). The Seattle Social Development Project: Effects of the first four years on protective factors and problem behaviors. In J. McCord & R. E. Tremblay (Eds.), *Preventing antisocial behavior: Interventions from birth through adolescence* (pp. 139–161). New York: Guilford Press.

Hawkins, J. D., Herrenkohl, T., Farrington, D. P., Brewer, D., Catalano, R. F., & Harachi, T. W. (1998). A review of predictors of youth violence. In R. Loeber & D. P. Farrington (Eds.), *Serious and violent juvenile offenders: Risk factors and successful interventions* (pp. 106–146). Thousand Oaks, CA: Sage.

Henggeler, S. W., Clingempeel, W. G., Brondino, M. J., & Pickrel, S. G. (2002). Four-year follow-up of multisystemic therapy with substance-abusing and substance-dependent juvenile offenders. *Journal of the American Academy of Child and Adolescent Psychiatry, 41,* 868–874.

Henry, B., Caspi, A., Moffitt, T., & Silva, P. (1996). Temperamental and familial predictors of violent and nonviolent criminal convictions: Age 3 to age 18. *Developmental Psychology, 32,* 614–623.

Herrenkohl, T. I., Maguin, E., Hill, K. G., Hawkins, J. D., Abbott, R. D., & Catalano, R. F. (2000). Developmental risk factors for youth violence. *Journal of Adolescent Health, 26,* 176–186.

Hill, K. G., Hawkins, J. D., Catalano, R. F., Kosterman, R., Abbott, R., & Edwards, T. (1996, November). *The longitudinal dynamics of gang membership and problem behavior: A replication and extension of the Denver and Rochester gang studies in Seattle.* Paper presented at the annual meeting of the American Society of Criminology, Chicago.

Hipwell, A. E., Loeber, R., Stouthamer-Loeber, M., Keenan, K., White, H. R., & Krone-Man, L. (2002). Characteristics of girls with early onset disruptive and antisocial behavior. *Criminal Behavior and Mental Health, 12,* 99–118.

Howell, J. C., & Hawkins, J. D. (1998). Prevention of youth violence. In M. H. Moore & M. Tonry (Eds.), *Youth violence. Crime and justice: A review of research* (Vol. 24, pp. 263–315). Chicago: University of Chicago Press.

Hudley, C. A. (1994). Perceptions of intentionality, feelings of anger, and reactive aggression. In M. J. Furlong & D. C. Smith (Eds.), *Anger, hostility, and aggression: Assessment, prevention, and intervention strategies for youth* (pp. 39–56). Brandon, VT: Clinical Psychology Publishing Company.

Huesmann, L. R., Eron, L. D., Lefkowitz, M. M., & Walder, L. O. (1984). Stability of aggression over time. *Developmental Psychology, 20,* 1120–1134.

Huizinga, D., Weiher, A. W., Espiritu, R., & Esbensen, F. (2003). Delinquency and crime: Some highlights from the Denver Youth Survey. In T. P. Thornberry & M. D. Krohn (Eds.), *Taking stock of delinquency: An overview of findings from contemporary longitudinal studies* (pp. 47–91). New York: Kluwer Academic/ Plenum Publishers.

Jang, S. J., & Smith, C. A. (1997). A test of reciprocal causal relationships among parental supervision, affective ties, and delinquency. *Journal of Research on Crime and Delinquency, 34,* 307–336.

Johnson, R. A., Hoffmann, J. P., Su, S. S, & Gerstein, D. R. (1997). Growth curves of deviant behavior in early adolescence: A multilevel analysis. *Journal of Quantitative Criminology, 13,* 429–467.

Kalb, L. M., & Loeber, R. (2003). Child disobedience and noncompliance: A review. *Pediatrics, 111,* 641–652.

Keenan, K., Loeber, R., Zhang, Q., Stouthamer-Loeber, M., & Van Kammen, W. B. (1995). The influence of deviant peers on the development of boys' disruptive and delinquent behavior: A temporal analysis. *Development and Psychopathology, 7,* 715–726.

Kelly, B. T., Thornberry, T. P., & Smith, C. A. (1997, August). In the wake of childhood maltreatment. *Juvenile Justice Bulletin* (NCJ 165257). Washington, DC: U.S. Department of Justice, Office of Juvenile Justice and Delinquency Prevention.

Kochanek, K. D., Murphy, S. L., Anderson, R. N., & Scott, C. (2004). Deaths: Final data for 2002. *National Vital Statistics Reports, 53*(5).

Kosterman, R., Graham, J. W., Hawkins, J. D., Catalano, R. F., & Herrenkohl, T. I. (2001). Childhood risk factors for persistence of violence in the transition to adulthood: A social development perspective. *Violence and Victims, 16,* 355–369.

Krohn, M. D., Thornberry, T. P., Rivera, C., & LeBlanc, M. (2001). Later delinquency careers. In R. Loeber & D. P. Farrington (Eds.), *Child delinquents: Development, intervention and service needs* (pp. 67–93). Thousand Oaks, CA: Sage.

Lahey, B. B., McBurnett, K., & Loeber, R. (2000). Are attention-deficit/hyperactivity disorder and oppositional/defiant disorder developmental precursors of conduct disorder? In A. J. Sameroff, M. Lewis, & S. M. Miller (Eds.), *Handbook of developmental psychopathology* (2nd ed., pp. 431–446). New York: Plenum Press.

Lansford, J. E., Dodge, K. A., Pettit, G. S., Bates, J. E., Crozier, J., & Kaplow, J. (2002). A 12-year prospective study of the long-term effects of early child physical maltreatment on psychological, behavioral, and academic problems in adolescence. *Archives of Pediatric and Adolescent Medicine, 156,* 824–830.

Laub, J. H., & Lauritsen, J. L. (1993). Violent criminal behavior over the life course: A review of the longitudinal and comparative research. *Violence and Victims, 8,* 235–252.

Laub, J. H., & Lauritsen, J. L. (1998). The interdependence of school violence with neighborhood and family conditions. In D. S. Elliott, B. A. Hamburg, & K. R. Williams (Eds.), *Violence in American schools* (pp. 127–155). Cambridge, England: Cambridge University Press.

LeBlanc, M., & Lanctot, N. (1998). Social and psychological characteristics of gang members according to the gang structure and its subcultural and ethnic make up. *Journal of Gang Research, 5,* 15–28.

Levendosky, A. A., & Graham-Bermann, S. A. (2001). Parenting in battered women: The effects of domestic violence on women and their children. *Journal of Family Violence, 16,* 171–192.

Lipsey, M. W., & Derzon, J. H. (1998). Predictors of serious delinquency in adolescence and early adulthood: A synthesis of longitudinal research. In R. Loeber & D. P. Farrington (Eds.), *Serious and violent juvenile offenders: Risk factors and successful interventions* (pp. 86–105). Thousand Oaks, CA: Sage.

Lochman, J. E., & Dodge, K. A. (1994). Social cognitive processes of severely violent, moderately aggressive, and nonaggressive boys. *Journal of Consulting and Clinical Psychology, 62,* 366–374.

Loeber, R., & Farrington, D. P. (2001). *Child delinquents: Development, intervention, and service needs.* Thousand Oaks, CA: Sage.

Loeber, R., Farrington, D. P., Stouthamer-Loeber, M., Moffitt, T. E., & Caspi, A. (1998). The development of male offending: Key findings from the first decade of the Pittsburgh Youth Study. *Studies in Crime and Crime Prevention, 7,* 141–172.

Loeber, R., & Hay, D. F. (1994). Developmental approaches to aggression and conduct problems. In M. Rutter & D. F. Hay (Eds.), *Development through life: A handbook for clinicians* (pp. 488–516). Oxford, England: Blackwell Science.

Loeber, R., & Hay, D. F. (1997). Key issues in the development of aggression and violence from childhood to early adulthood. *Annual Review of Psychology, 48,* 371–410.

Loeber, R., Keenan, K., & Zhang, Q. (1997). Boys' experimentation and persistence in developmental pathways toward serious delinquency. *Journal of Child and Family Studies, 6,* 321–357.

Loeber, R., Wei, E., Stouthamer-Loeber, M., Huizinga, D., & Thornberry, T. (1999). Behavioral antecedents to serious and violent juvenile offending: Joint analyses from the Denver Youth Survey, Pittsburgh Youth Study, and the Rochester Youth Development Study. *Studies on Crime and Crime Prevention, 8,* 245–263.

Loeber, R., Wung, P., Keenan, K., Giroux, B., Stouthamer-Loeber, M., & Van Kammen, W. B. (1993). Developmental pathways in disruptive child behavior. *Development and Psychopathology, 5,* 101–132.

Lynch, M., & Cicchetti, D. (1998). An ecological–transactional analysis of children and contexts: The longitudinal interplay among child maltreatment, community violence, and children's symptomatology. *Development and Psychopathology, 10,* 235–257.

Maguin, E., & Loeber, R. (1996). Academic performance and delinquency. In M. Tonry (Ed.), *Crime and justice: An annual review of research* (Vol. 20, pp. 145–264). Chicago: University of Chicago Press.

Maxfield, M. G., & Widom, C. S. (1996). The cycle of violence: Revisited 6 years later. *Archives of Pediatric and Adolescent Medicine, 150,* 390–395.

McCord, J. (1977). A comparative study of two generations of Native Americans. In R. F. Meier (Ed.), *Theory in criminology: Contemporary views* (pp. 83–92). Beverly Hills, CA: Sage.

McCord, J., & Conway, K. P. (2002). Patterns of juvenile delinquency and co-offending. In E. Waring & D. Weisburd (Eds.), *Crime and social organization:*

Advances in criminological theory (Vol. 10, pp. 15–30). New Brunswick, NJ: Transaction Publishers.

McCord, J., & Ensminger, M. (1995, November). *Pathways from aggressive childhood to criminality*. Paper presented at the annual meeting of the American Society of Criminology, Boston.

Mihalic, S., Irwin, K., Elliott, D., Fagan, A., & Hansen, D. (2001, July). Blueprints for violence prevention. *Juvenile Justice Bulletin* (NCJ 187079). Washington, DC: U.S. Department of Justice, Office of Juvenile Justice and Delinquency Prevention.

Moffitt, T. E. (1993). Adolescence-limited and life-course-persistent antisocial behavior: A developmental taxonomy. *Psychological Review, 100,* 674–701.

Moffitt, T. E., & Caspi, A. (2001). Childhood predictors differentiate life-course persistent and adolescent-limited antisocial pathways among males and females. *Development and Psychopathology, 13,* 355–375.

Moffitt, T. E., Caspi, A., Dickson, D., Silva, P., & Stanton, W. (1996). Childhood-onset versus adolescent-onset antisocial conduct problems in males: Natural history from ages 3 to 18 years. *Development and Psychopathology, 8,* 399–424.

Moffitt, T. E., Caspi, A., Harrington, H., & Milne, B. J. (2002). Males on the life-course-persistent and adolescent-limited antisocial pathways: Follow-up at age 26 years. *Development and Psychopathology, 14,* 179–207.

Morenoff, J. D., Sampson, R. J., & Raudenbush, S. W. (2001). Neighborhood inequality, collective efficacy, and the spatial dynamics of urban violence. *Criminology, 39,* 517–559.

Nagin, D., & Tremblay, R. E. (1999). Trajectories of boys' physical aggression, opposition, and hyperactivity on the path to physically violent and nonviolent juvenile delinquency. *Child Development, 70,* 1181–1196.

Nagin, D., & Tremblay, R. E. (2001). Parental and early childhood predictors of persistent physical aggression in boys from kindergarten to high school. *Archives of General Psychiatry, 58,* 389–394.

National Center for Injury Prevention and Control. (2002). *CDC injury research agenda*. Atlanta, GA: Centers for Disease Control and Prevention.

National Research Council. (1993). *Losing generations: Adolescents in high-risk settings*. Washington, DC: National Academy Press.

Oakes, J. (1990). *Multiplying inequities: The effects of race, social class, and tracking on opportunities to learn math and science*. Santa Monica, CA: Rand Corporation.

Olds, D. L. (2002). Prenatal and infancy home visiting by nurses: From randomization trials to community replication. *Prevention Science, 33,* 153–172.

Olds, D. L., Henderson, C. R., Jr., Cole, R., Eckenrode, J., Kitzman, H., Luckey, D., et al. (1998). Long-term effects of nurse home visitation on children's criminal and antisocial behavior: 15 year follow-up of a randomized controlled trial. *Journal of the American Medical Association, 280,* 1238–1244.

Olweus, D. (1979). Stability of aggressive reaction patterns in males: A review. *Psychological Bulletin, 86,* 852–875.

Patterson, G. R., Forgatch, M. S., Yoerger, K. L., & Stoolmiller, M. (1998). Variables that initiate and maintain an early-onset trajectory for juvenile offending. *Development and Psychopathology, 10,* 531–547.

Peterson, R. D., Krivo, L. J., & Vélez, M. B. (2001). Segregation and youth criminal violence. In S. O. White (Ed.), *Handbook of youth and justice* (pp. 277–286). Dordrecht, the Netherlands: Kluwer Academic.

Proctor, B. D., & Dalaker, J. (2003). *Poverty in the United States: 2002* (U.S. Census Bureau, Current Population Reports, P60-222). Washington, DC: U.S. Government Printing Office.

Raine, A., Farrington, D. P., Brennan, P., & Mednick, S. A. (Eds.). (1997). *Biosocial bases of violence.* New York: Plenum Press.

Reiss, A. J., & Farrington, D. P. (1991). Advancing knowledge about co-offending: Results from a prospective longitudinal survey of London males. *Journal of Criminal Law and Criminology, 82,* 360–395.

Reiss, A. J., Jr., & Roth, J. A. (Eds.). (1993). *Understanding and preventing violence* (Vol. 1). Washington, DC: National Academy Press.

Resnick, M. D., Ireland, M., & Borowsky, I. (2004). Youth violence perpetration: What protects? What predicts? Findings from the National Longitudinal Study of Adolescent Health. *Journal of Adolescent Health, 35,* 424.e1–424.e10.

Sampson, R. J., Morenoff, J. D., & Earls, F. (1999). Beyond social capital: Spatial dynamics of collective efficacy for children. *American Sociological Review, 64,* 633–660.

Sampson, R. J., Morenoff, J. D., & Gannon-Rowley, T. (2002). Assessing "neighborhood effects": Social processes and new directions in research. *Annual Review of Sociology, 28,* 443–478.

Sampson, R. J., Raudenbush, S. W., & Earls, F. (1997, August 15). Neighborhoods and violent crime: A multilevel study of collective efficacy. *Science, 277,* 918–924.

Shields, A., & Cicchetti, D. (1998). Reactive aggression among maltreated children: The contributions of attention and emotion dysregulation. *Journal of Clinical Child Psychology, 27,* 381–395.

Slaby, R. G., & Guerra, N. G. (1988). Cognitive mediators of aggression in adolescent offenders: I. Assessment. *Developmental Psychology, 24,* 580–588.

Small, M. L., Everett Jones, S., Barrios, L. C., Crossett, L. S., Dahlberg, L. L., Albuquerque, M. S., et al. (2001). School policy and environment: Results from the School Health Policies and Programs Study 2000. *Journal of School Health, 71,* 325–334.

Stattin, H., & Magnusson, D. (1989). The role of early aggressive behavior in the frequency, seriousness, and types of later crime. *Journal of Consulting and Clinical Psychology, 57,* 710–718.

Stattin, H., & Magnusson, D. (1996). Antisocial development: A holistic approach. *Development and Psychopathology, 8,* 617–645.

Stouthamer-Loeber, M., & Loeber, R. (2002). Lost opportunities for intervention: Undetected markers for the development of serious juvenile delinquency. *Criminal Behavior and Mental Health, 12*, 69–82.

Stouthamer-Loeber, M., Loeber, R., Wei, E., Farrington, D. P., & Wikström, P. H. (2002). Risk and promotive effects in the explanation of persistent serious delinquency in boys. *Journal of Consulting and Clinical Psychology, 70*, 111–123.

Stouthamer-Loeber, M., Wei, E. H., Homish, D. L., & Loeber, R. (2002). Which family and demographic factors are related to both maltreatment and persistent serious juvenile delinquency? *Children's Services: Social Policy, Research and Practice, 5*, 261–272.

Thornberry, T. P. (1994). *Violent families and youth violence* (Office of Juvenile Justice and Delinquency Prevention, Fact Sheet No. 21). Washington, DC: U.S. Department of Justice.

Thornberry, T. P. (1998). Membership in youth gangs and involvement in serious and violent offending. In R. Loeber & D. P. Farrington (Eds.), *Serious and violent juvenile offenders: Risk factors and successful interventions* (pp. 147–166). Thousand Oaks, CA: Sage.

Thornberry, T. P., Huizinga, D., & Loeber, R. (1995). The prevention of serious delinquency and violence: Implications from the program of research on the causes and correlates of delinquency. In J. Howell, B. Krisberg, D. Hawkins, & J. D. Wilson (Eds.), *A sourcebook: Serious, violent and chronic juvenile offenders* (pp. 213–237). Thousand Oaks, CA: Sage.

Thornberry, T. P., Krohn, M. D., Lizotte, A. J., Smith, C. A., & Tobin, K. (2003). *Gangs and delinquency in developmental perspective*. Cambridge, England: Cambridge University Press.

Thornberry, T. P., Lizotte, A. J., Krohn, M. D., Farnworth, M., & Jang, S. J. (1991). Testing interactional theory: An examination of reciprocal causal relationships among family, school, and delinquency. *Journal of Criminal Law and Criminology, 82*, 3–35.

Thornton, T. N., Craft, C. A., Dahlberg, L. L., Lynch, B. S., & Baer, K. (2000). *Best practices of youth violence prevention: A sourcebook for community action*. Atlanta, GA: Centers for Disease Control and Prevention, National Center for Injury Prevention and Control.

Tolan, P. H., & Gorman-Smith, D. (1998). Development of serious and violent offending careers. In R. Loeber & D. P. Farrington (Eds.), *Serious and violent juvenile offenders: Risk factors and successful interventions* (pp. 68–85). Thousand Oaks, CA: Sage.

Tolan, P. H., Gorman-Smith, D., & Loeber, R. (2000). Developmental timing of onsets of disruptive behaviors and later delinquency of inner-city youth. *Journal of Child and Family Studies, 9*, 203–220.

Toth, S. L., Cicchetti, D., & Kim, J. (2002). Relations among children's perceptions of maternal behavior, attributional styles, and behavioral symptomatology in maltreated children. *Journal of Abnormal Child Psychology, 30*, 487–501.

Tracy, P. E., & Kempf-Leonard, K. (1996). *Continuity and discontinuity in criminal careers*. New York: Plenum Press.

Tremblay, R. E. (2000). The development of aggressive behavior during childhood: What have we learned in the past century? *International Journal of Behavioral Development, 24*, 129–141.

U.S. Department of Health and Human Services. (2001). *Youth violence: A report of the surgeon general*. Washington, DC: U.S. Government Printing Office.

U.S. Department of Justice. (2003). *Age-specific arrest rates and race-specific arrest rates for selected offenses, 1993–2001* (Federal Bureau of Investigation, Uniform Crime Reports). Washington, DC: U.S. Government Printing Office.

U.S. Department of Justice. (2004). *Crime in the United States—2003* (Federal Bureau of Investigation, Uniform Crime Reports). Washington, DC: U.S. Government Printing Office.

Wasserman, G. A., & Seracini, A. M. (2001). Family risk factors and interventions. In R. Loeber & D. P. Farrington (Eds.), *Child delinquents: Development, intervention, and service needs* (pp. 165–189). Thousand Oaks, CA: Sage.

White, H. R., Bates, M. E., & Buyske, S. (2001). Adolescence-limited versus persistent delinquency: Extending Moffitt's hypothesis into adulthood. *Journal of Abnormal Psychology, 110*, 600–609.

Widom, C. S. (1989). Child abuse, neglect, and violent criminal behavior. *Criminology, 27*, 251–272.

Williams, K. R., Guerra, N. G., & Elliott, D. S. (1997). *Human development and violence prevention: A focus on youth*. Boulder, CO: Center for the Study and Prevention of Violence, Institute for Behavioral Science.

Wolfe, D. A., Crooks, C. V., Lee, V., McIntyre-Smith, A., & Jaffe, P. G. (2003). The effects of children's exposure to domestic violence: A meta-analysis and critique. *Clinical Child and Family Psychology Review, 6*, 171–187.

6

SCHOOL-BASED INTERVENTIONS FOR YOUTH VIOLENCE PREVENTION

ALBERT D. FARRELL AND SUZANNE CAMOU

Extensive media coverage of shootings at schools in Jonesboro, Arkansas, in 1998; Littleton, Colorado, in 1999; Santee, California, in 2001; and Red Lake, Minnesota, in 2005 has generated considerable concern about the safety of students in schools. Fortunately, such extreme events are relatively rare. For example, less than 1% of all homicides among children and adolescents in the first half of the 1998–1999 school year occurred on school property, on the way to or from school, or at a school-sponsored event (Small & Tetrick, 2001). Although data on violent crimes indicate that children are typically safer at school than they are elsewhere, rates of violent crimes at schools remain unacceptably high, and incidents involving fighting and weapons carrying are all too common (Elliott, Williams, & Hamburg, 1998). According to the Centers for Disease Control and Prevention's (CDC's) 2003 national survey of high school students, 17% of boys and 8% of girls had been involved in a physical fight at school in the past 12 months, 12% of boys and 7% of girls had been threatened or injured by someone with a weapon on school property in the past 12 months, and 9% of boys and 3% of girls had carried a weapon on school property in the past 30 days (Grunbaum et al., 2004). Students and teachers in many schools

125

experience high levels of less serious forms of violent crime and property theft that compromise instruction and create a ripple effect that interferes with the education of students (Crosse, Burr, Cantor, Hagen, & Hantman, 2001). Indeed, in many inner-city schools, students' sense of vulnerability may make academic work a lower priority than avoiding dangerous confrontations (Lorion, 1998).

Although schools may not be the most frequent setting in which violence occurs, they are a particularly appropriate setting for violence prevention efforts. Many of the risk and protective factors associated with violence and other problems, such as delinquency and drug use, are directly related to schools (e.g., school failure and failure to develop bonds or commitment to school), and other problems, such as peer influences and norms, are imbedded in the school environment (Gottfredson, 2001). Elliott et al. (1998), for example, noted that schools may unintentionally develop a climate that supports violence as a means of resolving conflict, achieving status, or addressing perceived wrongs. Similarly, Felner et al. (2001) argued that transitions into middle school or high school present numerous challenges that place many youths at risk for adjustment problems. This puts schools in a unique position to address many of these factors. More generally, because schools represent a primary context for social development, they provide natural opportunities for teachers and other staff to model appropriate behaviors and to reinforce the use of skills taught by prevention programs (Hawkins, Farrington, & Catalano, 1998). School-based programs also have the advantage of ready access to children throughout the developmental years (Gottfredson, 2001). Implementing programs in schools may thus avoid practical issues related to securing a location, providing transportation, and ensuring program attendance.

A GRID MODEL FOR CLASSIFYING PREVENTION STRATEGIES

School-based efforts to reduce youth violence have encompassed a variety of strategies ranging from the installation of metal detectors and security cameras to the implementation of programs to teach social, emotional, and behavioral skills. In this chapter, we highlight four particularly important dimensions that have been used to classify prevention strategies: (a) the level of social system the strategies attempt to change, (b) the extent to which the strategies focus on individuals at different levels of risk, (c) the developmental stage of the participants, and (d) the strategies' goals. Although each characteristic provides useful information about an intervention, the characteristics tend to interact such that a complete picture requires consideration of all four dimensions. This section presents a grid model for classifying violence prevention strategies on the basis of these dimensions (see Figure 6.1).

The first dimension in the grid is the social system targeted by the intervention. Tolan and Guerra (1994) presented a model of adolescent violence based on social ecological theory that differentiates among four social system levels. Interventions that focus on the individual level include those that teach specific social and emotional skills, problem solving, and conflict resolution. Interventions addressing close interpersonal relations typically focus on parents and peers. Other interventions focus on proximal social settings such as schools and neighborhoods. Finally, interventions may be directed at societal macrosystems by addressing such broad issues as policies related to gun regulations and sentencing guidelines.

A second dimension concerns the extent to which the intervention focuses on children at different levels of risk. Gordon (1987) suggested that prevention programs be classified into three categories: universal, selective, and indicated. *Universal* programs address an entire population (e.g., all students within a given grade level). *Selective* programs are designed for individuals at above average risk for being exposed to violence or engaging in violent behavior (e.g., students in neighborhoods with high rates of poverty and crime). Finally, *indicated* programs are designed for individuals who have already begun to exhibit aggressive behaviors (e.g., early-onset aggressive children). This division reflects the fact that children at different levels of risk may benefit from interventions that vary in their focus and intensity (Prinz, 2000).

The third dimension in the grid is the developmental stage of the target population. Optimum intervention strategies and the focus of prevention efforts are likely to differ across stages of development because risk factors play a different role at each stage (Dahlberg & Potter, 2001; Samples & Aber, 1998). Interventions designed for elementary school children should be fundamentally different from those for high school students. For example, whereas elementary school programs frequently involve parents, programs for adolescents are more likely to focus on peers because of their increasing influence (Wasserman & Miller, 1998). Interventions directed at different age groups may also reflect differences in the critical skills required at different stages of development. For example, an important focus for elementary school children is self-control and emotional awareness (Samples & Aber, 1998). Middle school interventions, in contrast, are more likely to focus on problem-solving skills for nonviolent conflict resolution and managing peer relations (Meyer, Farrell, Northup, Kung, & Plybon, 2000).

The choice of a particular prevention strategy will depend in large part on its goals. These may focus on reducing a specific type of violence, preventing a constellation of problem behaviors, or making broader efforts to promote positive development. Tolan and Guerra (1994) differentiated

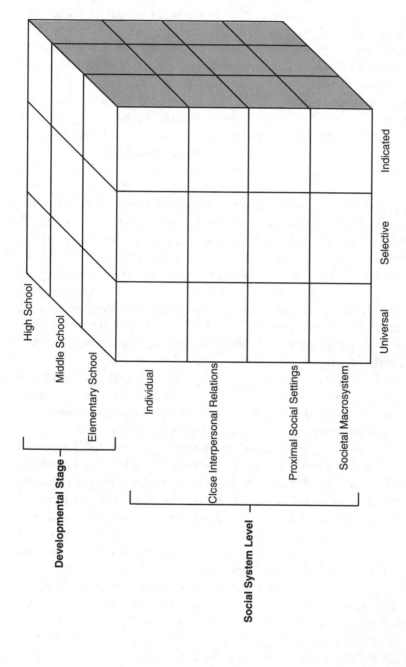

Figure 6.1. A grid model for classifying youth violence prevention efforts according to the level of social system, level of risk in the target population, and developmental stage. A fourth dimension is the goals of the program (e.g., reducing levels of specific types of violence, reducing problem behaviors more generally, and promoting positive youth development).

among four types of violence: situational violence, relationship or interpersonal violence, predatory violence, and psychopathological violence. They argued that these forms differ in their causes and the segment of the population most at risk. Each type may therefore require different approaches to prevention, and the optimal time to intervene may differ across types. Programs may also focus on less severe forms of aggression such as verbal and physical confrontations that may escalate to violence or on specific forms of violence, such as dating violence, that may be particularly salient at specific ages (Foshee et al., 1996). Some prevention efforts are broader in focus. Overlap among the risk and protective factors associated with violence and other forms of problem behavior (Gottfredson, 2001) suggests that programs directed at these factors may produce generalized effects across an array of problem behaviors. This is reflected in the number of programs initially developed to prevent drug use that have been identified as effective for violent behavior (e.g., U.S. Department of Health and Human Services [USDHHS], 2001). An alternative to focusing on preventing problem behaviors is to focus on promoting positive outcomes. Advocates of this perspective have argued that producing positive outcomes is not simply a matter of preventing problem behaviors. As Catalano, Berglund, Ryan, Lonczak, and Hawkins (2002) noted, "a successful transition to adulthood requires more than avoiding drugs, violence, or precocious sexual activity" (p. 9). In contrast, they argued, efforts that produce positive outcomes through promoting the development of social, emotional, cognitive, and behavioral skills may be the most effective approach to reducing problem behaviors.

For any given prevention program, identifying the social system level it is directed at and the nature and developmental stage of the target population will indicate its location within the grid model. Not all programs are located within a single cell in the grid. Interventions may target individual and higher level systems, include separate components for participants that differ in their level of risk, or span multiple grade levels. Equal attention has not been devoted to all the cells in the grid. For example, the majority of school-based programs have focused on the individual level (Gottfredson, 2001; Howard, Flora, & Griffin, 1999), and few attempts have been made to evaluate programs at the macrosystem level (Tolan & Guerra, 1994). Similarly, more programs have been implemented in elementary and middle schools and fewer in high schools (Gottfredson, 2001). The grid does not include all the relevant characteristics of prevention programs. For example, prevention programs may differ according to the characteristics of the target population and the specific risk and protective factors they address (Farrell, Meyer, Kung, & Sullivan, 2001). These other characteristics may be used to differentiate among prevention programs within each cell in the grid. Nonetheless, the grid provides a system for categorizing the scope of a given prevention effort and for guiding the development of a comprehensive effort that includes multiple components to achieve a specific prevention goal.

SCHOOL-BASED PREVENTION STRATEGIES

In this section, we provide an overview of violence prevention strategies at the elementary, middle, and high school levels. This section is not meant to be comprehensive but rather is intended to illustrate the variety of strategies that have been used and to discuss where these might fit within the grid model. It is important to note that not all of the programs mentioned have undergone rigorous evaluation, and evaluations of specific programs have not always produced consistent findings (e.g., Gottfredson, 2001; Howard et al., 1999; Samples & Aber, 1998). Because these descriptions are too brief to do justice to these efforts, interested readers should refer to the original sources for details.

Elementary School Programs

The period between the ages of 6 and 11 is an important time for developing normative beliefs about violence and aggression. It is an age when many children can test their own efficacy with violence as a problem-solving technique (Selman, Beardslee, Schultz, Krupa, & Poderesky, 1986). More generally, it is a critical time for learning important emotional, cognitive, and behavioral skills (Conduct Problems Prevention Research Group [CPPRG], 1999). Elementary school is therefore an opportune place to implement programs that help children develop these skills, encourage their use, and influence normative beliefs (Aber, Jones, Brown, Chaudry, & Samples, 1998). Because the peak period for more serious forms of violence does not occur until adolescence, prevention programs for elementary school children often focus on less extreme forms of aggression and delinquency (Elliott et al., 1998).

At the individual level, numerous curriculum-based prevention programs have been implemented in schools across the country. Examples include universal interventions such as the Second Step Program, which focuses on the development of skills related to empathy, impulse control, and anger management (Grossman et al., 1997), and the Resolving Conflict Creatively Program, which teaches skills such as perspective taking, assertiveness, identifying conflict, and active listening (Aber et al., 1998). Individual-level interventions have also been developed for selective and indicated populations. For example, the Anger Coping Program is an 18-session program designed to help aggressive boys identify their anger and improve their problem-solving and social interaction skills (Lochman, Curry, Dane, & Ellis, 2002).

Elementary school prevention programs directed at close interpersonal relations most often involve parents. For example, Linking the Interests of Families and Teachers is a universal multimodal violence prevention program for elementary schools that attempts to reduce aggression and violence by increasing parenting and communication skills (Eddy, Reid, & Fetrow, 2000). This program is linked to a violence prevention curriculum within the school through weekly newsletters describing family activities that complement the curriculum. The parent-training component of the Seattle Social Development Project is tailored to the needs of children at different ages (Hawkins, Catalano, Jones, & Fine, 1987). In the first and second grades, its focus is on family management training. In the second and third grades, it shifts to promoting healthy parent–child communication and making the home a positive learning environment. The focus in fifth and sixth grade is on encouraging drug resistance skills.

Other elementary school programs include components that focus on school climate. For example, PeaceBuilders is a universal prevention strategy directed at cultural changes at the school level (Embry, Flannery, Vazsonyi, Powell, & Atha, 1996). PeaceBuilders attempts to create a common language of acceptance and respect throughout the school, thus fostering a sense of belonging within the school community. Within this program, acceptance and adherence to prosocial norms is promoted by the acculturation of these values into daily school activities.

There are excellent examples of comprehensive prevention programs for elementary-school-age children. These programs cover multiple cells within the grid model. The Seattle Social Development Project was designed to promote positive changes and prevent substance abuse, violence, and aggressive behavior by promoting prosocial bonds and attachment to school (Hawkins et al., 1992). Various components of the intervention are implemented at different grade levels from first grade through sixth grade. At the individual level, a curriculum focuses on communication, decision making, negotiation, and conflict resolution. The parent component is tailored to the needs of children at different ages. At the school level, a teacher component focuses on proactive classroom management, interactive teaching, and cooperative learning in which students learn to work together in small groups. A second example is Fast Track, which represents a multicomponent school-based program that is comprehensive in scope and well-grounded in developmental theory (CPPRG, 1999). Although the program was designed to prevent conduct problems, its focus is on positive development with an emphasis on emotion regulation, self-control, and social problem-solving skills. Fast Track includes components directed at the individual, classroom, family, and school levels of influence. It also includes both universal and selective components to enhance the program's effects on the school environment. The universal intervention includes a curriculum taught by teachers beginning in the first grade. Lessons focus on emotional recognition and understanding, friendship skills, self-control skills, and social problem-solving skills. Additional selective components are implemented with students identified as highly aggressive. These children participate in social skills training groups, weekly tutoring, and an enrichment program held in the evenings. Parents of selective children are encouraged to participate in a parent group focusing on age-appropriate behavioral norms, appropriate and effective forms of punishment, and communication skills.

Middle School Programs

The transition to middle school or junior high co-occurs with important developmental changes. These include the onset or completion of puberty, changes in cognitive functioning, increasing importance of peers, increased expectations for achievement and autonomy, and a more distinct sense of self-identity (Crockett & Petersen, 1993). Changes also occur in the school environment as children move from smaller, more structured elementary schools into larger schools that require greater responsibility. These larger schools often serve a heterogeneous student population that provides more exposure to antisocial behaviors (Felner et al., 2001). These changes can result in escalations in problem behavior (Crosse et al., 2001) but can also provide important opportunities for prevention by focusing on the development of critical skills such as conflict resolution, problem solving, and managing peer relationships (Meyer & Farrell, 1998).

A variety of middle school programs focus on the individual level. Smart Talk, for example, is a computer-based intervention that teaches children conflict resolution, anger management, and perspective taking (Bosworth, Espelage, DuBay, Dahlberg, & Daytner, 1996). This innovative intervention can be individualized for each respondent. Because it provides anonymity, children are able to ask questions and explore issues that they may be too embarrassed to do in front of their peers or teachers. The Positive Adolescent Choices Training is a universal intervention specifically designed for African American adolescents (Hammond & Yung, 1990). This program includes an education component that provides information about risks associated with violence and teaches prosocial skills. Instructional techniques include videotaped vignettes, role plays, and discussions to teach skills related to giving positive and negative feedback, accepting negative feedback, resisting peer pressure, problem solving, and negotiating. Responding in Peaceful and Positive Ways (RIPP; Meyer et al., 2000) is a universal prevention program designed to address critical developmental issues during each grade of middle school. The RIPP program is based on a health promotion model that emphasizes the development of social–cognitive skills (Meyer & Farrell, 1998). The program uses an adult role model to teach knowledge, attitudes, and skills that promote nonviolence and is designed to be implemented with a peer-mediation program that attempts to promote school-level change.

Some youth violence prevention programs have attempted to decrease delinquent and violent behavior by focusing on peers. For example, Wiist, Jackson, and Jackson (1996) developed a program that attempted to change perceptions of violence as an acceptable form of problem solving by changing these perceptions in peer leaders. Peer leaders were indirectly nominated by students who were asked to identify the individuals in their grade whom they most looked up to, wanted to be like, and admired. The program was guided by social network theory and attempted to reduce school violence by altering behavioral norms through the natural peer leaders in the school.

Programs focusing on parents have also been developed for middle school students. The Adolescent Transitions Program (Dishion, Kavanagh, Schneiger, Nelson, & Kaufman, 2002) includes universal, selective, and indicated family intervention components that are offered through a Family Resource Room within the school. The goals of the program are to reduce a broad constellation of problem behaviors, including aggression, delinquent behavior, and drug use. Intervention components at the universal level include home visits, a videotape-based parent assessment that focuses on effective family management skills, and a 6-week curriculum that includes weekly newsletters and parent–child homework. The selective intervention involves a three-session intervention based on motivational interviewing targeted at students referred by their parents or by school staff because of concerns about their behavior, peer associations, or emotional adjustment. At the indicated level, the Family Resource Room offers family intervention services.

Comprehensive middle school programs designed to produce change at the school level have also been implemented. A variety of programs designed to address bullying behavior have focused on the school environment (see Orpinas & Horne, chap. 7, this volume). An excellent example is the Bully/Victim program, which includes schoolwide, classroom, and individual components (Olweus, 1993). This program attempts to restructure the school environment so that it will not tolerate bullying or aggressive behavior. Its focus is on both primary and secondary violence prevention in that it attempts to decrease aggressive behavior already evident in the school and prevent additional instances from occurring. The GREAT Schools and Family Program (Multisite Violence Prevention Project [MVPP], 2004b) represents an effort to produce schoolwide effects by incorporating multiple components. It includes a sixth-grade student curriculum, workshops and support groups for teachers, and a family intervention for students identified as high in aggression and peer influence.

High School Programs

During high school, adolescents struggle to find their own identity and strive for autonomy from adult norms (Samples & Aber, 1998). Important attachments shift from parents to peers, thus making it necessary for adolescents to revise their relationship with their parents and create and maintain meaningful peer relationships. It is also a time when adolescents try out adult behaviors and may mimic peers who appear to be mature by their acceptance and practice of forbidden behaviors, such as drinking and delinquency (Moffitt, 1993). Thus, prevention efforts for this age group frequently shift from primary to secondary prevention (Samples & Aber, 1998).

Although there is often overlap with individual-level programs developed for middle schools, some programs are specifically designed for high school. Safe Dates (Foshee et al., 1996) is an example of a universal intervention directed at the individual level that focuses specifically on dating violence. This program has been implemented with eighth and ninth graders and includes a theater production performed by peers, a 10-session curriculum, and a poster contest. The Violence Prevention Curriculum (Prothrow-Stith, 1987) is an individual-level program that highlights factual information about violence, provides alternative strategies for problem solving, and teaches how to analyze the costs and benefits of using violence as a means of resolving conflict. It has been used as both a universal and an indicated or selective intervention (e.g., Hausman, Pierce, & Briggs, 1996).

The School Transitional Environment Project is an example of a universal intervention designed to reduce violence in secondary schools by making environmental changes at the school level (Felner et al., 2001). Its goals are to reduce conditions in the school that contribute to maladaptive psychosocial vulnerabilities in students and to enhance the school environment and programs so that they encourage adaptive and healthy student behavior. This involves reorganizing the school social system and restructuring the role of homeroom teachers so they become more nurturing and involved. Reorganization involves assigning students to small units within the school that attend the same core classes. This simulates a small school environment, fosters supportive peer networks, and minimizes contact with upperclassmen to reduce the likelihood of victimization and negative influences (Felner et al., 2001).

High schools have also attempted to produce school-level changes through use of security devices such as metal detectors and security cameras.

Metal detectors have been found to have a moderate effect on reducing weapon-related violence in and around schools, but their ability to eliminate school violence is limited (CDC, 1993). Other methods for changing school environments have also been suggested. For example, the 2002 edition of *Safe Schools: A Planning Guide for Action*, published by the California Department of Education (2002), suggested making several physical changes in an effort to reduce violence and delinquency. These include limiting student access to lockers, having brightly lit hallways, and keeping bathrooms and walls clean and free from graffiti. Such measures are based on the assumption that making schools aesthetically pleasing fosters a sense of school pride and belonging, thus decreasing the incidence and tendency toward youth aggression and delinquency.

CURRENT STATUS AND REMAINING CHALLENGES

Increasing effort has been devoted to the development and evaluation of school-based programs to address youth violence. As the surgeon general noted, we have moved beyond the prevailing view from 10 years ago that nothing works for preventing and reducing youth violence (USDHHS, 2001). Nonetheless, "much of the money America spends on youth violence prevention is spent on ineffective—sometimes even harmful—programs and policies" (USDHHS, 2001, p. 99). This conclusion was echoed by Crosse et al. (2001), who conducted a national survey of principals representing 886 elementary and secondary schools and found that schools implemented a median of 14 activities to prevent problem behavior but that the quality of many of these programs was questionable. Schools typically placed a low priority on research-based sources of information in selecting activities. Only one third of the prevention activities involved methods or approaches found to be effective in the research literature.

Although developers of school-based interventions have been creative in developing a variety of strategies for reducing violence, the lack of credible evidence about the effectiveness of the majority of these programs makes it difficult for schools to make informed decisions about which programs are most likely to meet their goals. We have only begun to build the scientific base needed to address this problem, and considerable work is needed to move to the point at which effective programs can be implemented on a wide-scale basis (USDHHS, 2001). This effort must include the development of stronger, more comprehensive interventions; more rigorous and sophisticated evaluations; and ultimately, movement from efficacy studies to studies examining the impact of wide-scale implementation.

The Need for Better Interventions

Reviews of school-based violence prevention programs have concluded that much of what has been tried does not work, and that which does often produces modest effects that are not maintained over time (Gottfredson, 2001). The U.S. surgeon general's report on youth violence (USDHHS, 2001) and a review of positive youth development programs by Catalano et al. (2002) identified a fairly small number of programs as "model" or "effective." Only a subset of those found to be effective in reducing aggressive behaviors were school-based interventions. Similarly, the Blueprints Violence Prevention Initiative (Mihalic, Irwin, Elliott, Fagan, & Hansen, 2001) reviewed over 500 violence, drug use, and delinquency prevention programs, of which only 11 were designated model programs. Of these, 5 were primarily school-based programs, but only 3 of these focused on aggression. As Howard et al. (1999) noted, many of the positive effects reported in evaluation studies reflect changes in knowledge, attitudes, and responses to hypothetical situations rather than in actual behavior. This suggests the need for a stronger focus on training specific skills and ensuring that participants can generalize those skills to new situations. Often, effects are gender specific (e.g., Farrell & Meyer, 1997) or represent effects for subgroups of participants (e.g., Farrell, Meyer, & White, 2001; Metropolitan Area Child Study Research Group [MACSRG], 2002) or in classrooms where fidelity or dosage was particularly strong (Aber et al., 1998). Such effects are evident even among programs designated as model or exemplary. As previously noted, schools have the potential for playing an important role in reducing youth violence. Further work is clearly needed to develop more effective programs to realize this potential. Recent reviews of the literature have suggested several strategies that could potentially lead to stronger programs.

The quality of violence prevention programs could be improved by making greater use of theory. Howard et al. (1999) noted that most studies do not discuss how theory was used to guide development of the intervention. As Prinz (2000) argued, the failure to incorporate theory into the development and evaluation of prevention programs has seriously impeded progress: "Scientists and evaluators do not want to bounce randomly from one unsuccessful program to another, hoping to discover the right one" (p. 25). Once relevant risk and protective factors are identified, further effort is needed to determine the most effective approaches for altering these processes (Farrell, Meyer, et al., 2001). Research establishing not only the content of prevention programs but also the most effective delivery methods is urgently needed (Gottfredson, 2001).

The multiple influences that promote and support violent behavior make it likely that comprehensive efforts will be needed to address this problem (Gottfredson, 2001; Howard et al., 1999; Prinz, 2000). Within the context of the grid model, prevention programs need to address multiple levels of social systems (Elliott et al., 1998) and developmental stages (Wasserman & Miller, 1998). Changes at the individual level are not likely to persist if they are not supported within the environment (Elliott & Tolan, 1999). Similarly, arguments for early intervention (e.g., Dahlberg & Potter, 2001) do not imply that interventions should be restricted to early stages of development. As Guerra (1998) noted, further work is needed to establish the optimum age for specific types of interventions and booster sessions to support these interventions. Strong arguments can also be made for combining universal with selective or indicated interventions. For example, the CPPRG (1999) noted that more intensive intervention with higher risk students may reduce their disruptive impact and make it easier for other students to respond to a universal intervention. Finally, the dosage of prevention programs must also be sufficient to promote mastery of skills at the individual level or to produce significant changes in social settings (Dahlberg & Potter, 2001; Elliott & Tolan, 1999). The repeated failure of relatively brief, narrowly focused programs makes it clear that such efforts will do little to produce meaningful change.

The Need for Better Evaluations

Numerous reviews (e.g., Gottfredson, 2001; Howard et al., 1999; Samples & Aber, 1998) have noted that the majority of violence prevention programs have either not been evaluated or have been evaluated using weak research designs that make it difficult to draw clear conclusions about their effectiveness. Reviewers have repeatedly called for greater efforts to improve the quality of evaluations of these programs (e.g., Farrell, Meyer, et al., 2001; Tolan & Guerra, 1994). Howard et al. (1999), for example, in their review of school-based violence prevention programs published between 1993 and 1997, were able to identify only 44 school-based evaluation studies. Of these, only 13 met a minimum standard that involved either having a control group or including pre- and postmeasures of the same individuals. Similarly, Cooper, Lutenbacher, and Faccia (2000) could identify only 38 studies evaluating violence prevention programs for 7- to 14-year-old children that met minimum standards for methodological rigor; only 19 of the programs evaluated in these studies included a school-based component. Recent reviews have identified some of the methodological issues related to evaluating school-based programs in some detail (Catalano et al., 2002; Farrell, Meyer, et al., 2001; Gottfredson, 2001). In this section, we highlight several key issues.

Improvements are needed in the measures used to evaluate violence prevention programs. Studies have often included measures of knowledge, attitudes, and responses to hypothetical situations rather than actual behavior (Howard et al., 1999). Ideally, outcome batteries should include measures of primary outcome variables related to aggression, the mediating variables that represent the proximal effects of the intervention, and moderator variables that may influence intervention effects (Farrell, Meyer, et al., 2001). Evaluation studies should also include process measures to assess variations in treatment fidelity (Dumas, Lynch, Laughlin, Smith, & Prinz, 2001). Because each source of data (e.g., self-report, teacher ratings, school records, and behavioral observations) reflects a certain degree of bias, efforts should be made to include multiple sources. Measures must also meet minimum psychometric standards and be appropriate for the specific target population (Farrell, Meyer, et al., 2001). Because reviews of violence prevention require evidence of sustained effects (Mihalic et al., 2001), it is essential that follow-up data be collected.

One of the major design considerations in evaluating school-based prevention programs concerns the use of a within-school or a between-schools design (Farrell, Meyer, et al., 2001). Within-school designs involve the assignment of individuals or units within a school (e.g., classrooms) to experimental conditions. Between-schools designs involve assigning entire schools to conditions. Each has significant limitations. Within-school designs may introduce diffusion effects in that students in the control group may receive some benefit from the intervention through their interactions with peers, teachers, and others who are participating in the intervention. Such designs may also simply not be feasible for evaluating interventions that attempt to produce changes in peer norms or school climate. Between-schools designs eliminate many of these problems and more closely represent how programs are likely to be implemented in practice but require the participation of substantial numbers of schools. Gottfredson (2001) noted that although a minimum of 44 schools may be required to achieve sufficient statistical power to detect intervention effects, the studies of school or classroom-level interventions she reviewed involved an average of 12 schools, and the majority (85%) used fewer than 20. Most between-schools evaluations are thus underpowered, often result in nonequivalent intervention and control groups, and frequently fail to use appropriate methods of data analysis that focus on schools as the unit of analysis (Gottfredson, 2001). The use of between-schools designs may also complicate the interpretation of certain sources of data. For example, teachers' ratings of student behavior or referrals for disciplinary violations may be influenced by awareness that the school is participating in an intervention. Conversely, participation in an intervention may increase teachers' reports of aggressive behaviors because they become more aware of certain types of student behavior (e.g., bullying).

The field of violence prevention could benefit from more sophisticated designs that go beyond simple comparisons of intervention participants to a no-treatment control. For the most part, prevention programs have been evaluated as packages without any effort to determine the contribution of individual components (Gottfredson, 2001). A notable exception is the stepped design used by the Metropolitan Area Child Study Research Group (MACSRG; 2002). This study involved assignment of schools to four conditions: (a) no-intervention control; (b) classroom intervention; (c) classroom intervention and small-group intervention; and (d) classroom intervention, small-group intervention, and family intervention. A more recent example is the MVPP, in which 36 schools from four sites were randomly assigned to four conditions to compare the impact of a universal intervention, a targeted intervention, and the combined effects of both interventions with a no-treatment control condition (Henry, Farrell, & MVPP, 2004). Such designs provide a basis for examining the separate and additive effects of different approaches to intervention at the school level.

Trends and Future Directions

Researchers evaluating the impact of violence prevention programs have just begun to go beyond asking questions about whether a given program is effective. They are beginning to ask more challenging questions about the specific population for whom a program is effective and the conditions under which it is most likely to work. This situation parallels a similar development that began in the area of psychotherapy research some years back (Kiesler, 1966). Farrell, Meyer, Sullivan, and Kung (2003), for example, found that effects of the RIPP intervention on certain outcomes in a within-school design were only evident among students with high initial levels of aggression. Other evaluations have reported negative effects for some program participants (Catalano, Arthur, Hawkins, Berglund, & Olson, 1998), particularly when certain intervention strategies are used (e.g., Dishion, McCord, & Poulin, 1999). The characteristics of the intervention and school setting may also moderate program effects. For example, Aber et al. (1998) found that program effects for aggressive cognitions were moderated by classroom differences and neighborhood context. Similarly, the MACSRG (2002) reported that an early intervention program for high-risk students was associated with a decrease in aggression for schools in a midsize city and an increase for larger schools in an inner-city community.

More work is needed to replicate evaluations of prevention programs across multiple sites. What works in one setting will not necessarily work well in others. Characteristics of the interventionists, student population, school and community, and implementation issues may all contribute to a program's degree of impact. Efforts to replicate programs in new settings (e.g., Farrell, Valois, Meyer, & Tidwell, 2003) and multisite studies (e.g., CPPRG, 2002; MACSRG, 2002; MVPP, 2004b) provide opportunities to explore the potential role of setting variables on program impact. Such studies will initially be exploratory and may provide a basis for identifying critical variables through techniques such as meta-analysis (Hunter & Schmidt, 1990). More refined efforts that systematically manipulate setting characteristics using large numbers of schools will ultimately be needed to isolate specific variables that influence the impact of an intervention. Replications are also needed to determine the extent to which effects found in efficacy studies will be obtained when programs are implemented under more routine conditions. Schools willing to participate in randomized trials may not be representative of most schools. Rates of participation may also suffer for schools attempting to implement programs that assign extra activities to teachers or that attempt to involve parents in the absence of the types of incentives typically offered in efficacy studies. Gottfredson (2001) observed that there have been no systematic studies examining the quality of prevention programs as they are typically implemented in schools. Indeed, it has been argued that most schools are not likely to have the resources or technical expertise to implement most currently available programs (Samples & Aber, 1998). Similarly, little is known about what is needed to maintain a program's effectiveness when it is implemented on a wide scale (USDHHS, 2001).

Although increasing efforts to develop effective school-based programs to reduce youth violence have led to some initial progress, it is clear that much work remains to be done. Reviews have suggested that narrowly focused efforts are likely to have limited impact on this problem. Although the grid model described in this chapter may be used to classify specific intervention efforts, it may better serve as a guide to the construction of comprehensive efforts that address multiple levels of influence across multiple stages of development. These comprehensive efforts will likely involve school-based components, but they will form only one part of a larger effort. In comparison with intervention efforts directed at individuals, those directed at schools will require that evaluations be conducted on a large scale. In many cases this will involve multiple sites and multiple teams of investigators (e.g., CPPRG, 2002; MACSRG, 2002). Such efforts provide a basis for determining the extent to which findings can generalize across communities and have the added benefit of producing stronger studies through enhanced opportunities to collaborate among investigators. An excellent example is the MVPP, which represents the collaborative effort of investigators from four universities and the CDC (MVPP, 2004b). This project developed intervention components that built on the collaborative expertise of the entire team of investigators and is currently evaluating their impact in a randomized trial involving middle schools at four sites. Such efforts require substantial levels of funding. Obtaining the funds needed to conduct this work will require a substantial shift in priorities (MVPP, 2004a).

Even though violence prevention programs appear far more cost-effective than incarceration, federal spending on such programs pales in comparison with the funds provided for crime and drug control strategies such as policing and the construction of prisons (USDHHS, 2001). Moreover, funds that are available are often spent on programs that have not been proven to be effective or are ineffective (Gottfredson, 2001). This suggests that we may be being "penny wise and pound foolish" by not committing the funds needed to support the development, evaluation, and wider dissemination of more comprehensive violence prevention efforts.

REFERENCES

Aber, J. L., Jones, S. M., Brown, J. L., Chaudry, N., & Samples, F. (1998). Resolving Conflict Creatively: Evaluating the developmental effects of a school-based violence prevention program in neighborhood and classroom context. *Development and Psychopathology, 10,* 187–213.

Bosworth, K., Espelage, D., DuBay, T., Dahlberg, L., & Daytner, G. (1996). Using multimedia to teach conflict-resolution skills to young adolescents. *American Journal of Preventive Medicine, 12*(Suppl.), 65–74.

California Department of Education. (2002). *Safe schools: A planning guide for action.* Sacramento, CA: Author.

Catalano, R. F., Arthur, M. W., Hawkins, J. D., Berglund, M. L., & Olson, J. J. (1998). Comprehensive community- and school-based interventions to prevent antisocial behavior. In R. Loeber & D. P. Farrington (Eds.), *Serious and violent juvenile offenders: Risk factors and successful interventions* (pp. 248–283). Thousand Oaks, CA: Sage.

Catalano, R. F., Berglund, M. L., Ryan, J. A. M., Lonczak, H. S., & Hawkins, J. D. (2002). Positive youth development in the United States. Research findings on evaluations of the Positive Youth Development Programs. *Prevention and Treatment, 6,* Article 15. Retrieved August 12, 2002, from http://journals.apa.org/prevention/volume5/pre0050015a.html

Centers for Disease Control and Prevention. (1993, October 15). Violence-related attitudes and behaviors of high school students—New York City, 1992. *Morbidity and Mortality Weekly Report, 42,* 773–777.

Conduct Problems Prevention Research Group. (1999). Initial impact of the Fast Track prevention trial for conduct problems: II. Classroom effects. *Journal of Consulting and Clinical Psychology, 67,* 648–657.

Conduct Problems Prevention Research Group. (2002). The implementation of the Fast Track Program: An example of a large scale prevention science efficacy trial. *Journal of Abnormal Child Psychology, 30,* 1–17.

Cooper, W. O., Lutenbacher, M., & Faccia, K. (2000). Components of effective youth violence prevention programs for 7- to 14-year-olds. *Archives of Pediatric and Adolescent Medicine, 154,* 1134–1139.

Crockett, L., & Petersen, A. (1993). Adolescent development: Health risks and opportunities for health promotion. In S. Millstein, A. Petersen, & E. Night-engale (Eds.), *Promoting the health of adolescents* (pp. 13–37). New York: Simon & Schuster.

Crosse, S., Burr, M., Cantor, D., Hagen, C. A., & Hantman, I. (2001). *Wide scope, questionable quality: Drug and violence prevention efforts in American schools. Report on the Study on Youth Violence and Prevention.* Washington, DC: U.S. Department of Education.

Dahlberg, L. L., & Potter, L. B. (2001). Youth violence: Developmental pathways and prevention challenges. *American Journal of Preventive Medicine, 20*(Suppl. 1), 3–30.

Dishion, T. J., Kavanagh, K., Schneiger, A., Nelson, S., & Kaufman, N. K. (2002). Preventing early adolescent substance use: A family-centered strategy for the public middle school. *Prevention Science, 3,* 191–201.

Dishion, T. J., McCord, J., & Poulin, F. (1999). When interventions harm: Peer groups and problem behavior. *American Psychologist, 54,* 755–764.

Dumas, J. E., Lynch, A. M., Laughlin, J. E., Smith, E. P., & Prinz, R. (2001). Promoting intervention fidelity: Conceptual issues, methods, and preliminary results from the Early Alliance Prevention Trial. *American Journal of Preventive Medicine, 20*(Suppl. 1), 38–47.

Eddy, J. M., Reid, J. B., & Fetrow, R. A. (2000). An elementary school–based prevention program targeting modifiable antecedents of youth delinquency and violence: Linking the Interests of Families and Teachers (LIFT). *Journal of Emotional and Behavioral Disorders, 8,* 165–176.

Elliott, D. S., & Tolan, P. H. (1999). Youth violence prevention, intervention, and social policy: An overview. In D. J. Flannery & C. R. Huff (Eds.), *Youth violence prevention, intervention, and social policy* (pp. 3–46). Washington, DC: American Psychiatric Press.

Elliott, D. S., Williams, K. R., & Hamburg, B. (1998). An integrated approach to violence prevention. In D. S. Elliott, B. A. Hamburg, & K. R. Williams (Eds.), *Violence in American schools: A new perspective.* New York: Cambridge University Press.

Embry, D. D., Flannery, D. J., Vazsonyi, A. T., Powell, K. E., & Atha, H. (1996). PeaceBuilders: A theoretically driven, school-based model for early violence prevention. *American Journal of Preventive Medicine, 12*(Suppl.), 91–100.

Farrell, A. D., & Meyer, A. L. (1997). The effectiveness of a school-based curriculum for reducing violence among sixth grade students. *American Journal of Public Health, 87,* 979–984.

Farrell, A. D., Meyer, A. L., Kung, E. M., & Sullivan, T. N. (2001). Development and evaluation of school-based violence prevention programs. *Journal of Clinical Child Psychology, 30,* 207–220.

Farrell, A. D., Meyer, A. L., Sullivan, T. N., & Kung, E. M. (2003). Evaluation of the Responding in Peaceful and Positive Ways (RIPP) seventh grade violence prevention curriculum. *Journal of Child and Family Studies, 12,* 101–120.

Farrell, A. D., Meyer, A. L., & White, K. S. (2001). Evaluation of Responding in Peaceful and Positive Ways (RIPP): A school-based prevention program for reducing violence among urban adolescents. *Journal of Clinical Child Psychology*, 30, 451–463.

Farrell, A. D., Valois, R. F., Meyer, A. L., & Tidwell, R. (2003). Impact of the RIPP violence prevention program on rural middle school students. *Journal of Primary Prevention*, 24, 143–167.

Felner, R. D., Favazza, A., Shim, M., Brand, S., Gu, K., & Noonan, N. (2001). Whole school improvement and restructuring as prevention and promotion: Lessons from STEP and the Project on High Performance Learning Communities. *Journal of School Psychology*, 39, 177–202.

Foshee, V., Linder, G. F., Bauman, K. E., Langwick, S. A., Arriaga, X. B., Heath, J. L., et al. (1996). The Safe Dates Project: Theoretical basis, evaluation design, and selected baseline findings. *American Journal of Preventive Medicine*, 12(Suppl.), 39–47.

Gordon, R. (1987). An operational classification of disease prevention. In J. A. Steinberg & M. M. Silverberg (Eds.), *Preventing mental disorders: A research perspective* (pp. 20–26). Rockville, MD: National Institute of Mental Health.

Gottfredson, D. C. (2001). *Schools and delinquency*. New York: Cambridge University Press.

Grossman, D. C., Neckerman, H. J., Koepsell, T., Liu, P., Asher, K. N., Beland, K., et al. (1997). Effectiveness of a violence prevention curriculum among children in elementary school: A randomized control trial. *Journal of the American Medical Association*, 277, 1605–1642.

Grunbaum, J. A., Kann, L., Kincen, S. A., Hawkins, J., Ross, J. G., Lowry, R., et al. (2004, May 21). Youth risk behavior surveillance—United States, 2003. *Morbidity and Mortality Weekly Report*, 53(SS-2), 1–96.

Guerra, N. G. (1998). Serious and violent juvenile offenders: Gaps in knowledge and research priorities. In R. Loeber & D. P. Farrington (Eds.), *Serious and violent juvenile offenders: Risk factors and successful interventions* (pp. 389–404). Thousand Oaks, CA: Sage.

Hammond, W. R., & Yung, B. R. (1990). Preventing violence in at-risk African-American youth. *Journal of Health Care for the Underserved*, 2, 359–373.

Hausman, A., Pierce, G., & Briggs, L. (1996). Evaluation of a comprehensive violence prevention education: Effects on student behavior. *Journal of Adolescent Health*, 19, 104–110.

Hawkins, J. D., Catalano, R. F., Jones, G., & Fine, D. N. (1987). Delinquency prevention through parent training: Results and issues from work in progress. In J. Q. Wilson & G. C. Loury (Eds.), *From children to citizens: Families, schools, and delinquency prevention* (Vol. 13, pp. 186–204). New York: Springer-Verlag.

Hawkins, J. D., Catalano, R. F., Morrison, D. M., O'Donnell, J., Abbott, R. D., & Day, L. E. (1992). The Seattle Social Development Project: Effects of the first four years on protective factors and problem behaviors. In J. McCord & R. E.

Tremblay (Eds.), *Preventing antisocial behavior: Interventions from birth through adolescence* (pp. 139–161). New York: Guilford Press.

Hawkins, J. D., Farrington, D. P., & Catalano, R. F. (1998). Reducing violence through the schools. In D. S. Elliott, B. A. Hamburg, & K. R. Williams (Eds.), *Violence in American schools: A new perspective* (pp. 188–216). New York: Cambridge University Press.

Henry, D. B., Farrell, A. D., & Multisite Violence Prevention Project. (2004). The study designed by a committee: Design of the Multisite Violence Prevention Project. *American Journal of Preventive Medicine, 26*(Suppl. 1), 12–19.

Howard, K. A., Flora, J., & Griffin, M. (1999). Violence prevention programs in schools: State of the science and implications for future research. *Applied and Preventative Psychology, 8,* 197–215.

Hunter, J. E., & Schmidt, F. L. (1990). *Methods of meta-analysis: Correcting error and bias in research findings.* Newbury Park, CA: Sage.

Kiesler, D. J. (1966). Some myths of psychotherapy research and the search for a paradigm. *Psychological Bulletin, 65,* 110–136.

Lochman, J. E., Curry, J. F., Dane, H., & Ellis, M. (2002). The Anger Coping Program: An empirically-supported treatment for aggressive children. *Residential Treatment for Children and Youth, 18,* 63–73.

Lorion, R. P. (1998). Exposure to urban violence: Contamination of the school environment. In D. S. Elliott, B. A. Hamburg, & K. R. Williams (Eds.), *Violence in American schools: A new perspective* (pp. 293–311). New York: Cambridge University Press.

Metropolitan Area Child Study Research Group. (2002). A cognitive–ecological approach to preventing aggression in urban settings: Initial outcomes for high risk children. *Journal of Consulting and Clinical Psychology, 70,* 179–194.

Meyer, A. L., & Farrell, A. D. (1998). Social skills training to promote resilience and reduce violence in African American middle school students. *Education and Treatment of Children, 21,* 461–488.

Meyer, A. L., Farrell, A D., Northup, W., Kung, E. M., & Plybon, L. (2000). *Promoting non-violence in early adolescence: Responding in Peaceful and Positive Ways.* New York: Kluwer Academic.

Mihalic, S., Irwin, K., Elliott, D., Fagan, A., & Hansen, D. (2001, July). Blueprints for violence prevention. *Juvenile Justice Bulletin* (NCJ 187079). Washington, DC: Office of Juvenile Justice and Delinquency Prevention, U.S. Department of Justice. Retrieved July 8, 2005, from http://ncjrs.org/html/ojjdp/jjbul 2001_7_3/contents.html

Moffitt, T. E. (1993). Adolescent-limited and life-course-persistent antisocial behavior: A developmental taxonomy. *Psychological Review, 100,* 674–701.

Multisite Violence Prevention Project. (2004a). Lessons learned in the Multisite Violence Prevention Project collaboration: Big questions require large efforts. *American Journal of Preventive Medicine, 26*(Suppl. 1), 62–71.

Multisite Violence Prevention Project. (2004b). The Multisite Violence Prevention Project: Background and overview. *American Journal of Preventive Medicine*, 26(Suppl. 1), 3–11.

Olweus, D. (1993). *Bullying at school: What we know and what we can do*. Oxford, England: Blackwell Publishers.

Prinz, R. (2000). Research-based prevention of school violence and youth antisocial behavior: A developmental and educational perspective. In *Preventing school violence: Plenary papers of the 1999 Conference on Criminal Justice Research and Evaluation—Enhancing Policy and Practice Through Research* (Vol. 2, NCJ 180972, pp. 23–36). Washington, DC: U.S. Department of Justice, Office of Justice Programs, National Institute of Justice. Retrieved July 8, 2005, from http://www.ncjrs.org/pdffiles1/nij/180972.pdf

Prothrow-Stith, D. (1987). *Violence prevention curriculum for adolescents*. Newton, MA: Education Development Center.

Samples, F., & Aber, L. (1998). Evaluations of school-based violence prevention programs. In D. Elliott, B. Hamburg, & K. Williams (Eds.), *Violence in American schools* (pp. 217–252). New York: Cambridge University Press.

Selman, R. L., Beardslee, W., Schultz, L. H., Krupa, M., & Podoresky, D. (1986). Assessing adolescent interpersonal negotiation strategies: Toward the integration of structural and functional models. *Developmental Psychology, 22*, 450–459.

Small, M., & Tetrick, K. D. (2001). School violence: An overview. *Juvenile Justice, 8*, 3–12.

Tolan, P., & Guerra, N. (1994). *What works in reducing adolescent violence: An empirical review of the field*. Boulder, CO: Center for the Study and Prevention of Violence.

U.S. Department of Health and Human Services. (2001). *Youth violence: A report of the surgeon general*. Washington, DC: U.S. Department of Justice.

Wasserman, G. A., & Miller, L. S. (1998). The prevention of serious and violent juvenile offending. In R. Loeber & D. P. Farrington (Eds.), *Serious and violent juvenile offenders: Risk factors and successful interventions* (pp. 197–247). Thousand Oaks, CA: Sage.

Wiist, W. H., Jackson, R. H., & Jackson, K. W. (1996). Peer and community leader education to prevent youth violence. *American Journal of Preventive Medicine, 12*(Suppl.), 56–64.

7

BULLIES AND VICTIMS: A CHALLENGE FOR SCHOOLS

PAMELA ORPINAS AND ARTHUR M. HORNE

In a position statement on school violence, the National Association of School Psychologists (2001) stated that "schools must continue to strive to be havens of safety and security that permit all youth to thrive academically, socially, and emotionally" (¶1). It also stated that schools should minimize students' exposure not only to illegal acts such as assaults, theft, and sexual harassment but also to behaviors such as bullying that may cause emotional and psychological damage to students and may result in a negative school climate. Bullying affects a large number of children in schools, has negative short- and long-term consequences for students, and creates a climate that is not conducive to learning. However, adults should prevent and stop bullying not only because of its mental health and academic consequences but because it is in itself cruel and unfair to children. Children are entitled to grow up and study in a safe environment, and they should not have to spend either time or energy trying to defend themselves. Bullying can be preventable if the adults in the lives of children opt to make it so.

This chapter is composed of four sections. In the first section, we discuss the definition of bullying and differentiate it from aggression and violence. In the second section, we examine the prevalence of bullying in schools, and in the third section, we describe the consequences of bullying on the victims and the bullies. Finally, on the basis of the research on bullying, in the last section, we propose guidelines for schools and parents to reduce this problem.

DEFINITION OF BULLYING

The distinction among the terms *violence, aggression,* and *bullying* is not always clear. In general, *aggressive behaviors* are defined as acts intended to physically or emotionally hurt or injure another person. Aggressive behaviors are considered less extreme than violent behaviors (e.g., homicide, rape, robbery, and aggravated assault) and are not limited to physical harm. For many European and American researchers, bullying is a subset of aggression (Orpinas & Horne, 2006; Smith, Cowie, Olafsson, & Liefooghe, 2002). Bullying is a type of aggression in which the bully (or the aggressor) is stronger or more powerful than the victim, and the aggressive behaviors are committed intentionally, repeatedly, and over time. Therefore, a fight among gang members of equal power would be aggressive but not bullying, whereas pushing, teasing, or threatening a child who is younger, smaller, or somehow weaker would be bullying if the behavior is repeated over time. These distinctions are not, however, universally accepted, and sometimes they may be controversial as educators, researchers, and politicians develop their own definitions.

A key element in the definitions of violence, aggression, and bullying is the concept of intention. Thus, an act that hurts another person but is committed without the intention to hurt is not considered aggressive. For example, if a child falls on the playground and while falling hurts a peer, this behavior would not be considered aggressive even though it may have caused pain or even injury. However, if a child pretends to fall with the intent to trip a classmate, that behavior would be an act of aggression. Defining *intention* is not always an easy process, because children's games frequently escalate from playful to aggressive, and the intention to hurt may not be openly recognized. Frequently, children respond with aggression when they are hurt while playing hard with another child, and this process may escalate to a major fight. Defining intention may be especially difficult when dealing with emotional aggression, in particular when the aggressor denies any intention. Thus, the perception of intention may be very different in the eyes of the "doer" and the "viewer."

Problems arise not only in defining these terms but also in distinguishing what is normal or expected from what is aggressive. For example, when does rough-and-tumble play cross the line between play and aggression? Aggression is partially defined by the context in which it occurs. Although a certain level of pushing and tackling is expected on the football field, the same pushing is not acceptable in the school hallway and could prove deadly if coming from a rival gang member. Similarly, a certain level of rough play may be acceptable on the playground, but it would be at least considered disturbing when done in the classroom. The level of acceptable rough playing also depends on the level of friendship of the players.

Bullying is often divided into four categories: physical, verbal, relational, and sexual. The most recognized category is *physical bullying*, such as pushing, shoving, hitting, and other acts of physical aggression. *Verbal bullying* includes name calling, cursing, and threatening. *Relational bullying* refers to acts that damage the relationships among children, such as excluding peers from participating in social events (e.g., eating lunch together), gossiping about a child, or telling lies to have others avoid the victim. Finally, *sexual bullying* refers to any unwelcome and unsolicited words or conduct of a sexual nature.

Because bullying is most likely to occur in social situations when other peers are present, students may take several roles in the bullying process. The most common and recognized role is the *bully*, who usually initiates the aggression and assumes a leadership role. Thus, the bully is easily recognizable by teachers and peers. Bullies have two types of followers: *assistants* (who help the bully) and *reinforcers* (who reinforce the bully by cheering or simply laughing; Atlas & Pepler, 1998; Salmivalli, 1999; Sutton, Smith, & Swettenham, 1999). Bystanders who witness the aggression also fall into two categories: those who are part of the problem (e.g., instigate the fight, just watch, or are afraid to help) and those who are part of the solution (e.g., ask for help, help diffuse the problem, or provide assistance to the victim; Orpinas & Horne, 2006). By not opposing the bullying, outsiders allow the bullying to continue and implicitly approve it. Some children may not have the skills or the knowledge to stop the bullying and may feel guilty for not doing anything to stop it. Thus, they may become secondary victims of the bullying process (Newman, Horne, & Bartolomucci, 2000). Finally, the *victim* is the child who is systematically and repeatedly harassed or abused by the bully. Some have suggested that the term *victim* may not be the most appropriate because it connotes being a powerless recipient of the aggression and instead have offered the term *targets of aggression* (Stein, Gaberman, & Sjostrom, 1996).

Authors have distinguished among the different types of victims. Olweus (1993), on the basis of several studies conducted in the Scandinavian countries, described two types of victims: passive and provocative. Passive victims, who are the most common type, are those children picked on without provocation. They are characterized by being more anxious, quiet, and submissive than other children. They frequently have no lasting friendships in their classroom. Provocative victims, on the other hand, deliberately provoke the antagonism of the bullies, and sometimes of the entire classroom, by displaying a combination of anxious and aggressive behaviors (Olweus, 1993; Schwartz, Dodge, & Coie, 1993). They may associate with bullies to increase their social status (Boulton & Smith, 1994). Provocative victims are particularly deserving of attention because they are often the most rejected members of their peer group, and they are at increased risk for behavioral problems and dropping out of school (Pellegrini, 1998; Perry, Kusel, & Perry, 1988). The prevalence of students who act as bullies in one situation and as victims in another is unclear, with estimates ranging from a low of 4% (Boulton & Smith, 1994) to a high of 31% (Forero, McLellan, Rissel, & Bauman, 1999).

HOW BIG IS THE PROBLEM OF BULLYING?

Numerous factors influence the estimates of the prevalence of bullying. Thus, answering questions about how frequently and how intensely children are bullied at school is not easy. One of these factors is the wording of questions. Studies in other areas of interpersonal violence, such as intimate partner violence, have found that the prevalence of the problem is much higher when researchers ask questions about specific behaviors (e.g., shoving and punching) rather than a general question about being abused. Similarly, the prevalence of bullying may be lower when children answer questions about being bullied rather than questions regarding the frequency of specific aggressive behaviors, such as teasing or hitting.

The prevalence of bullying and victimization also varies by type of bullying behavior. Practitioners and researchers frequently underestimate the overall magnitude of bullying by not recognizing certain acts as bullying or by failing to evaluate them. As described in the prior section, bullying encompasses a large number of behaviors including physical (e.g., slapping, kicking, and destroying property), verbal (e.g., taunting and name-calling), and relational aggression (e.g., passing rumors and isolating) as well as sexual harassment (e.g., making sexual comments and sexual gestures). Teachers and students usually recognize physical bullying but do not think about social isolation or gossiping as bullying. Further, most studies have not assessed sexual harassment. An additional complication is that because bullying implies a power differential between the bully and the victim, researchers need to evaluate the relationship between the bully and the victim.

Comparisons across studies are difficult because researchers have used different time frames (e.g., ever, since school started, last term, prior month, or prior week) and different response categories. Some surveys request information about the specific number of times the behavior occurred, and others request information about the students' perception of the extent to which a specific problem applies to them (e.g., sometimes or most of the time). The prevalence of the problem also varies greatly by who is the respondent: children, teachers, or parents. Generally, the prevalence is much higher in students' self-reports of bullying than in teachers' or parents' reports (Stockdale, Hangaduambo, Duys, Larson, & Sarvela, 2002). Finally, international comparisons pose additional problems, as languages and cultures may ascribe different meanings to bullying. Recently, Smith and colleagues compared the concept of bullying in 14 countries with 13 different languages (Smith et al., 2002). The term *bullying* does not exist in all languages, and finding the best translation is a challenge for international research. As expected, the comprehension of the complexity and breadth of the term was much higher among adolescents than among younger children.

In spite of all of these methodological problems, educators and researchers search for an answer to the question, how big is the bullying problem? Overall, most studies have concluded that bullying increases during late elementary school, peaks in middle school (in particular among sixth graders), and then decreases through high school. Also, most of the literature concurs that physical and verbal bullying and victimization are higher among boys than girls (e.g., Nansel et al., 2001). Finally, studies have been inconclusive about how relational bullying and victimization—that is, covert forms of aggression directed at damaging peer relationships—varies by gender (Crick, Casas, & Ku, 1999; Prinstein, Boergers, & Vernberg, 2001; Tomada & Schneider, 1997).

In 1997–1998, the World Health Organization (WHO) coordinated the largest cross-national study on bullying, in which 30 countries participated. In each country, a survey was completed by a representative sample of 6th to 10th graders. Bullying was explained as follows:

> We say a student is BEING BULLIED when another student, or group of students, say or do nasty or unpleasant things to him or her. It is also bullying when a student is being teased repeatedly in a way that he or she doesn't like, but it is NOT BULLYING when two students of about the same strength quarrel or fight. (Nansel et al., 2001, p. 2095)

In the United States, 53% of the boys and 37% of the girls reported bullying someone at least once during the current term. Moreover, 13% of the boys and 5% of the girls admitted to bullying someone at least once a week. Slightly fewer children reported being the victims of bullying. Overall, 41% reported being bullied at least once during the current term, and 8% reported weekly victimization. Most common forms of bullying were physical aggression (mostly among boys) and belittlement about looks or speech, rumors, and sexual harassment (mostly among girls; Nansel et al., 2001).

The prevalence of bullying among the 13-year-olds in 27 of the participating countries is summarized in WHO's *World Report on Violence and*

Health (Mercy, Butchart, Farrington, & Cerdá, 2002). On average, 42% of these students reported having bullied someone at least once during the current school term. The prevalence ranged from under 15% in Sweden and England to over 60% in Lithuania, Greenland, Denmark, Germany, and Austria. The prevalence of weekly bullying ranged between 1% and 10% among countries.

The School Crime Supplement to the National Victimization Survey, which is conducted by the U.S. Department of Justice (DOJ), yielded very different results. Students were asked, "During the last 6 months, have you been bullied at school? That is, have any other students picked on you a lot or tried to make you do things you didn't want to like give them money?" (DeVoe et al., 2004, p. 156). Prevalence of bullying ranged from 14% of 6th graders to 2% of 12th graders. As in the WHO study, boys reported more victimization than girls, and victimization decreased as grade level increased. Surprisingly, the bullying prevalence in the DOJ study was much lower. Possible explanations for the difference are the context of the question (the DOJ study was a crime survey and the WHO study was a school survey) and the differences in the instructions given to the children.

An indirect estimate of bullying is students' perception of safety at school. In the 2003 Youth Risk Behavior Survey (YRBS), a national survey of high school students, 5% of students reported having felt too unsafe to go to school at least one day during the month preceding the survey (Grunbaum et al., 2004). The feeling of being unsafe at school may be influenced not only by the bullying that occurs at school but also by national events such as school shootings (Brener, Simon, Anderson, Barrios, & Small, 2002). In the same YRBS, 13% of the students reported having been in a fight on school property; 9% reported having been threatened or injured with a weapon on school property; and 6% reported having carried a weapon on school property. Not surprisingly, fights, threats, and weapon carrying were higher among boys than girls.

Prevalence of specific behaviors can be even higher. In a survey of over 9,000 inner-city, middle school students conducted in Texas (unpublished data from Students for Peace project; see Orpinas et al., 2000), students reported the frequency of specific aggressive behaviors during the week prior to the survey: 60% had called other students bad names, 55% had made fun of someone, 44% had pushed someone, 39% had kicked or slapped another student, and 36% had threatened to hurt or hit someone. Answering the same questions, upper elementary students have also reported high levels of aggression: 38% had called other students bad names, 38% had made fun of someone, 30% had pushed someone, 21% had kicked or slapped another student, and 26% had threatened to hurt or hit someone (Orpinas, Horne, & Staniszewski, 2003). Others studies have reported similar high levels of aggression and victimization (e.g., Kochenderfer & Ladd, 1997; Silvernail, Thompson, Yang, & Kopp, 2000).

School violence not only affects students; teachers may also be victimized. In a recent national survey sponsored by the U.S. Department of Education, almost 10% of the public school teachers reported that a student had threatened to injure them, and 4.2% reported that a student attack had occurred during the year prior to the survey (Gruber, Wiley, Broughman, Strizek, & Burian-Fitzgerald, 2002).

CONSEQUENCES OF BULLYING

Researchers have no doubt that bullying has negative consequences on the victims. Depending on the frequency and intensity of the bullying as well as the personal and social characteristics of the victim, consequences of being victimized can range from minor physical and psychological problems to its most tragic consequences, homicide and suicide. A study conducted by the U.S. Secret Service and the U.S. Department of Education found that almost three quarters of school shootings committed by students against other students had in common the acting out of anger or revenge for having been the victim of bullying at school (Vossekuil, Fein, Reddy, Borum, & Modzeleski, 2002).

Most commonly, the victim of bullying is likely to suffer from depression, somatic complaints (head- and stomachaches), common health problems, not sleeping well, bed wetting, and feelings of loneliness (Williams, Chambers, Logan, & Robinson, 1996; Wolke, Woods, Bloomfield, & Karstadt, 2001). Not surprisingly, in a meta-analysis of 20 years of research on several forms of psychological maladjustment caused by victimization, depression was the symptom most strongly related to victimization (Hawker & Boulton, 2000). The relation between bullying and self-esteem has some interesting nuances. In a large study conducted in Ireland, the lowest levels of self-esteem were found among students who were both victims and bullies, and self-esteem decreased as the frequency of victimization increased. However, the self-esteem of the *pure bullies*, that is, those who bullied others but were not victims, was not as affected (O'Moore & Kirkham, 2001). Students who are the target of aggression are also likely to have fewer good friends and thus feel lonely at school (Boulton & Underwood, 1992). The fact that they have few friends is likely to make them easy targets of aggression, and conversely, other children may avoid befriending them for fear of becoming themselves targets of the bullies. Victims are also likely to avoid going to school because they fear for their safety (Berthold & Hoover, 2000). Most worrisome, in a study of Finnish adolescents, depression and suicidal ideation were found among bullies and victims (Kaltiala-Heino, Rimpela, Marttunen, Rimpela, & Rantanen, 1999).

Although some victims do suffer the consequences of victimization as adults, bullies fare considerably worse as they get older. Bullies are more likely than nonbullies to do poorly in school, drop out of school, cheat on tests, and have problems with the legal system (Berthold & Hoover, 2000; Olweus, 1993). Students involved in school bullying and aggression have a number of familial, personal, and behavioral risk factors. In a study of fourth to sixth graders in the United States, bullies in comparison with nonbullies were more likely to spend time unsupervised at home, drink alcohol, use tobacco, and carry or have easy access to weapons (Berthold & Hoover, 2000).

REDUCING BULLYING IN SCHOOL

Bullying in schools is prevalent, unacceptable, and may have serious emotional and academic consequences on the child. Thus, schools need to develop policies and strategies to prevent bullying from occurring, to stop it when it does occur, to make the bullies accountable for their actions, to help the victims, and to foster a safe and positive school climate. Because bullying implies a power differential and the purposeful infliction of pain in a situation that is most frequently unprovoked, traditional conflict resolution strategies and mediation may not be effective. Victims of bullying are frequently unable to effectively defend themselves; otherwise, the bullying would have stopped. Thus, it is the role of the adults in the lives of children to assure that bullying does not happen.

The first and most well-known study on bullying prevention was implemented in Norway between 1983 and 1985. The concern for bullying was sparked by newspaper articles reporting three cases of children who had committed suicide, most likely as a result of severe bullying at school. In response to these tragic events, the Norwegian Ministry of Education launched a campaign against bullying in Grades 1 to 9, which started in the fall of 1983. As part of this movement, Dan Olweus developed a comprehensive schoolwide intervention that was evaluated in 42 schools in Bergen and included 2,500 boys and girls in fourth to seventh grades. Children were evaluated in late spring of 1983, 1984, and 1985. The intervention yielded an approximately 50% reduction in bullying (Limber, 2004; Olweus, 1993). Unfortunately, this magnitude of reduction has not been replicated in other studies, perhaps reflecting a time trend or cultural characteristics of Norwegian schools. A number of studies have been conducted in the past decade, with a reduction of bullying ranging between 15% and 35% (Olweus, Limber, & Mihalic, 2000); however, the evaluation of other projects is still in process. The largest number of evaluated programs has been in the area of school violence prevention (Mytton, DiGuiseppi, Gough, Taylor, & Logan, 2002). Fewer have been specific to bullying, such as the Seville Anti-Bullying in School Project (Ortega & Lera, 2000), the antibullying campaigns in the Netherlands (Limper, 2000), the Bully Busters program in the United States (Horne, Orpinas, Newman-Carlson, & Bartolomucci, 2004), the Sheffield Project in the United Kingdom (Sharp & Smith, 1991), and a sequence of different programs implemented in Norway (Roland, 2000). In the book, *Bullying Prevention: Creating a Positive School Climate and Developing Social Competence* (Orpinas & Horne, 2006), the authors proposed the "school social competence development and bullying prevention model." The book provides a step-by-step process to prevent bullying and provide a positive, caring school climate.

In the sections that follow, we summarize some of the most effective strategies to reduce bullying, which are organized in seven categories: commitment and awareness, school policies, support of teachers and school personnel, positive school climate, supervision, education of students, and education of parents.

Commitment and Awareness

The successful implementation of bullying prevention programs is not likely to occur without a strong commitment from the school principal, other administrators, and teachers (Orpinas et al., 1996). Limper (2000) described several conditions that must be met to effectively address the problem. Bullying must be seen as a problem by all members of the educational community; the school must be ready to discuss the problem with students, parents, and teachers and to take action to prevent it; all teachers must stand against it; and procedures must be in place in case bullying does happen. Schools that are not serious about solving the problem of bullying use a "yes, but . . ." approach, such as "bullying is bad, but we don't have a problem at our school," or "bullying is a serious problem, but we don't have the resources to address it" (Sullivan, 2000). Schools committed to the prevention of bullying devote resources to evaluate the magnitude of the problem, to train teachers and students, and to create a safe environment for all.

School personnel need to understand the magnitude of the bullying problem and be committed to solving the problem. An important mechanism to increase educators' commitment is to raise awareness of the problem by presenting data collected from students and teachers (Orpinas & Horne 2006). Survey data collected from students and teachers can provide information on students' perceptions of how big the problem is (frequency of bullying and victimization), where and how it occurs, and how much support victims receive from teachers. Results of the survey can be presented during an in-service meeting of the school community, including teachers, administrators, parents, and student representatives. At this meeting, it is also important to address common attitudes about bullying, such as denying that bullying exists ("it does not happen here"), normalizing bullying ("boys will be boys"; "bullying is just part of growing up"), putting the responsibility or even the blame on the victim ("students should stand up for themselves"; "they shouldn't act odd"), or denying the consequences of bullying ("we have all gone through it, and we are fine adults").

School Policies

If schools do not have clear policies about bullying and a plan of action to address the problem, victims are victimized twice: by the bullies and by the system. School policies should address all types of bullying: physical, verbal, relational, and sexual. Schools have been mostly concerned with physical fights. Fights at school, however, do not just happen; they are usually the end consequence of a series of events. Students most frequently resort to physical fights to retaliate because of teasing and rumors (Boulton, 1993).

School rules should be based on clear and stated school core values (Curwin & Mendler, 1997), such as "all members of the school deserve to be treated with respect" and "bullying, aggression, and violence are not acceptable" (Orpinas & Horne, 2006; Orpinas, Horne, & Multisite Violence Prevention Project, 2004). On the basis of those core values, rules indicate specific expected behaviors (e.g., "include others in your work" or "use respectful language") as well as consequences for breaking the rules.

Schools also need to provide venues for reporting bullying and violence, such as a reporting box. The reporting box can be located in the teachers' classroom, in the central office, in the media center, or another location. School personnel should check the box daily and act on any problems quickly and efficiently. Another option is to have a formal mechanism, such as a bullying prevention team formed by school community members, to receive and review complaints (Kelder et al., 1996). The team investigates complaints and recommends solutions as well as develops guidelines for teachers to intervene (e.g., see Ross, 2003). This team can also be in charge of developing and implementing the student survey and other schoolwide campaigns.

Support of Teachers and School Personnel

To date, students have expressed little faith in the value of school personnel's response to bullying (Boulton, 1997; Boulton & Underwood,

1992; Glover, Gough, Johnson, & Cartwright, 2000). Although most students recognize that teachers will intervene in cases of physical fights, significantly fewer believe that teachers will act in cases of pushing or tripping. In addition, most teachers do not recognize relational aggression as a form of bullying; thus, they are not likely to act on it. In one study, only one third of the students reported that teachers would do something to stop bullying (Boulton & Underwood, 1992). In a recent study by the authors, approximately one fourth of students reported that teachers ignored threats and teasing (Orpinas & Horne, 2006). Most worrisome, most students perceived teachers' interventions as unsuccessful and feared that reporting the incidents would worsen the problem (Glover et al., 2000). Students' perceptions are supported by the large number of teachers who do not feel confident handling bullying incidents (Boulton, 1997). Another source of concern is that even though most teachers report a sympathetic attitude toward stopping bullying, this attitude tends to diminish with years of service (Boulton, 1997). Thus, teachers need ongoing support and training to acknowledge the different types of bullying, understand the magnitude and consequences of the problem, and implement successful strategies to prevent bullying. When teachers do not establish consequences for bullying, they are inadvertently reinforcing the behavior.

To support teachers, schools should develop clear policies and provide teacher training for policy implementation and classroom management. In addition to traditional workshops, teachers can discuss in small groups their progress to eliminate bullying and develop creative solutions to specific problems. These support groups can be fundamental to help teachers reduce school bullying (Bambino, 2002; Ialongo et al., 1999). Training manuals to help teachers develop skills to reduce bullying and aggression have been developed and are in the process of being validated (e.g., Horne, Bartolomucci, & Newman-Carlson, 2003; Newman et al., 2000; Orpinas et al., 2004). Initial studies of the Bully Busters Program have shown that in-service training followed by teacher support groups significantly increased teachers' violence prevention knowledge, skills, and self-efficacy and reduced discipline referrals (Howard, Horne, & Jolliff, 2001; Newman & Horne, 2004).

Positive School Climate

Creating a positive school climate is an essential part of any violence or bullying prevention program (Greenberg et al., 2003; Orpinas & Horne, 2006). In a positive school climate, teachers model how to treat each other with respect, use frequent praise and positive feedback for good behaviors, establish positive relationships with students, and apply consequences for violating school policies. When bullying occurs, negative consequences are administered on the basis of social–cognitive theory's rules of punishment. (a) Negative consequences must always follow the behavior; thus, they need to be easy to administer. (b) Negative consequences must be related to the behavior; for example, if a student pushed a boy, causing him to drop his books, the bully would be required to pick up his books, pay for any damaged books, and carry the victim's books to the class. (c) Negative consequences must teach the correct behavior; thus, extra homework is not an appropriate punishment (Bandura, 1986). Teachers need to make a point to punish the behavior, not the person, and clearly state which behavior is not acceptable, how it violates the school values, and what the consequence will be. In addition to punishing inappropriate behaviors, schools should provide positive consequences for good behavior. To this effect, Newman et al. (2000) proposed the acronym "ActNICE": Notice when others are doing well; Increase focus on positive behavior; Create opportunities for positive class interaction; and Encourage all students to reduce aggression and increase prosocial behavior. Another strategy for rewarding positive behavior is the Good Behavior Game, which has shown long-term effects on reducing aggression when used as a component of classroom management (Ialongo, Poduska, Werthamer, & Kellam, 2001).

Supervision

Because bullying is most likely to occur when adults are not present (Glover et al., 2000), one of the most effective strategies to stop bullying is to increase adult supervision. Schools need to develop a supervision plan, so that a sufficient number of adults are always present in hallways, playgrounds, lunchrooms, buses, and any other critical location reported by students or teachers. Supervising adults not only need to be present, they need to be prepared to intervene effectively and quickly if bullying occurs. In addition, supervisors must communicate any bullying incidents to relevant classroom teachers and administrators.

Education of Students

Schools need to send a strong message to all members of the community that bullying is not acceptable. Teachers should educate students at least once per semester regarding types of unacceptable behaviors, the school policies on bullying, the reporting process, and the school's expectations regarding the behavior of bystanders. Olweus et al. (2000) proposed four basic school rules: Students will not bully others; students will help students who are bullied; students will include all students in their activities; and students will tell an adult if someone is being bullied. Children who are the targets of bullying should know that they can and should ask for help from their teacher and their parents. In addition, most students would benefit from learning and practicing behavioral skills to increase positive communication, manage negative emotions, and solve conflicts (Orpinas & Horne, 2006).

Bystanders play a critical role in the bullying process. Almost 90% of bullying occurs when other students are present (Hawkins, Pepler, & Craig, 2001), and the majority of students hold attitudes that do not support bullying (Whitney & Smith, 1993). However, their attitudes often are not consistent with their behavior. In observational studies of children, fewer than 20% of students actually do something to defend the victim or to stop the bullying (Hawkins et al., 2001), and a large number of students think that they should do something, but they do not (Charach, Pepler, & Ziegler, 1995). Most of the children who do intervene are successful at stopping the bullying; however, some do use aggressive strategies to accomplish this goal, which is also problematic (Hawkins et al., 2001). Thus, on the basis of these results, schools can build their bullying prevention programs on the fact that most students do not support bullying and educate students on successful strategies to stop it. First, students should not reinforce the bullying by laughing, cheering, or even gathering around to observe it. In fact, the school can provide negative consequences for these behaviors. Second, students can learn to stop bullying by using prosocial, nonaggressive strategies, such as speaking out against bullying, not reinforcing the behavior by laughing, including isolated children in school tasks and play, and being helpful and friendly toward victims. Third, it is important that children speak out and inform adults; students need to know that bullying thrives in the silence of the victims and bystanders.

Education of Parents

Schools need to educate parents in three areas. First, parents need to know the definition and characteristics of bullying, the school policies for reporting and handling bullying, and appropriate bystander behaviors. Second, parents need to know about parental behaviors that may increase the problem, such as supporting fighting and encouraging children to fight back (Orpinas, Murray, & Kelder, 1999). Finally, parents need to be able to recognize signs of victimization and understand the steps they need to take if their child reports that he or she is being bullied at school. Signs of being the target of bullying may include being afraid to go to school, having a sudden drop in grades, being anxious or depressed, having somatic complaints, having unexplained bruises or torn clothes, receiving phone calls that the child does not want to talk about, and "losing" possessions or money.

SUMMARY

Bullying is a type of aggression in which the aggressor is more powerful than the victim, and the aggressive acts are intentional and committed repeatedly and over time. Bullying behaviors may be physical (e.g., hitting, punching, and shoving), verbal (e.g., teasing and threatening to hit or hurt), relational (e.g., excluding someone from a group, breaking a secret, and withdrawing friendship), or sexual (e.g., telling sexual jokes, pulling someone's clothes, making suggestive comments or gestures, and engaging in inappropriate touching). Bullying can cause serious emotional problems for the victim, such as suicide attempts, assaulting the bully with a weapon as revenge, and depression. Bullying can also result in lower academic performance and may result in an increased likelihood of future delinquency. It is important that schools provide a safe place for children, not only because of the emotional and academic consequences of bullying but also because bullying is wrong and unfair to children. Schools need to take a strong position against bullying and develop clear policies that reflect this position. Teachers, students, and parents need to be educated on how to prevent bullying and how to stop it.

In spite of what is currently known about bullies and victims, numerous questions still remain that require further research. First, theoretical models that help understanding of the development and trajectory of bullying and the bully–victim relationship need further investigation. Second, more research is needed to understand the risk and protective factors of bullies and victims. Third, a better understanding of the strengths and limitations of the different methods to assess the problem will facilitate research. Finally and most important, in spite of what we know about interventions to address the problem, there is still a dearth of information about the efficacy of programs and strategies to prevent and reduce bullying at schools. More specifically, more research is needed on how to tailor the type and intensity of programs to the characteristics of schools and to the types of bullying problems.

REFERENCES

Atlas, R. S., & Pepler, D. J. (1998). Observations of bullying in the classroom. *Journal of Educational Research, 92,* 86–99.

Bambino, D. (2002). Critical friends. *Educational Leadership, 59,* 25–27.

Bandura, A. (1986). *Social foundations of thought and action: A social cognitive theory.* Englewood Cliffs, NJ: Prentice-Hall.

Berthold, K. A., & Hoover, J. H. (2000). Correlates of bullying and victimization among intermediate students in the midwestern USA. *School Psychology International*, *21*, 65–78.

Boulton, M. J. (1993). Proximate causes of aggressive fighting in middle school children. *British Journal of Educational Psychology*, *63*, 231–244.

Boulton, M. J. (1997). Teachers' views on bullying: Definitions, attitudes and ability to cope. *British Journal of Educational Psychology*, *67*, 223–233.

Boulton, M. J., & Smith, P. K. (1994). Bully/victim problems in middle school children: Stability, self-perceived competence, peer perceptions and peer acceptance. *British Journal of Developmental Psychology*, *12*, 315–329.

Boulton, M. J., & Underwood, K. (1992). Bully/victim problems among middle school children. *British Journal of Educational Psychology*, *62*, 73–87.

Brener, N. D., Simon, T. R., Anderson, M., Barrios, L. C., & Small, M. L. (2002). Effect of the incident at Columbine on students' violence- and suicide-related behaviors. *American Journal of Preventive Medicine*, *22*, 146–150.

Charach, A., Pepler, D. J., & Ziegler, S. (1995). Bullying at school: A Canadian perspective. *Education Canada*, *35*, 12–18.

Crick, N. R., Casas, J. F., & Ku, H. C. (1999). Relational and physical forms of peer victimization in preschool. *Developmental Psychology*, *35*, 376–385.

Curwin, R. L., & Mendler, A. N. (1997). *As tough as necessary: Countering violence, aggression, and hostility in our schools*. Alexandria, VA: Association for Supervision and Curriculum Development.

DeVoe, J. F., Peter, K., Kaufman, P., Miller, A. K., Noonan, M., Snyder, T. D., et al. (2004). *Indicators of school crime and safety: 2004*. Washington, DC: U.S. Departments of Education and Justice and U.S. Government Printing Office.

Forero, R., McLellan, L., Rissel, C., & Bauman, A. (1999). Bullying behaviour and psychosocial health among school students in New South Wales, Australia: Cross-sectional survey. *British Medical Journal*, *319*, 344–348.

Glover, D., Gough, G., Johnson, M., & Cartwright, N. (2000). Bullying in 25 secondary schools: Incidence, impact, and intervention. *Educational Research*, *42*, 141–156.

Greenberg, M. T., Weissberg, R. P., O'Brien, M. U., Zins, J. E., Fredericks, L., Resnik, H., et al. (2003). Enhancing school-based prevention and youth development through coordinated social, emotional, and academic learning. *American Psychologist*, *58*, 466–474.

Gruber, K. J., Wiley, S. D., Broughman, S. P., Strizek, G. A., & Burian-Fitzgerald, M. (2002). *School and staffing survey, 1999–2000: Overview of the data for public, private, public charter, and Bureau of Indian Affairs elementary and secondary schools* (Report No. NCES 2002-313). Washington, DC: U.S. Department of Education, National Center for Education Statistics.

Grunbaum, J. A., Kann, L., Kinchen, S., Ross, J., Hawkins, J., Lowry, R., et al. (2004, May 21). Youth risk behavior surveillance—United States, 2003. *Morbidity and Mortality Weekly Report*, *53*, 1–96.

Hawker, D. S., & Boulton, M. J. (2000). Twenty years' research on peer victimization and psychosocial maladjustment: A meta-analytic review of cross-sectional studies. *Journal of Child Psychology and Psychiatry, 41*, 441–455.

Hawkins, D. L., Pepler, D. J., & Craig, W. M. (2001). Naturalistic observations of peer interventions in bullying. *Social Development, 10*, 512–527.

Horne, A. M., Bartolomucci, C. L., & Newman-Carlson, D. (2003). *Bully Busters: A teacher's manual for helping bullies, victims, and bystanders (Grades K–5).* Champaign, IL: Research Press.

Horne, A. M., Orpinas, P., Newman-Carlson, D., & Bartolomucci, C. (2004). Elementary school Bully Busters program: Understanding why children bully and what to do about it. In D. L. Espelage & S. M. Swearer (Eds.), *Bullying in American schools: A social–ecological perspective on prevention and intervention* (pp. 297–325). Mahwah, NJ: Erlbaum.

Howard, N. M., Horne, A. M., & Jolliff, D. (2001). Self-efficacy in a new training model for the prevention of bullying in schools. *Journal of Emotional Abuse, 2*, 181–191.

Ialongo, N., Poduska, J., Werthamer, L., & Kellam, S. (2001). The distal impact of two first-grade preventive interventions on conduct problems and disorder in early adolescence. *Journal of Emotional and Behavioral Disorders, 9*, 146–160.

Ialongo, N. S., Werthamer, L., Kellam, S., Brown, C. H., Wang, S., & Lin, Y. (1999). Proximal impact of two first-grade preventive interventions on the early risk behaviors for later substance abuse, depression, and antisocial behavior. *American Journal of Community Psychology, 27*, 599–641.

Kaltiala-Heino, R., Rimpela, M., Marttunen, M., Rimpela, A., & Rantanen, P. (1999). Bullying, depression, and suicidal ideation in Finnish adolescents: School survey. *British Medical Journal, 319*, 348–351.

Kelder, S. H., Orpinas, P., McAlister, A., Frankowski, R., Parcel, G. S., & Friday, J. (1996). The Students for Peace Project: A comprehensive violence-prevention program for middle school students. *American Journal of Preventive Medicine, 12*, 22–30.

Kochenderfer, B. J., & Ladd, G. W. (1997). Victimized children's responses to peers' aggression: Behaviors associated with reduced versus continued victimization. *Development and Psychopathology, 9*, 59–73.

Limber, S. (2004). Implementation of the Olweus bullying prevention program in American schools: Lessons learned from the field. In D. L. Espelage & S. M. Swearer (Eds.), *Bullying in American schools: A social–ecological perspective on prevention and intervention* (pp. 351–363). Mahwah, NJ: Erlbaum.

Limper, R. (2000). Cooperation between parents, teachers, and school boards to prevent bullying in education: An overview of work done in the Netherlands. *Aggressive Behavior, 26*, 125–134.

Mercy, J. A., Butchart, A., Farrington, D., & Cerdá, M. (2002). Youth violence. In E. G. Crug, L. L. Dahlberg, J. A. Mercy, A. B. Zwi, & R. Lozano (Eds.), *World report on violence and health* (pp. 23–56). Geneva, Switzerland: World Health Organization.

Mytton, J. A., DiGuiseppi, C., Gough, D. A., Taylor, R. S., & Logan, S. (2002). School-based violence prevention programs—Systematic review of secondary prevention trials. *Archives of Pediatrics and Adolescent Medicine, 156,* 752–762.

Nansel, T. R., Overpeck, M., Pilla, R. S., Ruan, W. J., Simons-Morton, B., & Scheidt, P. (2001). Bullying behaviors among US youth—Prevalence and association with psychosocial adjustment. *Journal of the American Medical Association, 285,* 2094–2100.

National Association of School Psychologists. (2001). *Position statement on school violence.* Retrieved March 5, 2005, from http://www.nasponline.org/information/pospaper_violence.html

Newman, D. A., & Horne, A. M. (2004). Bully Busters: A psychoeducational intervention for reducing bullying behavior in middle school students. *Journal of Counseling and Development, 82,* 259–268.

Newman, D. A., Horne, A. M., & Bartolomucci, C. L. (2000). *Bully Busters: A teacher's manual for helping bullies, victims, and bystanders.* Champaign, IL: Research Press.

Olweus, D. (1993). *Bullying at school: What we know and what we can do.* Cambridge, MA: Blackwell Publishers.

Olweus, D., Limber, S., & Mihalic, S. (2000). *Bullying prevention program* (Report No. 9, Blueprints for violence prevention). Boulder: University of Colorado at Boulder, Institute of Behavioral Science, Center for the Study and Prevention of Violence.

O'Moore, M., & Kirkham, C. (2001). Self-esteem and its relationship to bullying behaviour. *Aggressive Behavior, 27,* 269–283.

Orpinas, P., & Horne, A. M. (2006). *Bullying prevention: Creating a positive school climate and developing social competence.* Washington, DC: American Psychological Association.

Orpinas, P., Horne, A. M., & Multisite Violence Prevention Project. (2004). A teacher-focused approach to prevent and reduce students' aggressive behavior—The GREAT Teacher Program. *American Journal of Preventive Medicine, 26,* 29–38.

Orpinas, P., Horne, A. M., & Staniszewski, D. (2003). School bullying: Changing the problem by changing the school. *School Psychology Review, 32,* 431–444.

Orpinas, P., Kelder, S., Frankowski, R., Murray, N., Zhang, Q., & McAlister, A. (2000). Outcome evaluation of a multi-component violence-prevention program for middle schools: The Students for Peace project. *Health Education Research, 15,* 45–58.

Orpinas, P., Kelder, S., Murray, N., Fourney, A., Conroy, J., McReynolds, L., et al. (1996). Critical issues in implementing a comprehensive violence prevention program for middle schools: Translating theory into practice. *Education and Urban Society, 28,* 456–472.

Orpinas, P., Murray, N., & Kelder, S. (1999). Parental influences on students' aggressive behaviors and weapon carrying. *Health Education and Behavior, 26,* 774–87.

Ortega, R., & Lera, M. J. (2000). The Seville Anti-Bullying in School Project. *Aggressive Behavior, 26,* 113–123.

Pellegrini, A. D. (1998). Bullies and victims in school: A review and call for research. *Journal of Applied Developmental Psychology, 19,* 165–176.

Perry, D. G., Kusel, S. J., & Perry, L. C. (1988). Victims of peer aggression. *Developmental Psychology, 24,* 807–814.

Prinstein, M. J., Boergers, J., & Vernberg, E. M. (2001). Overt and relational aggression in adolescents: Social–psychological adjustment of aggressors and victims. *Journal of Clinical Child Psychology, 30,* 479–491.

Roland, E. (2000). Bullying in school: Three national innovations in Norwegian schools in 15 years. *Aggressive Behavior, 26,* 135–143.

Ross, D. M. (2003). *Childhood bullying, teasing, and violence: What school personnel, other professionals, and parents can do* (2nd ed.). Alexandria, VA: American Counseling Association.

Salmivalli, C. (1999). Participant role approach to school bullying: Implications for interventions. *Journal of Adolescence, 22,* 453–459.

Schwartz, D., Dodge, K. A., & Coie, J. D. (1993). The emergence of chronic peer victimization in boys' play groups. *Child Development, 64,* 1755–1772.

Sharp, S., & Smith, P. (1991). Bullying in UK schools: The DES Sheffield Bullying Project. *Early Child Development and Care, 77,* 47–55.

Silvernail, D. L., Thompson, A. M., Yang, Z., & Kopp, H. J. P. (2000). *A survey of bullying behavior among Maine third graders.* Gorham: University of Southern Maine, Maine Center for Educational Policy, Applied Research and Evaluation. Retrieved March 5, 2005, from http://lincoln.midcoast.com/~wps/against/finalreport.html

Smith, P. K., Cowie, H., Olafsson, R. F., & Liefooghe, A. P. D. (2002). Definitions of bullying: A comparison of terms used, and age and gender differences, in a fourteen-country international comparison. *Child Development, 73,* 1119–1133.

Stein, N., Gaberman, E., & Sjostrom, L. (1996). *Bullyproof: A teacher's guide on teasing and bullying for use with fourth and fifth grade students.* Wellesley, MA: Wellesley College Center for Research on Women.

Stockdale, M. S., Hangaduambo, S., Duys, D., Larson, K., & Sarvela, P. D. (2002). Rural elementary students', parents', and teachers' perceptions of bullying. *American Journal of Health Behavior, 26,* 266–277.

Sullivan, K. (2000). *The anti-bullying handbook.* Auckland, New Zealand: Oxford University Press.

Sutton, J., Smith, P. K., & Swettenham, J. (1999). Social cognition and bullying: Social inadequacy or skilled manipulation? *British Journal of Developmental Psychology, 17,* 435–450.

Tomada, G., & Schneider, B. H. (1997). Relational aggression, gender, and peer acceptance: Invariance across culture, stability over time, and concordance among informants. *Developmental Psychology, 33,* 601–609.

Vossekuil, B., Fein, R., Reddy, M., Borum, R., & Modzeleski, W. (2002). *The final report and findings of the safe school initiative: Implications for the prevention of school attacks in the United States*. Washington, DC: U.S. Department of Education, Office of Elementary and Secondary Education, Safe and Drug-Free Schools Program, and U.S. Secret Service, National Threat Assessment Center.

Whitney, I., & Smith, P. K. (1993). A survey of the nature and extent of bullying in junior/middle and secondary schools. *Educational Research, 35,* 3–25.

Williams, K., Chamgers, M., Logan, S., & Robinson, D. (1996). Association of common health symptoms with bullying in primary school children. *British Medical Journal, 313,* 17–19.

Wolke, D., Woods, S., Bloomfield, L., & Karstadt, L. (2001). Bullying involvement in primary school and common health problems. *Archives of Disease in Childhood, 85,* 197–201.

II

DEVELOPING RESEARCH ARENAS: INTIMATE PARTNER VIOLENCE AND SUICIDE

SECTION INTRODUCTION:
INTIMATE PARTNER
VIOLENCE PREVENTION

As noted in the introduction to chapter 8, there are several terms that are used to express violence between adults or teens in partner relationships. One of the most common and the one used in this book is *intimate partner violence* (IPV). In chapter 8, Arias and Ikeda provide the rationale for the term and explain to whom it applies. They also address the public health model and how it is used in the prevention of IPV. As with child maltreatment, there are problems of surveillance in understanding the incidence of IPV because of the need for uniform definitions. In chapter 8, Arias and Ikeda describe some of the Centers for Disease Control and Prevention efforts in working toward uniform definitions. Though there are problems of definition, it is apparent that IPV affects a large number of women in the United States, including those who fall victim to homicide. Additionally, it is estimated that almost 8% of women are sexually assaulted by an intimate partner at some time in their lives. More difficult to determine, but also a problem, is psychological IPV, an area also addressed in chapter 8.

Arias and Ikeda examine the etiology of IPV and review three prominent theories: attachment, feminist, and resource theory. It should be noted that the empirical support for these theories is limited. Of particular interest is the observation that men who were exposed to child maltreatment and other forms of family violence are more likely to become perpetrators of IPV than men who did not have such exposure. Thus, as with youth violence, it appears that child maltreatment begins a pathway to other forms of violence.

In chapter 8, Arias and Ikeda also look at sociocultural factors that appear to play a role in IPV. In addition to the more predictable variable of under- and unemployment as a factor, the authors draw attention to data suggesting that there are higher rates of IPV among partners who have no religious affiliation. Thus, there appear to be a host of etiologic factors that may drive IPV. The more information gleaned through robust research, the better the likelihood that effective prevention programs can be developed and evaluated.

Interventions in IPV are covered in chapter 9 by Sullivan. It quickly becomes apparent that there is a paucity of robust science in IPV interventions. Nonetheless, Sullivan reviews what is currently available. Historically, the oldest "interventions" for IPV have been shelters, environments designed to keep women safe from partner perpetrators, but environments that in fact make research difficult. In chapter 9, Sullivan notes the few evaluations of shelters and further notes that attrition is a serious problem in trying to study outcomes. In one evaluation, there have been changes in self-esteem and similar variables of the participating women but no measures of the degree to which the participants have been protected from future violent episodes by their perpetrators.

Another vehicle for intervening in IPV is advocacy. This is another area with limited evaluations. In one fairly robust study, however, researchers found that women who worked with advocates over time experienced less violence than those who did not have advocates. Criminal legal-focused interventions, which the author notes have not been experimentally evaluated, are also covered in this chapter.

Programs aimed at either legal solutions or behavior change have been attempted with batterers. These are known as *batterer intervention prevention programs* (BIPPs). The data from the few evaluations of these programs have been disappointing in terms of recidivism (subsequent abuse) by perpetrators who have and have not participated in BIPPs. Dropout is a major problem with BIPPs, especially among men of color. Thus, clearly, cultural issues may not have been adequately addressed. Additionally, interventions using groups might conceivably be counterproductive with respect to participants modeling to each other poor attitudes toward women. Also, the approaches in these groups tend to be entirely cognitive or educational rather than teaching skills that may avert aggressive responding in perpetrators.

Another intervention covered in chapter 9 is coordinating councils, which are made up of representatives of service agencies that try to combine resources to offer services to battered women. Robust evaluation of such programs is lacking. In fact, as noted by Sullivan, robust evaluation research is extremely rare at this stage of IPV prevention research and programming. Thus, there is much room for the development of new programs and much more sophisticated evolution of extant IPV prevention programs.

8

ETIOLOGY AND SURVEILLANCE OF INTIMATE PARTNER VIOLENCE

ILEANA ARIAS AND ROBIN M. IKEDA

Intimate partner violence (IPV) refers to the use of actual or threatened physical or sexual violence or psychological or emotional abuse by current or former spouses, boyfriends, or girlfriends (including heterosexual and same-sex partners; Saltzman, Fanslow, McMahon, & Shelley, 1999). Some of the terms commonly used to describe IPV include *domestic violence, marital violence, spouse abuse, dating violence, courtship violence,* and *couple violence.* However, each of these alternatives is limited to certain forms of violence and excludes others. For example, domestic violence is limited to violence between married and cohabiting partners, excluding nonmarried heterosexual partners and gay and lesbian partners. The phrase *intimate partner violence* is preferred because it captures physical, sexual, and psychological violence among intimately related partners regardless of marital status, sexual orientation, or cohabitation status. Although both men and women report IPV victimization, victimization is more prevalent and frequent among women

This chapter was authored by employees of the United States government as part of official duty and is considered to be in the public domain. Any views expressed herein do not necessarily represent the views of the United States government, and the authors' participation in the work is not meant to serve as an official endorsement.

than men, and differences between women's and men's rates of victimization become greater as the severity of assault increases (Stets & Straus, 1990). Further, women are significantly more likely than men to sustain an injury, receive medical care, be hospitalized, receive counseling, and lose time from work (Tjaden & Thoennes, 2000). Accordingly, the focus of IPV prevention efforts traditionally has been on men's perpetration of IPV against women.

Medical and mental health professionals gave little empirical attention to family or intimate violence until the 1960s. Publication of an article on the battered child syndrome by Kempe, Silverman, Steele, Droegmueller, and Silver in 1962 led to immediate keen interest in documenting and preventing family violence and treating its victims. Early efforts focused almost exclusively on child abuse. However, investigations into the widespread occurrence of child abuse led to detection and subsequent interest in violence among other family members, including married partners. Straus and his colleagues (see Straus, 1980) alarmed professionals and lay consumers in 1975 by showing that approximately 28% of married couples experienced physical violence at some time during the course of their marriages. Just as research on child abuse led to the detection of physical violence between marital partners, research on marital violence led to detection of physical violence between other intimately related heterosexual couples, such as dating couples (Arias, Samios, & O'Leary, 1987; Makepeace, 1983), and between gay and lesbian partners (Kelly & Warshafsky, 1987).

Initial empirical attention to IPV was primarily the domain of sociologists and family studies scholars. The major focus of this original work was on the assessment of relationship quality and functioning and macrosystemic variables with potential etiologic significance, such as socioeconomic factors. During the 1970s, there was an increased interest among psychologists in family and relationship functioning in response to the documented negative impact of divorce on individual adjustment and the inability to effectively address child psychopathology without taking marital factors into account (O'Leary, 1987). Psychological research on IPV shifted the focus from macrovariables to microvariables such as intrapersonal characteristics and interpersonal interactions. This new wave of research concentrated first on identifying the consequences of IPV and then on identifying etiologic and maintaining factors to guide the development of psychological interventions. More recently, a public health perspective has been applied to understanding and preventing IPV.

PUBLIC HEALTH AND ITS CONTRIBUTION

Identifying and controlling factors that affect morbidity and mortality among men and women across the life span are the objectives of public health. Traditionally, public health practitioners and researchers have focused on infectious diseases in controlling morbidity and mortality. However, the relevance of infectious diseases in controlling morbidity and mortality has decreased over time while the relevance of chronic diseases has increased (Schneiderman & Speers, 2001). Behavioral, psychosocial, and sociocultural factors associated with lifestyles have been found to be major contributors to the leading causes of death (Schneiderman & Speers, 2001). Thus, although it was not considered a traditional public health problem in the past, IPV is now a priority among public health problems because of its impact on morbidity and mortality and because, like smallpox and many other infectious diseases, it is a problem that can be understood and perhaps prevented through the application of epidemiological methods (Rosenberg, 1989). Incorporating a public health perspective into violence prevention makes sense because both physical and emotional health are affected by violence. But even beyond this focus on health, the public health approach brings other unique and valuable contributions to the problem.

Traditionally, the functions of public health in the United States have been described as "assessment, assurance, policy development, and evaluation" (Institute of Medicine, 1988, p. 7). In the United States, the government (federal, state, and local) has had the lead responsibility for these functions, because many of them require the exercise of authority and because the government is obligated to ensure that the public interest is served by any policy decisions. More recently, a public health model that moves beyond the traditional notion of public health as a function of government agencies focused on assurance and the provision of individual-level services has been described (Mercy, Rosenberg, Powell, Broome, & Roper, 1993). This model describes a comprehensive approach to address significant health problems, placing an increased emphasis on the development and dissemination of interventions at the community level and explicitly encouraging input from others outside the public sector and from multiple disciplines. The four steps of this model are (a) problem description, (b) research regarding risk and protective factors, (c) development and evaluation of preventive interventions, and (d) large-scale implementation of effective prevention programs and dissemination of scientific findings. Ideally, movement in this model occurs from the first to the fourth step, with data obtained from the earlier steps used to guide and inform the later ones. In reality, action in all steps may occur simultaneously or proceed in a nonlinear fashion. Each of the four steps is described below.

Problem description includes those activities that help define health issues of importance and identify needs. *Public health surveillance*, often defined as the "ongoing systematic collection, analysis, and interpretation of outcome-specific data for use in the planning, implementation, and evaluation of public health practice" (Thacker & Berkelman, 1988, p. 164), falls into this category. Public health surveillance systems are designed to provide data regarding the incidence and prevalence of health problems and general descriptive information about who is impacted by the event under surveillance (person) and where and when these events are occurring (place and time). Although this information may generate hypotheses about why these events are occurring, it is important to note that surveillance systems are not designed to test hypotheses but rather to document the distribution of health problems and to monitor changes over time. Current public health surveillance efforts specific to IPV are described later in this chapter.

Etiologic and epidemiologic research to determine modifiable risk factors and protective factors constitutes the second step. On the basis of information from the first two steps, possible avenues for prevention are identified and developed further in the third step. This step also includes evaluation of interventions for both efficacy and effectiveness. The fourth and final step of the public health model is the widespread implementation and dissemination of effective interventions. Evaluation is considered an essential aspect to all steps in the model—ongoing evaluation of surveillance systems regarding their usefulness is advocated by the Centers for Disease Control and Prevention (CDC) and other health agencies. Likewise, there is growing recognition that implementation and dissemination efforts can and should be studied in a scientific fashion. This public health model has been successfully applied to a number of different public health problems, both injury- and non-injury-related.

In addition to the functions outlined in this model, one strength of public health is its emphasis on primary prevention, or preventing health problems such as IPV, before they occur. As described above, earlier prevention efforts in this area have primarily concentrated on victims of abuse and thus are not considered primary prevention. However, there is general agreement in the field that future activities need to move in the direction of primary prevention, perhaps by studying risk and protective factors associated with perpetration. Etiologic research efforts in this area are described at the end of this chapter.

Another strength of public health is its multidisciplinary approach to health problems. Public health has a long-standing tradition of collaborating with partners from different perspectives and areas of expertise, in part because of its history of both providing services and overseeing regulatory functions. This is particularly useful for violence prevention given the myriad contributing factors and the equally diverse consequences that span the behavioral, physical, and emotional. Input from fields such as psychology, sociology, anthropology, medicine, and criminal justice are all necessary to prevent IPV.

INTIMATE PARTNER VIOLENCE SURVEILLANCE

Although the eradication of IPV through prevention and intervention may be the ultimate goal, attempts to establish accurate estimates of prevalence and incidence have been at the forefront of IPV research. Accurate estimates based on empirically sound methodologies are necessary to determine the scope of the problem and to be able to monitor and assess changes in response to prevention and intervention efforts. As mentioned earlier, the primary purpose of public health surveillance is to provide descriptive epidemiologic information and to monitor trends over time. This information can be used to inform public health activities by identifying at-risk groups, suggesting hypotheses, and assessing the impact of preventive interventions. This is distinct from research efforts that are generally designed to test specific hypotheses and contribute to generalizable scientific knowledge. Thus, data collection needs for these two types of efforts are different. The data gathered by surveillance systems for any single event are usually relatively limited, in contrast to data collected for research purposes, which are often extensive. Another distinguishing feature of surveillance data collection is the ability to compare across time and geographic location, which requires ongoing use of uniform definitions and data elements. Again, this is different from research studies in which, depending on the hypothesis being tested, different definitions or data elements may be used.

Traditionally, surveillance involves systematic, ongoing collection, analysis, and interpretation of data already available from sources such as emergency departments, hospital discharge records, or health departments. In IPV surveillance, potential sources of data include emergency departments, hospitals, social services, police departments, and shelters for battered women and their children. Although information from these sources is collected for other agency-related purposes, it can be used for surveillance purposes, allowing examination of trends over time. These "passive" data collection methods are inexpensive relative to "active" methods such as surveys and interviews because the data already exist.

Over the years, the Division of Violence Prevention of the National Center for Injury Prevention and Control (NCIPC) at the CDC has been involved in a number of efforts to advance such surveillance efforts for IPV. In 1996, a working group of experts met to develop a set of recommended data elements needed for surveillance of IPV (Saltzman et al., 1999). The group also developed a glossary of terms (uniform definitions) to be used with the set of recommended data elements. The purpose of developing these definitions and elements was to support and facilitate standardized data collection across jurisdictions in hopes of improving the consistency and quality of the data. The CDC additionally convened experts to develop recommendations for building data systems to facilitate IPV surveillance (CDC, 2000). The CDC subsequently provided funding to initiate state-based surveillance systems in three states: Massachusetts, Michigan, and Rhode Island. The purpose of these systems was to determine and pilot test the best methods for conducting this type of data collection. As part of their funding support from the CDC, the three states were asked to pilot test both the definitions and the recommended data elements and provide insight into their utility and feasibility. Feedback from the three states (CDC, in press) was used to refine the recommended uniform definitions and data elements and serves to inform future state-based and national surveillance efforts related to IPV. Since the initial three states were funded, the CDC has funded an additional four states to initiate similar systems. Recipients of these funds include Kentucky, Minnesota, Oklahoma, and Oregon. Lessons learned from these additional states will be used to further revise the recommended uniform definitions and data elements.

Challenges for Traditional Intimate Partner Violence Surveillance

As with any endeavor involving the collection of data, there are a number of challenges to implementing and conducting public health surveillance for IPV. Some of these challenges are specific to surveillance itself, given the unique features of this type of data collection, whereas others result from the sensitive and complex nature of the topic under surveillance. Each of these is described briefly below.

The need to use consistent definitions and data elements over time and location raises the first set of challenges—how to achieve consensus about definitions and data elements from jurisdictions with different data needs and capabilities. Related is the question of what is the optimal balance of the practical and the ideal. In other words, in the process of agreeing on common definitions and elements, what is the best mix between what is possible to collect and what is desired? Although this is a pertinent issue for any data collection effort, it is an especially difficult one for surveillance data collection because selection of data elements is not driven by specific hypotheses to be tested but rather by the much more general purpose of monitoring trends over time and providing descriptive characteristics. In addition, it is often difficult to anticipate how the surveillance data might be used in the future, which may encourage developers of these systems to err on the side of being more inclusive.

The second set of challenges is largely a result of the sensitive and complex nature of IPV. Although many other public health events under surveillance are of a sensitive nature, this is particularly true for IPV. Not only is there social stigma associated with the event, many victims may also be reluctant to disclose such events for fear this will exacerbate the abusive behavior should their partners find out about the disclosure. Likewise, there is no incentive for perpetrators to report their behavior; in fact, quite the opposite, given that there are serious legal repercussions if they are identified as perpetrators. All of these factors may result in significant underreporting of IPV. Again, this is not a problem unique to this health issue or to public health surveillance overall, but because the purpose of surveillance is to monitor events over time, changes in social norms and reporting behaviors may pose special problems for this type of data collection that are different from those faced by researchers.

Another aspect of IPV that complicates public health surveillance efforts is the complexity of the problem. Unlike many other health issues under surveillance that involve a single person (patient) with a specific disease entity, IPV by definition involves at least two people, victim and perpetrator. Thus, characteristics of both these individuals and descriptive information about the relationship between them and the circumstances that resulted in violence are all elements to be included in any surveillance system. The involvement of two people complicates the surveillance efforts in ways that differ from surveillance efforts for many other health events. Similarly, IPV includes a number of distinctly different categories—physical, sexual, and emotional abuse—which further complicates decisions about the definitions to be used for surveillance and discussions about which data elements are appropriate to collect. Another aspect is the fact that incidents of IPV may occur once or multiple times and may be perpetrated by a single partner or by multiple partners over time. Again, this is different from most other health events under surveillance in which incidence and prevalence can be more easily separated. Finally, because the event under surveillance may come to the attention of both the health and the law enforcement systems, there are a number of different data systems that could potentially be used to gather surveillance information. Although the availability of multiple data systems can lead to the acquisition of more complete data, it is not without its own set of problems. Data from these systems may be collected for purposes other than public health and thus may not fully satisfy public health needs. Because data may be from nontraditional public health sources, relationships and collaborative partnerships must be developed before efficient data sharing can take place.

Findings From State-Based Surveillance Systems

Despite the many challenges, the seven states funded by the CDC to conduct this type of surveillance have all successfully implemented systems and collected data. Summary reports from Minnesota, Kentucky, Michigan, Oklahoma, and Oregon provide descriptive information from these efforts and underscore the utility of collecting the data. For example, in Minnesota, the overall rate of persons treated in hospitals for injuries resulting from IPV was 23 per 100,000 population during 2000 (Minnesota Department of Health, 2002).[1] Not surprisingly, the rate was much higher for women than for men, 44 per 100,000 compared with 2 per 100,000. The average charge for a patient receiving treatment for resulting injuries was $739, and the majority of fatal incidents involved a firearm. In Kentucky, an estimated half million women aged 18 and over reported experiencing threats, physical abuse, or sexual abuse by a current or recent intimate partner, with more than 760,000 women reporting emotional abuse by their intimate partner in 2000 (Kentucky Department of Health, 2000). Data from 19 hospitals in Michigan identified 711 confirmed cases of IPV during 2000. Many of these patients were cohabitating with the perpetrator, and in more than half, the perpetrator was a current boyfriend (Martin, Tan-Schriner, Petrona, Fiedler, & Wojcik, 2000). On the basis of data collected in Oklahoma, an estimated 30,700 women are assaulted each year by their partners. Rates of IPV among African Americans and Native Americans were more that two times rates among Whites (Oklahoma State Department of Health, 2000). In addition to highlighting the magnitude of the problem and providing descriptive characteristics, the data collected in Oregon were used to alert clinicians and others to the problem in the state and to encourage both screening for IPV and documentation of abuse in the medical record (Oregon Department of Human Services, 2002). Analysis of the data also helped identify differences between fatal and nonfatal events (Sullivan, 2002).

ALTERNATIVES TO TRADITIONAL INTIMATE PARTNER VIOLENCE SURVEILLANCE

Because it relies on existing sources of data established for other purposes, traditional surveillance limits the types of information available. Information on possible risk factors such as a history of child abuse or on the psychological impact of IPV may not be available from hospital records completed for a woman visiting the emergency department with a detached retina. Additionally, only incidents of IPV that lead to injuries for which victims seek treatment or incidents to which the police or criminal justice system respond would be captured by traditional surveillance methods. Many women do not contact the police or sectors of the criminal justice system in response to their victimization (Fleury, Sullivan, Bybee, & Davidson, 1998), and many assaults do not produce injuries that require medical attention (CDC, 2003). Surveys are often relied on to complement informa-

---

[1] Numerator and denominator limited to those aged 15 and older.

tion obtained through traditional surveillance methods. Unlike record abstraction, surveys involve systematic data collection from a representative sample of the population of interest for analysis and interpretation. Survey data are collected directly from individuals affected by the condition under surveillance and allow flexibility in the types of questions that can be asked and the level of detail of information that can be collected. Although more expensive, survey methods yield more complete data necessary to estimate prevalence and incidence of IPV.

Crime Surveys

Physical and sexual assaults by intimate partners are crimes in the United States. Crime victim surveys such as the National Crime Victimization Survey (NCVS) have been used to find rates of IPV (Gaquin, 1977–1978). The Bureau of Justice Statistics of the U.S. Department of Justice administers the NCVS annually. Data are obtained from a nationally representative sample of roughly 50,000 households comprising nearly 100,000 persons on the frequency, characteristics, and consequences of criminal victimization in the United States, including physical and sexual assaults against women perpetrated by intimate partners. Records indicate that IPV made up 20% of violent crime against women in 2001 (Rennison, 2003). According to estimates from the NCVS, there were 588,490 nonfatal IPV victimizations during 2001. Because the NCVS is administered annually, it has been used to establish trends in IPV. The rate of nonfatal IPV against women declined significantly between 1993 and 2001, dropping by nearly half (49%). Information from the Federal Bureau of Investigation's Uniform Crime Reports has been used to address the prevalence of fatal IPV victimization or homicide. In 2000, 1,247 women were killed by an intimate partner, accounting for approximately 33% of female murder victims. The number of women murdered by intimate partners decreased 22% between 1976 and 2000 (Rennison, 2003).

Family Surveys

The rates found by crime surveys are thought to vastly underestimate the incidence of IPV, because the focus of these surveys is on crime, and as noted above, respondents may consider assaults by an intimate partner, especially a spouse, to be a "family problem" rather than a "crime." Most instances of IPV therefore are not reported (Kantor & Straus, 1990). Family studies have been conducted in attempts to overcome this barrier and generate more accurate estimates of IPV. The first population-based survey of family violence was conducted by Straus and colleagues in 1975 (Straus, Gelles, & Steinmetz, 1980) and replicated in 1985 (Straus & Gelles, 1986).

The 1975 survey included 2,143 families and assessed perpetration and victimization of physical IPV by husbands and wives. Approximately 12% of the women had been victims of IPV during the year preceding the survey. In 1985, in a readministration of the survey to 3,520 families, approximately 12% of the women again reported IPV victimization during the preceding 12-month period.

National Violence Against Women Survey

Sample sizes used in previous surveys typically had not been large enough or representative enough of the United States population to be able to generate reliable estimates of the prevalence of IPV. To address some of these deficiencies, the NCIPC at the CDC, through collaboration with the National Institute of Justice, provided funding to design and conduct a survey to provide reliable estimates of the prevalence and incidence of physical assault and rape by intimate partners, related injuries, and medical costs including costs for mental health services (CDC, 2003). The National Violence Against Women Survey (NVAWS) was conducted from November 1995 to May 1996 and consisted of a national probability sample of 8,000 women and 8,000 men aged 18 and older. *Physical assault* was defined as any behavior that threatens to, attempts to, or actually does inflict physical harm, such as throwing something at the victim; pushing, grabbing, or shoving; pulling hair; slapping or hitting; kicking or biting; choking or trying to drown; hitting with objects; beating up; or threatening with a gun or knife. *Rape* was defined as the use of force (without the victim's consent) or threat of force to penetrate the victim's vagina or anus by penis, tongue, fingers, or object or the victim's mouth by penis.

Physical Intimate Partner Violence

The lifetime prevalence of physical assault of women by an intimate partner was 22.1%. Accordingly, it was estimated that 22,254,037 women are physically assaulted by their intimate partners at some point in their lifetime. The 12-month prevalence rate for physical assault was 1.3%, suggesting that 1,309,061 women are physically assaulted annually by an intimate partner. Women who were physically assaulted reported an average of 3.4 victimizations annually.

Among women who were physically assaulted, 41.5% were injured during the most recent victimization. The majority of women who were injured during the most recent physical IPV episode sustained relatively minor injuries, such as scratches, bruises, and welts. Relatively few women sustained more serious types of injuries, such as lacerations, broken bones, dislocated joints, head or spinal cord injuries, chipped or broken teeth, or internal injuries. Of the women who were injured during their most recent IPV physical assault, 28% had received some type of medical treatment (e.g., ambulance or paramedic services, treatment in a hospital emergency facility, or physical therapy), and 26% of physical IPV victims reported they had consulted with a mental health professional, for an average of 12.9 visits.

Sexual Intimate Partner Violence

The lifetime prevalence of sexual assault of women by an intimate partner was 7.7%. It was estimated that 7,753,669 women are sexually assaulted by an intimate partner at some point in their lifetime. The 12-month prevalence rate was 0.2%, suggesting that 201,394 are raped annually by an intimate partner. Women who were sexually assaulted reported an average of 1.6 rapes.

Among women who were victims of sexual assault, 36.2% sustained an injury (other than the rape itself). Again, women reported relatively minor injuries and few serious injuries. Of sexual IPV victims who were injured by an intimate partner, 31% had received some type of medical treatment, and 33% of rape victims reported they had consulted with a mental health professional, for an average of 12.4 visits.

Psychological Intimate Partner Violence

Psychological aggression or abuse is typically defined as verbal and nonverbal acts that symbolically hurt the partner or psychological trauma caused by acts, threats of acts, or coercive tactics (Saltzman et al., 1999; Straus, 1979). Analysis of NVAWS data yielded a lifetime prevalence of psychological victimization by an intimate partner of 27% of women (Coker et al., 2002). This may have occurred in the context of physical or sexual victimization as well. The lifetime prevalence of psychological victimization alone (no other form of IPV) was 14%. Among women, 4% reported psychological violence alone by a current intimate partner. As was true of the mental health consequences of physical violence, analysis of data from the NVAWS suggested that women who were victims of psychological violence only were also at higher risk for depression, alcohol use, and medication use including antidepressants, tranquilizers, painkillers, and unlike victims of physical violence, recreational drugs. Victims of psychological abuse were at higher risk for exhibiting posttraumatic stress disorder symptoms (Basile, Arias, Desai, & Thompson, 2004). Psychological abuse is emerging as an important focus for prevention of IPV. Psychological violence appears to be a precursor to physical violence, and physical violence rarely occurs in the absence of psychological violence (Ronfeldt, Kimerling, & Arias, 1998). Additionally, psychological abuse appears to be related to negative outcomes equally or more so than physical assault, and some women are only psychologically abused (Arias & Pape, 1999).

It appears that IPV is a substantial public health problem. However, surveys that have attempted to determine the extent of the problem have produced varying estimates. Some of these estimates may be overestimates or underestimates of the true prevalence of IPV. Several variations across surveys may be responsible for the different estimates and the inability to decide on a "true" and final estimate (CDC, 2003). For example, there has not been consensus on the operational definition of IPV in previous surveys. In some studies, IPV includes only acts that may cause pain or injury, ignoring behaviors designed to control or intimidate, such as stalking; humiliation; verbal abuse; imprisonment; and denial of access to money, shelter, or services. Sampling strategies and the stated purpose of a survey have differed and may affect how participants answer survey questions. For example, a respondent on the National Crime Victimization Survey may not acknowledge being the victim of IPV if he or she does not believe IPV is a crime. However, the same respondent might disclose IPV victimization on a survey about family conflict. Some studies have focused either on married or cohabiting couples, and others have included other types of intimate relationships such as dating relationships. Because methodological differences such as those described here can affect the findings of a survey or study, researchers must explain the choice of a particular methodology, define terms used, and clearly explain how information was gathered (CDC, 2000).

ETIOLOGY OF INTIMATE PARTNER VIOLENCE

The success of IPV prevention and intervention efforts is determined in large part by the extent to which they address factors that cause and influence IPV. Accordingly, research focusing on factors that may be related to the etiology of IPV has also been a priority. Numerous theories have been proposed to account for the development of IPV and to guide research on causal factors. Theories differ on the level of analysis. Some focus on individual psychological factors; some focus on relationship and family factors; and others focus on contextual, sociocultural factors. For example, three popular theories of IPV that vary along this dimension are (a) attachment theory, (b) resource theory, and (c) feminist theory.

Attachment is defined by the quality and strength of the bond a child develops to his or her caretaker, usually the mother (Bowlby, 1977). Secure attachment increases with consistent positive treatment (Dutton & Painter, 1993). Later disruption of this connection through actual or psychological separation, rejection, or deprivation can cause anxiety, anger, and violence (Alexander, 1992; Ehrensaft, Langhinrichsen-Rohling, Heyman, O'Leary, & Lawrence, 1999; Kesner, Julian, & McKenry, 1997). Poor mother–child attachment can create a frustrated emotional dependency in which the child's needs are never fulfilled. During adulthood, the emotionally frustrated adult tends to replicate the mother–child relationship by creating the same emotional dependency on and subsequent frustration with his current intimate partner (Buttell & Jones, 2001). This frustration may potentially result in abuse of intimate partners. It is theorized that as a result of the insecure attachment experienced during childhood, batterers are particularly sensitive to rejection from their intimate partners. Insecurely attached individuals may rely on violence as a coping mechanism for dealing with perceived rejection by the intimate partner and also when dealing with an intimate partner who develops autonomy (Dutton, 1998; Ehrensaft et al., 1999; Kesner et al., 1997). In essence, IPV becomes a technique to avoid rejection or perceived vulnerability to rejection.

Resource theory encompasses some aspects of the social exchange control model of IPV, which suggests that battering is dictated by the principle of costs and rewards: Violence and abuse are used when the rewards are higher than the costs (Gelles, 1993; Hampton, Vandergriff-Avery, & Kim, 1999). When a man who is engaged in an intimate relationship feels he has relinquished or lost control, power, and dominance and simultaneously views the costs for engaging in abuse as being greatly overshadowed by the rewards, battering becomes a reasonable course of action (Gelles, 1993; Hampton et al., 1999). Thus, according to the social exchange model of IPV as seen through the lens of resource theory, IPV is used as a negotiation strategy in the relationship when motivating factors and anticipated outcomes are stronger and more beneficial than any perceived losses as consequences of IPV.

Feminist theory regards IPV as a consequence of a patriarchal society that promotes male coercive power and domination over women through sexism and economic inequality (Dobash & Dobash, 1979; Stets, 1988; Yllo, 1993; Yllo & Bograd, 1988). According to feminist theory, IPV can be directly attributed to the influence of the patriarchal society (Dobash & Dobash, 1979; Yllo, 1993). Most social institutions, including the law, marriage, medicine, the military, and the sports industry, promote male dominance (Kurz, 1993). Feminist theory incorporates the notion that economic inequalities between men and women contribute to the legitimization of male domination and abuse of females (Fagan & Browne, 1994). Men have too much power in society, and because patriarchal social norms incorporate and accept male violence, both power and violence are sustained at a societal level (Yllo & Bograd, 1988). Reflective in greater society is the endorsement of the use of aggression and violence by men to denote power and control, and this entitlement is transferred to the relationship with their intimate partner. Thus, IPV, from a feminist perspective, is a product of the male and female sex roles, which form an inherently imbalanced dichotomy (Taylor, Davis, & Maxwell, 2001). It is argued that batterers feel they are justified for engaging in IPV, especially when their female partners fail to conform to standard societal stereotypes such as being a "good wife" and keeping the house clean (Kurz, 1993).

There is no consensus on any single theory to completely account for IPV, and there is significant overlap among the various theories that have been proposed. Some theorists have attempted to integrate various single theories to account for the complex and multidimensional nature of IPV. For example, Dutton (1995) has proposed a comprehensive nested ecological model of IPV. According to his model, attitudes and beliefs are the result of contextual sociocultural variables, such as cultural values and norms that allow the development of IPV. Factors at various levels, such as stress and social isolation at the community level, communication and conflict at the relationship or family level, and personality and skills at the individual level, exert a combined influence. Comprehensive theories such as Dutton's do not focus on any single variable or type of variable but attempt to identify and integrate different types of factors that influence behavior.

Although not guided by any particular theory, etiologic research has focused on the identification of intrapersonal, interpersonal, and sociocultural factors included in comprehensive models of IPV. Specifically, research has focused on the identification of intrapersonal, interpersonal, and sociocultural characteristics of perpetrators. Characteristics or correlates of victim status such as low self-esteem and depression have been identified (Arias, 1999). However, it is difficult to assess the extent to which such characteristic differences between victims and nonvictims of IPV are antecedents or consequences of marital violence. Hotaling and Sugarman (1986, 1990) concluded that the best predictors of whether a woman will be assaulted by an intimate partner are characteristics of her male partners.

Intrapersonal Factors

Studies have shown that IPV perpetration is negatively related to age (Pagelow, 1981; Schumacher, Feldbau-Kohn, Smith Slep, & Heyman, 2001; Straus et al., 1980). Men who were victims of child maltreatment or were exposed to IPV and other forms of family violence are more likely to perpetrate IPV than men without such histories (Kalmuss, 1984; Malone, Tyree, & O'Leary, 1989). Perpetrators of IPV have been found to be characterized by higher levels of stressful events in their lives than nonperpetrators

(Julian & McKenry, 1993; McKenry, Julian, & Gavazzi, 1995; Straus et al., 1980). Unfortunately, perpetrators are also more likely than nonperpetrators to be characterized by deficits in resources to respond to stress. Perpetrators of IPV have been found to have low levels of self-esteem (Murphy, Meyer, & O'Leary, 1994) and self-efficacy (Prince & Arias, 1994). Relative to nonperpetrators, perpetrators of IPV are unassertive with their partners (Dutton & Strachan, 1987; O'Leary & Curley, 1986). Higher rates of alcohol and drug use and abuse are found among violent men (Danielson, Moffitt, Caspi, & Silva, 1998; Fagan, Stewart, & Hansen, 1983; Leonard & Senchak, 1993). Violent, relative to nonviolent, men are more likely to make dysfunctional and blaming attributions for their partners' behavior (Holtzworth-Munroe & Hutchinson, 1993); have more irrational beliefs and hostile attributional biases (Eckhardt, Barbour, & Davison, 1998); exhibit high levels of pathological jealousy (Walker, 1979), narcissism (Hastings & Hamberger, 1988), and anger (Heyman, O'Leary, & Jouriles, 1995; Maiuro, Cahn, & Vitaliano, 1988); and be more approving of violence (Straus, 1980). A recent meta-analytic review of the existing empirical literature on risk factors for IPV perpetration by Stith, Smith, Penn, Ward, and Tritt (2004) identified large effect sizes for perpetration of emotional abuse and forced sex, accepting attitudes condoning IPV, and illicit drug use; moderate effect sizes were identified for traditional sex-role attitudes, anger and hostility, alcohol use, depression, and life and work stress.

Interpersonal Factors

Interpersonal factors that have been found to distinguish male IPV perpetrators from nonviolent men include interpersonal conflict and relationship dissatisfaction (O'Leary et al., 1989), poor communication skills (Jacobson et al., 1994; Margolin, John, & Gleberman, 1988), and one-sided allocation of decision-making responsibilities (Straus et al., 1980). Margolin et al. (1988) were the first to demonstrate that during conflictual discussions, violent husbands show greater negative affect and arousal and greater reciprocity of negative affect than do nonviolent husbands. Babcock, Waltz, Jacobson, and Gottman (1993) further demonstrated that violent husbands, relative to dissatisfied nonviolent and satisfied nonviolent husbands, are more likely to be characterized by a pattern of communication wherein the husband demands and pursues the wife while she withdraws from him during conflictual discussions. Straus et al. (1980) have shown that violence is most likely in households in which decision-making power is solely in the hands of the husband and least likely in democratic homes. The results of Stith et al.'s (2004) meta-analysis of IPV perpetration risk factors identified a large effect size for relationship dissatisfaction and a moderate effect size for history of IPV.

Sociocultural Factors

Men with low occupational status and income, unemployment, and job dissatisfaction are at risk for engaging in IPV (Gelles & Cornell, 1985; Straus et al., 1980). African American (Hampton, Gelles, & Harrop, 1989) and acculturated Mexican American and Puerto Rican American men are also at higher risk for IPV perpetration (Kantor, Jasinski, & Aldarondo, 1994). Cohabitation relative to marriage is associated with higher rates of relationship aggression (Hotaling & Sugarman, 1986). Rates of violence are higher among partners who report no religious affiliation (Straus et al., 1980). Among those who do report some religious affiliation, the lowest rates of violence are found among Jewish men, and the highest rates are found among husbands who are members of nonmainstream fundamentalist religious groups (Straus et al., 1980). Social isolation (Pagelow, 1981) and a greater number of dependent children in the home (Straus et al., 1980) are associated with an increased risk for IPV.

CONCLUSION

Empirical attention to IPV is relatively recent. The field is still struggling with the lack of consensus on a definition of IPV that in turn affects progress in measurement, identification of causal and maintaining mechanisms, and effective prevention. Additionally, there is lack of consensus on theories that would be productive in guiding etiologic and prevention research and development. These problems notwithstanding, progress has been made. With input from experts across a variety of disciplines, the CDC developed and proposed standard definitions for IPV (Basile & Saltzman, 2002; Saltzman et al., 1999). Various theories of IPV etiology have been proposed. No single theory appears to adequately account for the multidimensional nature of IPV. Accordingly, the field has moved to consider comprehensive ecological theories that address potential etiologic variables at various levels of analysis. The results of research on risk factors for IPV perpetration support relying on such comprehensive theories to develop programs for prevention and intervention. Public health has been the latest contributor to the effort to conceptualize, explain, and prevent IPV. The multidisciplinary nature of the public health approach to prevention is a major strength and makes the approach especially suited for addressing IPV prevention.

REFERENCES

Alexander, P. C. (1992). Application of attachment theory to the study of sexual abuse. *Journal of Consulting and Clinical Psychology, 60,* 185–194.

Arias, I. (1999). Women's responses to physical and psychological abuse. In X. B. Arriaga & S. Oskamp (Eds.), *Violence in intimate relationships* (pp. 139–161). Thousand Oaks, CA: Sage.

Arias, I., & Pape, K. T. (1999). Psychological abuse: Implications for adjustment and commitment to leave violent partners. *Violence and Victims, 14,* 55–67.

Arias, I., Samios, M., & O'Leary, K. D. (1987). Prevalence and correlates of physical aggression during courtship. *Journal of Interpersonal Violence, 2,* 82–90.

Babcock, J. C., Waltz, J., Jacobson, N. S., & Gottman, J. M. (1993). Power and violence: The relation between communication patterns, power discrepancies, and domestic violence. *Journal of Consulting and Clinical Psychology, 61,* 40–50.

Basile, K. C., Arias, I., Desai, S., & Thompson, M. P. (2004). The differential association of intimate partner physical, sexual, psychological, and stalking violence and posttraumatic stress symptoms in a nationally representative sample of women. *Journal of Traumatic Stress, 17,* 413–421.

Basile, K. C., & Saltzman, L. E. (2002). *Sexual violence surveillance: Uniform definitions and recommended data elements.* Atlanta, GA: National Center for Injury Prevention and Control, Centers for Disease Control and Prevention.

Bowlby, J. (1977). The making and breaking of affectional bonds. *British Journal of Psychiatry, 130,* 201–210.

Buttell, F. P., & Jones, C. (2001). Interpersonal dependency among court-ordered domestic violence offenders: A descriptive analysis. *Journal of Family Violence, 16,* 375–384.

Centers for Disease Control and Prevention. (2000, October 27). Building data systems for monitoring and responding to violence against women: Recommendations from a workshop. *Morbidity and Mortality Weekly Report, 49*(RR-11), 1–18.

Centers for Disease Control and Prevention. (2003). *Costs of intimate partner violence against women in the United States.* Atlanta, GA: National Center for Injury Prevention and Control.

Centers for Disease Control and Prevention. (in press). *Intimate partner violence (IPV) surveillance: Guidance from three state pilot projects.* Atlanta, GA: National Center for Injury Prevention and Control.

Coker, A. L., Davis, K. E., Arias, I., Desai, S., Sanderson, M., Brandt, H. M., & Smith, P. H. (2002). Physical and mental health effects of intimate partner violence for men and women. *American Journal of Preventive Medicine, 23,* 260–268.

Danielson, K. K., Moffitt, T. E., Caspi, A., & Silva, P. A. (1998). Comorbidity between abuse of an adult and *DSM–III–R* mental disorders: Evidence from an epidemiological study. *American Journal of Psychiatry, 155,* 131–133.

Dobash, R. E., & Dobash, R. P. (1979). *Violence against wives.* New York: Free Press.

Dutton, D. G. (1995). *The domestic assault of women: Psychological and criminal justice perspectives.* Vancouver, Canada: University of British Columbia Press.

Dutton, D. G. (1998). *The abusive personality: Violence and control in intimate relationships*. New York: Guilford Press.

Dutton, D. G., & Painter, S. (1993). Emotional attachments in abusive relationships: A test of traumatic bonding theory. *Violence and Victims, 8*, 105–120.

Dutton, D. G., & Strachan, C. E. (1987). Motivational needs for power and spouse-specific assertiveness in assaultive and non-assaultive men. *Violence and Victims, 2*, 145–156.

Eckhardt, C. L., Barbour, K. A., & Davison, G. C. (1998). Articulated thoughts of martially violent men and nonviolent men during anger arousal. *Journal of Consulting and Clinical Psychology, 66*, 259–269.

Ehrensaft, M. K., Langhinrichsen-Rohling, J., Heyman, R. E., O'Leary, K. D., & Lawrence, E. (1999). Feeling controlled in marriage: A phenomenon specific to physically aggressive couples? *Journal of Family Psychology, 13*, 20–32.

Fagan, J., & Browne, A. (1994). Violence between spouses and intimates: Physical aggression between women and men in intimate relationships. In A. J. Reiss Jr. & J. A. Roth (Eds.), *Understanding and preventing violence: Vol. 3. Social influences* (pp. 115–292). Washington, DC: National Academy Press.

Fagan, J. A., Stewart, D. K., & Hansen, K. V. (1983). Violent men or violent husbands. In D. Finkelhor, R. J. Gelles, G. Hotaling, & M. A. Straus (Eds.), *The dark side of families: Current family violence research* (pp. 49–67). Beverly Hills, CA: Sage.

Fleury, R. E., Sullivan, C. M., Bybee, D. I., & Davidson, W. S. (1998). Why don't they just call the cops? Reasons for differential police contact among women with abusive partners. *Violence and Victims, 13*, 333–346.

Gaquin, D. A. (1977–1978). Spouse abuse: Data from the National Crime Survey. *Victimology, 2*, 632–643.

Gelles, R. J. (1993). Through a sociological lens: Social structure and family violence. In R. J. Gelles & D. R. Loseke (Eds.), *Current controversies on family violence* (pp. 31–46). Newbury Park, CA: Sage.

Gelles, R. J., & Cornell, C. P. (1985). *Intimate violence in families*. Beverly Hills, CA: Sage.

Hampton, R. L., Gelles, R. J., & Harrop, J. W. (1989). Is violence in Black families increasing? A comparison of 1975 and 1985 national survey rates. *Journal of Marriage and the Family, 51*, 969–980.

Hampton, R. L., Vandergriff-Avery, M., & Kim, J. (1999). Understanding the origins and incidence of spousal violence in North America. In T. P. Gullotta & S. J. McElhaney (Eds.), *Violence in homes and communities: Prevention, intervention, and treatment* (pp. 39–70). Thousand Oaks, CA: Sage.

Hastings, J. E., & Hamberger, L. K. (1988). Personality characteristics of spouse abusers: A controlled comparison. *Violence and Victims, 3*, 31–38.

Heyman, R. E., O'Leary, K. D., & Jouriles, E. N. (1995). Alcohol and aggressive personality styles: Potentiators of serious physical aggression against wives? *Journal of Family Psychology, 9*, 44–57.

Holtzworth-Munroe, A., & Hutchinson, G. (1993). Attributing negative intent to wife behavior: The attributions of maritally violent men versus nonviolent men. *Journal of Abnormal Psychology, 102,* 206–211.

Hotaling, G., & Sugarman, D. (1986). An analysis of risk markers in husband-to-wife violence: The current state of knowledge. *Violence and Victims, 1,* 101–124.

Hotaling, G., & Sugarman, D. (1990). A risk marker analysis of assaulted wives. *Journal of Family Violence, 5,* 1–13.

Institute of Medicine. (1988). *The future of public health.* Washington, DC: National Academy Press.

Jacobson, N. S., Gottman, J. M., Waltz, J., Rushe, R., Babcock, J., & Holtzworth-Munroe, A. (1994). Affect, verbal content, and psychophysiology in the arguments of couples with a violent husband. *Journal of Consulting and Clinical Psychology, 62,* 982–988.

Julian, T. W., & McKenry, P. C. (1993). Mediators of male violence toward female victims. *Journal of Family Violence, 8,* 39–56.

Kalmuss, D. (1984). The intergenerational transmission of marital aggression. *Journal of Marriage and the Family, 46,* 11–19.

Kantor, G. K., Jasinski, J. L., & Aldarondo, E. (1994). Sociocultural status and incidence of marital violence in Hispanic families. *Violence and Victims, 9,* 207–222.

Kantor, G. K., & Straus, M. A. (1990). Response of victims and the police to assaults on wives. In M. A. Straus & R. J. Gelles (Eds.), *Physical violence in American families: Risk factors and adaptations to violence in 8,145 families* (pp. 473–487). New Brunswick, NJ: Transaction Publishers.

Kelly, E. E., & Warshafsky, L. (1987, July). *Partner abuse in gay male and lesbian couples.* Paper presented at the Third National Conference for Family Violence Researchers, Durham, NH.

Kempe, C. H., Silverman, F. N., Steele, B. F., Droegmueller, W., & Silver, H. K. (1962). The battered child syndrome. *Journal of the American Medical Association, 181,* 105–112.

Kentucky Department of Health. (2000). *Intimate partner violence in the lives of Kentucky women.* Lexington: Kentucky Injury Prevention and Research Center.

Kesner, J. E., Julian, T., & McKenry, P. C. (1997). Application of attachment theory to male violence toward female intimates. *Journal of Family Violence, 12,* 211–228.

Kurz, D. (1993). Physical assaults by husbands: A major social problem. In R. J. Gelles & D. R. Loseke (Eds.), *Current controversies on family violence* (pp. 88–103). Newbury Park, CA: Sage.

Leonard, K. E., & Senchak, M. (1993). Alcohol and premarital aggression among newlywed couples. *Journal of Studies on Alcohol, 11,* 96–108.

Maiuro, R., Cahn, T., & Vitaliano, P. (1988). Anger, hostility, and depression in domestically violent men versus generally assaultive men and nonviolent control subjects. *Journal of Consulting and Clinical Psychology, 56,* 17–23.

Makepeace, J. M. (1983). Life events stress and courtship violence. *Family Relations*, *32*, 101–109.

Malone, J., Tyree, A., & O'Leary, K. D. (1989). Generalization and containment: Different effects of past aggression for wives and husbands. *Journal of Marriage and the Family*, *51*, 687–697.

Margolin, G., John, R. S., & Gleberman, L. (1988). Affective responses to conflictual discussions in violent and nonviolent couples. *Journal of Consulting and Clinical Psychology*, *56*, 24–33.

Martin, A., Tan-Schriner, C., Petrona, L., Fiedler, J., & Wojcik, C. (2000). *Intimate partner violence surveillance system: Aggregate report for nineteen reporting hospitals, 2000.* Lansing: Michigan Department of Community Health & The Center for Collaborative Research in Health Outcomes and Policy.

McKenry, P. C., Julian, T. W., & Gavazzi, S. M. (1995). Toward a biopsychosocial model of domestic violence. *Journal of Marriage and the Family*, *57*, 307–320.

Mercy, J. A., Rosenberg, M. L., Powell, K. E., Broome, C. V., & Roper, W. L. (1993). Public health policy for preventing violence. *Health Affairs*, *12*, 7–29.

Minnesota Department of Health. (2002). *Violence data brief: Intimate partner violence 1998 to 2001.* St. Paul: Minnesota Department of Health Injury and Violence Prevention Unit.

Murphy, C. M., Meyer, S. L., & O'Leary, K. D. (1994). Dependency characteristics of partner assaultive men. *Journal of Abnormal Psychology*, *103*, 729–735.

Oklahoma State Department of Health. (2000). *Injury update: Intimate partner violence.* Oklahoma City: Oklahoma State Department of Health Injury Prevention Service.

O'Leary, K. D. (1987). The emergence of marital assessment. In K. D. O'Leary (Ed.), *Assessment of marital discord: An integration of research and practice* (pp. 1–11). Hillsdale, NJ: Erlbaum.

O'Leary K. D., Barling, J., Arias, I., Rosenbaum, A., Malone, J., & Tyree, A. (1989). Prevalence and stability of spousal aggression. *Journal of Consulting and Clinical Psychology*, *57*, 263–268.

O'Leary, K. D., & Curley, A. D. (1986). Assertion and family violence: Correlates of spouse abuse. *Journal of Marital and Family Therapy*, *12*, 281–289.

Oregon Department of Human Services. (2002). *CD summary—Ask the hard questions: Intimate partner violence and health-care providers.* Salem: Oregon Office of Communicable Disease and Epidemiology.

Pagelow, M. D. (1981). *Woman-battering: Victims and their experiences.* Beverly Hills, CA: Sage.

Prince, J. E., & Arias, I. (1994). The role of perceived control and the desirability of control among abusive and nonabusive husbands. *American Journal of Family Therapy*, *22*, 126–134.

Rennison, C. M. (2003). *Intimate partner violence, 1993–2001* (NCJ 197838). Washington, DC: U.S. Department of Justice, Bureau of Justice Statistics.

Ronfeldt, H. M., Kimerling, R., & Arias, I. (1998). Relationship power satisfaction and perpetration of dating violence in the context of paternal marital violence. *Journal of Marriage and the Family, 60,* 70–78.

Rosenberg, M. L. (1989). Violence is a public health problem. In R. C. Maulitz (Ed.), *Unnatural causes: The three leading killer diseases in America* (pp. 147–168). New Brunswick, NJ: Rutgers University Press.

Saltzman, L. E., Fanslow, J. L., McMahon, P. M., & Shelley, G. A. (1999). *Intimate partner violence surveillance: Uniform definitions and recommended data elements.* Atlanta, GA: National Center for Injury Prevention and Control, Centers for Disease Control and Prevention.

Schneiderman, N., & Speers, M. A. (2001). Behavioral science, social science, and public health in the 21st century. In N. Schneiderman, M. A. Speers, J. M. Silva, H. Tomes, & J. H. Gentry (Eds.), *Integrating behavioral and social sciences with public health* (pp. 3–28). Washington, DC: American Psychological Association.

Schumacher, J. A., Feldbau-Kohn, S., Smith Slep, A. M., & Heyman, R. E. (2001) Risk factors for male-to-female partner physical abuse. *Aggression and Violent Behavior, 6,* 281–352.

Stets, J. E. (1988). *Domestic violence and control.* New York: Springer-Verlag.

Stets, J. E., & Straus, M. A. (1990). Gender differences in reporting marital violence and its medical and social consequences. In M. A. Straus & R. J. Gelles (Eds.), *Physical violence in American families: Risk factors and adaptations to violence in 8,145 families* (pp. 151–166). New Brunswick, NJ: Transaction Publishers.

Stith, S. M., Smith, D. B., Penn, C. E., Ward, D. B., & Tritt, D. (2004). Intimate partner physical abuse perpetration and victimization risk factors: A meta-analytic review. *Journal of Aggression and Violent Behavior, 10,* 65–98.

Straus, M. A. (1979). Measuring intrafamily conflict and violence: The Conflict Tactics (CT) Scales. *Journal of Marriage and the Family, 41,* 75–88.

Straus, M. A. (1980). Victims and aggressors in marital violence. *American Behavioral Scientist, 23,* 681–704.

Straus, M. A., & Gelles, R. J. (1986). Societal change and change in family violence from 1975 to 1985 as revealed by two national surveys. *Journal of Marriage and the Family, 48,* 465–479.

Straus, M. A., Gelles, R. J., & Steinmetz, S. (1980). *Behind closed doors: Violence in the American family.* Garden City, NY: Anchor Press/Doubleday.

Sullivan, A. (2002). *Intimate partner violence surveillance in Oregon: Comparison of fatal and traumatic non-fatal intimate partner violence in Oregon, 1999–2000.* Retrieved May 5, 2003, from http://www.dhs.state.or.us/publichealth/ipv/hcdv2002/index.cfm

Taylor, B. G., Davis, R. C., & Maxwell, C. D. (2001). The effects of a group batterer treatment program in Brooklyn. *Justice Quarterly, 18,* 170–201.

Thacker, S. B., & Berkelman, R. L. (1988). Public health surveillance in the United States. *Epidemiologic Reviews, 10,* 164–190.

Tjaden, P., & Thoennes, N. (2000). Prevalence and consequences of male-to-female and female-to-male intimate partner violence as measured by the National Violence Against Women Survey. *Violence Against Women, 6,* 142–161.

Walker, L. E. (1979). *The battered woman.* New York: Harper & Row.

Yllo, K. (1993). Through a feminist lens: Gender, power, and violence. In R. J. Gelles & D. R. Loseke (Eds.), *Current controversies on family violence* (pp. 47–62). Newbury Park, CA: Sage.

Yllo, K., & Bograd, M. (1988). *Feminist perspectives on wife abuse.* Newbury Park, CA: Sage.

9

INTERVENTIONS TO ADDRESS INTIMATE PARTNER VIOLENCE: THE CURRENT STATE OF THE FIELD

CRIS M. SULLIVAN

Although it is difficult to believe today, interventions to address intimate partner violence were virtually nonexistent before the mid-1970s.[1] The serious problem of domestic violence was first recognized and named in the United States in large part as a result of the women's liberation movement, in conjunction with the civil rights movement and the anti-poverty movement. Feminists, other community activists, and survivors of domestic violence worked together to open the first emergency shelters designed to provide safety and support for battered women (Schechter, 1982). The first shelters were often no more sophisticated than women opening their homes to other women, but as public awareness of this problem increased, shelters proliferated throughout the country so that today there are

---

[1] Although some couples engage in mutual combat or low-level violence that does not alter the power dynamics within the relationship, the larger social problem of battering includes a pattern of behavior, generally committed by men against women, that results in the perpetrator gaining an advantage of power and control (Dobash, Dobash, Wilson, & Daly, 1992; Johnson, 1995). In this chapter, I focus on interventions that address intimate partner violence against women.

over 2,000 domestic violence programs across the United States (National Research Council, 1998).

The first domestic-violence-focused interventions were, by necessity, targeted toward ensuring victims' immediate safety from abuse. Women who were abused often had nowhere to turn, and there were few laws or policies in place to protect them. Lack of public awareness in general regarding the causes and consequences of this problem led to inadequate or even harmful responses to women's formal and informal help seeking (Gondolf, 1988; Sullivan, 1991a). It was never assumed, however, that emergency shelter would be enough to end this widespread social problem. Interventions continued to be created not only to address victims' immediate needs but also to address their emotional, economic, health-related, educational, and spiritual needs as well. There was also an understanding that domestic violence would continue until batterers were held accountable for their actions and prevented from recidivating (National Research Council, 1996). And finally, many efforts have been focused on educating the general public about this issue and creating systems change, with the recognition that society as a whole must oppose intimate partner violence in order for it to be ultimately prevented.

No single book chapter can adequately describe all of the many interventions currently being implemented to address this complex issue. I do provide an overview of the most common types of interventions being provided in the United States as well as discuss the empirical evidence, if available, supporting these efforts. The majority of interventions that are currently in place to address intimate partner violence fall into four broad categories: community-based programs to assist victims (and often their children), criminal legal-system-based programs to assist victims or hold batterers accountable, batterer intervention programs, and coordinating councils designed to bring systems together to respond effectively to this problem.

COMMUNITY-BASED INTERVENTIONS FOR BATTERED WOMEN

As understanding about the dynamics of intimate partner violence has increased, so too have the types of community-based programs for survivors. Empirical studies that have involved listening to survivors themselves have reported that whether seeking help to end the violence while maintaining the relationship or seeking help to end the relationship as well as the violence, women turn to a variety of community systems to protect themselves and their children. Women turn to informal help sources such as family and friends but also to formal sources such as the police, health care professionals, religious leaders, and the social service system (Allen, Bybee, & Sullivan, 2004; Caralis & Musialowski, 1997; Gondolf, 1988; Sullivan, 1991a, 1997; Wauchope, 1988). Unfortunately, women often have been unsuccessful in obtaining the help needed from the very agencies and institutions designed to provide it (Baker, Cook, & Norris, 2003; Binney, Harkell, & Nixon, 1981; Dobash, Dobash, & Cavanaugh, 1985; Epstein, 1999; Stark & Flitcraft, 1996; Sullivan, 1997).

To redress the often inadequate or ineffective responses battered women have traditionally received from their communities, many community-based programs engage in various forms of advocacy on women's behalf (Peled & Edleson, 1994). Many such services are now being offered not just within grassroots domestic violence programs but also across a variety of systems throughout communities. Programs can now be found in health care settings, in family service organizations, in faith communities, and on college campuses, just to name a few. What these programs share is a focus on providing emotional support and practical assistance to survivors of domestic violence. Probably the most recognized community-based service for battered women is the domestic violence shelter program.

Victim Service Shelter Programs

Although the earliest shelter programs offered little more than beds and short-term support, today community-based shelter programs are likely to provide emergency shelter, 24-hour crisis lines, support groups, counseling services, advocacy, and programs for children. Unfortunately, the number of programs available is still much lower than the need. Shelters are less likely to be available to women in rural areas, and most struggle continually for enough money to stay open. The National Coalition Against Domestic Violence (NCADV) estimates that for every woman who receives shelter, three are turned away for lack of space (R. Smith, NCADV, personal communication, 2002).

Shelter programs have been found to be one of the most supportive, effective resources for women with abusive partners according to the residents themselves (Bennett, Riger, Schewe, Howard, & Wasco, 2004; Bowker & Maurer, 1985; Gordon, 1996; Sedlak, 1988; Straus, Gelles, & Steinmetz, 1980; Tutty, Weaver, & Rothery, 1999). Most programs provide all services free of charge and were created to empower and respect women (Ridington, 1977–1978; Schechter, 1982). For example, Berk, Newton, and Berk (1986) reported that for women who were actively attempting other strategies at the same time, a stay at a shelter dramatically reduced the likelihood of further violence.

One intervention that is commonly provided within domestic violence shelter programs (and sometimes through other community-based organizations) is the *support group*. Although these groups were initially created by shelter programs to provide women with a supportive atmosphere through which to discuss their experiences and to share information about resources with other survivors, such groups have expanded in breadth and scope over time. Now many groups are available that either target specific populations of abused women (e.g., Latinas, lesbians, or mothers) or focus on particular circumstances (e.g., groups for women still in the relationship or for women who are no longer being abused but who still seek support for dealing with the aftereffects). Evaluations of such groups have been quite limited. One notable exception is Tutty, Bidgood, and Rothery's (1993) evaluation of 12 closed support groups (i.e., not open to new members once begun) for survivors. The 10-to-12-week closed support group is a common type of group offered to survivors and typically focuses on safety planning, offering mutual support and understanding, and discussion of dynamics of abuse. Tutty et al.'s evaluation involved surveying 76 women before, immediately after, and 6 months following the group. Significant improvements were found in women's self-esteem, sense of belonging, locus of control, and overall stress over time; however, fewer than half of the original 76 women completed the 6-month follow-up assessment ($n = 32$), and there was no control or comparison group for this study. Hence, these findings should be interpreted with extreme caution.

It is important to note that although shelters receive high effectiveness ratings in general by their residents, not all women feel that shelters are options for them, and some are distrustful of the experiences they might have there. Lesbian women, for example, are much more likely to have negative shelter experiences and to believe that shelters are for heterosexual women only (Irvine, 1990; Renzetti, 1992). Some women of color, regardless of sexual orientation, also hesitate to use shelters for various reasons. Many shelters are staffed primarily by White women who may be insensitive to needs and issues within cultures other than their own. Even if insensitivity is not an issue, some women of color simply prefer being with other women from their own culture and background, and this may not be provided by their local shelter program. Language barriers prevent some women from seeking shelter, as do shelter policies that are more comfortable to those from the majority culture (e.g., chores needing to be done at specific times and the ban on corporal punishment of children). Migrant women often work far from their homes and face multiple language, cultural, and structural barriers (e.g., lack of transportation and lack of documented status) preventing their use of shelter programs as well as other services (Rodriguez, 1998). Immigrant women face language, cultural, and sometimes legal (e.g., documented status) barriers to accessing services (Bauer, Rodriguez, Quiroga, & Flores-Ortiz, 2000; Dasgupta, 1998). Domestic violence victim service programs continue to struggle with these issues as they seek to design and provide culturally competent services (Donnelly, Cook, Van Ausdale, & Foley, 2005). However, a great deal more work needs to be done in this area before all survivors will receive the services they need.

Transitional Housing Programs

Batterers often use finances as a means of controlling women during and after the relationship. Some batterers deny their victims access to money or prevent them from working outside the home (Lloyd, 1997). Others harass their victims at work until they are fired (Lein, Jacquet, Lewis, Cole, & Williams, 2001; Lloyd & Taluc, 1999), or they damage their homes, causing women to be evicted (Menard, 2001).

One result of these tactics is that some battered women either have no credit or their credit is so badly marred that it represents too large a risk to landlords. The long-term results for many battered women include being unable to secure and maintain permanent, affordable housing independent of their abusers. Transitional housing programs for survivors of domestic violence were designed to offer an important alternative to living with an abusive partner and have proven a vital resource for many poor battered women striving to become free from abuse (Melbin, Sullivan, & Cain, 2003). Although still few in number, today there are transitional housing programs for battered women in every state in the nation. All offer women housing in which they can live for a set period of time (usually 1 to 2 years) or until they can obtain permanent housing. Women often pay a small percentage of their income for rent, and most transitional housing programs also include support services such as counseling, housing assistance, and employment assistance (National Council of Juvenile and Family Court Judges, 1998).

Davis and Srinivasan (1995) conducted nine focus groups among women participating in support groups for domestic violence survivors in seven cities in a Midwestern state. All of the women praised transitional housing programs as important resources. Melbin et al. (2003) interviewed women who had participated in six different transitional housing programs. Many women noted that had the transitional housing program not been available, they would have either returned to their assailants, been homeless, resorted to prostitution, or been incarcerated. Given the scarcity of low-income housing across the nation and the continued danger many women face from their assailants even after they end the relationship, transitional housing programs hold great promise for enhancing economic stability for battered women.

Community-Based Advocacy

The majority of domestic violence service programs engage in some form of activities they identify as advocacy (Peled & Edleson, 1994). These efforts generally involve paraprofessionals working collaboratively and respectfully with individual survivors who guide the focus of the intervention to meet their specific needs and desires. Systems-level advocacy efforts are generally targeted at the criminal justice system, the health care system, the welfare system, and other such institutions. Activities identified by programs as being individual-level advocacy have ranged from helping a woman locate housing to accompanying women through the court process. Such community-based advocacy interventions have received scant evaluation, and the belief in their effectiveness has largely been predicated on anecdotal evidence.

In response to this dearth of information about the effectiveness of advocacy for women with abusive partners, I designed and experimentally evaluated a community-based advocacy intervention for women after they exited a domestic violence shelter program (Bybee & Sullivan, 2002; Sullivan, 1991b, 2000; Sullivan & Bybee, 1999). The Community Advocacy Project involved providing advocates to work one-on-one with women who had recently exited a domestic violence shelter, working in their communities with them 6 to 8 hours a week over a period of 10 weeks. Advocates were trained in helping women obtain a variety of community resources, including housing, employment, legal assistance, transportation, education, child care, health care, material goods and services, financial assistance, services for the children (e.g., tutoring and counseling), and social support (e.g., making new friends and joining clubs or groups).

A true experimental design was used to evaluate the impact of the Community Advocacy Project wherein women were randomly assigned to either the intervention group or the control group (services as usual). All 278 women, regardless of group assignment, were interviewed preintervention, 10 weeks later (postintervention for those in the experimental group), and again every 6 months over 2 years. At each time point, 94% or more of the women were located and interviewed.

Women who had worked with advocates experienced less violence over time, reported higher quality of life and social support, and had less difficulty obtaining community resources over time. For the women who had worked with advocates, 1 out of 4 (24%) experienced no physical abuse by the original assailant or by any new partners across the 24 months of postintervention follow-up. Only 1 out of 10 women (11%) in the control group remained completely free of violence during the same period. This low-cost, short-term intervention using unpaid advocates appears to have been effective not only in reducing women's risk of reabuse but also in improving their overall quality of life. It is important to remember, however, that although the provision of advocates reduced the risk of further violence by a partner or ex-partner, many women (76% who worked with advocates and 89% who did not) were abused at least once over the 2-year time span. No single intervention will be a panacea for this complex social problem, and many abusive men continue their violence in spite of the strategies women use to protect themselves. Systems-level and individual-level advocacy should be viewed as important components of an overall comprehensive community approach to ending intimate violence against women.

Interventions in Health Care Settings

Approximately 1.5 million women seek medical treatment for injuries sustained from abusive partners each year (Straus, 1986). Women also turn to their health care providers for help with symptoms related to the stress of being abused by a partner (Campbell, 1998). In response to this, several researchers and practitioners have outlined interventions health care providers can implement to assist survivors of intimate partner violence (Campbell & Lewandowski, 1997; Dutton, Haywood, & El-Bayoumi, 1997; Naumann, Langford, Torres, Campbell, & Glass, 1999). These interventions include providing emotional support and mental health counseling, safety planning, patient education, legal advocacy, referral to community services, and consistent documentation of abuse history. Some hospitals and clinics are collaborating with their local domestic violence shelter programs so that trained advocates housed within the health care setting can have easier and faster access to women who have been identified as survivors of intimate partner violence. Although hospital-based domestic abuse programs have been in existence since the mid-1970s (Sheridan, 1998), none to date have received rigorous evaluation. Although most health care settings still lack this level of intervention, at the very least medical professionals can validate women's experiences by creating a nonjudgmental, supportive atmosphere and can have information about local domestic violence services readily available.

Criminal Legal-Focused Interventions

Some communities have implemented programs within police stations, prosecutors' offices, or legal offices to reach women in need of legal assistance, legal advocacy, or direct assistance. One innovative strategy for providing free legal advocacy to survivors of intimate partner violence has been to locate such services within law schools. Over 40 law schools now have programs in which law students work as legal advocates (Goelman & Valente, 1997; Murphy, 1997; Schneider, 2000), and the number is growing. Although legal advocacy programs are also sometimes offered through domestic violence service programs or prosecutors' offices, using law students not only increases the likelihood of survivors being paired with especially knowledgeable advocates but also serves to educate future lawyers about the many barriers facing battered women. The only evaluation of a legal advocacy program to date is Bell and Goodman's (2001) quasi-experimental study conducted in Washington, DC. Their research found that women who had worked with advocates reported decreased abuse 6 weeks later as well as marginally higher emotional well-being compared with women who had not worked with advocates. Their qualitative findings also supported the use of paraprofessional legal advocates. All of the women who had worked with advocates talked about them as being very supportive and knowledgeable, and the women who had not worked with advocates mentioned wishing they had had that kind of support while they were going through this difficult process.

Another intervention that involves providing advocacy and support at the time the violence occurs is the first response team, which can be, but does not necessarily need to be, housed within the criminal justice system. First response teams generally consist of trained advocates or social workers who either accompany police officers on domestic violence calls or are called to the scene after an arrest has been made. Limited evaluations of this intervention suggest it may be meeting its intended goal of providing supportive services and information to survivors of domestic violence. Carr (1982) surveyed survivors 1 year after a first response team was implemented and reported that 79% found the service to be helpful. Corcoran, Stephenson, Perryman, and Allen (2001) surveyed 219 police officers in a locale that used a first response team, and again, 79% found the team to be useful.

Although a first response team can provide immeasurable assistance to women after the police have been called, such help is limited if the police, prosecutors, judges, and probation officers are not cooperative in holding perpetrators accountable for their behavior. In response to this, an increasing number of communities have designed what the Minneapolis Domestic Abuse Project first termed *community intervention projects* (CIPs). Under many different names across the country, these projects bring together multiple community partners to respond more effectively to domestic violence. The police agree to contact the CIP after responding to a domestic violence call, and perpetrators are held in jail for a set period of time (usually at least overnight). The CIP then sends female volunteers to the survivor's home and sends male volunteers to visit the perpetrator in jail. Survivors are given information, referrals, and transportation to a shelter if needed, and perpetrators are encouraged to accept responsibility for their actions and to attend a batterer intervention program. Prosecutors agree to pursue domestic violence charges aggressively, and judges agree to order presentence investigations and to mandate jail time or batterer intervention or both. Probation officers also play an important role in this coordination. They agree to incorporate the perpetrator's violent history and the survivor's wishes in the presentence investigation, and they sentence perpetrators to jail time if they do not attend their mandatory batterer intervention meetings.

CIPs have been evaluated in three suburbs in Minnesota (Gamache, Edleson, & Schock, 1988); in Lincoln, Nebraska (Steinman, 1990); and in Minneapolis, Minnesota (Syers & Edleson, 1992). The trisuburb Minnesota evaluation focused on whether change had occurred in arrest, prosecution, and sentencing after CIPs were initiated, and the Lincoln and Minneapolis studies focused on the effects of CIPs on batterers' continued use of violence.

Gamache et al. (1988) examined the number of domestic violence calls to the police, number of arrests, and court outcomes over a 22-month period as CIPs were introduced into their communities. Across all three communities, they found a significant increase in arrests relative to calls received, increased successful prosecution, and an increase in the number of perpetrators mandated into batterer intervention programs. This study provides powerful evidence that CIPs can have a significant positive impact on the criminal justice response to abuse of women.

Whereas Gamache and colleagues examined the institutional impact of CIPs, Steinman (1990) and Syers and Edleson (1992) evaluated their effectiveness in deterring reabuse. Steinman's research found that when police action was coordinated with other systems, a critical component of coordinated community intervention, perpetrators were significantly less likely to reoffend. Equally important, he found that when police action was not coordinated with other components of the system, perpetrators actually seemed to increase their use of violence against women. Syers and Edleson (1992) corroborated these findings. On the basis of data collected from survivors, police reports, and advocacy records across three time points (time of police report and 6- and 12-month follow-ups), they found that arrest followed by mandated intervention resulted in the lowest recidivism among the perpetrators. Men who were arrested but not mandated into batterer intervention were more likely to recidivate, and the group most likely to batter again was the group of men who were not arrested at all. These findings strongly support the contention that men's use of violence against women with whom they are involved is related to how the community responds to them. Lack of arrest, as well as arrests that lead to no sanctions, sends a clear signal to perpetrators that they can abuse their partners with impunity.

INTERVENTIONS TARGETED TOWARD ASSAILANTS

Early efforts to hold batterers accountable generally focused on increasing the arrest rate and successfully prosecuting perpetrators (National Research Council, 1996). However, it soon became clear that the most common sentence that perpetrators received (probation or minimal jail time), if they were even arrested, prosecuted, and sentenced at all, was inadequate as a strategy for changing batterers' behavior. There were also concerns that the criminal processing system unfairly targeted men of color and low-income men. In the 1980s, batterer intervention programs (commonly referred to as "BIPs") were developed as a means of reeducating and rehabilitating perpetrators. Today BIPs are quite prevalent, with many courts across the country mandating convicted batterers into such programs.

Although BIPs differ in philosophy, duration of program, and curricula, the majority of the well-established programs adhere to the following three guidelines: (a) complying with state standards, (b) collaborating with victim service programs to ensure women's safety, and (c) using or modifying a well-established cognitive–behavioral-focused curriculum (Gondolf, 1999; Kivel, 1992; Pence & Paymar, 1993). Most men in BIPs have been mandated by the court, with far fewer attending voluntarily.

The extent to which BIPs are effective in reducing or ending men's violence is still open to debate. Only two large-scale randomized experiments have been conducted testing the effectiveness of BIPs, one in Broward County, Florida (Feder & Forde, 2000), and the other at a San Diego naval base (Dunford, 2000). Neither found significant differences between the subsequent abusiveness of men who attended batterer intervention and men who received probation or community service. However, there is some evidence to suggest that this type of program may be at least somewhat effective for some perpetrators who complete the majority of sessions (Bennett & Williams, 2002; Edleson & Syers, 1990; Feder & Forde, 2000; Gondolf, 1991, 1997, 1999; Saunders, 1996; Tolman & Bennett, 1990; Tolman & Edleson, 1995), especially for men with a higher stake in conformity (e.g., those who are employed, married, have higher incomes, and own their own homes).

In addition to studies comparing BIPs with other sanctions (e.g., probation and community service), a number of studies have compared BIPs with each other. Communities are interested in knowing not just if BIPs are an improvement over services as usual but if some programs are better than others. Two controlled experimental designs (Edleson & Syers, 1990; Saunders, 1996) failed to find significant differences in assault rates between men in programs following different philosophies (cognitive–behavioral vs. discussion group). However, as Gondolf (1999) noted of these and other studies, "It is difficult to compare these studies and the different components they examine because the samples, instruments, and methodologies differ" (p. 42). The only study to compare four well-established programs in geographically disparate cities has concluded that program duration and content do not appear to impact reassault rate, threat rate, or victim quality of life. The longest program offering the most comprehensive approach, however, did result in a lower rate of severe violence compared with the other sites (Gondolf, 1997, 1999).

It is important to note that the completion rate of men of color in many BIPs is lower than that of their White counterparts (Tolman & Edleson, 1995; Williams, 1992; Williams & Becker, 1994). Williams (1992, 1994) and others have pointed to the lack of cultural competence in many of the well-established programs as the reason for this. Some communities now are designing and implementing their own culturally relevant BIPs, including Alianza (Latino Alliance for the Elimination of Domestic Violence) and Evolve (located in Connecticut and specifically for men of color), although evaluation data are not available from these programs. These efforts are nonetheless extremely important, as it is imperative that BIPs be relevant and meaningful to the men participating in them if success is to be achieved.

COORDINATING COUNCILS

Coordinating councils have proliferated since the mid-1990s as a means of creating or enhancing a coordinated community response to violence against women (Clark, Burt, Schulte, & Maguire, 1996; Hart, 1995). These councils typically consist of representatives from numerous service systems and organizations that are considered important to intervening in cases in which women are being abused. Councils often include, but are not limited to, representatives from domestic violence victim service programs, BIPs, the police, the prosecutor's office, probation offices, the health care system, the religious community, other social service agencies, universities, and child welfare agencies. There is evidence to suggest that coordinating councils in general play a role in encouraging interorganizational exchanges, developing more highly integrated service delivery systems, and enhancing communication among the agencies involved (Abbott, Jordan, & Murtaya, 1995). Although there is relatively little research on the application of this model to domestic violence intervention, there is some evidence to suggest that this intervention strategy may lead to increased coordination among agencies responding to domestic violence. In a study conducted in San Francisco, the presence of a coordinating council was found to facilitate interactions between agencies, promote broader institutional change, and increase the responsiveness of the service system to the needs of battered women (Clark et al., 1996). Another study of domestic violence coordinating councils in Michigan found that perceived effectiveness of councils was related to their internal climate and membership (Allen, 2005). Specifically, those councils encompassing strong leadership, a shared mission, shared power, and a membership extending across more fields were perceived to be more effective in accomplishing their goals. Although these findings provide early evidence of the usefulness of these councils, more rigorous large-scale evaluations are needed to identify whether they are working, how they are working, and how they can be improved and disseminated across communities.

THE NEED FOR MORE RIGOROUS EVALUATIONS

The National Research Council (1998) has identified evaluation of domestic violence interventions as "one of the most critical needs of this field" (p. 59). A great deal of the research and evaluation in the field to date has suffered from a variety of methodological problems, including, but not limited to, small sample sizes and samples with limited generalizability (e.g., shelter samples and predominantly White samples), nonexperimental designs, cross-sectional designs that preclude identifying causal relationships, and measures lacking established validity and reliability. Since the Violence Against Women Act was enacted in 1994, a considerable influx of dollars has entered communities. It is essential that programs and policies be guided by sound empirical evidence in order for those funds to be best used.

To date, there has been only one experimental evaluation of advocacy services for battered women (Bybee & Sullivan, 2002; Sullivan, 1991b, 2000; Sullivan & Bybee, 1999). There have also been few large-scale rigorous evaluations of BIPs (exceptions include Dunford, 2000; Feder & Forde, 2000; Gondolf, 1997, 1999). Notably, each of the experimental, longitudinal studies was accomplished with large federal grants that spanned multiple years. More funds and larger designations of funds per study are needed in order for more rigorous research to be conducted. Conducting research involving safely locating and interviewing battered women (as was done in some of the aforementioned studies) and including longitudinal designs is not inexpensive. Only by funding additional large-scale, rigorous evaluations will our knowledge base considerably increase.

It is also important to focus research and evaluation in communities of color and to involve knowledgeable researchers from those communities. Many of the published studies to date lack adequate representation of people of color, which is sometimes but not always reflective of the services currently being provided. A great deal more work must occur to ensure that culturally competent and culturally relevant research guides our programmatic efforts. Similarly, more work is needed to understand the effectiveness of interventions for lesbians and gay men, for immigrants and refugees, for those with disabilities or multiple needs, and for other traditionally marginalized groups.

Evaluating the effects of coordinated community responses presents another daunting task. However, as Shepard (1999) pointed out, it is difficult to understand the efficacy of one component of a coordinated community response without examining all interrelated components. Therefore, a multi-level analysis approach is needed (Sullivan & Allen, 2001). Specifically, evaluation efforts must investigate the degree to which change has occurred on the community level and the degree to which these community-level efforts are resulting in meaningful change in the lives of survivors. A multiple-level framework includes the individual and family levels (i.e., the survivor's safety and well-being), the community level (e.g., coordinating councils, criminal justice system, health care system, and social service providers), and the state and federal levels (i.e., laws and policies governing the response to violence against women and children). This multilevel framework allows for an examination of accountability at both the community and state and federal levels while simultaneously examining how these policies and practices impact the safety and well-being of women and their children.

In conclusion, the past 30 years have borne witness to an explosion of interventions designed to address and eliminate intimate partner violence. There is evidence to suggest that at least some of these interventions are resulting in positive change for survivors of intimate partner violence. Unfortunately, there is still a great deal more that we do not know about what works, how it works, and for whom it works. The National Research Council (1996, 1998) has identified a number of recommendations that would ideally lead to more and better research and evaluation in this field. Given the complexity of this issue, rigorous evaluations conducted in collaboration with practitioners and survivors are needed to help focus efforts on implementing those interventions most likely to enhance victim safety and offender accountability.

REFERENCES

Abbott, B., Jordan, P., & Murtaya, N. (1995). Interagency collaboration for children's mental health services: The San Mateo County model for managed care. *Administration and Policy in Mental Health, 22*, 301–313.

Allen, N. E. (2005). A multi-level analysis of community coordinating councils. *American Journal of Community Psychology, 35*, 49–63.

Allen, N. E., Bybee, D. I., & Sullivan, C. M. (2004). Battered women's multitude of needs: Evidence supporting the need for comprehensive advocacy. *Violence Against Women, 10*, 1015–1035.

Baker, C. K., Cook, S. L., & Norris, F. H. (2003). Domestic violence and housing problems: A contextual analysis of women's help-seeking, received informal support, and formal system response. *Violence Against Women, 9*, 754–783.

Bauer, H. M., Rodriguez, M. A., Quiroga, S. S., & Flores-Ortiz, Y. G. (2000). Barriers to health care for abused Latina and Asian immigrant women. *Journal of Healthcare for the Poor and Underserved, 11*, 33–44.

Bell, M. E., & Goodman, L. A. (2001). Supporting battered women involved with the court system: An evaluation of a law-school-based advocacy intervention. *Violence Against Women, 7*, 1377–1404.

Bennett, L., Riger, S., Schewe, P., Howard, A., & Wasco, S. (2004). Effectiveness of hotline, advocacy, counseling and shelter services for victims of domestic violence: A statewide evaluation. *Journal of Interpersonal Violence, 19*, 815–829.

Bennett, L., & Williams, O. (2002). *Controversies and recent studies of batterer intervention program effectiveness.* Retrieved September 28, 2002, from http://www.mincava.umn.edu/vawnet/ar_bip.htm

Berk, R. A., Newton, P. J., & Berk, S. F. (1986). What a difference a day makes: An empirical study of the impact of shelters for battered women. *Journal of Marriage and the Family, 48*, 481–490.

Binney, V., Harkell, G., & Nixon, J. (1981). *Leaving violent men: A study of refuges and housing for battered women.* Leeds, England: Women's Aid Federation.

Bowker, L. H., & Maurer, L. (1985). The importance of sheltering in the lives of battered women. *Response to the Victimization of Women and Children, 8*, 2–8.

Bybee, D. I., & Sullivan, C. M. (2002). The process through which an advocacy intervention resulted in positive change for battered women over time. *American Journal of Community Psychology, 30*, 103–132.

Campbell, J. C. (1998). Making the health care system an empowerment zone for battered women: Health consequences, policy recommendations, introduction, and overview. In J. C. Campbell (Ed.), *Empowering survivors of abuse: Health care for battered women and their children* (pp. 3–22). Thousand Oaks, CA: Sage.

Campbell, J. C., & Lewandowski, L. A. (1997). Mental and physical health effects of intimate partner violence on women and children. *Psychiatric Clinics of North America, 20*, 353–374.

Caralis, P. V., & Musialowski, R. (1997). Women's experiences with domestic violence and their attitudes and expectations regarding medical care of abuse victims. *Southern Medical Journal, 90*, 1075–1080.

Carr, J. (1982). *The abusive partner: An analysis of domestic battering.* New York: Van Nostrand Reinhold.

Clark, S. J., Burt, M. R., Schulte, M. M., & Maguire, K. (1996). *Coordinated community responses to domestic violence in six communities: Beyond the justice system.* Washington, DC: Urban Institute.

Corcoran, J., Stephenson, M., Perryman, D., & Allen, S. (2001). Perceptions and utilization of a police–social work crisis intervention approach to domestic violence. *Families in Society, 82*, 393–398.

Dasgupta, S. D. (1998). Women's realities: Defining violence against women by immigration, race, and class. In R. K. Bergen (Ed.), *Issues in intimate violence* (pp. 209–219). Thousand Oaks, CA: Sage.

Davis, L. V., & Srinivasan, M. (1995). Listening to the voices of battered women: What helps them escape violence. *Affilia, 10*, 49–69.

Dobash, R. E., Dobash, R. P., & Cavanaugh, K. (1985). The contact between battered women and social and medical agencies. In J. Pahl (Ed.), *Private violence and public policy: The needs of battered women and the response of the public services* (pp. 142–165). London: Routledge & Kegan Paul.

Dobash, R. P., Dobash, R. E., Wilson, M., & Daly, M. (1992). The myth of sexual symmetry in marital violence. *Social Problems, 39*, 71–91.

Donnelly, D. A., Cook, K. J., Van Ausdale, D., & Foley, L. (2005). White privilege, color blindness, and services to battered women. *Violence Against Women, 11*, 6–37.

Dunford, F. W. (2000). The San Diego Navy Experiment: An assessment of interventions for men who assault their wives. *Journal of Consulting and Clinical Psychology, 68*, 468–476.

Dutton, M. A., Haywood, Y., & El-Bayoumi, G. (1997). Impact of violence on women's health. In S. J. Gallant, G. P. Keita, & R. Royak-Schaler (Eds.), *Health care for women: Psychological, social, and behavioral influences* (pp. 41–56). Washington, DC: American Psychological Association.

Edleson, J. L., & Syers, M. (1990). The relative effectiveness of group treatments for men who batter. *Social Work Research and Abstracts, 26*, 10–17.

Epstein, D. (1999). Effective intervention in domestic violence cases: Rethinking the roles of prosecutors, judges and the court system. *Yale Journal of Law and Feminism, 11*, 3–50.

Feder, L., & Forde, D. R. (2000). *A test of the efficacy of court-mandated counseling for domestic violence offenders: The Broward experiment.* Washington, DC: National Institute of Justice.

Gamache, D. J., Edleson, J. L., & Schock, M. D. (1988). Coordinated police, judicial, and social service response to woman battering: A multi-baseline evaluation across three communities. In G. T. Hotaling, D. Finkelhor, J. T. Kirkpatrick, & M. Straus (Eds.), *Coping with family violence: Research and policy perspectives* (pp. 193–209). Newbury Park, CA: Sage.

Goelman, D., & Valente, R. (1997). *When will they ever learn? Educating to end domestic violence: A law school report.* Chicago: American Bar Association.

Gondolf, E. W. (1988). *Battered women as survivors: An alternative to learned helplessness.* Lexington, MA: Lexington Books.

Gondolf, E. W. (1991). A victim-based assessment of court-mandated counseling for batterers. *Criminal Justice Review, 16*, 214–226.

Gondolf, E. W. (1997). Patterns of reassault in batterer programs. *Violence and Victims, 12*, 373–387.

Gondolf, E. W. (1999). A comparison of four batterer intervention systems: Do court referral, program length, and services matter? *Journal of Interpersonal Violence, 14*, 41–61.

Gordon, J. S. (1996). Community services for abused women: A review of perceived usefulness and efficacy. *Journal of Family Violence, 11*, 315–329.

Hart, B. J. (1995). *Coordinated community approaches to domestic violence*. Retrieved January 31, 2000, from http://www.mincava.umn.edu

Irvine, J. (1990). Lesbian battering: The search for shelter. In P. Elliott (Ed.), *Confronting lesbian battering* (pp. 25–30). St. Paul: Minnesota Coalition for Battered Women.

Johnson, M. P. (1995). Patriarchal terrorism and common couple violence: Two forms of violence against women. *Journal of Marriage and the Family, 57*, 283–294.

Kivel, P. (1992). *Men's work: How to stop the violence that tears our lives apart*. Center City, MN: Hazelden.

Lein, L., Jacquet, S., Lewis, C., Cole, P., & Williams, B. (2001). With the best intentions: Family violence option and abused women's needs. *Violence Against Women, 7*, 193–210.

Lloyd, S. (1997). The effects of domestic violence on women's employment. *Law and Policy, 19*, 139–165.

Lloyd, S., & Taluc, N. (1999). The effects of male violence on female employment. *Violence Against Women, 5*, 370–392.

Melbin, A., Sullivan, C. M., & Cain, D. (2003). Transitional supportive housing programs: Battered women's perspectives and recommendations. *Affilia, 18*, 445–460.

Menard, A. (2001). Domestic violence and housing: Key policy and program challenges. *Violence Against Women, 7*, 707–720.

Murphy, A. (1997, May 7). Court, bar ready anti-domestic violence clinic in Maywood: Free protection orders. *Chicago Daily Law Bulletin*, p. 3.

National Council of Juvenile and Family Court Judges. (1998). *Family violence: Emerging programs for battered mothers and their children*. Reno, NV: Author.

National Research Council. (1996). *Understanding violence against women*. Washington, DC: National Academy Press.

National Research Council. (1998). *Violence in families: Assessing prevention and treatment programs*. Washington, DC: National Academy Press.

Naumann, P., Langford, D., Torres, S., Campbell, J., & Glass, N. (1999). Women battering in primary care practice. *Family Practice, 16*, 343–352.

Peled, E., & Edleson, J. L. (1994). Advocacy for battered women: A national survey. *Journal of Family Violence, 9*, 285–296.

Pence, E., & Paymar, M. (1993). *Education groups for men who batter: The Duluth model*. New York: Springer Publishing Company.

Renzetti, C. M. (1992). *Violent betrayal: Partner abuse in lesbian relationships*. Newbury Park, CA: Sage.

Ridington, J. (1977–78). The transition process: A feminist environment as reconstitutive milieu. *Victimology: An International Journal, 2*, 563–575.

Rodriguez, R. (1998). Clinical interventions with battered migrant farm worker women. In J. C. Campbell (Ed.), *Empowering survivors of abuse: Health care for battered women and their children* (pp. 271–279). Thousand Oaks, CA: Sage.

Saunders, D. (1996). Feminist–cognitive–behavioral and process–psychodynamic treatments for men who batter: Interaction of abuser traits and treatment models. *Violence and Victims, 11*, 393–414.

Schechter, S. (1982). *Women and male violence: The visions and struggles of the battered women's movement.* Boston: South End Press.

Schneider, E. M. (2000). *Battered women and feminist lawmaking.* New Haven, CT: Yale University Press.

Sedlak, A. J. (1988). Prevention of wife abuse. In V. B. Van Hasselt, R. L. Morrison, A. S. Bellack, & M. Hersen (Eds.), *Handbook of family violence* (pp. 319–358). New York: Plenum Press.

Shepard, M. (1999). Evaluating a coordinated community response. In M. Shepard & E. Pence (Eds.), *Coordinated community response to domestic violence: Lessons from the Duluth model* (pp. 169–191). Newbury Park, CA: Sage.

Sheridan, D. J. (1998). Health-care-based programs for domestic violence survivors. In J. C. Campbell (Ed.), *Empowering survivors of abuse: Health care for battered women and their children* (pp. 23–31). Thousand Oaks, CA: Sage.

Stark, E., & Flitcraft, A. (1996). *Women at risk: Domestic violence and women's health.* Thousand Oaks, CA: Sage.

Steinman, M. (1990). Lowering recidivism among men who batter women. *Journal of Police Science and Administration, 17*, 124–132.

Straus, M. A. (1986). Medical care costs of intrafamily assault and homicide. *Bulletin of the New York Academy of Medicine, 62*, 556–561.

Straus, M. A., Gelles, R. J., & Steinmetz, S. K. (1980). *Behind closed doors: Violence in the American family.* New York: Anchor Press.

Sullivan, C. M. (1991a). Battered women as active helpseekers. *Violence Update, 1*(12), 1, 8, 10–11.

Sullivan, C. M. (1991b). The provision of advocacy services to women leaving abusive partners: An exploratory study. *Journal of Interpersonal Violence, 6*, 41–54.

Sullivan, C. M. (1997). Societal collusion and culpability in intimate male violence: The impact of community response toward women with abusive partners. In A. P. Cardarelli (Ed.), *Violence between intimate partners: Patterns, causes, and effects* (pp. 154–164). Needham Heights, MA: Allyn & Bacon.

Sullivan, C. M. (2000). A model for effectively advocating for women with abusive partners. In J. P. Vincent & E. N. Jouriles (Eds.), *Domestic violence: Guidelines for research-informed practice* (pp. 126–143). London: Jessica Kingsley.

Sullivan, C. M., & Allen, N. E. (2001). Evaluating coordinated community responses for abused women and their children. In S. A. Graham-Bermann & J. L. Edleson (Eds.), *Domestic violence in the lives of children: The future of research, intervention, and social policy* (pp. 269–282). Washington, DC: American Psychological Association.

Sullivan, C. M., & Bybee, D. I. (1999). Reducing violence using community-based advocacy for women with abusive partners. *Journal of Consulting and Clinical Psychology, 67*, 43–53.

Syers, M., & Edleson, J. L. (1992). The combined effects of coordinated criminal justice intervention in woman abuse. *Journal of Interpersonal Violence, 7,* 490–502.

Tolman, R. M., & Bennett, L. W. (1990). A review of quantitative research on men who batter. *Journal of Interpersonal Violence, 5,* 87–118.

Tolman, R. M., & Edleson, J. L. (1995). Intervention for men who batter: A research review. In S. M. Stith & M. A. Straus (Eds.), *Understanding partner violence: Prevalence, causes, consequences, and solutions* (pp. 163–173). Minneapolis, MN: National Council on Family Relations.

Tutty, L. M., Bidgood, B. A., & Rothery, M. A. (1993). Support groups for battered women: Research on their efficacy. *Journal of Family Violence, 8,* 325–343.

Tutty, L. M., Weaver, G., & Rothery, M. (1999). Residents' views of the efficacy of shelter services for assaulted women. *Violence Against Women, 5,* 898–925.

Wauchope, B. (1988, March). *Help-seeking decisions of battered women: A test of learned helplessness and two stress theories.* Paper presented at a meeting of the Eastern Sociological Society, Durham, NH.

Williams, O. J. (1992). Ethnically sensitive practice to enhance treatment participation of African American men who batter. *Families in Society, 73,* 588–595.

Williams, O. J. (1994). Group work with African American men who batter: Toward more ethnically sensitive practice. *Journal of Comparative Family Studies, 25,* 91–103.

Williams, O. J., & Becker, L. R. (1994). Partner abuse programs and cultural competence: The results of a national study. *Violence and Victims, 9,* 287–295.

SECTION INTRODUCTION: SUICIDE PREVENTION AND CROSSCUTTING ISSUES

As noted in chapter 1, intimate partner violence (IPV) and suicide prevention are developing areas of violence prevention research. Though the science of violence prevention is relatively new overall and is necessarily an interdisciplinary field, more intervention and prevention research has been conducted in child maltreatment and youth violence prevention than suicide prevention. Thus, in chapter 10, Bell, Richardson, and Blount address etiology, surveillance, and intervention in suicide prevention. In chapter 11, O'Leary and Woodin cover the need for bringing violence prevention arenas together, particularly child maltreatment and IPV.

That adolescents have the fastest rising suicide rate should be of great concern to professionals and the public. In chapter 10, the authors provide data to substantiate this and argue convincingly for the need for prevention programs. Bell and colleagues also address the alarming suicide rates in other age groups and the especially high rates among American Indians and Alaskan Natives. Risk factors include biological, psychological and psychiatric, and sociological factors, which, along with environmental factors can also be protective if they are positive rather than negative. Each factor receives attention in chapter 10.

Universal, selective, and integrated interventions are detailed in chapter 10, including the apparent efficacy of medication both alone and in combination with other therapies. As with interventions for other problems, suicide interventions face many barriers, such as stigma, financial concerns, and health care system problems. These are addressed by Bell and colleagues.

In chapter 10, the authors also provide a brief review of the Institute of Medicine's (IOM's) 2002 report on reducing suicide and note the recommendation that the National Institute of Mental Health should develop a network of suicide population laboratories aimed at interdisciplinary research in suicide prevention. Other recommendations by the IOM are highlighted as well as recommendations from the 1999 surgeon general's report, such as training for several kinds of individuals in the recognition of signs of suicidality and in interventions. Such training would include clergy, teachers, correctional workers, and others. Bell and colleagues also suggest individuals such as coaches, hairdressers, school personnel, and so on. Chapter 10 ends with the call for much more evaluation research.

Child maltreatment, youth violence, violence against women, and suicide are problems whose pathways are related more often than they are not. As noted elsewhere in this volume, being the victim of child maltreatment is a risk factor for becoming a perpetrator of youth, intimate partner, and sexual violence and a victim of suicide. In chapter 11, the authors briefly address the pathways regarding youth violence and suicide: O'Leary and Woodin tie partner abuse and child maltreatment together and lament the degree to which these two fields have been separate in their terminology, theories, journals, research agendas, and experts. Child and partner abuse appear to covary in 31% of cases. The authors make a number of recommendations as to the rationale for and mechanisms to accomplish joint efforts in child maltreatment and IPV prevention. They also suggest that agencies serving victims of IPV and child maltreatment must begin a functional partnership. One of the problems addressed is the dearth of funding available for researchers who might want to blend IPV and child maltreatment research.

As has also been noted frequently in this volume, most intervention programs are more likely to offer approaches that are aimed at changing knowledge and attitudes rather than at teaching skills to change behaviors. Additionally, IPV intervention programs often lack outcome measures of perpetration and victimization.

Too few child maltreatment and IPV interventions have addressed comorbid problems of perpetrators, such as substance abuse and community and social–ecological variables. O'Leary and Woodin thus suggest that because this is the case, researchers should consider prevention programs that address both forms of violence by targeting youths who show some of these common risk factors. In a similar prevention-related vein, the authors recommend that professionals give frequent consideration to universal as opposed to targeted youth violence prevention programs while continuing to offer targeted programs for youths and adults with elevated risk factors. Finally, these authors make a number of provocative suggestions for bridging the gaps between IPV and child maltreatment researchers.

Another crosscutting issue is the role of culture in research and service in violence prevention. In chapter 12, Reese, Vera, and Caldwell review several concerns over how culture may be defined and how it affects assessment, research, and service in violence prevention. The authors offer a broadened perspective of the role of culture and how to address it in violence prevention activities.

10

SUICIDE PREVENTION

CARL C. BELL, JEROME RICHARDSON, AND MORRIS A. BLOUNT JR.

In this chapter, we discuss the epidemiology of suicide, risk and protective factors for suicide, identification and treatment of at-risk suicidal individuals, and barriers to treatment. Despite the etiologic complexity of this lethal behavior, we believe that a public health approach to psychiatric disorders can reduce this problem in the 21st century.

EPIDEMIOLOGY OF SUICIDE

Statistics indicate that 815,000 people throughout the world died of suicide in 2000 (World Health Organization [WHO], 2004b), and the WHO estimates that by 2020 suicides will claim as many as 1.5 million lives (WHO, 2004a). Over the past 50 years, there has been a downward shift in the age of completed suicides worldwide. Accordingly, individuals age 44 and younger account for a greater percentage of completed suicides, and suicide is now among the three leading causes of death for young men and women in the 15 to 34 age group (WHO, 2001). Although several indicators suggest that the national suicide rate has improved (Gibbons, Hur, Bhamumik, & Mann, 2005), the most recent suicide data indicate that

217

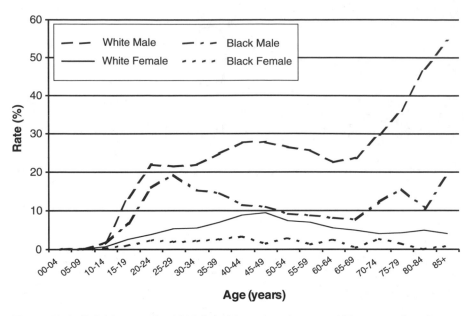

Figure 10.1. Suicide rates for 2002 for African Americans and European Americans. Data from Centers for Disease Control and Prevention (2004).

several populations are still at risk, specifically elderly White American and Native American men. (Kochanek, Murphy, Anderson, & Scott, 2004).

Suicide was the 11th leading cause of death in 2002 (Centers for Disease Control and Prevention [CDC], 2004) but the 2nd leading cause of death for 25- to 34-year-olds and the 3rd leading cause of death among 10- to 24-year-olds (CDC, 2004). There was also an incremental increase in the ratio of male to female suicides among 10- to 24-year-olds. The ratio (males:females) was 3.1:1 for 10- to 14-year-olds, 5:5 for 15- to 19-year-olds, and 6.2:1 for 20- to 24-year-olds (CDC, 2004). The national ratio was 5.6:1 (males:females). Most suicides in the United States in 2002 were committed by European American men (19.98 per 100,000), closely followed by Native American and Alaskan Native men (16.31 per 100,000). During adolescence and throughout adulthood, including later life (15–68 years old), the crude rate of suicide was greater among Native American and Alaskan Native males than European American males. In Figure 10.1, suicide rates for 2002 (the most recent year that complete national vital statistics data are available) are compared between European Americans and African Americans by age and gender. This graph reveals that starting at age 40 until age 85 and older, the crude suicide rate among European American men was at least double that of African American men for each consecutive age group. Younger European American and African American men, however, had similar rates of suicide—a pattern that has been fairly consistent

(Griffith & Bell, 1989). It also reveals the historically low rates of female African American suicide.

RISK FACTORS

Suicide deaths and attempts are complex phenomena that are promoted by biological, psychological or psychiatric, and social–ecological risk factors.

Biological Factors

Some of the neurobiological aspects that may contribute to suicidal behavior include dysregulation of the body's primary stress response systems, the hypothalamic–pituitary–adrenal axis, and changes in the system of monoamines such as dopamine, norepinephrine, and serotonin (Institute of Medicine [IOM], 2002). In addition, there is evidence of an association between suicidality and genetics. For example, high rates of suicide have been found among biological families, adopted children whose biological families have elevated rates, and identical versus fraternal twins (IOM, 2002).

Psychological or Psychiatric Factors

Affective Disorder

The most frequently cited percentage of individuals with major depression that would eventually die of suicide (15%) is based on a meta-analysis conducted some time ago by Guze and Robins (1970). More recent studies have reported much smaller estimates using current statistical modeling approaches. For example, Blair-West, Mellsop, and Eyeson-Annan (1997) found 3.4%, and Inskip, Harris, and Barrclough (1998) found 6%. The prevalence of major depression in individuals who have died by committing suicide depends on the age and gender of the population (U.S. Public Health Service, 1999). Conwell et al. (1996) found that among suicide victims ages 21 to 97, unipolar major depression increased with age.

Schizophrenia

The suicide risk among individuals with schizophrenia is high. It has been estimated that at least 10% of persons with schizophrenia die by committing suicide (Roy, 2000), but this percentage is even higher (25%–33%) among people with schizophrenia in psychiatric hospitals. Most of them tend to be young, unmarried men who exhibit depressive symptoms and have made previous suicide attempts (IOM, 2002).

Substance Use Disorders

Suicide victims ages 16 to 19 were more likely than 13- to 15-year-olds to be intoxicated with alcohol and to meet criteria for substance abuse disorder (Brent, Baugher, Bridge, Chen, & Chiappetta, 1999; Conwell et al., 1996). Suicide victims for whom heavy alcohol consumption is an important factor are also prevalent among populations such as Native Americans and Alaska Natives (May et al., 2002).

Sociological Factors

Data on suicide rates by levels of education and marital status are not regularly examined by any U.S. government agency. A few studies exist, and differences in education and marital status have been shown to be associated with varying suicide rates. In some studies, less education and divorce was associated with higher suicide rates (IOM, 2002). The National Institute for Occupational Safety and Health (2000) has examined differences in suicide by occupation, and depending on which variables are controlled, different occupations have higher rates than others. The most well-known sociologic theoretical explanation for the motivations behind suicide was proposed by Durkheim (1951), who divided these motivations into four types: egoistic, altruistic, anomic, and fatalistic. Although this theory is purported to help explain different suicide rates in various populations (Bell & Clark, 1998), there are no data to support these explanations.

Suicide rates for men in jails are about 9 to 15 times higher than rates for the general population. Prison suicide rates are about one and one half times higher than rates in the general population (Bell, 2005). A comprehensive study by Felitti et al. (1998) showed strong and graded relationships between adverse childhood experiences (psychological abuse, physical abuse, sexual abuse, violence against the mother, living with household members who were substance abusers, living with household members who were mentally ill or suicidal, and living with household members who were ever imprisoned) and risk for attempted suicide. Persons who experienced four or more categories of childhood exposure to adverse experiences, compared with those who had experienced none, had a 12.2-fold increase in suicide attempts.

RESILIENCY: PROTECTIVE FACTORS

Hopelessness, depression, and various levels of stress are correlated with suicidal ideation and suicide. Similarly, protective factors that inoculate against suicidal behavior are multifaceted and consist of factors that are biological, psychological, social, and environmental. Resilience in people has been defined as including "intrapsychic strengths" of trust, self-regulation, autonomy, self-esteem, empathy, altruism, an internal locus of control, flexibility, optimism, invulnerability, and aspects of health or social competence (Zigler & Trickett, 1978) and being "stress-resistant" (Masten, 1989). Investigators also measure the absence of psychopathology or maladaptive behavior as an indicator of resilience against high-risk conditions (Rutter & Quinton, 1984). Apfel and Simon (1996) and Wolin and Wolin (1996) have provided comprehensive characteristics of resiliency, and Bell (2001) has suggested more esoteric characteristics of resiliency found in other cultures.

Biological Protective Factors

There has been considerable biogenetic and heritability research on dimensional models of personality functioning. The heritability of neuroticism is typically estimated to be approximately 50%; the heritability of extraversion is estimated at 60%; and the domains of agreeableness, openness, and conscientiousness are estimated to have a heritability of 40% (Plomin & Caspi, 1999). Thus, despite being thought of as psychological attributes, intellectual ability (Masten, 1989) and personality traits (Tedeschi & Calhoun, 1996) have genetic and biological underpinnings, and as a result, are currently unalterable. However, evidence suggests that facilitating the physiologic pattern of toughness increases tolerance to stressors, emotional stability, and immune system enhancement (Dienstbier, 1991). Thus, through stress inoculation, acquired biological correlates of resiliency can be cultivated.

Psychological Protective Factors

Individuals use conscious cognitive strategies (Lazarus & Folkman, 1984) that may be protective from suicidal behavior. In addition, they may rely on involuntary mental mechanisms to reduce subjective stress. Intrapsychic protective factors, for example, include the manner in which individuals perceive themselves (e.g., perceptions of self-reliance, resilience, and invulnerability or vulnerability). Self-perceptions may also be positively shaped by living through trauma, which can create a sense of competence or stress inoculation. Behavioral parent-training techniques, with other interventions based in family systems theory designed to improve family relations, may strengthen intrapsychic protective factors (Borowsky, Ireland, & Resnick, 2001; Tolan & Mitchell, 1989).

Most cognitive theories of depression suggest that depressed individuals view the future in a pessimistic light (Kuiper, Derry, & MacDonald, 1982).

Similarly, helplessness theorists view low expectancies for the occurrence of highly desired outcomes as the proximal cause of a wide range of depressive deficits (Seligman, 1975). Antithetical to these notions are emotional protective factors that enhance a sense of emotional well-being (Fredrickson, 1998). Such positive emotions stem from the feeling resulting from one's psychological needs being met, optimism, hope, happiness, trust, and life-satisfaction. Thus, emotional well-being is likely a significant protective factor for attempting suicide.

Social Protective Factors

Individual characteristics may assist some individuals in being better able to maintain social support systems than others. There is evidence of the beneficial effects of positive attitudes and interpersonal orientations (such as sociability) on protecting against depression (Antonucci, Fuhrer, & Dartigues, 1997). The role of interpersonal skills in protecting against stress is supported by empirical data and descriptive qualitative reports (Luthar, 1991; Murphy & Moriarty, 1976). These findings are given greater importance considering that the implementation of school-based programs can enhance children's social skills and thereby inoculate them against the deleterious effects of stressful life events (Weissberg, Barton, & Shriver, 1997). Resnick et al. (1997) noted that a perceived parental and family connectedness was significantly protective against suicide for youth. Evidence suggests that socially supportive relationships can promote psychological and physical health and therefore are an important aspect of resiliency (Sarason, Sarason, & Pierce, 1990). Religious practices may also impact of the availability of social support systems (IOM, 2002).

Environmental Protective Factors

Finally, there are environmental protective factors, such as positive life events (Luthar, 1991; Rutter & Quinton, 1984) and socioeconomic status. The IOM's (2002) recent report on suicide highlights the historically low rates of suicide in African American women despite the abundance of risk factors in this population. Unfortunately, research on what protects African American women from the risks of suicide is limited, and much more research needs to be conducted in this area.

INTERVENTIONS

Intervention practices in the United States are usually divided into universal prevention strategies for the general population, selective prevention strategies for population subsets, and indicated prevention strategies for high-risk individuals. There are also integrated prevention methods that combine any or all these categories (IOM, 2002).

Universal Prevention Strategies

Universal strategies include media campaigns aimed at widespread education about suicide and components to improve media response to suicide, with the purpose of diminishing or eliminating imitation and modeling of suicidal behavior. Studies have shown that imitation and modeling do occur with suicidal behavior in the forms of temporal clusters of suicides in a particular community or culture, suicide among family members, and suicide following exposure to media presentation of a real or fictional suicide (Gould, 2001). In fact, media attention about a real or fictional suicide is associated with an increase in suicide deaths 1 to 2 weeks after the story is released (Bell & Clark, 1998). In response to the imitation that occurs after media portrayal of suicide, various agencies have collaborated to offer guidelines to correct this problem (IOM, 2002). Some of the suggestions that have been offered are that accounts of suicide should neither romanticize nor normalize suicide, nor should suicide be portrayed as heroic or romantic (American Foundation for Suicide Prevention, 2001).

Another aspect of universal prevention is the reduction of access to means of suicide. Some strategies have focused on acetaminophen overdose, prescription drug overdose, jumping from buildings and bridges, automobile carbon monoxide inhalation, and railway suicides (IOM, 2002). Other strategies have targeted the use of firearms, the most common method of suicide for all demographic groups in the United States (CDC, 1994).

Changes in packaging of pills and limiting the number of pills sold in one package have been shown to possibly reduce morbidity and mortality of acetaminophen overdose, which is more lethal than aspirin because of liver toxicity. Likewise, the use of blister packs, which separate the pills individually and make opening the packs more difficult, has also been shown in some studies to make a difference in suicide rates from acetaminophen overdose, the most common over-the-counter medication used for suicide (IOM, 2002). With prescription drugs, the higher the number of per capita physicians, the higher the suicide rates from these methods, a fact attributed primarily to the number of physicians available to write prescriptions (Forster & Frost, 1985). The interventions of limiting the amount of drug prescribed at one time and using less lethal drugs (such as the use of selective serotonin reuptake inhibitors [SSRIs] as opposed to tricyclic antidepressants) have resulted in a decrease in suicide by this method (Gibbons et al., 2005).

Inhalation of automobile exhaust fumes is also a common method of suicide and is correlated with the availability of automobiles (Ostrom,

Thorson, & Eriksson, 1996). This form of suicide is often impulsive and frequently occurs under the influence of alcohol (Skopek & Perkins, 1998). Suggestions to decrease lethality in this form of suicide include detoxifying emissions, having idling automobiles cut off after a certain amount of time, and modifying the ends of tail pipes to make it more difficult to attach hoses (Ostrom et al., 1996).

Interventions for railway suicides, which entail impulsivity and high fatality rates, involve physically separating passengers from train beds, improved surveillance of passengers by station staff, liaison to hospitals for areas with a high density of patients with mental illness, availability of emergency hotline telephones, redesign of train bumpers, and use of slow approaches to stations (Beskow, Thorson, & Ostrom, 1994).

Several studies have shown that the presence of a gun in the home is highly predictive of its use for completed suicide. Conversely, if a gun is not in the home, it is used for suicide infrequently (Beautrais, Joyce, & Mulder, 1996). Higher risk is associated with handguns than long guns, loaded guns than unloaded guns, and unlocked guns than locked guns (Brent et al., 1993). One possible intervention is widespread stricter firearm legislation, because the firearm suicide rate and the overall suicide rate are related to the strictness of gun control laws and the prevalence of gun ownership (Killias, 1993; Loftin, McDowall, Wiersema, & Cottey, 1991; Sloan et al., 1990).

There is limited research on the effectiveness of hotlines and crisis centers in actually reducing suicide, but usage is high (IOM, 2002). Services offered include anonymous or nonanonymous phone counseling for suicidal people and family members and friends as well as face-to-face counseling and referrals by staff with various types of training. Research on effectiveness of hotlines shows either reductions in suicide rates (Bagley, 1968) or no change in suicide rates (Lester, 1990). There has been no documentation of increased suicide rates (IOM, 2002).

Selective Prevention Strategies

Selective interventions include screening programs to identify and assess at-risk groups and gatekeeper training, consultation, and education services (IOM, 2002). The identification of at-risk individuals can be accomplished when the screening is routine and occurs in a setting where these individuals can be found. For example, adolescents can be screened at school with a screening tool such as the Suicide Ideation Questionnaire (Reynolds, 1998). Research has suggested that screening combined with supportive intervention can work to decrease suicidal behaviors (Thompson, Eggert, Randell, & Pike, 2001).

For adolescents, gatekeeper training can involve training school professionals on assessment and intervention with at-risk adolescents (Eggert, Randell, Thompson, & Johnson, 1997). Two such programs, Living Works Suicide Intervention Workshop and Suicide Options Awareness and Relief (Project SOAR), have been studied and show that trained gatekeepers are more likely to recognize warning signs of suicide (Eggert et al., 1997; King & Smith, 2000). Likewise, primary care clinicians can serve as gatekeepers for both the adolescent and adult population (IOM, 2002). One Swedish study showed that structured educational programs for general medicine physicians with topics of recognition and treatment of depressive disorders resulted in lower suicide rates (Rutz, von Knorring, & Walinder, 1989).

Indicated Prevention Strategies

Indicated prevention involves working with population subsets that evidence early warning signs of suicide risk and includes family support training, skill-building support groups, case management, and referral resources for crisis intervention and treatment for at-risk individuals (IOM, 2002). The understanding of indicated prevention strategies for at-risk individuals, that is, treatment of psychiatric disorders, is much further developed than the understanding of universal, selective, or integrated strategies.

Assessment

Although risk factors for suicide identify many false positive and false negative cases that affect their usefulness in long-term prediction of suicide, they are helpful in short-term prediction of suicide and are useful in the assessment interviews of psychiatric patients. It is important to assess current suicidal symptoms (including ideation, intent, and plans) and current abilities to cope with acute or chronic stress (Frierson, Melikian, & Wadman, 2002; IOM, 2002).

Treatment

Following assessment, interventions may include psychoactive medications, electroconvulsive therapy (ECT), and psychotherapy. Although there is evidence showing that medication effects on suicidality may be independent from effects on the mental illness (IOM, 2002), 90% of suicide occurs in people with mental disorders, so treating the underlying disorder may reduce risk. Major categories of drugs used to prevent suicide are antidepressants, mood stabilizers, anxiolytic medications, and antipsychotic medications.

Antidepressant medications (SSRIs, in particular) have been shown in several studies to reduce suicide rates (Rich, 1999). More recently, however,

SSRIs have been implicated in promoting increased suicidal behaviors (Fergusson et al., 2005), and such findings have resulted in the Food and Drug Administration's insisting on putting a black box warning on antidepressants (Newman, 2004); however, these findings are being contested (Mitchell, 2005). Tricyclics are effective for treatment of depressive symptoms but are lethal in overdose; thus, their use in suicidal patients causes concern (Gibbons et al., 2005). Lithium carbonate (a mood stabilizer) has been shown to reduce suicide rates in patients treated for bipolar disorder, an effect that was shown to be separate from its antidepressant and anti-manic effects (Tondo, Hennen, & Baldessarini, 2001). The anticonvulsants (valproic acid, divalproex, and carbamazepine), though used for bipolar disorder, have not been studied for their effectiveness on suicide. Anti-psychotic medications may also be effective for reducing suicidal behavior when suicidality is a feature of psychosis (IOM, 2002). Several studies have shown clozapine to be particularly effective in reducing suicidal behavior in schizophrenic patients (Meltzer, 1999). Data relating anxiolytics (e.g., benzodiazepines) to suicide are limited, though some reports suggest that use of benzodiazepines is associated with increased risk of suicide. Causality is unknown in these situations (Neutel & Patten, 1997).

Medicine alone is not sufficient for effective outcomes in individuals who need to be supported while pursuing adequate care for mental disorders that put them at risk for suicide (IOM, 2002). Unfortunately, evaluations of long-term therapeutic interventions are rare. Though many studies show cognitive–behavioral therapy is effective in treating mental disorders such as depression and posttraumatic stress disorder, which can increase suicide risk, few have shown cognitive–behavioral therapy to be effective for actual suicidal behavior and intent (Linehan, 1997). One recent development in this area, however, is showing promise. Beck and colleagues (e.g., Henriques, Beck, & Brown, 2003) are currently conducting a randomized clinical trial of a brief cognitive intervention for adolescents and adults who attempt suicide. The 10-session protocol being tested focuses on replacing maladap-tive coping strategies (e.g., suicidal behaviors) with adaptive coping strate-gies. Preliminary results report that the intervention is associated with a reduction in subsequent suicide attempts of approximately 50% over an enhanced services-as-usual condition (Henriques et al., 2003).

Research has shown ECT to have some short-term effect on suicidality because of its rapid onset of effectiveness. There is, however, no evidence that ECT has a long-term effect on the suicide rate (Goodwin & Jamison, 1990; Prudic & Sackeim, 1999).

Suicide is the most common precipitant for psychiatric inpatient admis-sion (Friedman, 1989). However, there have not been randomized clinical trials to determine if hospitalization of high-risk patients saves lives (Ameri-can Academy of Child and Adolescent Psychiatry, 2001). The purpose of hospitalization is to reduce suicidal thoughts, anxiety, and other symptoms associated with suicide attempts, though some patients remain suicidal if symptoms improve without resolution of life stressors (IOM, 2002). The postdischarge period is also important because it is a period of significantly increased risk of suicide (Appleby, Dennehy, Thomas, Faragher, & Lewis, 1999). These rates are lowered if discharged patients are compliant with treatment (Modestin, Schwarzenbach, & Wurmle, 1992).

Integrated Prevention Methods

Integrated approaches include incorporating all levels of prevention and include the targets of reduction of mental illness and the promotion of mental health using macro- to microlevel changes in social policy and media training. They also establish coordinated services and improve data gathering and surveillance systems. Examples of programs are the Prevention of Suicide in Primary Care Elderly: Collaborative Trial (PROSPECT; Bruce et al., 2004), Maryland Youth Suicide Prevention Strategy (IOM, 2002), and the Suicide Prevention Programs for Rural American Indian Communities (Oldsmith, Pellmar, Kleinman, & Bunney, 2002). A multicenter trial funded by the National Institute of Mental Health, PROSPECT uses primary-care-based depression care managers to conduct a structured screening and treatment intervention versus usual care on depressive symptoms, suicidal ideation, hopelessness, and functional and quality-of-life measures. At 8 months, 70% of intervention patients who had suicidal thoughts at the outset were free of them compared with 44% of usual care patients (Bruce et al., 2004). The State of Maryland implemented a comprehensive suicide prevention model in the middle 1980s and later chose to focus on reducing youth suicide. In the 15- to 24-year-old age group, there was a 21.4% drop in suicide rates, although the national rate increased 11% during the decade (Westray, 2001). Similar integrated programs have been instituted over the past 3 decades for rural American Indian communities (Levy, 1988). The suicide rate per 100,000 fell from 173.1 in 1972 through 1976 to 21.5 in 1977 through 1980 (May, 1987).

BARRIERS TO TREATMENT

Barriers to effective treatment include stigma of mental illness, financial barriers, mental health system barriers, clinician barriers to treatment, and patient barriers (IOM, 2002).

Stigma

Stigma causes people to fear, reject, and distance themselves from people with mental illness (Corrigan & Penn, 1998; Hinshaw & Cicchetti,

2000). Stigma promotes public discrimination against people with mental illness in housing and employment plus discrimination in payment for treatment (Corrigan & Penn, 1998; Hanson, 1998). As a result, many Americans are less likely to seek mental health treatment for themselves, even though they generally support mental health treatment for people with mental disorders (Pescosolido et al., 2000). The stigma of mental illness may also inhibit patients from bringing up mental health concerns to primary care physicians and discourage patients who begin mental health treatment from continuing it (Sirey et al., 2001; U.S. Department of Health and Human Services [USDHHS], 2001). Moreover, just as the families of people with mental illness may conceal the illness or not seek treatment because of stigma, so may the families of suicidal people tend to conceal suicidal behavior, hoping to avoid shame or embarrassment or societal perception that they are to blame (U.S. Public Health Service, 2001).

Financial Barriers

The demand for mental health services is more responsive to price than other types of health services (Taube, Kessler, & Burns, 1986). This creates problems for the uninsured and even for individuals with insurance. People without insurance experience more barriers to care, have more delay in seeking care, and have more unmet mental health needs (Ayanian, Weissman, Schneider, Ginsburg, & Zalslavsky, 2000). Having health insurance, however, does not guarantee receipt of services, because of disparities in mental health coverage by insurance companies (USDHHS, 1999). Over the past decade, disparities in mental health coverage by insurance companies have led to a 50% decrease in the mental health portion of total health care costs paid by insurance companies (Hay Group, 1998).

Health Care System Barriers

Separate funding streams, varying eligibility rules, and disparate administrative sources creating artificial boundaries between treatment settings and sectors all contribute to a fragmented system with additional barriers to mental health treatment (IOM, 2002; Ridgely, Goldman, & Willenbring, 1990). Patients with the dual diagnoses of substance abuse and mental health problems are the most affected. They are also at increased risk for suicide (USDHHS, 1999). There are problems with the linkages between mental health care and primary care, emergency department care, substance abuse care, and school-based programs. The linkage between inpatient care and community-based care needs to be improved because the time period after discharge and before the first outpatient appointment is when many suicides occur (Appleby et al., 1999).

There are clinician barriers to treatment, including nondetection of suicidal thoughts days before suicide. A systematic review of published studies found that 16% to 20% of completed suicide victims had had contact with primary care just days before their suicides (Pirkis & Burgess, 1998). Physicians often do not ask patients about suicidal thoughts for fear of triggering suicidal behavior (Michel, 2000), and there have been few guidelines for suicide assessments by professional organizations (IOM, 2002). The lack of clinical training is another reason that at-risk patients may not be identified (Bernstein, Feldberg, & Brown, 1991).

Each at-risk group also has barriers that are specific to that group. For the elderly, some of the barriers are Medicare limits on office visits and hospitalization (USDHHS, 1999) and noncoverage of prescription drugs. One fourth of the elderly report they would not seek mental health services if needed (Mickus, Colenda, & Hogan, 2000). Limited transportation and stigma play a role (USDHHS, 1999). For adolescents, who typically access care in emergency departments, the low rate of aftercare follow-up is common (IOM, 2002). Lack of correctional mental health care is another societal barrier contributing to the problem of suicide (Bell, 2005).

Although there are a number of barriers, there are some bright spots. Research on the barriers within the mental health system has resulted in the development of better models for the delivery of more integrated mental health care. These include multisystemic treatment, programs for children and adolescents, assertive community treatment programs, and combined programs for people with substance abuse and mental health disorders (USDHHS, 1999).

CONCLUSION

The IOM's (2002) report on reducing suicide made several recommendations for beginning to solve the problem of suicide within the United States. The first recommendation was that the "National Institute of Mental Health (in collaboration with other agencies) should develop and support a national network of suicide research Population Laboratories devoted to interdisciplinary research on suicide and suicide prevention across the life cycle" (p. 427). The second recommendation was that "national monitoring of suicide and suicidality should be improved" (p. 433), and the report listed concrete steps to accomplish this goal. The report also suggested that primary care providers, who are often the first and only medical contact for suicidal patients, should be trained on tools for recognition and screening of patients at risk for suicide. And finally, the report suggested that "programs for suicide prevention should be developed, tested, expanded, and implemented through funding from appropriate agencies including NIMH [National Institute of

Mental Health], DVA [Division of Veterans' Affairs], CDC, and SAMHSA [Substance Abuse and Mental Health Services Administration]" (p. 438). Actualizing the IOM recommendations would greatly improve the methodology for basic suicide research as well as improve prevention and intervention research. Methodologically, such recommendations may fix the problem of studying a rare phenomenon by ensuring that large-scale stratified surveys are conducted regularly so that more accurate data on suicidal behavior, including the risk and protective factors, are provided.

The recommendations made by the surgeon general (U.S. Public Health Service, 1999) should be incorporated into those made by the IOM. Some of the surgeon general's recommendations are that interventions could be improved by training the clergy, teachers, correctional workers, and social workers about suicide management and aftercare interventions. Family members should be trained to recognize, respond to, and refer people showing signs of suicide risk. This training should be extended to coaches, hairdressers, faith leaders, and others. Schools, community care facilities, and workplaces need to be used as access points for mental and physical health services and to provide support to families and friends of individuals who commit suicide. To advance the science of suicide prevention, mental health professionals require a better understanding of risk and protective factors, their interaction, and their effects on suicide and suicidal behaviors. In addition, more research is needed on effective clinical treatments for suicidal individuals and culture-specific interventions. Mental health professionals also need to ensure that evaluation components are included in all suicide prevention programs so that successful programs can be replicated.

REFERENCES

American Academy of Child and Adolescent Psychiatry. (2001). Summary of the practice parameters for the assessment and treatment of children and adolescents with suicidal behavior. *Journal of the American Academy of Child and Adolescent Psychiatry, 40,* 495–499.

American Foundation for Suicide Prevention. (2001). *Reporting on suicide: Recommendations for the media.* Retrieved September 11, 2002, from http://www.afsp.org//index-1.htm

Anderson, R. (2002). Deaths: Leading causes. *National Vital Statistics Reports, 50,* 1–86.

Antonucci, T. C., Fuhrer, R., & Dartigues, J. F. (1997). Social relations and depressive symptomatology in a sample of community-dwelling French older adults. *Psychological Aging, 12,* 189–195.

Apfel, R. J., & Simon, B. (Eds.). (1996). *Minefields in their hearts: The mental health of children in war and communal violence.* New Haven, CT: Yale University Press.

Appleby, L., Dennehy, J. A., Thomas, C. S., Faragher, E. B., & Lewis, G. (1999). Aftercare and clinical characteristics of people with mental illness who commit suicide: A case-control study. *Lancet, 353,* 1397–1400.

Ayanian, J. Z., Weissman, J. S., Schneider, E. C., Ginsburg, J. A., & Zalslavsky, A. M. (2000). Unmet health needs of uninsured adults in the United States. *Journal of the American Medical Association, 284,* 2061–2069.

Bagley, C. (1968). The evaluation of a suicide prevention scheme by an ecological method. *Social Science and Medicine, 2,* 1–14.

Beautrais, A. L., Joyce, P. R., & Mulder, R. T. (1996). Access to firearms and the risk of suicide: A case control study. *Australian and New Zealand Journal of Psychiatry, 30,* 741–748.

Bell, C. C. (2001). Cultivating resiliency in youth. *Journal of Adolescent Health, 29,* 375–381.

Bell, C. C. (2005). Correctional psychiatry. In B. J. Sadock & V. A. Sadock (Eds.), *Comprehensive textbook of psychiatry* (8th ed., Vol. 2, pp. 4002–4012). Baltimore: Williams & Wilkins.

Bell, C. C., & Clark, D. (1998). Adolescent suicide. *Pediatric Clinics of North America, 45,* 365–376.

Bernstein, R. M., Feldberg, C., & Brown, R. (1991). After-hours coverage in psychology training clinics. *Professional Psychology: Research and Practice, 22,* 204–208.

Beskow, J., Thorson, J., & Ostrom, M. (1994). National suicide prevention programme and railway suicide. *Social Science and Medicine, 38,* 447–451.

Blair-West, G. W., Mellsop, G. W., & Eyeson-Annan, M. L. (1997). Down-rating lifetime suicide risk in major depression. *Acta Psychiatrica Scandinavica, 95,* 259–263.

Borowsky, I. W., Ireland, M., & Resnick, M. D. (2001). Adolescent suicide attempts: Risks and protectors. *Pediatrics, 107,* 485–493.

Brent, D. A., Baugher, M., Bridge, J., Chen, T., & Chiappetta, L. (1999). Age- and sex-related risk factors for adolescent suicide. *Journal of the American Academy of Child and Adolescent Psychiatry, 38,* 1497–1505.

Brent, D. A., Perper, J. A., Moritz, G. M., Baugher, M., Schweers, J., & Roth, C. (1993). Firearms and adolescent suicide. A community case-control study. *American Journal of Diseases of Children, 147,* 1066–1071.

Bruce, M. L., Ten Have, T. R., Reynolds, C. F., Katz, I. I., Schulberg, H. C., Mulsant, B. H., et al. (2004). Reducing suicidal ideation and depressive symptoms in depressed older primary care patients. *Journal of the American Medical Association, 291,* 1081–1091.

Centers for Disease Control and Prevention. (1994). Deaths resulting from firearm and motor-vehicle related injuries—United States, 1968–1991. *Journal of the American Medical Association, 271,* 495–496.

Centers for Disease Control and Prevention. (2004). Web-based Injury Statistics Query and Reporting System (WISQARS) [Data file]. Retrieved March 3, 2005, from www.cdc.gov/ncipc/wisqars

Conwell, Y., Duberstein, P. R., Cox, C., Herrmann, J. H., Forbes, N. T., & Caine, E. D. (1996). Relationship of age and Axis I diagnoses in victims of completed suicide: A psychological autopsy study. *American Journal of Psychiatry, 153,* 1001–1008.

Corrigan, P. W., & Penn, D. L. (1998). Lessons from social psychology on discrediting psychiatric stigma. *American Psychologist, 54,* 765–776.

Dienstbier, R. A. (1991). Behavioral correlates of sympathoadrenal reactivity: The toughness model. *Medicine and Science in Sports and Exercise, 23,* 846–852.

Durkheim, E. (1951). *Suicide: A study in sociology* (J. A. Spaulding & G. Simpson, Trans.). New York: Free Press.

Eggert, L. L., Randell, B. P., Thompson, E. A., & Johnson, C. L. (1997). *Washington state youth suicide prevention program: Report of activities.* Seattle: University of Washington.

Felitti, V. J., Anda, R. F., Nordenberg, D., Williamson, D. F., Spitz, A. M., Edwards, V., et al. (1998). Relationship of child abuse and household dysfunction to many of the leading causes of death in adults: The adverse childhood experiences (ACE) study. *American Journal of Preventive Medicine, 14,* 245–258.

Fergusson, D., Doucette, S., Glass, K. C., Shapiro, S., Healy, D., Herbert, P., & Hutton, B. (2005). Association between suicide attempts and selective serotonin reuptake inhibitors: Systematic review of randomised controlled trials. *British Medical Journal, 330,* 396–399.

Forster, D. P., & Frost, C. E. (1985). Medicinal self-poisoning and prescription frequency. *Acta Psychiatrica Scandinavica, 71,* 567–574.

Fredrickson, B. L. (1998). What good are positive emotions? *Review of General Psychology, 2,* 300–319.

Friedman, R. S. (1989). Hospital treatment of the suicidal patient. In D. G. Jacobs & H. P. Brown (Eds.), *Suicide: Understanding and responding* (pp. 379–402). Madison, CT: International Universities Press.

Frierson, R. I., Melikian, M., & Wadman, P. C. (2002). *Principles of suicide risk assessment: How to interview depressed patients and tailor treatment.* Retrieved September 20, 2002, from http://www.postgradmed.com/issues/2002/09_02/frierson4.htm

Gibbons, R. D., Hur, K., Bhamumik, D. K., & Mann, J. J. (2005). The relationship between antidepressant medication use and rate of suicide. *Archives of General Psychiatry, 62,* 165–172.

Goodwin, F. K., & Jamison, K. R. (1990). *Manic-depressive illness.* New York: Oxford University Press.

Gould, M. S. (2001). Suicide and the media. In H. Hendin & J. J. Mann (Eds.), *Annals of the New York Academy of Sciences: Vol. 932. The clinical science of suicide prevention* (pp. 200–224). New York: New York Academy of Sciences.

Griffith, E. H., & Bell, C. C. (1989) Recent trends in suicide and homicide among Blacks. *Journal of the American Medical Association, 262,* 2265–2269.

Guze, S. B., & Robins, E. (1970). Suicide and primary affective disorders. *British Journal of Psychiatry, 117,* 437–438

Hanson, K. W. (1998). Public opinion and the mental health parity debate: Lessons from the survey literature. *Psychiatric Services, 49,* 1059–1066.

Hay Group. (1998). *Health care plan design and cost trends: 1988 through 1997.* Washington, DC: Author.

Henriques, G., Beck, A. T., & Brown, G. K. (2003). Cognitive therapy for adolescent and young adult suicide attempters. *American Behavioral Scientist, 46,* 1258–1268.

Hinshaw, S. P., & Cicchetti, D. (2000). Stigma and mental disorder: Conceptions of illness, public attitudes, personal disclosure and social policy. *Development and Psychopathology, 12,* 555–598.

Inskip, H. M., Harris, E. C., & Barrclough, B. (1998). Lifetime risk of suicide for affective disorder, alcoholism and schizophrenia. *British Journal of Psychiatry, 172,* 35–37.

Institute of Medicine. (2002). *Reducing suicide: A national imperative.* Washington, DC: National Academy Press.

Killias, M. (1993). International correlations between gun ownership and rates of homicide and suicide. *Canadian Medical Association Journal, 148,* 1721–1725.

King, K. A., & Smith, J. (2000). Project SOAR: A training program to increase school counselors' knowledge and confidence regarding suicide prevention and intervention. *Journal of School Health, 70,* 402–407.

Kochanek, K. D., Murphy, S. L., Anderson, R. N., & Scott, C. (2004). *National vital statistics reports: Vol. 53. Deaths: Final data for 2002.* Hyattsville, MD: National Center for Health Statistics.

Kuiper, N. A., Derry, P. A., & MacDonald, M. R. (1982). Self-reference and person perception in depression: A social cognition perspective. In G. Weary & H. Mirels (Eds.), *Integrations of social and clinical psychology* (pp. 79–103). New York: Oxford University Press.

Lazarus, R., & Folkman, S. (1984). *Stress, appraisal, and coping.* New York: Springer Publishing Company.

Lester, D. (1990). Was gas detoxification or establishment of suicide prevention centers responsible for the decline in the British suicide rate? *Psychological Reports, 66,* 286.

Levy, J. E. (1988). The effects of labeling on health behavior and treatment programs among North American Indians. *American Indian and Alaska Native Mental Health Research Monograph, 1.*

Linehan, M. M. (1997). Behavioral treatments of suicidal behaviors. Definitional obfuscation and treatment outcomes. In *Annals of the New York Academy of Sciences: Vol. 836. The neurobiology of suicide: From the bench to the clinic* (pp. 302–328). New York: New York Academy of Sciences.

Loftin, C., McDowall, D., Wiersema, B., & Cottey, T. J. (1991). Effects of restrictive licensing of handguns on homicide and suicide in the District of Columbia. *New England Journal of Medicine, 325*, 1615–1620.

Luthar, S. S. (1991). Vulnerability and resilience: A study of high-risk adolescents. *Child Development, 62*, 600–616.

Masten, A. S. (1989). Resilience in development: Implications of the study of successful adaptation for developmental psychopathology. In D. Cicchetti (Ed.), *Rochester Symposium on Developmental Psychopathology: Vol. 1. The emergence of a discipline* (pp. 261–294). Hillsdale, NJ: Erlbaum.

May, P. A. (1987). Suicide and self-destruction among American Indian youths. *American Indian and Alaska Native Mental Health Research, 1*, 52–69.

May, P. A., Van Winkle, N. W., Williams, M. B., McFeeley, P. J., DeBruyn, L. M., & Serna, P. (2002). Alcohol and suicide death among American Indians: 1980–1998. *Suicide and Life-Threatening Behavior, 32*, 240–255.

Meltzer, H. Y. (1999). Suicide and schizophrenia: Clozapine and the InterSePT study. *Journal of Clinical Psychiatry, 60*, 47–50.

Michel, K. (2000). Suicide prevention and primary care. In K. Hawton & K. van Heeringen (Eds.), *International handbook of suicide and attempted suicide* (pp. 661–674). Chichester, England: Wiley.

Mickus, M., Colenda, C. C., & Hogan, A. J. (2000). Knowledge of mental health benefits and preferences for type of mental health providers among the general public. *Psychiatric Services, 51*, 199–202.

Mitchell, A. J. (2005). Do selective serotonin reuptake inhibitors cause suicide? Data seem to be incorrect. *British Medical Journal, 330*, 1149–1150.

Modestin, J., Schwarzenbach, F. A., & Wurmle, O. (1992). Therapy factors in treating severely ill psychiatric patients. *British Journal of Medical Psychology, 65*, 147–156.

Murphy, L. B., & Moriarty, A. E. (1976). *Vulnerability, coping and growth.* New Haven, CT: Yale University Press.

National Center for Health Statistics. (2005). *Health, United States, 2001 with urban and rural health chartbook.* Hyattsville, MD: Author.

National Institute for Occupational Safety and Health. (2000). *Worker health chartbook, 2000.* Retrieved September 11, 2002, from http://www.cdc.gov/noish/pdfs/2000-127.pdf

Neutel, C. I., & Patten, S. B. (1997). Risk of suicide attempts after benzodiazepine and/or antidepressant use. *Annals of Epidemiology, 7*, 568–574.

Newman, T. B. (2004). A black-box warning for antidepressants in children? *New England Journal of Medicine, 351*, 1595–1598.

Oldsmith, S. K., Pellmar, T. C., Kleinman, A. M., & Bunney, W. E. (Eds.). (2002). *Reducing suicide: A national imperative.* Washington, DC: National Academy Press.

Ostrom, M., Thorson, J., & Eriksson, A. (1996). Carbon monoxide suicide from car exhausts. *Social Science and Medicine, 42*, 447–451.

Pescosolido, B. A., Martin, J. K., Link, B. G., Kikuzawa, S., Burgos, G., Swindle, R., et al. (2000). *Americans' views of mental health and illness at century's end: Continuity and change*. (Public Report on the MacArthur Mental Health Module, 1996 General Social Survey). Bloomington: Indiana University, Indiana Consortium of Mental Health Services Research, and New York: Columbia University, Joseph P. Mailman School of Public Health.

Pirkis, J., & Burgess, P. (1998). Suicide and recovery of health care contacts: A systematic review. *British Journal of Psychiatry, 173*, 462–474.

Plomin, R., & Caspi, A. (1999). Behavioral genetics and personality. In L. A. Pervin & O. P. John (Eds.), *Handbook of personality* (2nd ed., pp. 251–276). New York: Guilford Press.

Prudic, J., & Sackeim, H. A. (1999). Electroconvulsive therapy and suicide risk. *Journal of Clinical Psychiatry, 60*, 104–110.

Resnick, M. D., Bearman, P. S., Blum, R. W., Bauman, K. E., Harris, K. M., Jones, J., et al. (1997). Protecting adolescents from harm—Findings from the national longitudinal study on adolescent health. *Journal of the American Medical Association, 278*, 823–832.

Reynolds, W. M. (1998). *Suicide Ideation Questionnaire: A professional manual*. Odessa, FL: Psychological Assessment Resources.

Rich, C. L. (1999). Relationship between antidepressant treatment and suicide. *Journal of Clinical Psychiatry, 60*, 340.

Ridgely, M. S., Goldman, H. H., & Willenbring, M. (1990). Barriers to the care of persons with dual diagnoses: Organizational and financing issues. *Schizophrenia Bulletin, 16*, 123–132.

Roy, A. (2000). Suicide. In B. J. Sadock & V. A. Sadock (Eds.), *Comprehensive textbook of psychiatry* (7th ed., Vol. 2, pp. 2031–2041). Philadelphia: Williams & Wilkins.

Rutter, M., & Quinton, D. (1984). Long-term follow-up of women institutionalized in childhood: Factors promoting good functioning in adult life. *British Journal of Developmental Psychology, 18*, 225–234.

Rutz, W., von Knorring, L., & Walinder, J. (1989). Frequency of suicide on Gotland after systematic postgraduate education of general practitioners. *Acta Psychiatrica Scandinavica, 80*, 151–154.

Sarason, B. R., Sarason, R. G., & Pierce, G. R. (1990). Traditional views of social support and their impact on assessment. In B. Sarason, I. Sarason, & G. Pierce (Eds.), *Social support: An interactional view* (pp. 1–26). New York: Wiley.

Seligman, M. E. P. (1975). *Helplessness: On depression, development, and death*. San Francisco: Freeman.

Sirey, J. A., Bruce, M. L., Alexopoulos, G. S., Perlick, D. A., Raue, P., Friedman, S. J., et al. (2001). Perceived stigma as a predictor of treatment discontinuation in young and older outpatients with depression. *American Journal of Psychiatry, 158*, 479–481.

Skopek, M. A., & Perkins, R. (1998). Deliberate exposure to motor vehicle exhaust gas: The psychosocial profile of attempted suicide. *Australian and New Zealand Journal of Psychiatry, 32,* 830–838.

Sloan, J. H., Rivara, F. P., Reay, D. T., Ferris, J. A. J., Path, M. R. C., & Kellermann, A. L. (1990). Firearms regulations and rates of suicide: A comparison of two metropolitan areas. *New England Journal of Medicine, 322,* 369–373.

Taube, C. A., Kessler, L. G., & Burns, B. J. (1986). Estimating the probability and level of ambulatory mental health services use. *Health Services Research, 21,* 321–340.

Tedeschi, R. G., & Calhoun, L. G. (1996). The posttraumatic growth inventory: Measuring the positive legacy of trauma. *Journal of Traumatic Stress, 9,* 455–471.

Thompson, E. A., Eggert, L. L., Randell, B. P., & Pike, K. C. (2001). Evaluation of indicated suicide risk prevention approaches for potential high school dropouts. *American Journal of Public Health, 91,* 742–752.

Tolan, P. H., & Mitchell, M. E. (1989). Families and the therapy of antisocial delinquent behavior. *Journal of Psychotherapy and the Family, 6,* 29–48.

Tondo, L., Hennen, J., & Baldessarini, R. J. (2001). Lower suicide risk with long-term lithium treatment in major affective illness: A meta-analysis. *Acta Psychiatrica Scandinavica, 104,* 163–172.

U.S. Department of Health and Human Services. (1999). *Mental health: A report of the surgeon general.* Rockville, MD: Author.

U.S. Department of Health and Human Services. (2001). *Mental health: Culture, race and ethnicity—A supplement to mental health: A report of the surgeon general.* Rockville, MD: Author.

U.S. Public Health Service. (1999). *The surgeon general's call to action to prevent suicide.* Washington, DC: U.S. Department of Health and Human Services.

U.S. Public Health Service. (2001). *National strategy for suicide prevention: Goals and objectives for action.* Rockville, MD: U.S. Department of Health and Human Services.

Weissberg, R. P., Barton, H. A., & Shriver, T. P. (1997). The social-competence promotion program for young adolescents. In G. W. Albee & T. P. Gullotta (Eds.), *Primary prevention exemplars: The Lela Rowland Awards* (pp. 268–290). Thousand Oaks, CA: Sage.

Westray, H., Jr. (2001, October). *The Maryland suicide prevention model: A caring community saves lives.* Paper presented at the 13th Annual Maryland Youth Suicide Prevention Conference, Baltimore.

World Health Organization. (2001). Choosing to die—A growing epidemic among the youth. *Bulletin of the World Health Organization, 79.* Retrieved September 4, 2002, from http://www.who.int/bulletin/pdf/2001/issue12/79(12)1175-1177.pdf

World Health Organization. (2004a). *For which strategies of suicide prevention is there evidence of effectiveness?* Retrieved March 1, 2005, from http://www.euro.who.int/document/E83583.pdf

World Health Organization. (2004b). *Suicide huge but preventable public health problem, says WHO*. Retrieved March 1, 2005, from http://www.who.int/media centre/news/releases/2004

Wolin, S., & Wolin, S. J. (1996). The challenge model: Working with strengths in children of substance-abusing parents. *Child and Adolescent Psychiatric Clinics of North America, 5*, 243–256.

Zigler, E., & Trickett, P. K. (1978). IQ, social competence, and evaluation of early childhood intervention programs. *American Psychologist, 33*, 789–798.

11

BRINGING THE AGENDAS TOGETHER: PARTNER AND CHILD ABUSE

K. DANIEL O'LEARY AND ERICA M. WOODIN

Historically, both research and clinical services in the child abuse and partner abuse areas have been separate, although there is now need for integration across areas. As noted by Chalk and King (1998) in the introduction to their book, *Violence in Families: Assessing Prevention and Treatment Programs*, the partner and child abuse areas (as well as elder abuse) each has its own terminology, theories, experts, funding sources, data collection efforts, research instruments, and scholarly journals. As has often been observed, those who study domestic violence rarely communicate with or read the journals of those who study child abuse. Similarly, practitioners in child abuse agencies rarely meet with or talk to practitioners in the partner abuse agencies (i.e., shelters for battered women, programs for batterers, and advocacy and counseling for battered women).

The separatist phenomenon is well entrenched, as exemplified by books on child abuse and partner abuse in which abuse in one realm is rarely covered in the other. For example, Lutzker's (1998) *Handbook of Child Abuse Research and Treatment* did not list partner abuse, wife abuse, wife battering, or husband abuse in the subject index. Similarly, the compendium *Programs for Men Who Batter: Interventions and Prevention Strategies in a Diverse Society* by Aldarondo and Mederos (2002) provided an excellent summary of the types and diversity of programs for men who batter, but had only four entries under topics related to children, and those entries covered only six pages.

Nonetheless, there are some recent efforts to foster more connections between child abuse and partner abuse services (e.g., Edleson, 1999) and to empirically examine the co-occurrence of child and partner abuse (e.g., Appel & Holden, 1998). In this chapter, we address several issues regarding the schism of the partner and child abuse fields. More specifically, we address the following: (a) Why have the fields of partner and child abuse been so independent? (b) What evidence exists that supports an integration of the area? and (c) What are the preventive implications of integrating the child and partner abuse fields?

WHY HAVE THE FIELDS OF PARTNER AND CHILD ABUSE BEEN SO INDEPENDENT?

There are a number of reasons for the relatively distinct areas of child and partner violence. We now discuss three of them: (a) different theoretical conceptualizations of child and partner abuse; (b) laws requiring reporting of child abuse that steer clinicians away from assessing parenting practices of batterers and physically abused women in shelters; and (c) the relative dearth of funding for research on child and partner violence, especially for integrative research.

Theoretical Conceptualizations of Partner and Child Abuse

Partner Abuse Models

As noted elsewhere (K. D. O'Leary & Vega, 2005), there are two major conceptual frameworks of partner abuse in intimate relationships: feminist (e.g., Adams, 1989; Yllo, 1993) and cognitive–behavioral (e.g., Hamberger & Lohr, 1989). These two views are not necessarily contradictory, and in fact, they often complement one another. Indeed, Rosenbaum and Maiuro (1989) have used variants of these two conceptual frameworks in their integrative approaches.

Power and control are dominant concepts in almost all of the feminist models, and proponents describe the manner in which the male aggressor uses coercive acts to intimidate and undermine the female victim. Men's aggressive behavior is not simply physical in nature; it is psychological as well. Psychological aggression serves to undermine the self-esteem of female victims (Schechter, 1982). Moreover, psychological abuse is often more predictive of a battered woman's traumatic responses than is physical violence (Dutton, Goodman, & Bennett, 2001).

The cognitive–behavioral model, building on feminist concepts, introduces an emphasis on goal-directed, self-produced patterns of behavior that are "under the control of the batterer" (Hamberger & Lohr, 1989, p. 66). This model emphasizes control of aggression through changes in physiological, cognitive, and behavioral processes and the need to address issues such as anger, anxiety, and stress (Hamberger & Lohr, 1989). The feminist model places more emphasis on protection of battered women than on aiding men. As Pence (1989) stated, the goal of the Duluth program is "protection of the battered women, not fixing of batterers" (p. 30). It involves challenging the attitudes of men and their views of women and encouraging the notion of equality in relationships, but it also emphasizes an interagency focus with methods of handling all domestic abuse calls, jail for all domestic violence offenders, and judges' orders to promote victim safety (Pence, 2002).

Treatment of partner abuse almost singularly focuses on men, though in recent years a number of service agencies have developed programs for physically aggressive women as well (Dowd, 2001; Hamberger & Potente, 1994). This relative lack of services for aggressive women, however, reflects a long-term schism between theory and research on partner abuse. Scores of studies in community and clinical samples show that physical aggression by women against their male partners is as common as physical aggression by men against their female partners (Archer, 2000), yet feminist writings almost always portray men as the sole physical aggressors. If aggression by women is discussed in feminist models, it is usually in the context of self-defense (Yllo, 1993). We recognize that among women in shelter samples, physical aggression against them is probably much more frequent and intense than their aggression toward men. Further, there are considerable data showing that men murder women more frequently than women murder men (K. D. O'Leary, 2000). However, battered women in shelters and murdered women represent a very small proportion of all physical aggression victims.

Part of the problem in this area is the need to better understand the diversity of physical aggression in relationships. *Partner aggression* often refers to any act of aggression against a partner, whether that aggression is a mild push or an assault with a knife or other weapon. The field was probably initially helped by the casting of a wide net when attempting to document the prevalence of partner abuse (e.g., Straus, Gelles, & Steinmetz, 1980), but we now have evidence showing that physical aggression against partners is best understood by examining different types of aggression (e.g., Holtzworth-Munroe & Stuart, 1994) and by understanding that physical aggression in nationally representative samples (Straus & Gelles, 1990) and marital clinic samples (K. D. O'Leary, Vivian, & Malone, 1992) is engaged in by both genders (often referred to as *mutual aggression*). In contrast, *battering* involves fear and intimidation and is primarily something men do to women (Jacobson & Gottman, 1998). Battering should not be considered synonymous with any physical aggression against a partner.

In our opinion, a major problem with the absence of female aggression in the feminist conceptualizations of partner abuse is that women are often the ones who engage in child physical abuse. In fact, the 1990 National Family Violence Survey found no difference in child physical abuse rates by fathers and mothers (Straus & Gelles, 1990). If women who engage in physical aggression against their partner are at significant risk for engaging in aggression against their children, the conceptualization of what could be called *family violence* becomes a reality. We return to the issue of family violence later.

Child Abuse Models

As Azar (1997) noted, the conceptual frameworks dominating the child abuse field are now largely integrative ones, such as the cognitive–behavioral and ecological models. The field has moved away from single-factor models such as stress or frustration aggression, and some have moved away altogether from aggression as the organizing construct. In fact, the child abuse field has moved farther from single- or few-model construct theories than has the partner abuse field. The cognitive–behavioral and ecologically based models are multifaceted, both in terms of the etiological views as well as the targets for interventions.

Azar (1997) developed a metamodel of child maltreatment that encompasses physical abuse, sexual abuse, and neglect. Her model is one of parenting competence with a continuum of incompetence to competence. Five general areas of parental disturbance are posited: (a) cognitive disturbances, (b) parenting-skill problems, (c) impulse control problems, (d) stress management problems, and (e) social skill problems (Azar & Twentyman, 1986). Further, Azar and Siegel (1990) have posited a framework that involves a set of unique tasks at each developmental level. This model is attractive because it brings possible interventions to mind.

Ecological models of child abuse (e.g., Lutzker, Bigelow, Doctor, Gershater, & Greene, 1998) have also significantly impacted the way in which researchers and clinicians understand child abuse. These models were promoted by the work of Belsky (1980), who placed parenting in a larger social context. The ecological views were developed in part to help explain why many parents with poor parenting skills or who are under tremendous stress do not abuse their children. The ecological conceptualizations also brought into focus risk factors such as poverty, joblessness, and the skill deficits of children and created a framework for multifaceted interventions.

In sum, partner abuse models have been more limited in scope than child abuse models. The dominant partner abuse conceptualizations have focused largely on power and control issues, and individual psychopathology issues have been ignored or even seen as irrelevant (e.g., Pence, 2002). The cognitive–behavioral models of partner abuse are more integrative with openness to mental health problems, patterns of drug and alcohol abuse, and past medical history (Hamberger, 2002). Nonetheless, the child abuse models are more expansive, with a greater emphasis on social factors that can contribute to child abuse such as poverty, lack of job skills, and lack of social support. Some of the etiological models of partner aggression that have looked at issues of dating aggression and aggression in early marriage are more expansive than the intervention models, and in particular, the problem of physical aggression by women is faced more directly in such models. However, the intervention models that inform batterer treatment see aggression by women as self-defense, a position that is clearly not the case in dating and early marriage in community samples.

Laws Requiring Action on Child and Partner Abuse

The duty to report child abuse presents a problem for those therapists who see adults who have serious problems with anger and aggression. In programs for men who batter their wives, if the men are assessed in detail for the use of physical aggression toward their children, it is quite likely that the clinician will discover some evidence of child abuse. Similarly, if one assessed the parenting practices of women in shelters for battered women, it is quite likely that there would be child abuse in some families. In either case, clinicians feel cautious in assessing parenting practices because they worry about the need and legal duty to report child abuse. Thus, many instances of overlapping abuse may go unreported.

Research on child and partner abuse uncovers similar issues. If the informed consent document warns parents about the consequences of reporting any suspected physical abuse to a child, then any parent fully understanding the informed consent may simply withhold information that would lead to a report to a child protective agency. This concern about reporting child abuse contributes to the exclusion of child abuse variables in partner abuse research and vice versa. There are methods of collecting data with fully informed consent that allow investigators to gather data from parents about aggression toward a child or partner in a manner that provides confidentiality of information. The methodology by which this can be accomplished is complex. However, our own approach to this problem, in a sample of 450 fathers and mothers of 3- to 7-year-olds in which aggression toward the partner and child was assessed, basically entailed providing a method of anonymous reporting (Slep & O'Leary, 2005).

Dearth of Funding Opportunities

A majority of the funding for investigator-initiated research in the child abuse and partner abuse areas comes from the National Institute of Mental Health (NIMH), the Centers for Disease Control and Prevention (CDC), and the National Institute for Child Health and Human Development (NICHD). An examination of these three agencies illustrates a critical need for integrative research across the partner and child abuse areas as well as a need for more research on partner abuse overall.

Our search of currently funded NIMH projects indicated that support for partner abuse research and research on the overlap between partner and child abuse is quite meager. We conducted a search of the database Computer Retrieval of Information for Scientific Projects (CRISP; http://crisp.cit.nih.gov), using the search phrases "child abuse," "domestic violence," "partner aggression," "partner violence," and "wife abuse." At NIMH, 36 researchers obtained investigator-initiated awards (i.e., R01s) funded during the 5-year period from 2000 to 2005. Twenty-two of those awards were for child abuse and 11 were for partner abuse. Only 3 of these grants targeted the overlap between partner and child abuse.

The CDC has a mandate to provide surveillance (monitoring) of the prevalence of abuse of women. For example, the CDC is the lead agency for Healthy People 2010, Injury and Violence Prevention (U.S. Department of Health and Human Services, 2000), the goal of which is "to reduce injuries, disabilities, and deaths due to unintentional injuries and violence" (p. 15-3). However, a search of the CRISP database parallel to our search of NIMH with identical search terms indicated that CDC funded only two partner abuse investigator-initiated awards and no child abuse awards in the 2000–2005 period.

At NICHD, between the years 2000 and 2005, researchers obtained a total of 19 investigator-initiated awards: 10 for child abuse, 6 for partner abuse, and 3 for the overlap between partner abuse and child abuse. Although NICHD is an agency with an emphasis on child health and development, the agency also seems to be addressing partner abuse issues as they relate to the impact of such abuse on children.

Overall, a significant problem faces the fields of both partner abuse and child abuse. Currently there is not enough funding for investigator-initiated research to sustain a core cadre of researchers, an essential component if the areas are to grow and prosper. We hope that at least 20 investigators will be funded for research on the etiology and treatment of both child and partner abuse making up approximately 40 grants and that many of these grants will address the overlap of these two frequently independent areas. Further, the striking lack of funding for investigator-initiated awards for partner abuse research at NIMH and CDC in particular makes any progress difficult and makes integration between the partner and child abuse areas much less likely.

WHAT EVIDENCE EXISTS TO SUPPORT INTEGRATION?

Overall, there are several ways in which empirical evidence can be brought to bear on the issue of integration. First, one can examine the overlap or co-occurrence of child and partner abuse (e.g., Appel & Holden, 1998). Second, one can address the conditional probability of one form of abuse given another form (e.g., K. D. O'Leary, Slep, & O'Leary, 2000). Third, one can assess whether arguments about child rearing lead to arguments between partners and, in turn, partner abuse. Similarly, one can assess whether arguments and physical aggression between partners leads to physical aggression toward children. Fourth, one can examine the extent to which the correlates and risk factors for child and partner abuse are similar (e.g., Slep & O'Leary (2001).

Co-Occurrence of Child and Partner Abuse

The exact percentages of co-occurrence will vary depending on the definitions of child and partner abuse. Although there are now *Diagnostic and Statistical Manual of Mental Disorders* (4th ed.; American Psychiatric Association, 1994) definitions of child abuse (Knutson & Schwartz, 1997) and partner abuse (K. D. O'Leary & Jacobson, 1997), they are relatively recent. In addition, much of the research on family violence does not occur in a mental health context but rather through state agencies such as court systems and child protective services in which definitions of abuse vary by state. Thus, precision regarding definitions is lacking; consensus definitions are rare (K. D. O'Leary et al., 2000); and service providers are plagued by definitional problems (Portwood, Reppucci, & Mitchell, 1998). Although there has been variability in the definitions of child and partner abuse, fortunately several recent reviews have precisely defined the terms used in studies that have evaluated co-occurrence.

Appel and Holden (1998) published a comprehensive review of co-occurrence of child and partner abuse. *Child abuse* referred to severe acts of aggression against the child, and parents were considered abusive if (a) they engaged in any severe acts of physical aggression toward a child on the Conflict Tactics Scale (Straus, 1990) or (b) if they were in the top 10% of the sample in terms of use of physical aggression against a child. On the basis of two different representative samples from the National Family Violence Surveys of 1975 and 1985 (Hotaling, Straus, & Lincoln, 1990), the rates of child abuse were determined to be 23% and 18%, respectively. *Partner abuse* was defined as occurring when the individual had engaged in any act of physical aggression against the partner in the past year (a zero-tolerance definition). Using this definition, researchers found that 16% to 18% of the respondents reported that they or their spouse had engaged in partner aggression. Using these definitions, the co-occurrence of child and partner abuse among families with at least one minor in the house was 6% to 7%.

Severe aggression against children and partners was examined in a sample of 453 randomly recruited parents of 3- to 7-year-old children in Suffolk County, New York (S. G. O'Leary, 2003). On the basis of the revised Conflict Tactics Scales (Straus, Hamby, & Boney-McCoy, 1996), the rates of severe husband-to-wife aggression and wife-to-husband aggression were 13% and 20%, respectively. The rates of severe father-to-child and severe mother-to-child aggression were 7% and 8%, respectively. The co-occurrence of husband-to-wife and father-to-child aggression was 2%, and the co-occurrence of wife-to-husband and mother-to-child was 3%. The co-occurrence rates noted by Appel and Holden (1998) and S. G. O'Leary (2003) may not seem high enough to warrant an integration of agendas for child and partner abuse. However, we turn now to two other ways one can conceptualize the association between child and partner abuse, namely conditional probabilities and common risk markers.

Conditional Probabilities of Child and Partner Aggression

Using the same National Family Violence Surveys data as noted above, we examined the conditional probability of one kind of abuse, given that the other exists (K. D. O'Leary et al., 2000). The definitions of *child abuse* and *partner abuse* were identical to those just mentioned. When partner abuse was present, the conditional probability of child abuse was 31%. Coincidentally, the conditional probability of partner abuse when child abuse was present was also 31%. On the basis of the severe partner and child aggression data noted earlier in the sample of 453 randomly recruited parents of 3-to 7-year-olds (S. G. O'Leary, 2003), when there was severe aggression to the wife, the probability of severe aggression to the child by the father was 15%. When there was severe aggression to the child by the father, the probability of severe aggression to the wife was 30%. We consider these conditional probabilities to be especially relevant to clinicians, because clinicians are usually presented with one form of a clinical problem and then must be alert to other problems.

Indicative of the conditional probability of child abuse given partner abuse in samples of battered women in a shelter, O'Keefe (1995) found that 34% of the children of these mothers had been physically abused by their fathers. Similarly, McClosky, Figueredo, and Koss (1995) found that 43% of the children of battered women in a shelter had been abused by their fathers. In sum, children in homes of battered women in shelters were at significant risk for being abused by their fathers. Moreover, if both the father and the mother's actions toward the child were considered, the risk of child abuse was even higher (67%; O'Keefe, 1995).

Data from samples of abused children revealed a similarly elevated risk. Specifically, McKibben, De Vos, and Newberger (1989) showed that in hospital records of physically abused children, 59% of mothers were also classified as victims of partner abuse. In addition, Carlson (1991) found that 50% of the adolescents in a residential treatment program who were victims of child abuse had observed interparental violence. In short, the presence of child abuse elevates the risk of partner abuse by the parents.

Common Risk Markers

In the partner and child abuse areas, the following are demographic factors repeatedly found to be risk markers: low income, young age, race, and unemployment. Poverty has long been seen as a key predictor of child abuse, along with being a young single mother (Wolfe, 1987). Most demographic factors are seen as risk markers for other variables rather than being causes of the aggression per se. However, poverty has been such a consistent and large predictor of child abuse that some see poverty as a key causal factor itself.

In addition to demographic risk factors, family factors such as violence in the family of origin and arguments about children, as well as individual factors such as alcohol abuse and anger problems, are important risk factors that have been repeatedly associated with partner and child abuse. Moreover, these risk factors are generally thought to have at least moderate effect sizes in both the partner (Schumacher, Feldbau-Kohn, Slep, & Heyman, 2001) and child abuse arenas (Slep & Heyman, 2001).

Violence in the Family of Origin

The most commonly studied variable providing information about a family-level link between child and partner abuse is violence in the family of origin. This variable is often discussed in the context of the cycle of violence or the intergenerational transmission of violence and refers to the belief that if one comes from a family of violence, there is a greater likelihood of that individual repeating the cycle of violence in his or her own family. Meta-analyses document that family-of-origin violence and violence in one's home as an adult are definitely correlated (Stith et al., 2000). However, the effect across studies was only .18, a small to medium effect size. In addition, the effect size was about the same for witnessing interparental violence (r = .18) and being the victim of interparental violence (r = .16). Men growing up in a violent home were more likely than women to be perpetrators of aggression, though there was a significant effect for both genders. Further, clinical samples showed stronger associations than community samples. Finally, being a victim of child abuse was a stronger predictor of interpartner victimization than observing violence, and growing up in a violent home had a stronger effect on being a victim for women than men.

One of the largest studies of the risk for intimate partner violence looked at the violent childhood experiences of 8,629 individuals in a large health maintenance organization (Whitfield, Anda, Dube, & Felitti, 2003). They found that childhood physical and sexual abuse increased the likelihood of risk of victimization of women and perpetration of intimate partner abuse by men by approximately twofold. Approximately 25% of men and women met criteria for having been physically abused as children, and approximately 5% of women and 4% of men met the definition of being at risk for victimization or at risk for perpetration of interpartner violence, respectively. Individuals who reported being pushed, grabbed, slapped, or having had something thrown at them as a child had a risk of perpetrating violence or of victimization that was 2.3 and 2.5 times greater for men and women, respectively.

Substance Abuse

Substance abuse has been examined as a risk factor in many studies of partner violence; however, the conclusions reached depend on the sample. The association between alcohol abuse and partner abuse is much stronger in populations of arrested men than in representative populations. For example, in approximately two thirds of arrests for partner violence, the male perpetrator was abusing alcohol and cocaine on the day of the assault (Brookoff, O'Brien, Cook, Thompson, & Williams, 1997). However, in representative samples, only 25% of the instances of partner aggression have been associated with alcohol use or abuse (Kantor & Straus, 1989).

Analyses of data by K. D. O'Leary and Schumacher (2003) from a representative sampling of United States citizens indicated that it is not alcohol use per se but rather alcohol abuse that is a clinically important risk factor for partner violence. For instance, data from physically abused women across eight emergency room departments indicated that problem alcohol use immediately preceding the assault was associated with injury to the female partner in approximately 52% of the cases (Kyriacou et al., 1999). The link of substance abuse with child abuse has been given less attention than its link with partner abuse, but substance abuse is considered to be a significant risk factor for child abuse as well (Slep & O'Leary, 2001).

Anger

Anger is a controversial topic in the partner abuse field because many feminist scholars and service delivery personnel do not approve of anger management as an intervention for batterers. As Rosenbaum and Leisring (2001) noted, feminist-based proponents feel that referring to a program as "anger management" mislabels the problem and refocuses the issue as an anger problem rather than a power and control problem. This seems unscientific to us, first because there is evidence that men who engage in physically aggressive acts against their partners do have elevated anger levels (Boyle & Vivian, 1996) and second because anger problems are risk factors for both child and partner abuse (Slep & O'Leary, 2001).

Arguments With Spillover Effects

Although there are certainly a host of topics that can lead to an argument in intimate relationships, arguments over child rearing have been shown to be one of the most common precipitants of partner violence. Straus et al. (1980) found that although one of the least frequent arguments couples reported engaging in was about child rearing, these were the most likely to lead to physical aggression against a partner. Couples actually fought more frequently about topics such as housekeeping, sex, social activities, and money than children, and the greater the conflict about any of these issues, the greater the risk for partner aggression. However, conflict over children was most likely to lead to partner aggression. We suggest that aggression may be more likely to surround conflicts over children because of the intensity of the emotions associated with child rearing.

PREVENTIVE IMPLICATIONS OF INTEGRATING THE CHILD AND PARTNER ABUSE FIELDS

Thus far, we have proposed that child and partner abuse are often related problems, with significant co-occurrence and common risk factors. This overlap helps shed light on important clinical issues related to the prevention of both problems. Unfortunately, up to this point, efforts to prevent partner and child abuse have followed separate, though somewhat parallel, tracks. We first provide a brief overview of prevention efforts aimed specifically toward either partner or child abuse and then present our rationale for an effective merging of the two endeavors.

Prevention efforts are considered either universal or targeted at populations at risk. Universal prevention programs are broad based and directed at all individuals in a population (such as an entire high school or all students in their first year of college). Targeted prevention programs, in contrast, are directed at populations who appear to be at higher risk (such as teen mothers or couples with high levels of marital discord) or who evidence low-level forms of a problem. Although universal programs avoid stigmatizing particular individuals, targeted programs are often more effective at allocating resources to those at greatest risk of abuse. Generally, partner abuse prevention has followed a universal prevention model, whereas child abuse prevention has focused more on targeted groups. Legal or intense clinical interventions for individuals who have already evidenced severe abuse also are needed to reduce existing levels of aggression and to prevent such aggression from escalating. We discuss such interventions (sometimes called *indicated interventions*—interventions for individuals with an existing severe problem or who are at very high risk for a problem or disorder such as battering or injury of a partner) later in this chapter.

Prevention of Partner Abuse

Efforts to prevent abuse by intimate partners consist primarily of universal school-based programs conducted at the junior and senior high school and college levels. The feminist perspective has been strongly influential in the development of many partner abuse prevention programs, a key focus of which is often to promote equity in dating relationships and to challenge gender stereotypes and sexist attitudes. In addition, nearly all of the programs aim to increase participants' knowledge about the problem of partner abuse, the various kinds and warning signs of abuse, and the availability of community resources for both victims and perpetrators. Similarly, several of the programs also include a focus on communication and conflict management skills and strengthening communication and interaction between families, students, schools, and the surrounding community (Avery-Leaf & Cascardi, 2002; K. D. O'Leary, Woodin, & Fritz, in press). There have also been attempts to examine the utility of existing marriage preparation programs that provide instruction in effective communication and conflict management skills (e.g., Markman, Renick, Floyd, Stanley, & Clements, 1993) to prevent partner abuse, as well as programs targeted to engaged couples at higher risk for partner abuse that include specific attention to increasing knowledge, changing attitudes, and preventing conflict escalation (e.g., Neidig, 1989). Although most programs are successful in changing adolescents' and young adults' knowledge levels and attitudes toward partner abuse as well as their behavioral intentions in hypothetical conflict situations, there has been little systematic evaluation of changes in actual partner abuse perpetration and victimization rates (K. D. O'Leary et al., in press).

Prevention of Child Abuse

The prevention of child abuse, in contrast to efforts to prevent partner abuse, tends to target resources to individuals (primarily mothers) who may be at greatest risk for abusing their child as a result of factors such as adolescent pregnancy (e.g., Budd, Stockman, & Miller, 1998) and poverty (e.g., Wasik, 1998). Efforts to prevent child abuse generally focus on improving parenting knowledge, attitude, and skills as well as decreasing the use of corporal punishment. Outcome results mirror those of partner abuse programs, with significant improvements in knowledge and attitudes but little measured evidence for reduced rates of child abuse (Reppucci, Woolard, & Fried, 1999). More recent conceptualizations of child abuse prevention are increasingly focusing on the context in which the family lives and are providing services to multiple domains within the community (e.g., child care, home safety, support groups, alcohol use referrals, parent education, and financial counseling) to reduce the risk of abuse both directly and indirectly through increased community support (Lutzker et al., 1998; Reppucci et al., 1999).

An Integration of Partner and Child Abuse Prevention

Because there is a great deal of overlap in risk factors for partner and child abuse (e.g., substance use, anger control problems, and impoverished circumstances) and because prevention programs for both forms of abuse typically target adolescents and young adults, an effective solution to preventing both problems may be to identify individuals who display elevated levels of known risk factors and then to implement programs that address both forms of abuse in tandem. Further, low levels of aggression (e.g., slapping or shoving a partner once) may be used as indicators for the implementation of programs aimed at preventing future aggressive behavior toward the partner as well as to maximize the likelihood that the violence does not generalize to the child as well. A cohesive approach would reduce stress and conflict within the family as well as provide skills needed to manage both interpersonal conflict and parenting stresses.

Figure 11.1 depicts a multilevel prevention scheme designed to provide increasing intensities of prevention and intervention services that are based on level of risk for abuse and that are founded on programs that have received the most empirical support in other violence prevention areas

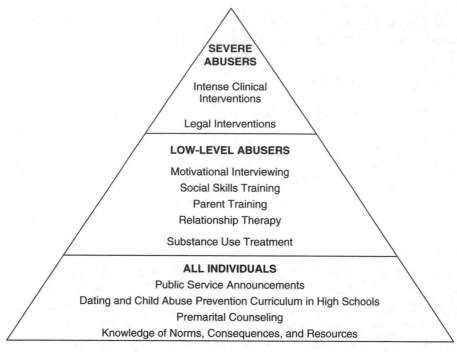

Figure 11.1. An integrated, multitargeted model of partner and child abuse prevention.

(e.g., Gottfredson, 1997). Prevention of partner and child abuse, as well as attempts to curb ongoing abuse, would occur on various levels.

The universal prevention program for all individuals would be the least costly component and would serve as an initial gateway before more intensive interventions were provided. Although universal prevention programs often have lower efficacy than targeted efforts, primarily as a result of brief implementation periods and small base rates of aggression in the general population (e.g., Lipsey, 1992), universal programs are useful in introducing concepts of nonabusive relationships and creating an environment that does not condone violence. The intervention would be designed for disbursement to the entire community, with any presentations being in a large-group format. The program would impart information regarding (a) norms for appropriate behavior and communication techniques in interpersonal and parenting situations, (b) the risks and negative consequences associated with aggression toward either the partner or the child (including harm to the victim and legal repercussions for the perpetrator), and (c) services available to get help if partner or child abuse occurs (for both the aggressor and the victim).

For individuals with elevated risk or low levels of partner or child abuse at either the adolescent or young-adult ages, we suggest a targeted prevention program of moderate cost and intensity, with sessions of moderate length. The targeted interventions could involve various components such as motivational interviewing, social skills building, parenting classes, relationship therapy, and substance use treatment. First, small groups of individuals could undergo social skills training classes in which the lessons introduced in the universal prevention program could be extended and intensified, and more individualized attention and feedback could be provided. Second, individual motivational feedback interviews could be conducted to (a) directly contrast the individual's potential for abusiveness with normative behavior, (b) assess for awareness of the consequences of such behavior, and (c) provide individualized recommendations and advice for methods to change. Third, support services such as parent training, relationship therapy, and substance use treatment would be used to reduce stress and conflict and promote healthy family relationships.

Finally, for those individuals who display persistent or severe partner or child abuse, interventions should entail adequate assessment and treatment for both types of abuse. Perpetrators and victims who are referred to treatment for either type of abuse should be considered at high risk for other forms of family-related abuse, and professionals should be trained to detect the patterns of abuse within families. For example, in cases in which abuse is occurring between partners, the impact of that abuse on the child should be assessed. Impact may be direct, as in observation of interparental abuse, or indirect, through increased stress and discord that might precipitate abuse toward the child as well. Given the large number of interventions for men who batter and for parents who abuse their children, it would be extremely helpful if such programs collected data not just on the primary target of change (i.e., wife abuse or child abuse) but on the secondary target as well, (i.e., aggression toward children in programs directed at reducing partner abuse, and aggression toward partners in programs directed at reducing aggression toward children).

SUMMARY

The fields of partner and child abuse have remained separate in part because of different theoretical conceptualizations of the etiology of abuse, laws that discourage the assessment of child abuse in clinical settings, and a dearth of funding opportunities in both the partner and child abuse fields. Evidence to support increasing integration of the two fields includes a high co-occurrence of partner and child abuse (particularly in clinical settings), high conditional probabilities of one kind of abuse given the other, and a host of common risk factors (including violence in the family of origin, substance use, anger, and arguments regarding child rearing). The prevention of partner abuse consists primarily of universal programs for adolescents or engaged couples, whereas the prevention of child abuse is often targeted toward more high-risk groups (e.g., teen mothers and families living in poverty). A more integrative approach to the prevention of these two problems would ideally entail a multilevel program focused on the common risk factors for both partner and child abuse in adolescent and young adult populations, with a series of increasingly targeted programs designed to address both issues in tandem.

From a research perspective, greater integration of the child and partner abuse prevention fields is sorely needed. Several means of integration seem worthwhile: (a) having think tank groups from the two fields meet to consider means of conceptual integration and joint data collection, (b) holding miniconferences of 12 to 15 presenters to address integration and ultimately to produce a book addressing integration across the two fields, (c) publishing a special journal issue addressing integration, and (d) making treatment grants available to researchers who wish to develop and evaluate interventions addressing core risk factors common to both child maltreatment and partner abuse. Activities such as these will help to raise awareness and provide structure for the promotion of a more integrative perspective on the understanding and prevention of partner and child abuse.

REFERENCES

Adams, D. (1989). Feminist-based interventions for battering men. In P. L. Caesar & L. K. Hamberger (Eds.), *Treating men who batter: Theory, practice and programs* (pp. 3–23). New York: Springer Publishing Company.

Aldarondo, E., & Mederos, F. (2002). *Programs for men who batter: Intervention and prevention strategies in a diverse society.* Kingston, NJ: Civic Research Institute.

American Psychiatric Association. (1994). *Diagnostic and statistical manual of mental disorders* (4th ed.). Washington, DC: Author.

Appel, A., & Holden, G. W. (1998). The co-occurrence of spouse and physical child abuse: A review and appraisal. *Journal of Family Psychology, 12,* 578–599.

Archer, J. (2000). Sex differences in aggression between heterosexual partners: A meta-analytic review. *Psychological Bulletin, 126,* 651–680.

Avery-Leaf, S., & Cascardi, M. (2002). Dating violence education: Prevention and early intervention strategies. In P. A. Schewe (Ed.), *Preventing violence in relationships* (pp. 79–106). Washington, DC: American Psychological Association.

Azar, S. T. (1997). A cognitive behavioral approach to understanding and treating parents who physically abuse their children. In D. A. Wolfe, R. J. McMahon, & R. D. Peters (Eds.), *Child abuse: New directions in prevention and treatment across the life span* (pp. 79–101). Thousand Oaks, CA: Sage.

Azar, S. T., & Siegel, B. R. (1990). Behavioral treatment of child abusers: A developmental perspective. *Behavior Modification, 14,* 279–300.

Azar, S. T., & Twentyman, C. T. (1986) Cognitive–behavioral perspectives on the assessment and treatment of child abuse. In P. C. Kendall (Ed.), *Advances in cognitive–behavioral research and therapy* (Vol. 5, pp. 237–267). New York: Academic Press.

Belsky, J. (1980). Child maltreatment: An ecological integration. *American Psychologist, 35,* 320–335.

Boyle, D. J., & Vivian, D. (1996). Generalized versus spouse-specific anger/hostility and men's violence against intimates. *Violence and Victims, 11,* 293–317.

Brookoff, D., O'Brien, K., Cook, C. S., Thompson, T. D., & Williams, C. (1997). Characteristics of participants in domestic violence. *Journal of the American Medical Association, 277,* 1369–1373.

Budd, K. S., Stockman, K. D., & Miller, E. N. (1998). Parenting issues and interventions with adolescent mothers. In J. R. Lutzker (Ed.), *Handbook of child abuse research and treatment* (pp. 357–376). New York: Plenum Press.

Carlson, B. E. (1991). Outcomes of physical abuse and observation of marital violence among adolescents in placement. *Journal of Interpersonal Violence, 6,* 526–534.

Chalk, R., & King, P. A. (1998). *Violence in families: Assessing prevention and treatment programs.* Washington, DC: National Academy Press.

Dowd, L. (2001). Female perpetrators of partner aggression: Relevant issues and treatment. *Journal of Aggression, Maltreatment, and Trauma, 5,* 73–104.

Dutton, M. A., Goodman, L. A., & Bennett, L. (2001). Court-involved battered women's responses to violence: The role of psychological, physical, and sexual abuse. In K. D. O'Leary & R. D. Maiuro (Eds.), *Psychological abuse in violent domestic relations* (pp. 177–195). New York: Springer Publishing Company.

Edleson, J. L. (1999). Interventions and issues in the co-occurrence of child abuse and domestic violence. *Child Maltreatment, 4,* 91–182.

Gottfredson, D. C. (1997). School-based crime prevention. In L. Sherman, D. C. Gottfredson, D. McKenzie, J. Eck, P. Reuter, & S. D. Bushway (Eds.), *Preventing crime: What works, what doesn't, what's promising.* College Park: University of Maryland, Department of Criminology and Criminal Justice.

Hamberger, L. K. (2002). The men's group—A community-based, cognitive–behavioral, profeminist intervention program. In E. Aldarondo & F. Mederos (Eds.), *Programs for men who batter: Intervention and prevention strategies in a diverse society* (pp. 7-1–7-43). Kingston, NJ: Civic Research Institute.

Hamberger, L. K., & Lohr, J. M. (1989). Proximal causes of spouse abuse: A theoretical analysis for cognitive–behavioral interventions. In P. L. Caesar & L. K. Hamberger (Eds.), *Treating men who batter: Theory, practice, and programs.* (pp. 53–76). New York: Springer Publishing Company.

Hamberger, L. K., & Potente, T. (1994). Counseling heterosexual women arrested for domestic violence: Implications for theory and practice. *Violence and Victims, 9,* 125–137.

Holtzworth-Munroe, A., & Stuart, G. L. (1994). Typologies of male partner violent men: Three subtypes and the differences among them. *Psychological Bulletin, 116*, 476–497.

Hotaling, G. T., Straus, M. A., & Lincoln, A. J. (1990). Intrafamily violence and crime and violence outside the family. In M. A. Straus & R. J. Gelles (Eds.), *Physical violence in American families* (pp. 431–466). New Brunswick, NJ: Transaction Publishers.

Jacobson, N. S., & Gottman, J. M. (1998). *When men batter women.* New York: Simon & Schuster.

Kantor, G., & Straus, M. A. (1989). Substance abuse as a precipitant of wife abuse victimizations. *American Journal of Drug and Alcohol Abuse, 15*, 173–189.

Knutson, J. G., & Schwartz, H. A. (1997). Physical abuse and neglect of children. In T. A. Widiger, A. J. Frances, H. A. Pincus, R. Ross, M. G. First, & W. Davis (Eds.), *DSM–IV sourcebook* (Vol. 3, pp. 713–804). Washington, DC: American Psychological Association.

Kyriacou, D. N., Anglin, D., Taliaferro, E., Stone, S., Tubb, T., Linden, J. A., et al. (1999). Risk factors for injury to women from domestic violence. *New England Journal of Medicine, 341*, 1892–1898.

Lipsey, M. W. (1992). Juvenile delinquency treatment: A meta-analytic inquiry into the variability of effects. In T. D. Cook, H. Cooper, D. S. Cordray, H. Hartman, L. V. Hedges, R. V. Light, et al. (Eds.), *Meta-analysis for explanation* (pp. 83–127). Beverly Hills, CA: Sage.

Lutzker, J. R. (1998). *Handbook of child abuse research and treatment.* New York: Plenum Press.

Lutzker, J. R., Bigelow, K. M., Doctor, R. M., Gershater, R. M., & Greene, B. F. (1998). An ecobehavioral model for the prevention and treatment of child abuse and neglect: History and applications. In J. R. Lutzker (Ed.), *Handbook of child abuse research and treatment* (pp. 357–376). New York: Plenum Press.

Markman, H. J., Renick, M. J., Floyd, F. J., Stanley, S. M., & Clements, M. (1993). Preventing marital distress through communication and conflict management training: A 4- and 5- year follow-up. *Journal of Consulting and Clinical Psychology, 61*, 70–77.

McCloskey, L. A., Figueredo, A. J., & Koss, M. P. (1995). The effects of systemic family violence on children's mental health. *Child Development, 66*, 1239–1261.

McKibben, L., De Vos, E., & Newberger, E. H. (1989). Victimization of mothers of abused children: A controlled study. *Pediatrics, 84*, 531–535.

Neidig, P. H. (1989). *Stop Anger and Violence Escalation (SAVE) instructor's guide.* Atlanta, GA: Behavioral Science Associates.

O'Keefe, M. (1995). Predictors of child abuse in maritally violent families. *Journal of Interpersonal Violence, 10*, 3–25.

O'Leary, K. D. (2000). Are women really more aggressive than men in intimate relationships? Comment on Archer (2000). *Psychological Bulletin, 126*, 685–689.

O'Leary, K. D., & Jacobson, N. (1997). Partner relational problems with physical abuse. In T. A. Widiger, A. J. Frances, H. A. Pincus, R. Ross, M. G. First, & W. Davis (Eds.), *DSM–IV sourcebook* (Vol. 3, pp. 673–692). Washington, DC: American Psychological Association.

O'Leary, K. D., & Schumacher, J. A. (2003). The association between alcohol use and intimate partner violence: Linear effect, threshold effect, or both? *Addictive Behaviors, 28,* 1575–1585.

O'Leary, K. D., Slep, A. M. S., & O'Leary, S. G. (2000). Co-occurrence of partner and parent aggression: Research and treatment implications. *Behavior Therapy, 31,* 631–648.

O'Leary, K. D., & Vega, E. M. (2005). Can partner aggression be stopped with psychosocial interventions? In W. Pinsoff (Ed.), *State of the art in family research* (pp. 243–263). Washington, DC: American Psychological Association.

O'Leary, K. D., Vivian, D., & Malone, J. (1992). Assessment of physical aggression in marriage: The need for a multimodal method. *Behavioral Assessment, 14,* 5–14.

O'Leary, K. D., Woodin, E. M., & Fritz, P. T. (in press). Can we prevent the hitting? Recommendations for preventing intimate partner violence between young adults. In S. Stith & D. Trit (Eds.), *Prevention of violence.* Binghamton, NY: Hayworth Press.

O'Leary, S. G. (2003, March). *Physical aggression in families: Links between parent-to-child and parent-to-parent aggression.* Paper presented at pediatric grand rounds, Children's Hospital at Buffalo, Buffalo, NY.

Pence, E. (1989). Batterer programs: Shifting from community collusion to community confrontation. In P. L. Caesar & L. K. Hamberger (Eds.), *Treating men who batter: Theory, practice, and programs* (pp. 24–50). New York: Springer Publishing Company.

Pence, E. (2002). The Duluth Domestic Abuse Intervention Project. In E. Aldarondo & F. Mederos (Eds.), *Programs for men who batter: Intervention and prevention strategies in a diverse society* (pp. 6-1–6-46). Kingston, NJ: Civic Research Institute.

Portwood, S. G., Reppucci, N. D., & Mitchell, M. S. (1998). Balancing rights and responsibilities: Legal perspectives on child maltreatment. In J. R. Lutzker (Ed.), *Handbook of child abuse research and treatment* (pp. 31–52). New York: Plenum Press.

Reppucci, N. D., Woolard, J. L., & Fried, C. S. (1999). Social, community, and preventive interventions. *Annual Review of Psychology, 50,* 387–418.

Rosenbaum, A., & Leisring, P. A. (2001). Group intervention programs for batterers. *Journal of Aggression, Maltreatment, and Trauma, 5,* 57–71.

Rosenbaum, A., & Maiuro, R. D. (1989). Eclectic approaches in working with men who batter. In P. L. Caesar & K. L. Hamberger (Eds.), *Treating men who batter: Theory, practice, and programs* (pp. 65–195). New York: Springer Publishing Company.

Schechter, S. (1982). *Women and male violence: The visions and struggles of the battered women's movement.* Boston: South End.

Schumacher, J. A., Feldbau-Kohn, S., Slep, A. M. S., & Heyman, R. E. (2001). Risk factors for male-to-female partner physical abuse. *Aggression and Violent Behavior, 6,* 281–352.

Slep, A. M. S., & Heyman, R. E. (2001). Where do we go from here? Moving toward an integrated approach to family violence. *Aggressive and Violent Behavior, 6,* 353–356.

Slep, A. M. S., & O'Leary, S. G. (2001). Examining partner and child abuse: Are we ready for a more integrated approach to family violence? *Clinical Child and Family Psychology Review, 4,* 87–107.

Slep, A. M. S., & O'Leary, S. G. (2005). Parent and partner violence in families with young children: Rates, patterns, and connections. *Journal of Consulting and Clinical Psychology, 73,* 435–444.

Stith, S. M., Rosen, K. H., Middleton, K. A., Busch, A. L., Lundeberg, K., & Carlton, R. P. (2000). The intergenerational transmission of spouse abuse: A meta-analysis. *Journal of Marriage and the Family, 62,* 640–654.

Straus, M. A. (1990). The Conflict Tactics Scale and its critics: An evaluation and new data on validity and reliability. In M. A. Straus & R. J. Gelles (Eds.), *Physical violence in American families: Risk factors and adaptation to violence in 8,145 families* (pp. 3–16). New Brunswick, NJ: Transaction Publishers.

Straus, M. A., & Gelles, R. J. (Eds.). (1990). *Physical violence in American families: Risk factors and adaptation to violence in 8,145 families.* New Brunswick, NJ: Transaction Publishers.

Straus, M. A., Gelles, R. J., & Steinmetz, S. K. (1980). *Behind closed doors: Violence in the American family.* Garden City, NY: Anchor Books/Doubleday.

Straus, M. A., Hamby, S. L., & Boney-McCoy, S. (1996). The revised Conflict Tactics Scales (CTS2): Development and preliminary psychometric data. *Journal of Family Issues, 17,* 283–316.

U.S. Department of Health and Human Services. (2000). Injury and violence prevention. In *Healthy people 2010: Understanding and improving health* (2nd ed., pp. 15-1–15-60). Washington, DC: U.S. Government Printing Office.

Wasik, B. H. (1998). Implications for child abuse and neglect interventions from early educational interventions. In J. R. Lutzker (Ed.), *Handbook of child abuse research and treatment* (pp. 519–542). New York: Plenum Press.

Whitfield, C. L., Anda, R. F., Dube, S. R., & Felitti, V. J. (2003). Violent childhood experiences and the risk of intimate partner violence in adults: Assessment in a large health maintenance organization. *Journal of Interpersonal Violence, 18,* 166–185.

Wolfe, D. A. (1987). *Child abuse: Implications for child development and psychopathology.* Newbury Park, CA: Sage.

Yllo, K. A. (1993). Through a feminist lens: Gender, power, and violence. In R. J. Gelles & D. R. Loseke (Eds.), *Current controversies on family violence* (pp. 47–62). Newbury Park, CA: Sage.

12

THE ROLE AND FUNCTION OF CULTURE IN VIOLENCE PREVENTION PRACTICE AND SCIENCE

LE'ROY E. REESE, ELIZABETH M. VERA, AND LEON D. CALDWELL

Over the past decade, the role and meaning of culture in public health research and practice has received significant attention (Betancourt, Green, Carrillo, & Ananeh-Firempong, 2003). This attention has come from public health professionals, institutions, and advocacy groups representing the diverse constituents served by public health in the United States. Similar to efforts in the applied areas of psychology and other areas of social and behavioral sciences, much of the impetus to carefully examine the meaning of culture in public health is the result of two important observations. First, the disproportionate incidence and prevalence of many diseases and health indicators ranging from cardiovascular disease to violence experienced by ethnic minority communities in the United States is overwhelming. Such trends result in the disproportionate morbidity and premature mortality rates

This chapter was coauthored by an employee of the United States government as part of official duty and is considered to be in the public domain. Any views expressed herein do not necessarily represent the views of the United States government, and the author's participation in the work is not meant to serve as an official endorsement.

experienced by members of these communities. Second, prevention and intervention efforts wherein ethnic minority communities and the poor have been the focus have shown a mixed record of effectiveness and sustainability (i.e., high levels of attrition, poorly measured outcomes, and effects that are not sustained over time), hence the continued health disparities observed among these groups (Nation et al., 2003; Weissberg, Kumpfer, & Seligman, 2003). The combination of these factors and others, such as the lack of social cohesion and social capital in these communities, underscores the importance of understanding culture in the manifestation and prevention of health problems.

Recently, the U.S. Department of Health and Human Services (USDHHS; 2000) identified the elimination of health disparities as the central objective of its Healthy People 2010 campaign. Additionally, the National Institutes of Health created the National Center on Minority Health and Health Disparities, whose focus is on improving the health of ethnic minority communities in the United States and eliminating health disparities. Initiatives such as these can play a critical role over time in elucidating the causes of health disparities in communities of color. Yet for scientists and practitioners in the field of violence prevention, there is a greater urgency to understand the role of culture in a health crisis that has immediate life and death consequences, because violence has had a distinctive impact on particular cultural groups' primarily poor ethnic minority communities.

The focus of this chapter is on culture and its relation to the prevention of violence. In referring to *violence*, we include child maltreatment, youth violence, suicide, and intimate partner violence. An understanding of what culture means or could mean within the context of violence prevention research efforts is examined, and recommendations for violence prevention researchers and practitioners are offered.

The current zeitgeist in public health and psychology has been to use terms such as *cultural competence*, *cultural sensitivity*, and *cultural relevance* to communicate an effort to address issues of culture for a particular demographic group in prevention research and practice. Important limitations to this dialogue about culture include the absence of clear conceptualizations about how culture is being defined, the ways in which culture is believed to mediate changes in behavior and attitudes, and testable or tested hypotheses to support claims about the role of culture in violence prevention. Indeed, one of the strongest arguments for understanding the role of cultural competency and sensitivity in violence prevention is the paucity of empirical research on these issues despite the continued speculation about the role of cultural competency and sensitivity in prevention. Thus, for example, studies providing clear and guiding evidence of how cultural considerations influence the prevention of violence are needed. Kirby (1997) reported that pregnancy prevention programs that were tailored (e.g., culturally specific examples and statistics) to the culture of participants were more effective than nondescript interventions. Lerner (1995) also discussed the importance of tailoring interventions to the specific cultural norms and attitudes of the targeted community as a means of promoting positive outcomes.

Culture can be defined broadly as common traditions, norms, and values shared among a group of people (USDHHS, 1999). The definition of *culture* we use here, however, is not limited to ethnic group membership but is influenced by gender, socioeconomic status, sexual orientation, and geography, which we acknowledge is markedly different from the view held by disciplines such as cultural anthropology. To understand the role of culture in violence prevention, we examine the worldview dominant in the theory and methods of Western prevention science and practice, discuss components of culture and their real or potential importance to effective violence prevention, and offer recommendations for advancing effective research and practice wherein the role and influence of culture are clarified.

IS CULTURE IMPORTANT IN VIOLENCE PREVENTION?

The complexity of culture must be fully considered to understand its potential role and function in violence prevention. Despite the lack of a central definition of culture, researchers agree that culture, often referred to as worldview or the manner in which people understand the nature of their existence and relations to others and the environment, provides a mechanism through which each generation transfers to its members information, skills, and traditions from which to interpret and act on their environment (Matsumoto, 1994; Ponterotto & Pedersen, 1993; Triandis, 1994). Nichols (1976) proposed philosophical characteristics of epistemology, logic, axiology, and process as variables that can vary across different cultural groups. Regardless of the definition of culture to which one ascribes, culture metaphorically and in reality is omnipresent. In sum, a culture-free society does not exist. This realization is important for prevention researchers and practitioners because they must constantly ask from what cultural worldview their interventions, research methodologies, and evaluation procedures operate. We assert that the consideration of culture is fundamental to violence prevention programs if they are to be effective.

A number of studies in the cross-cultural literature have investigated culture along easily measurable characteristics, typically ethnicity (e.g., African American, Asian American, and Latino) and nationality (e.g., American, Japanese, and African). Although phenotype and geographical location are measurable, culture's complexity is lost when only definitions that are psychological, not biological, are considered (Matsumoto, 1994).

For example, a violence prevention intervention for an African American cultural group (as demonstrated below) could look very different from an intervention for another cultural group wherein issues of identity confusion and diffusion and acculturative stress exist. Although the description of the first type of intervention for a cultural group (using only ethnicity) provides an identifiable target, it also assumes a monolithic cultural experience and perspective. The other type of intervention for a cultural group in this example, although not including an ethnic descriptor, accounts for intracultural differences and provides greater specificity for developing the intervention for those who may have similar psychological as well as phenotypic characteristics. In the former, it is conceivable that other racial and national groupings could be included. For this reason, we urge practitioners and researchers to consider with care the definition of culture they adopt as we advance understanding of constructs such as cultural competence, cultural relevance, and cultural responsiveness in the context of violence prevention.

CONCEPTUALIZING AND OPERATIONALIZING CULTURE IN VIOLENCE PREVENTION

Operationalizing culture in violence prevention can and should be included in the conception, implementation, and evaluation of an intervention. As prevention interventions are developed, researchers and practitioners should consider the adaptive interactions or natural prevention strategies (e.g., involvement of extended family and support of faith institutions), the shared life perspectives of the collective (e.g., history of cultural resilience), and modes of communication (e.g., music and spoken word) contemporarily and through generations (Triandis, 1994) of the target cultural group. Understanding a particular cultural group's adaptive interactions; methods of organizing and communicating information; development and use of symbols, patterns of behavior, and rituals; and intellectual, moral, and aesthetic standards is critical. Knowledge of the shared elements will assist a practitioner in how to implement an intervention. Having an understanding of how the cultural group interacts with other cultural groups and how subcultures are created can assist in determining where to target an intervention. For example, understanding the evolution of the hip-hop culture can help in developing interventions that employ this medium for adolescents in a manner that promotes healthy behavior and life choices. Finally, violence prevention interventions can be strengthened if interventions use methods of communication that are culturally meaningful. For example, developing interventions that require verbal expression of deep feelings may not be appropriate for some Native American communities. Conversely, the use of more symbolic modes of communication may be received as more effective and sensitive to a particular group. Subjecting such ideas to empirical investigation is an important step in determining their true relevance to the identified group.

Practitioners and researchers should consider the complexity of culture at each step as they develop and train interventionists and implement and evaluate interventions. Resisting overly simplistic definitions of culture is strongly encouraged. Instead, it has been suggested that culture should be approached from a perspective that considers a "deep structure" analysis of how culture may influence the way in which interventions are developed and evaluated. Examples that reflect such an approach include factors such as cultural consciousness (e.g., awareness of cultural history as evidenced by behavior and values), acculturative stress (e.g., being a first generation immigrant), or worldview (e.g., monocultural vs. multicultural perspective), which can be useful in understanding some of the psychological characteristics of a particular group (Matsumoto, 1994; Sue & Sue, 1999; Triandis, 1994).

CULTURE AND VIOLENCE PREVENTION

Among African American youths ages 15 to 24, homicide has been the leading cause of death for more than a decade, and homicide has been the second leading cause of death for Hispanic youths during the same period (USDHHS, 2001). Suicide continues to be the leading cause of death for youths among the indigenous groups of the United States (USDHHS, 2001). In child maltreatment, African American and poor children are disproportionately reported to be victims of child neglect and physical abuse according to government reporting agencies (USDHHS, 2003). Current epidemiological trends in intimate partner violence suggest that ethnic minority women are disproportionately the victims of violence by their male partners (Tjaden & Thoennes, 2000). In the United States, these epidemiological trends have all been calculated when comparing different demographic groups (i.e., by ethnic status) with the broadly defined majority ethnic group (European Americans). So, are such trends the result of the cultures of these groups? Specifically, do the values, attitudes, and traditions of these ethnic groups encourage and support such behaviors and experiences?

Some have made the perhaps simplistic argument (see Ani, 1999; Sue, 1978) that the disproportionate experience of violence and other poor health outcomes by ethnic minority communities is indeed a by-product of their culture and less a result of the influence of their unique sociocultural histories in the United States. Although it is important that the dialogue on effective violence prevention as it concerns the experiences of minority groups not be limited by sociopolitical sensibilities, it is equally critical that those serious about understanding and ameliorating these trends understand the complexity of these phenomena within the broader context of these groups' current and historical experiences in the United States. The experience of many minority groups in the United States has been predicated on sociocultural experiences in which discrimination institutionally (e.g., in employment, health care, and education), legally (e.g., jim crow laws and disproportionate adjudication and confinement), and societally (e.g., violent caricatures and stereotypes) has shaped their individual and collective experiences regarding violence (see Reese, Vera, & Hasbrouck, 2003).

In sum, the experience of many ethnic minority groups with respect to violence (similar to other quality-of-life indicators such as income equity and health care) is embedded within their broader experiences in the United States. The multicontextual nature of culture in the United States and the influence of various social, political, and economic realities on specific demographic groups require critical discussions of culture in the context of violence prevention if the role of culture is to be understood in a manner conducive to preventing premature morbidity and mortality caused by violence.

Many scholars have promulgated the need for culturally appropriate prevention programming as a key aspect of successful intervention efforts. For example, Nation et al. (2003) argued that prevention program relevance depends on the extent to which local community norms and cultural beliefs and practices of the participants have been integrated. Kumpfer, Alvarado, Smith, and Bellamy (2002) argued that including cultural relevance in prevention programs improves recruitment, retention, and outcome effectiveness. Yet, to achieve cultural relevance, it is unclear what researchers must attempt to accomplish. Cultural relevance is difficult to elucidate without discussing culture itself. Leading scholars within the applied areas of psychology advocate a definition of culture that is holistic and inclusive of the influences of gender, social class, race, ethnicity, sexual orientation, religion, and geography as influencing one's worldview (Sue & Sue, 1999). As referenced earlier in this chapter, definitions of culture are often discipline specific (e.g., anthropology and sociology), and we elect to use a broader view of culture given the context (i.e., prevention) that it is being considered. Given the breadth of the definition, one can understand why researchers have had a difficult time measuring all of the salient aspects of culture while simultaneously attempting to understand the impact of culture on various health phenomena. In fields such as anthropology and ethnic studies, culture has been considered along several dimensions including ontology, cosmology, and epistemology. These have importance for violence prevention researchers interested in developing more culturally relevant interventions by taking into account the worldviews of the targeted prevention group as well as the methods through which such groups learn and change (see Myers, 1988).

CULTURAL COMPETENCE

Recently, the concept of cultural competence has been discussed in disciplines such as medicine, psychology, public health, and social work. *Cultural competence* has been defined by Lopez (1997) as the ability to balance culture-specific (i.e., emic) and cultural-general (i.e., etic) norms. Emic norms are derived from group-focused research that attempts to clarify the specific histories, rituals, customs, and practices of a particular ethnic community. Etic norms are considered to be universal characteristics of the human experience that generalize across groups. For example, findings from the resiliency literature suggest that the presence of a caring adult not only helps children from resource-poor families or communities but is also linked to positive developmental outcomes for all children (Masten, 2001).

Lopez (1989, 1997) has demonstrated that cultural incompetence generally results in one of two errors. The first error is overpathologizing groups of people who are culturally different from the cultural group that is being used as the norm and who do not behave in ways consistent with the worldview of the majority (see also Sue, 1978). For example, a Chinese American male adolescent may be uncomfortable expressing anger verbally, perhaps largely as a result of his gender and ethnic socialization. Assuming that this difficulty is a psychological deficit is an example of an error reflecting a clinician's lack of emic knowledge. Such an error may also result in culturally incongruent intervention efforts with this youth, such as using assertiveness training or building emotional competencies.

The second error to which Lopez (1989) referred is minimizing the actual dysfunctional behavior of individuals instead of attributing their behavior or symptoms as normative given their culture. For example, such an error would be made if a clinician refrains from intervening with a client who is in an abusive relationship because of assumptions about her ethnic background (e.g., assuming that partner violence is a cultural norm in Latino marriages). This situation reflects a consideration of cultural factors but also an overgeneralization or reliance on stereotyping to make clinical decisions. In violence prevention, it can be dangerous to assume that the use of interpersonal violence is a cultural norm of any ethnic group or to assume that the overrepresentation of violent behavior in a particular cultural group suggests the behavior is condoned culturally.

Given the risk of making such errors in judgment when developing prevention programs for specific ethnic or racial groups, how do research and practice in violence prevention become culturally competent? Although many training programs in psychology and public health incorporate aspects of cultural competence and sensitivity into their curricula by requiring courses on cultural diversity or ethnic populations, there has yet to be agreement on which outcomes might signify that someone has attained such competence in research or clinical practice. Although this larger question is one related to training, licensing boards, and the work of research review boards, the overall issue of adapting interventions and research methods to reflect cultural relevance and competence is of equal importance. Thus, how do issues of culture come to be reflected in the conceptualization of interventions, implementation strategies, and evaluation techniques? Part of this answer may lie within new guidelines that were adopted by the American Psychological Association (APA).

THE AMERICAN PSYCHOLOGICAL ASSOCIATION'S MULTICULTURAL GUIDELINES

Recently, the APA adopted "Guidelines on Multicultural Education, Training, Research, Practice, and Organizational Change for Psychologists" (APA, 2003). These guidelines attempt to underscore the importance of cultural competence in the field of psychology and to make recommendations that guide psychologists in engaging in culturally competent practices. These guidelines are generally applicable to violence-related disciplines.

The first guideline states that psychologists must recognize that as cultural beings we may hold beliefs and attitudes that negatively bias our perception of ethnically and racially different persons. Such biases may lead to miscommunication across cultures because behaviors valued in one context may be misunderstood by individuals from different cultures (APA, 2003). In prevention science and practice, bias can manifest in the way that researchers interpret behavioral patterns related to health problems. For example, a researcher may see African American and Latino male youths' gang membership as an indication of community norms that support violence (or individual belief systems that justify the use of violence). Within these particular communities, youths may affiliate with gangs to gain protection from random community violence and may perceive gang involvement as a way to feel safer (i.e., so one is not bullied by peers; Vera, Reese, Paikoff, & Jarrett, 1996). Depending on one's interpretation of gang involvement, interventions designed to prevent violence (e.g., encouraging youths to "walk away" from their gangs) may be viewed as culturally inappropriate unless framed in culturally and contextually meaningful ways (e.g., identifying other culturally acceptable ways to reduce conflict while not appearing vulnerable to one's peers). This example illustrates some of the complexity of understanding culture when context, youth development, and perhaps ethnicity may be interacting to influence behavior.

The second guideline recognizes the importance of having culture-specific knowledge about the populations with whom psychologists and intervention programs work. This guideline supports the contention of Lopez (1997) and others who define cultural competence as having and using emic norms in addition to etic information. For violence prevention contexts, such as the gang context described above, having such information would allow professionals to design intervention programs that incorporate the realities of many communities (e.g., the "rules" that dictate gang disaffiliation). As another example, Hage (2000) suggested that intimate partner violence prevention practitioners take into account the role of environmental stressors such as racism and poverty as they affect women's perceptions of their ability to control their environments. Thus, the sociocultural history of women of color influences women's view of their self-agency when they experience violent relationships. As a result, some women may experience more violence in their relationships because of feeling disempowered in their relationships, communities, and the larger society.

Guideline 4 of the APA research guidelines encourages psychologists to conduct culture-centered research with people of ethnic, racial, and linguistic minority backgrounds. In prevention research, for research to be culture centered, the investigator must have familiarity with the community of focus to (a) have access to community members, (b) develop a positive working relationship with community members, and (c) develop programs that are valued by the community. These are important steps because most prevention researchers and some practitioners are "outsiders" to the community members with whom they work. As a result, it may be important to spend time in the community or make other valued contributions to the community before, as well as during and after, intervention research begins, consistent with models of community participatory research (Lerner, 1995). Examples might include volunteering in schools, community centers, or other important community focal points as a means of not only giving researchers an inside view of cultural norms but also assisting researchers to demonstrate their commitment to the community, which may translate into social capital important to the success of interventions and their evaluation. With regard to having programs that are valued by the community, it becomes important to create opportunities for members of the community to participate (e.g., have focus groups or community advisory boards) in the strategies used to develop, implement, and evaluate interventions.

Another practice guideline (Guideline 5) encourages psychologists to apply culturally appropriate skills in applied practice. Although the recommendation made in the guideline discussion focuses on individual, group, or family interventions in therapeutic settings, some extrapolation can be made for use in prevention settings. For example, psychologists are encouraged to use culturally appropriate assessment tools (see Suzuki & Ponterotto, 2001) and to have a broad repertoire of interventions (see Center for the Study and Prevention of Violence, Centers for Disease Control and Prevention [CDC], 2000) responsive to the worldview of the target group (APA, 2003). Prevention science uses program evaluation tools, and thus researchers must take care in selecting measures that were developed, previously used, and normed on the populations with whom they are working. For example, an initiative by the CDC's Division of Violence Prevention that focused on developing and evaluating interventions for the reduction of intimate partner violence and sexual violence among ethnic minority women encountered this challenge. Specifically, 10 projects that included youths and adults from African American, Hispanic, Asian American and Pacific Islander, and American Indian communities had great difficulty in identifying measures with appropriate psychometric properties (e.g., varying degrees of reliability and validity) with the populations with whom they were to be used. As a result, some of the measures used in these projects have been used in an exploratory and developmental manner to assess their validity and reliability with these communities.

The types of interventions used also must have been found to be culturally appropriate. For example, it may be culturally appropriate to use group-based interventions with ethnic minority parents when designing parenting programs (Reese et al., 2003) because such programs have been found to be more palatable to such parents. This does not mean that individual approaches would never be effective, but rather, participation is likely to be greater in a group context. Formative research plays a critical function in helping to determine if an intervention or implementation strategy is culturally appropriate for a given community. For example, community participatory research methods have been found to be effective in determining the appropriateness of interventions, implementation procedures, as well as evaluation and dissemination strategies (Lerner, 1995). What this type of research requires, however, is time devoted to relationship building that promotes collaboration, encourages community buy-in, and establishes the validity of intervention goals prior to beginning an intervention.

The last guideline encourages psychologists to use organizational change processes to support culturally informed policy development (APA, 2003). In violence prevention, environmentally focused interventions often target policies or laws that may serve as barriers to positive mental health and health promotion for culturally diverse communities. Examples of such policies are policing strategies that convey respect and affirmation to community residents in their practices while zealously and appropriately addressing violence (e.g., intimate partner violence, youth violence, suicide, or child maltreatment). This might also include community-sanctioned policies about the availability of resources to respond to violence, such as domestic violence shelters, or the availability of health-promoting resources for youths.

One of the superficial ways in which cultural adaptations have been made in violence prevention efforts has been what Resnicow, Solar, Braithwaite, Ahluwalia, and Butler (2000) termed "surface structure modifications." Such efforts could include merely translating intervention materials into the primary language of the participants or hiring program staff who have similar ethnic backgrounds as the participants. Such modifications would not necessarily be culturally inappropriate because it might be highly advantageous to have participants of the program communicate with program staff in their first languages or to interact with interventionists of the same ethnicity or gender. However, when program content does not reflect the reality of the participants' experience, interventions delivered by racially or linguistically similar intervention staff will not make the program relevant and most importantly effective.

It is the "deep structure modifications" (Resnicow et al., 2000) that determine cultural relevance. The use of the term *modifications* may be somewhat misleading, however. Often, the adaptations required for a prevention program to be culturally relevant result in a program that may be substantively different from its prototype. Dryfoos (1990), Lerner (1995), and Reiss and Price (1996), among others, have suggested that the most effective, culturally relevant prevention work includes the program participants (i.e., constituent groups) in the planning, implementation, and evaluation of the program. If this approach were followed, the content of the program (e.g., examples used in program content and reference group data) would not only become more relevant but the very structure of the program would also look significantly different from that of a program designed for a culturally dissimilar population. For example, if one were attempting to design a program to prevent partner violence for poor unemployed immigrant women versus a group of nonimmigrant working women, the intervention would have to consider the ramifications of encouraging women to leave their partners in each context. For poor immigrant women, the financial and extended family resources to make it on their own may be greatly constrained. As another example, a multisite school-based violence prevention study supported by the CDC found that modifications had to be made to the examples used in various components of the intervention because some examples were deemed culturally inappropriate at some study sites (Meyer, Allison, Reese, Gay, & the Multisite Violence Prevention Project, 2004). Some of the issues in this instance included geographically specific examples (i.e., urban vs. rural contexts) and differences by ethnicity (i.e.,

White, African American, and Hispanic) confounded by geography and other considerations such as language (e.g., translating intervention examples into Spanish).

Often, ethnic health disparities require population-specific approaches to violence prevention. Because statistical disparities may reflect epidemiological differences in the manifestation of problems, different risk or protective factors will be relevant when developing interventions. Yet, as useful as statistics are in elucidating group differences and describing the magnitude of a problem in a given population, the reasons such differences exist are often less clear. For example, in some research, racial or ethnic patterns may emerge that have been confounded by socioeconomic status, geography, immigration status, or other important aspects of the culture of the participants or the experiences of those groups in the broader society. Sue and Sue (1999), among others, have been critical of research that fails to define the culture of the participants in a more sophisticated manner. For example, if one were to find elevated levels of reported child abuse in Mexican American communities, one could speculate that this might reflect a cultural difference in social norms regarding acceptable parenting strategies by Mexican Americans or an increased level of stress related to poorer living conditions or linguistic barriers encountered during investigations of abuse. With these multiple interpretations all being plausible, prevention specialists could go about designing intervention strategies in a variety of ways. Yet, when research does not measure covariates of cultural variables (e.g., beliefs about parents, acculturative stress, or primary language) or has limited variability on such variables in the sample (e.g., surveying Mexican Americans who are all monolingual, low income, and recent immigrants), it is difficult to answer such questions.

SOCIAL EPIDEMIOLOGY AND ECOLOGY

In response to some of the issues described here, the field of social epidemiology has emerged in recent years to provide important contextual data on epidemiological trends that have helped researchers and practitioners make meaningful interpretations about reported rates (see Kawachi & Berkman, 2000). Practically, social epidemiology helps us understand under what circumstances and in what context violence occurs. Berkman and Kawachi (2000) described social epidemiology as a scientific approach to understanding the social determinants of health (e.g., discrimination, income inequality, and socioeconomic position) that may be related to particular health outcomes. They contend that by developing a thorough understanding of social determinants, it is then possible to truly address these variables in intervention strategies that reflect the complexity of peoples' lives, thus producing greater likelihood of positive and sustained outcomes. Such approaches argue that cultural competence is not served by merely attending to the uniqueness of a given demographic group but that broader macrolevel examinations are also important as they directly impinge on the experiences of certain groups as they relate to health outcomes such as violence.

Ecological models of development and prevention (e.g., Bronfenbrenner, 1979) suggest that rather than attempting to pinpoint the source of cause and effect for health problems such as the use of violence, one is better served assuming the causes are multiple, with influences residing in the microsystem (e.g., family, peer group, and community), macrosystem (e.g., society and cultural norms), and internal system of the individual. Although such conceptualizations are more complicated than assuming violent behavior results primarily from skills deficits or attitudes supportive of the use of aggression, the intervention options of such an approach are expanded versus limited. Such an approach reflects the realities of what is known about the origins of violence, that in fact, its occurrence is influenced by multiple factors and that most successful interventions reflect this complexity. The general consensus among violence prevention researchers supports the contention that the most effective prevention strategies are those that intervene at multiple systemic levels (e.g., individual, peer, family, and community targeted interventions; Catalano, Berglund, Ryan, Lonczak, & Hawkins, 1998). Because the ultimate goal of violence prevention researchers and practitioners is to reduce the premature morbidity and mortality caused by the various manifestations of violence, psychologists' efforts cannot be constrained by the challenges that more sophisticated approaches present. A review of the extant violence prevention literature suggests that in general, the same groups (e.g., the poor generally and poor African Americans and Latinos in particular) continue to be "studied" and remain the focus of intervention efforts in the different topical areas of violence (e.g., youth violence and child maltreatment), with little appreciable change in the disparities these groups experience. Such observations support the assertions made earlier in this chapter regarding the limited efficacy of many prevention efforts with these populations. Thus, there should be an impetus to work differently, building on what is already known to prevent violence to change the experience of these communities with violence and reduce health disparities in this area.

CONCLUSION

We have attempted to articulate that the role and influence of culture is neither clear nor simple to understand in violence prevention efforts. To illustrate this point, one study that assessed the degree of agreement on elements of culture to include in interventions with African Americans among peer-nominated experts in research and clinical practice with African Americans agreed on constructs important to cultural competence but could not agree on the particulars of these constructs (Cunningham, Foster, & Henggeler, 2002). And although these experts did agree on a small subset of variables, such findings illustrate the need for clearer guiding research on this topic. The importance of empirical research is accentuated in the face of numerous theoretical, yet untested, propositions arguing the importance of culture as a mediator of behavior and attitude change (see Bell & Mattis, 2000; Betancourt et al., 2003; Ridley, Baker, & Hill, 2001; Roosa, Dumka, Gonzales, & Knight, 2002; Sue, 2001). At the same time, some of the most promising and rigorous research in the prevention of youth violence, for example, contends that the consideration of culture is important to positive behavioral outcomes (see Henggeler, Mihalic, Rone, Thomas, & Timmons-Mitchell, 1998), and the influence of culture is highlighted as a central feature of all of the interventions evaluated and identified as model programs by the Center for the Study and Prevention of Violence. It is the variability in the ways in which culture is considered that holds both its challenge and its promise as a mediator of positive change in violence prevention.

We recommend that researchers and interventionists make a determined effort to understand culture and its role in prevention and begin to develop conceptualizations of cultural competence at both the construct level and within the theoretical models informing their interventions. Specifically, to advance our understanding of cultural competence, we argue that such conceptualizations be developed in a manner that allows their theoretical precepts to be empirically examined. The most significant limitation to arguments about the importance of cultural competence in violence prevention is the absence of empirical evidence supporting its effect as a mediating factor of positive change. The extant literature does not currently provide clear guidance with respect to empirically valid and reliable conceptualization of cultural competence, responsivity, and relevance.

Another recommendation involves the inclusion of these conceptualizations in the theoretical and measurement models guiding the development and evaluation of violence prevention interventions. This is being done increasingly, helping to refine our understanding of this construct and its role in violence prevention. For example, a CDC multisite school violence prevention project is investigating how the demographic characteristics (e.g., ethnicity, age, and gender) of interventionists and their experience working with certain demographic groups (e.g., inner-city vs. rural and different ethnic minority groups) may mediate some of the outcomes of that study. Although representative of only one conceptualization of cultural competence, such efforts have the potential to contribute to this dialogue in ways that move it beyond theory. There are also a growing number of measures available to prevention researchers representing different conceptualizations of cultural competence (e.g., Boyle & Springer, 2001). What many such measures lack is evidence of their psychometric properties confirming their validity and reliability when used repeatedly and across different contexts in violence prevention efforts. Although such validation needs to be pursued in the development and piloting of such measures, there are opportunities here for partnerships to be developed between violence prevention researchers and the developers of these measures.

In addition to the recommendations above, a framework is needed that can assist violence prevention researchers, practitioners, policy makers, and consumers in understanding the inclusion of culture in a systematic manner. This is important, because the epidemiology and intervention literature supports the assertion that violence is preventable when it is not approached in a piecemeal fashion (Mercy, Krug, Dahlberg, & Zwi, 2003). We believe that the public health model described in detail earlier in this volume provides a framework that with the minor modifications described in Figure 12.1 can allow culture, directly and indirectly, to be included in violence prevention efforts in an organized manner.

The first step in the public health model is to describe the magnitude of the problem. Typically this is done using traditional epidemiological methods that often do little to contextualize the magnitude of the problem in a manner reflective of who is really impacted by violence beyond ethnicity, gender, and sometimes geographical considerations (e.g., rural vs. urban). We suggest that this approach be augmented with the methods of social epidemiology briefly described earlier to inform our understanding of who is impacted and under what circumstances people are impacted by violence as either victims or perpetrators. By taking such an approach, researchers are better positioned to identify and understand the risks and protective factors specific to the communities of people with whom they work, which is the second step in the model. As discussed earlier, there can be and often are different risk and protective factors at work in different demographic groups. A one-size-fits-all approach will result in interventions that are poorly matched to the developmental and unique life experiences of the groups with which they are implemented. It is also important to address here the somewhat unchallenged notion that ethnicity is a risk factor for violence. As described here and elsewhere, members of ethnic minority communities are disproportionately victimized by violence, and most often the perpetrators of that violence are members of those same communities. This is an important issue requiring critical consideration if efforts to reduce and prevent violence are to be successful, and as has been argued, culture, whatever its manifestation, is a complex enterprise not to be oversimplified. Psychology has previously been criticized for the pejorative diagnostic views it held toward gay men, lesbians, and women, views that were subsequently

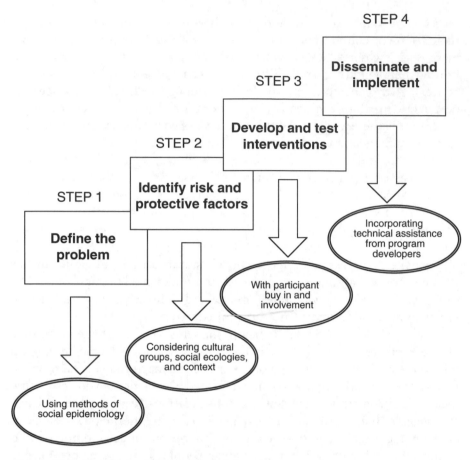

STEP 4

STEP 3

Disseminate and implement

Develop and test interventions

STEP 2

Identify risk and protective factors

STEP 1

Define the problem

Incorporating technical assistance from program developers

With participant buy in and involvement

Considering cultural groups, social ecologies, and context

Using methods of social epidemiology

Figure 12.1. Modified public health model.

acknowledged as sexist, homophobic, and insensitive to the unique experiences of those groups in the United States. We argue that ethnicity and violence should be viewed in a similar vein—that perhaps, as the surgeon general's report on youth violence suggested, race "may" be a risk marker for violence in certain socioecological contexts, but by itself is not a risk factor for youth violence (USDHHS, 2001).

The next step in the public health model involves the development, implementation, and evaluation of interventions. We discussed a number of issues specific to these steps earlier in this chapter. The central ideas presented in this discussion were that issues of culture need to be included in each step in the process. For example, it is simply unacceptable to have interventionists who are similar ethnically and linguistically implementing an intervention but use theories and techniques that are inconsistent with the worldview of the targeted group and then to call the intervention culturally sensitive or competent. A number of prevention elements (e.g., skill building) are most likely universal in their applicability to different demographic populations, and empirical evidence exists in some areas of violence prevention supporting their efficacy. Thus, we are not arguing for an approach wherein the proverbial wheel is reinvented, but instead, an approach that is more critical and attentive to how interventions are developed and evaluated.

The last step in the public health approach involves efforts to replicate and disseminate effective intervention components and interventions. The previous discussion regarding modifications to existing interventions is relevant here as is the role of technical assistance in effective dissemination efforts. The role of technical assistance is only now being fully explored in violence prevention. For example, the Center for the Study and Prevention of Violence and the Office of Juvenile Justice and Delinquency Prevention have a program in which technical assistance is provided by the developers of interventions with demonstrated empirical evidence that have been replicated at another intervention site. In this instance, technical assistance occurs when these interventions are replicated in targeted populations or in social contexts that are significantly different from the original samples. The program developers are available to assist in any modification of the essential features of the intervention to be responsive to the new community as well as to consider appropriate implementation strategies. As another example, the CDC is currently replicating an effective parenting intervention in communities in South Carolina that are markedly different from the communities where the original research was conducted. The developer of the intervention is actively involved in each step of the study to assist with any needed modifications. Efforts such as those described here allow effective interventions to be disseminated while simultaneously attending to some of the challenges of replication with different demographic groups. In the best case scenario, technical assistance involves not only the interventionists but also members of the targeted community.

The goals of this chapter were to raise for the reader's consideration the complexity of culture and the importance of understanding that complexity in efforts to reduce the morbidity and mortality caused by violence. The arguments and suggestions offered here may at times appear obvious, yet the state of the theoretical and empirical literature is underdeveloped such that a more functional and systematic approach is required if the construct of cultural competence is to have the impact theorized here and elsewhere on the prevention of violence. We believe the public health approach with the caveats described above offers such an approach. Violence is a preventable phenomenon, and although there is not room here for in-depth attention to be given to any specific form of violence, many of the ideas we have presented cut across the various manifestations of violence and thus have relevance for future violence prevention efforts with diverse populations. In sum, our perspective is that cultural competence in violence prevention equates with effective and sustained positive changes in prevention research and practice. Finally, because public policy is often the bellwether guiding the health and experience of citizens in the United States, we advocate for the development of violence prevention policies wherein issues of cultural competence are explicitly addressed and endorsed by supporting research.

REFERENCES

American Psychological Association. (2003). Guidelines on multicultural education, training, research, practice, and organizational change for psychologists. *American Psychologist, 58,* 377–402.

Ani, M. (1999). *Yurugu: An African-centered critique of European cultural thought and behavior.* Trenton, NJ: Africa World Press.

Bell, C. C., & Mattis, J. (2000). The importance of cultural competence in ministering to African American victims of domestic violence. *Violence Against Women, 6,* 515–532.

Berkman, L. F., & Kawachi, I. (Eds.). (2000). *Social epidemiology.* New York: Oxford University Press.

Betancourt, J. R., Green, A. R., Carrillo, J. E., & Ananeh-Firempong, O. (2003). Defining cultural competence: A practical framework for addressing racial/ethnic disparities. *Public Health Reports, 118,* 293–302.

Boyle, D. P., & Springer, A. (2001). Toward a cultural competence measure for social work with specific populations. *Journal of Ethnic and Cultural Diversity in Social Work, 9,* 53–71.

Bronfenbrenner, U. (1979). *The ecology of human development.* Cambridge, MA: Harvard University Press.

Catalano, R. F., Berglund, M. L., Ryan, J. A. M., Lonczak, H. C., & Hawkins, J. D. (1998). *Positive youth development in the United States: Research findings on evaluations of positive youth development programs.* Washington, DC: U.S. Department of Health and Human Services, National Institute for Child Health and Human Development.

Center for the Study and Prevention of Violence, Centers for Disease Control and Prevention. (2000). *Best practices of youth violence prevention: A sourcebook for community action.* Atlanta, GA: Author.

Cunningham, P. B., Foster, S. L., & Henggeler, S. W. (2002). The elusive concept of cultural competence. *Children's Services: Social, Policy, Research, and Practice, 5,* 231–243.

Dryfoos, J. (1990). *Adolescents at risk: Prevalence and prevention.* New York: Oxford University Press.

Hage, S. M. (2000). The role of counseling psychology in preventing male violence against female intimates. *Counseling Psychologist, 28,* 797–828.

Henggeler, S. W., Mihalic, S. F., Rone, L., Thomas, C., & Timmons-Mitchell, J. (1998). *Blueprints for violence prevention: Multisystemic therapy.* Boulder: University of Colorado.

Kawachi, I., & Berkman, L. F. (2000). Social cohesion, social capital, and health. In L. F. Berkman & I. Kawachi (Eds.), *Social epidemiology* (pp. 174–190). New York: Oxford University Press.

Kirby, D. (1997). *No easy answers: Research findings on programs to reduce teen pregnancy.* Washington, DC: National Campaign to Prevent Teen Pregnancy.

Kumpfer, K. L., Alvarado, R., Smith, P., & Bellamy, N. (2002). Cultural sensitivity and adaptation in family based interventions. *Prevention Science, 3,* 241–246.

Lerner, R. M. (1995). *America's youth in crisis: Challenges and options for programs and policies.* Thousand Oaks, CA: Sage.

Lopez, S. (1997). Cultural competence in psychotherapy: A guide for clinicians and their supervisors. In C. E. Watkins (Ed.), *Handbook of psychotherapy supervision* (pp. 570–587). New York: Wiley.

Lopez, S. R. (1989). Patient variable biases in clinical judgment: A conceptual overview and methodological considerations. *Psychological Bulletin, 106,* 184–203.

Lopez, S., & Hernandez, P. (1987). When culture is considered in the evaluation and treatment of Hispanic patients. *Psychotherapy, 24,* 120–126.

Masten, A. S. (2001). Ordinary magic: Resiliency processes in development, *American Psychologist, 56,* 227–238.

Matsumoto, D. (1994) *People: Psychology from a cultural perspective.* Prospect Heights, IL: Waveland Press.

Mercy, J. A., Krug, E. G., Dahlberg, L. L., & Zwi, A. B. (2003). Violence and health: The United States in a global perspective. *American Journal of Public Health, 92,* 256–261.

Meyer, A. L., Allison, K. W., Reese, L. E., Gay, F. N., & the Multisite Violence Prevention Project. (2004). Choosing to be violence free in middle school: The student component of the GREAT schools and families universal program. *American Journal of Preventive Medicine, 26,* 20–28.

Myers, L. J. (1988). *Understanding an Afrocentric world view: Introduction to an optimal psychology.* Dubuque, IA: Kendall.

Nation, M., Crusto, C., Wandersman, A., Kumpfer, K. L., Seybolt, D., Morrissey-Kane, E., & Davino, K. (2003). What works in prevention: Principles of effective prevention programs. *American Psychologist, 58,* 449–456.

Nichols, E. (1976). *The philosophical aspects of cultural differences.* Ibadan, Nigeria: World Psychiatric Association.

Ponterotto, J. G., & Pedersen, P. B. (1993). *Preventing prejudice: A guide for counselors and educators.* Thousands Oaks, CA: Sage.

Reese, L. E., Vera, E. M., & Hasbrouck, L. (2003). Examining the impact of violence on ethnic minority youth, their families, and communities: Issues for prevention practice and science. In G. Bernal, J. E. Trimble, A. K. Burlew, & F. T. L. Leong (Eds.), *Handbook of racial and ethnic minority psychology* (pp. 465–484). Thousand Oaks, CA: Sage.

Reiss, D., & Price, R. H. (1996). National research agenda for prevention research: The National Institute of Mental Health report. *American Psychologist, 51,* 1109–1115.

Resnicow, K., Solar, R., Braithwaite, R., Ahluwalia, J., & Butler, J. (2000). Cultural sensitivity in substance abuse prevention. *Journal of Community Psychology, 28,* 271–290.

Ridley, C. R., Baker, D. M., & Hill, C. L. (2001). Critical issues concerning cultural competence. *The Counseling Psychologist, 29,* 822–832.

Roosa, M. W., Dumka, L. E., Gonzales, N. A., & Knight, G. P. (2002). Cultural/ethnic issues and the prevention scientist in the 21st century. *Prevention and Treatment, 5,* 1–13.

Sue, D. W. (1978). World views and counseling. *Personnel and Guidance Journal, 56,* 458–462.

Sue, D. W. (2001). The superordinate nature of cultural competence. *The Counseling Psychologist, 29,* 850–857.

Sue, D. W., & Sue, D. (1999). *Counseling the culturally different: Theory and practice.* New York: Wiley.

Suzuki, L., & Ponterotto, J. G. (Eds.). (2001). *Handbook of multicultural assessment: Clinical, psychological, and educational applications* (2nd ed.). San Francisco: Jossey-Bass.

Tjaden, P., & Thoennes, N. (2000). *Extent, nature, and consequences of intimate partner violence* (Publication NIJ 181869). Washington, DC: U.S. Department of Justice.

Triandis, H. C. (1994). *Culture and social behavior.* New York: McGraw-Hill.

U.S. Department of Health and Human Services. (1999). *Mental health: A report of the surgeon general.* Rockville, MD: Author.

U.S. Department of Health and Human Services. (2000). *Healthy people 2010.* Washington, DC: U.S. Government Printing Office.

U.S. Department of Health and Human Services. (2001). *Youth violence: A report of the surgeon general.* Rockville, MD: Author.

U.S. Department of Health and Human Services. (2003). *Child maltreatment 2001.* Rockville, MD: Author.

Vera, E. M., Reese, L. E., Paikoff, R. L., & Jarrett, R. L. (1996). Contextual factors in sexual risk-taking in urban African American preadolescent children. In B. J. Ross-Leadbeater & N. Way (Eds.), *Urban girls: Resisting stereotypes, creating identities* (pp. 291–304). New York: New York University Press.

Weissberg, R. P., Kumpfer, K. L., & Seligman, M. E. P. (2003). Prevention that works for children and youth: An introduction. *American Psychologist, 59,* 425–432.

13

VIOLENCE PREVENTION IN THE 21ST CENTURY: MERGING AGENDAS AND CREATING IMPACT

JOHN R. LUTZKER, JENNIFER M. WYATT, AND PHAEDRA S. CORSO

At the beginning of the 20th century, diseases such as polio and smallpox killed millions of people. At that time, the possibility that these diseases would be virtually eradicated by the end of the century would not have been predicted either by the public or by many scientists, save for some dreamers and thinkers. Science, medicine, and technology advanced in those 100 years by geometric proportions, thereby producing dramatic decreases in the incidence and prevalence of such diseases.

Violence, on the other hand, increased in much of the world and certainly in the United States throughout most of the 20th century. Although the late 1990s and beginning of the 21st century saw some decline

This chapter was authored by employees of the United States government as part of official duty and is considered to be in the public domain. Any views expressed herein do not necessarily represent the views of the United States government, and the authors' participation in the work is not meant to serve as an official endorsement.

in violence in the United States, the numbers cited in the introductory chapter of this volume and in several of the chapters herein speak to the degree to which violence directly affects far too many people. The numbers do not address the economic or extended social suffering produced from any given incident of violence. How much does it cost society in dollars when a child is abused? There are medical and mental health costs that could and do endure for that child's lifetime (Edwards, Anda, Felitti, & Dube, 2004; Thompson, Arias, Basile, & Desai, 2002). Legal and social service costs also likely continue to accrue well beyond the initial event. Further, given that being the victim of child maltreatment (CM) often is a pathway to becoming a perpetrator of youth violence (YV) and adult violence (including partner abuse and CM) and can increase suicide risk, the effects of one type of violent victimization can extend across time and across types of violent perpetration and victimization for a single individual. Also, a single instance of intimate partner violence (IPV) will only appear as one data point in IPV surveillance systems. However, the effects of that single incident likely extend beyond the victim and perpetrator(s): The trauma experienced by the child witnesses may affect their mental health and development, and the worried family members of the victim may feel the need to seek mental health services. Examples such as these could fill many pages. The point is that even one violent incident is not as simple as a number from a database and can have more extensive effects beyond the specific incident.

Polio is preventable. Smallpox is preventable. Unintentional injuries are preventable. Violence, too, is preventable. Testimony for this comes, in part, from chapters in this volume that describe effective intervention and prevention programs in CM and YV and some promising directions in programs in trying to reduce and prevent IPV and suicide. Thus, if sufficient advocacy, policies, programs, funding, and dissemination efforts are made, perhaps a volume such as this written near the beginning of the 22nd century could reflect (in a manner similar to the mention here of smallpox and polio in the 20th century) that in this century there was a dramatic reduction in these forms of violence.

COMMON ISSUES

There are some common themes from each topic area that run through this book, and the field of violence prevention needs to attend to each of these themes to further advance research and service. This section addresses those commonalities.

Surveillance

In the public health model, the first step involves surveillance of the problem at hand: systematically collecting, analyzing, and interpreting data to define the extent of violent perpetration and victimization. What becomes clear for each topic area covered here is that improvements to current surveillance efforts would allow for the collection of more accurate data on the people involved in and the circumstances surrounding violent incidents over time. More accurate data, in turn, would facilitate the design and implementation of more effective prevention efforts. The chapters on surveillance in this book suggest two significant obstacles that impact systematic data collection on multiple types of violence: biases in official reporting systems and the need for uniform definitions.

The problems with relying on child protective services (CPS) data as the primary or only tool for counting CM cases (some of which are discussed in chap. 2, this volume) cut across all phases of the child protection process: reporting, investigating, substantiating, and adjudicating cases. Research using CPS records has repeatedly documented overrepresentation of certain groups (e.g., poor families and minority families) in rates of reported, investigated, and substantiated maltreatment that may not accurately reflect actual maltreatment rates (Ards, Myers, Chung, Malkis, & Hagerty, 2003; Drake & Zuravin, 1998; Garbarino, 1989; Hampton & Newberger, 1989). Therefore, one must use caution when drawing conclusions about differential maltreatment rates among different populations.

The lack of standardized definitions for what constitutes CM also contributes to problems in all four phases of the child protection system. Individuals within the community (and even professionals who work with children) vary with respect to what should be reported. Caseworkers vary with respect to what should be investigated. Differing legislation at the state or county level or even differing agency policies can lead to different substantiation requirements and adjudication decisions. Therefore, any figures citing incidence and prevalence from child protection records must be considered with caution because of the inconsistencies inherent in the current system. Serious efforts have been made to gather CM experts to address uniform definitions, but the pace has been slow. Although these experts have not yet come to consensus on definitional issues, there is a general agreement among professionals that the data reflect underestimates of the actual incidence of CM.

As with estimates of CM, estimates of IPV are also plagued by underreporting because of the desire and power of perpetrators to keep their behavior from becoming known and the characteristics of how IPV incidents come to the attention of professionals. With IPV, there are neither mandated reporters nor a centralized system of reporting as exists with CM. Therefore, official records (what Arias and Ikeda call "passive" data collection methods in chap. 8, this volume) of IPV incidents must be culled from hospitals, emergency departments, mental health and social service agencies, shelters, and police reports, to name a few. Thus, in addition to differing definitions among reports from the same type of setting (e.g., hospitals in one county vs. another), IPV surveillance is further complicated by differing definitions across different types of settings (e.g., police reports vs. social service reports). The Centers for Disease Control and Prevention (CDC) is currently undertaking substantial efforts to pilot test and revise a set of uniform definitions regarding IPV derived from a working group of experts in the field (CDC, 2000; Saltzman, Fanslow, McMahon, & Shelley, 1999, 2002). Large-scale studies such as the National Crime Victimization Survey and the National Violence Against Women Survey have helped provide estimates of the incidence and prevalence of IPV that are not biased in the same ways as official records (see chap. 8, this volume). Unfortunately, data such as these are more costly to obtain, reducing the frequency with which they can be collected.

The most common preexisting data sources for YV are police records of juvenile arrests and school records of violent incidents. The issue of inconsistent definitions plagues research using school records of violent behaviors, which may vary from school to school, even within a particular district. Population-based surveys such as the Youth Risk Behavior Surveillance System (CDC, 2004) provide more systematic data, especially across time, but are based on youth self-report of violent behaviors and experiences; thus, they must be considered in light of the usual biases associated with self-report data.

Hospital and emergency room data and death certificates can assist in determining the extent to which different types of violence result in injuries or death; these records are most often the basis for data on attempted and completed suicides. Given that actual cause of death cannot always be determined, death certificate data are generally considered to underestimate the number of completed suicides. The stigma associated with attempting suicide likely biases how well hospital and emergency room data estimate suicidal behaviors, because patients may not be willing to disclose their intent to inflict self-harm, and physicians may not be willing to document an injury as self-directed without convincing evidence (see chap. 10, this volume).

Etiology

Poverty emerges as the clearest common risk factor in CM and YV (see chaps. 2 and 5, respectively). This is in no way to suggest that middle-class parents do not engage in CM and that middle-class youths are not perpetrators of measurable violence. These societal ills cut across class, but there is little question that they are considerably more prevalent within impoverished communities. Poverty is also a common bond among the different types of CM. In addition to ample data showing that poverty increases the likelihood that children will be victimized by perpetrators of violence, researchers have also amassed evidence of the variables that mediate and moderate the effects of poverty on CM and YV, such as unemployment, residential stability, parental stress, parental monitoring, social isolation, and social norms regarding violence. Not surprisingly, many of these mediators and moderators have also been shown to increase or decrease the risk of IPV and suicide. Although researchers have typically studied these four areas of violence separately, the time has clearly arrived for more in-depth investigations of etiological factors that crosscut types of violent behavior and multipronged prevention and intervention efforts, rather than continuing to target programs separately to each type of violence.

Further, many of the chapters have discussed how victimization increases the likelihood of future victimization and perpetration. The pathways from being a victim of CM to becoming a perpetrator of CM, YV, and IPV and of becoming a victim later in life of suicide are perhaps the most obvious. Other pathways that have been examined are between victimization of *peer abuse* or bullying (see chaps. 2 and 7, this volume) and later likelihood of engaging in violence aimed at others (e.g., IPV, YV, or CM) or toward oneself (suicide) and the pathways between being a child witness to IPV— even if the child suffers no direct physical abuse—and later perpetration and victimization (see chap. 8, this volume). As noted more than once in this volume, the issue of pathways speaks all the louder for the need for crosscutting intervention and prevention research aimed at looking at identified victims of or those at risk of violence at earlier life stages and what can be accomplished from an individual, social ecological, and community perspective to prevent the pathways to perpetration or victimization later in life.

Social rejection or social isolation and lack of social support represent a set of interrelated risk factors that cut across areas of concern. Several chapters discussed the need for individuals to have more positive connections with helpful, involved, and concerned others to reduce the risk for violence. Parents who maltreat their children are more socially isolated in the community than other parents (whether by their own choice or by other circumstances) and report less social support from their friends and families. Couples who are involved in IPV are more often than not in this same situation. Children engaging in early aggressive and violent behaviors are quickly rejected by nonaggressive peers and are more likely than nonaggressive children to come from families that are socially isolated. Finally, those who engage in self-inflicted violence report extremely low levels of perceived social support. These issues suggest that interventions intended to increase the social connectedness of individuals, families, and communities may be a fruitful avenue to pursue in the course of engaging in truly primary prevention.

Though social ecological factors clearly are relevant risk factors for violent behavior, individual characteristics cannot be ignored and are often common to multiple types of violence covered here. Children with disabilities and children who exhibit disruptive and oppositional behaviors are more likely to be maltreated by their caregivers (see chap. 2, this volume) and are more likely to act out violently toward others (see chap. 5, this volume). Adults with a history of mental health and substance abuse problems are more likely than those without to be violent toward children, intimate partners, or themselves. Last, individuals who engage in any form of violence tend to report distorted attributions of others' behavior and higher levels of approval of violence than individuals who are not violent. Thus, the need becomes clear for better and early detection and assessments and for prevention approaches that intervene at multiple levels (i.e., individual, family, and social ecological). Such programs might be universal or targeted or a combination of both and must be evidence based.

Evaluation

There are a number of broad evaluation issues that traverse the topic areas of violence prevention covered here. Knowledge, attitudes, self- or other-reported behavior change, and direct observation of behavior change are important outcomes to examine in prevention and intervention research. Such data can shed light on the degree to which a given program has immediate effects on these variables. But unless data on reductions of violence can be shown, the overall impact of programs must be questioned. Outcome measures ultimately need to reflect clear change, that is, reductions of the prevalence of CM, YV, IPV, and suicide. In CM, for example, data from CPS (i.e., the number of county- or state-reported, substantiated incidents of CM) should be used in any applied research seeking to evaluate prevention or intervention programs in CM.

However, given the previously discussed biases in official records for all four types of violence, rigorous evaluation designs should also include outcome data from other sources (e.g., population-based or sample-specific survey data and service use data) to strengthen confidence in the results, conclusions, and future recommendations. As noted earlier in this chapter and other chapters in this volume, definition plays an important role in these outcome measures, because definitions are only useful if they can be operationalized and measured meaningfully. We therefore need to focus not only on developing new measures but also on continuing to improve extant core measures. In addition, in chapter 12, Reese, Vera, and Caldwell argue for the need to incorporate considerations of culture into evaluations to better understand the interplay of a complex array of cultural variables (i.e., beyond the one question about racial or ethnic background) with the intervention being evaluated, the outcome measures being used, and any resulting behavior change.

Participant attrition represents a serious problem for service programs and applied research programs alike (Hansen, Warner-Rogers, & Hecht, 1998). In many violence-related programs, 50% retention rates are the norm. That means that the sample is inherently biased in ways we might not understand and that at least one half of potential participants do not receive what may be an effective program for reducing violence. Thus, there is a need to formally study variables that affect attrition and retention in various populations and communities. The same rigorous empirical standards that should dictate outcome research in violence prevention should dictate efforts at understanding and improving recruitment and retention in these programs.

Overlooked by too many researchers and requests for proposals is the need for either formative research (i.e., evaluations intended to inform programmatic improvements) to lay the foundations for more sophisticated comparative outcome studies or the use of single-case research designs to serve a similar developmental purpose. Too frequently, interventions that have shown some efficacy may show little effectiveness because nuances of procedural or participant-related variables have not been examined or solved. The scope of this chapter and volume precludes a lengthy discussion of how such efforts could enhance subsequent outcome research, but the reader is referred to the following sources for a more complete presentation of the argument suggested here: Poling and Fuqua (1986); Rossi, Lipsey, and Freeman (2003); Shadish, Cook, and Leviton (1991).

The gold standard of evaluation in health promotion and disease prevention research has traditionally been the true experimental design (Chaffin, 2004). This is good, because such a design maximizes researchers' control over and ability to make causal inferences about the intervention being studied. There are a number of challenges in applied research on violence prevention that make randomization of individual participants to treatment and control groups and strict control over the intervention received difficult or less desirable. Hence, the experimental design must often be eschewed in favor of more feasible and palatable evaluation designs. For example, schools and service agencies (frequent settings for violence prevention programs) are rarely set up to allow a research team to randomly assign individuals to groups. Certain types of violence prevention programs are intended to target whole groups or communities (e.g., schoolwide bullying-prevention programs) rather than individuals, such that randomizing individuals would not actually test the hypothesis that an intervention can impact preexisting groups. In these and similar cases, group-randomized designs can be used if the researcher has access to a large enough sample to provide adequate statistical power to detect change. Alternatively, researchers often use a nonequivalent control group design, which becomes more rigorous as preexisting between-groups variance is reduced by careful group selection and statistical control over variables on which the groups differ.

The second main ingredient in the experimental design, strict control over the intervention being tested, also becomes more complicated in applied research compared with medical or clinical trials. With pharmaceutical studies, for example, clinical researchers ensure that participants receive the exact dosage (e.g., 30 mg, once per day) of the specified treatment. In the case of a program intended to decrease negative and increase positive parenting techniques, in contrast, applied researchers may not be able or willing to mandate either attendance or actual participation. Thus, the dosage of the intervention may differ greatly across participants, potentially reducing the impact of the intervention. Although a limitation to efficacy studies, this issue promotes the generalizability of the evaluation findings to how a program will perform in the real world, where program implementers are likely to face inconsistent participation and attendance rates with at least a small proportion of program participants.

Fidelity and Training

Any scientist with training in basic research design is aware of two possible errors in drawing inferences from a set of results. A Type I error has occurred when an effect is detected but none exists in the population (i.e., we conclude a program "worked" when it actually had no effect), whereas a Type II error has occurred when an effect is present in the population but was not detected by the methods used (i.e., we conclude that a program "did not work" when it did have the intended effect). However, it is quite likely that a program of applied research might appear to fail not because of design flaws or because the independent variable did not have potency but because of two other possible errors. One is the failure of those who implement the protocols to do so in the manner in which the protocols were designed or prescribed (Dobson & Cook, 1980). This is the problem of fidelity. To ensure fidelity, data must be collected on the reliable implementation of the independent variable. This should occur periodically throughout intervention, and interventionists must be corrected and retrained if fidelity is below acceptable levels. Thus, when there is independent variable integrity (intervention fidelity), if a program succeeds, there is more certainty that change has to do with the correctly implemented independent variable. Fidelity should include direct observation of the intervention by trained experts, and when possible, reliability data should be collected on the independent and dependent variables.

The second error that can occur is in the failure of those responsible for implementing the intervention to have met training criteria in the first place. For interventions that require individuals to interact with recipients of that program (e.g., parent training programs, anger management programs, and social skills programs), preset criteria for training should be established through validation by content experts or the use of master videotapes that show criterion performance. We recommend a protocol whereby the trainee first is exposed to written information on the independent variable and then must pass quizzes measuring knowledge of the material with a score of at least 90%. Scoring below 90% should require a review of the materials and alternative versions of the quizzes. After knowledge is demonstrated by passing the verbal (written) criteria, the trainee should be exposed to modeled (live or video) simulations of the intervention. Then, the trainee should be required to demonstrate these skills to a criterion of being able to perform the skills five times consecutively without corrective feedback. Finally, a trained interventionist should then shadow the newly trained interventionist in the field and provide corrective feedback until the new trainee is performing to criterion in the field. After that point, scheduled fidelity measures and possible booster training occurs. Applied research in violence prevention would be improved with adherence to this training model.

Efficacy, Effectiveness, and Dissemination

Efficacy has been defined as positive program outcomes and impacts when studied under controlled conditions; *effectiveness* has been defined as positive program outcomes and impacts when delivered in the real world (Flay, 1986). However, it is sometimes difficult to establish any clear lines between efficacy and effectiveness in applied research. For example, if efficacy is narrowly defined as a highly controlled environment, would a school-based YV prevention program that showed significant changes in outcome measures from a quasi-experimental design comparing only a few schools be considered an efficacious or effective program? What defines *highly controlled* will determine the answer. Schools are, experimentally speaking, very "sloppy" environments. Given the lack of control over dosage (because of student absences and moves into and out of a school) and content (because of differential buy-in or educational philosophies of teachers implementing the program) of the intervention, it is difficult to conceive of an applied school-based program that could truly be considered highly controlled. Yet, under rigid definitions, such research would not be defined as showing effectiveness, either, because of the small sample size and therefore extremely limited generalizability. Thus, perhaps another rubric and conceptual framework may be necessary in considering the continuum from program development, pilot or formative research, single-case research designs, small well-controlled studies, small less well-controlled studies, and large studies using a variety of appropriate quasi-experimental and experimental research designs to the process of "scaling-up" such work to much broader dissemination and replication efforts (Filene, Lutzker, Hecht, & Silovsky, 2005; Glasgow, Lichtenstein, & Marcus, 2003).

Replication and dissemination present a special set of research and evaluation considerations that impact how likely nonresearchers are to adopt programs with demonstrated efficacy or effectiveness. For example, if a suicide prevention program has had a number of positive outcomes with robust research designs and large sample sizes, but the programs have been run exclusively by university researchers, what variables influence whether whole school districts or community-based agencies are willing and able to replicate the program without the support of a university research base? A literature has developed stressing the numerous issues involved in accomplishing such a level of dissemination. A limited list of these issues includes organizational capacity to implement the program, acceptability of the program (to administrators, to those responsible for implementation, and to potential participants), the relative importance of different components to program outcomes, and cultural appropriateness of the program and its delivery methods (Filene et al., 2005). Thus, in the course of conducting efficacy and effectiveness studies, researchers should anticipate these and other issues related to future replication and dissemination and include relevant variables in the evaluations.

Economic Evaluation

In addition to information on efficacy and effectiveness, decisions to implement prevention programs should similarly be based on an intervention's economic efficiency. A program is economically efficient if benefits of the program are maximized while at the same time minimizing costs. Information on efficiency provides answers to such questions as what type of parenting intervention should be used to maximize the prevention of cases of CM, what is the proper mix of interventions that target batterers and interventions that target victims to reduce the overall incidence of IPV in the community, and what is the best way to allocate scarce public health resources across the population to ameliorate the rise of injuries and deaths associated with violence. Economic evaluation is one tool to answer questions regarding efficiency. Economic evaluation, which includes cost–benefit analysis (CBA), cost-effectiveness analysis (CEA), and cost-utility analysis (CUA) as a special variant of CEA, provides valuable information on costs and benefits that can be used by decision makers to assess program returns on investment (Haddix, Teutsch, & Corso, 2003; Owens, 2002).

All economic evaluations include some measure of costs, which can include the resources expended or forgone as a result of the intervention, for example, programmatic costs associated with a parenting program. Program costs from an economic perspective should be distinguished from those collected from a financial perspective. Financial costs typically include only those tangible goods and services that are itemized in a program's budget for which money has exchanged hands—for example, salaries and rent. Economic costs are the opportunity costs of the resources used to implement the intervention, for example, the value of resources such as volunteer time, had they been used for another purpose. Thus, program costs that include economic costs provide a more complete estimate of the resources required to implement a public health policy or program.

Another type of cost that can be included in an economic evaluation is the cost of the health outcome averted. Cost of illness or injury (COI) averted typically includes direct medical and nonmedical costs and productivity losses associated with lost time from work and loss of lifetime earnings because of premature mortality (Hodgson & Meiners, 1982; Rice, 1967; Rice, Hodgson, & Kopstein, 1985). For acute diseases and injury-related outcomes, measuring COI can be relatively straightforward, because the disease or injury period is short and involves very specific and easily defined medical and nonmedical resources. Measuring COI for chronic diseases or health outcomes that have latent effects, such as those associated with violent outcomes, can be more challenging (Daro, 1988; Fromm, 2001; Health Services Research, 2000; Irazuzta, McJunkin, Danadian, Arnold, & Zhang, 1997; Joint State Government Commission, 1995; Miller, Cohen, & Wiersema, 1996; Rovi, Chen, & Johnson, 2004).

For example, immediate and easily quantifiable costs associated with an incident of severe CM might include the use of medical care services such as inpatient and outpatient costs. Immediate and more difficult costs to quantify might include the use of CPS, the legal system, and productivity losses. However, CM might result in other lifetime costs that are not immediately apparent. For example, adults who were abused as children might experience lower earnings and more reliance on governmental support and services. A complete assessment of costs associated with a case of CM should presumably include all costs that occur over the child's lifetime that are both directly and indirectly caused by the adverse event(s). Further, COI analyses may be considered by some as an extreme underestimate of true costs because they do not include the value of hard-to-quantify costs such

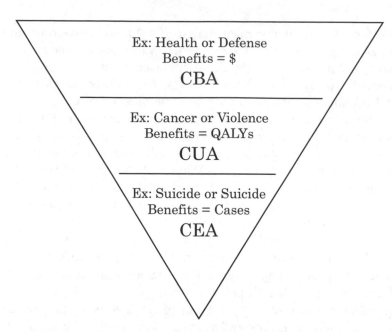

Figure 13.1. Tier of policy making, with examples from the broadest level through the narrowest level of funding decisions. The broadest level is where funding decisions are made between programs that do not necessarily have a common outcome measure. The second level is where funding decisions are made between programs that are similar in emphasis on health but dissimilar on outcome. The third, narrowest, level is where decisions are made between programs with similar outcomes. Ex = example; CBA = cost–benefit analysis; QALYs = quality-adjusted life years; CUA = cost-utility analysis; and CEA = cost-effectiveness analysis.

as pain and suffering. As such, alternative measures have been developed, including those that attempt to measure society's willingness to pay to reduce the risk of morbidity or mortality associated with a disease or injury.

The benefits of a program or intervention that prevents violent outcomes can be measured in monetary units, health-related units, or some other natural or physical unit. The valuation of program benefits depends on the type of economic evaluation being conducted, CBA, CUA, or CEA, which is determined in part by the perspective of the policymaker and the funding decisions that are required.

Figure 13.1 depicts three levels of policy making that differ on the basis of one's perspective and the programs and interventions between which funding decisions are made. At the broadest level of policy making, funding decisions are made between interventions that do not have a common outcome measure, such as programs intended to improve the public's health versus programs intended to bolster national security. To compare the costs and benefits of these disparate programs, benefits are converted into a common metric such as dollars for use in CBAs. The program with the greatest net benefits (i.e., program benefits less program costs) receives funding priority.

At the second level of policy making, funding decisions are made between interventions that are similar in their emphasis on health but dissimilar in their emphasis on health outcomes, such as cancer screening versus violence prevention. In this case, outcomes must be converted into a common health index, such as quality-adjusted life years (QALYs) for use in CUAs. The QALY index combines measures of survival (length of life) and morbidity (quality of life). The program with the greatest cost per QALY saved receives funding priority.

At the lowest level of policymaking, funding decisions are made between interventions with similar emphasis on health, such as between a school-based and a mass media suicide prevention program. In this case, outcomes do not need to be, but still could be, converted into dollars (for use in a CBA) or a health index (for use in CUAs). Instead, the outcome of interest remains in natural units, for use in CEAs, such that the program with the lowest cost per case prevented receives funding priority.

Although information on efficiency as measured by economic evaluation is increasingly recognized as essential for making violence prevention research more policy relevant, the research methods that have been used to date have generated a literature that says little about how much a program costs or about which programs deliver the best outcome for the least money.

At a minimum, program costs should be collected alongside any intervention that is being evaluated for effectiveness. For violence prevention interventions, in particular, a concerted effort should be made to collect and include the costs for participants, because attrition rates, especially for programs targeted to perpetrators, are likely to run high. Unfortunately, receiving federal grant money is not contingent on collecting program costs in most violence prevention interventions. And federal or other grant allotments are in many cases a poor proxy for total program dollars expended, including donated space and volunteer time.

It is often the case that when program costs are collected, they are only minimally compared with program benefits (Armstrong, 1983; Brooten et al., 1986; Karoly et al., 1998; Olds, Henderson, Phelps, Kitzman, & Hanks, 1993). This leads to a paucity of economic evaluations in the violence prevention community. One reason for this phenomenon might be that there is little evidence of effectiveness for most interventions, and therefore it is not timely to conduct an economic evaluation. Second, where evidence of effectiveness does exist, valuing benefits and costs might be too time and resource intensive and require expertise not readily available. For example, CUAs that use QALYs as the outcome measure may be scarce because of the problems with measuring quality of life in victims of violence. Additionally, measuring children's value of quality of life has inherent cognitive challenges that for other health outcomes, such as childhood cancers, can be avoided by having parents provide proxy values. But, in the case in which a child is maltreated by the parent, one cannot elicit values for a child's health from that parent. In CBA, benefits estimation is equally challenging.

More work has been done in the area of COI analyses, perhaps because this information is most often used to appeal for more prevention funding (Finkelstein & Corso, 2003). Most COI analyses have been limited, however, in their singular focus on the immediate health care impacts of violence and their limited focus on modeling lifetime costs. The broader macroeconomic impact of violent outcomes on family, community, and international behavior are rarely investigated.

Economic evaluation can easily be adapted to answer questions about the efficiency of violence prevention interventions. Unfortunately, a paucity of data regarding the application of economic evaluation to violence prevention still exists (Corso & Lutzker, in press). More investment in research dollars should be made to justify expenditure of scarce public health dollars toward violence prevention and to inform practitioners, researchers, and policymakers in this area.

Cultural Issues

In chapter 12, Reese, Vera, and Caldwell lay out many of the important concerns about the need to tailor programs and protocols that serve ethnic minority communities. These authors address the critical issue of applying science to cultural tailoring. Experts need to validate curricula that are adapted from forms that might not have been applied to a particular group. The development of new curricula for specific communities needs to undergo rigorous validation and testing processes. This issue also relates to the evaluation issues covered above. It would seem imprudent to develop any curriculum without conducting small systematic analyses of outcome before testing it at a broader group or community level. By conducting smaller analyses, problems with the curriculum can be corrected before implemented at the broader level.

Community input from the inception of a curriculum, a set of protocols, or an assessment tool is essential to improve the likelihood of stronger validation and community buy-in to a program. Additionally, there is no reason why training for interventionists or evaluators in cultural issues specific to a given racial or ethnic group cannot and should not be accomplished in a systematic fashion, addressing the same issues of training criteria and fidelity monitoring that should occur for the independent variable delivery. That is, in addition to independent variable integrity as discussed earlier, integrity to cultural issues can also be systematically monitored and corrective measures taken if interventionists and evaluators have fallen below criteria. Doing such would increase the likelihood of truly culturally relevant and responsive programs. Failure to design culturally relevant programs seriously reduces the likelihood of successful outcomes.

FUTURE RESEARCH AND PRACTICE IN VIOLENCE PREVENTION

Crosscutting Efforts

It would surely seem that with increased discussion of the practical relevance of attending to the crosscutting issues in violence prevention research (see chap. 3, this volume), subsequent service applications would spring forth. Failure to do so will inhibit the most effective prevention and intervention programs from being developed and evaluated. O'Leary and Woodin (chap. 11, this volume) mention the need for crosscutting efforts between CM and IPV. As noted in several places in this volume, the need for suicide prevention efforts to stem from research and service also relates to CM victimization, IPV victimization, YV victimization, and perpetration prevention. As etiology and surveillance data advance in the areas of violence prevention covered here, so should improved crosscutting research.

Primary Prevention

Violence itself is a negative event with negative medical, mental health, economic, and societal consequences and should be stopped. But, given that earlier experiences with violence (either as victim or as perpetrator) are often precursors of later experiences with violence (again, as victim or as perpetrator), the need for primary prevention becomes paramount. That is, by effectively preventing one type of violence (e.g., CM) before it occurs, the risk of a later type of violence (e.g., YV) occurring is decreased. Therefore, successful primary prevention should play a large part in future efforts to avert violence.

Elder Abuse

As the size of the elderly population has increased in recent years and is expected to continue to increase, mental health professionals must be ready to face an increase in cases of elder mistreatment. Research suggests that many of the same factors that influence the types of violence covered by this book also influence violence toward elders by their caregivers: poverty, social isolation, stress, mental health and substance abuse issues, and a history of experiencing or exhibiting violence (Ingram, 2004). It therefore follows that the same methods used to describe, define, and prevent CM, YV, IPV, and suicide can and should be applied to the study of elder abuse. Currently, the greatest research needs in this area fall into the early stages of the public health model: surveillance, etiology, and intervention research.

CONCLUSION

Violence prevention is a relatively young field and one that is clearly multidisciplinary. Comprehensive violence prevention will require increased collaboration across disciplines and between researchers and practitioners. More energy from advocacy groups and commitment from policymakers are needed, as well as a well-informed and committed public, who can add to the advocacy and commitment to change. Stronger efforts in surveillance, basic etiologic research; robust program, outcome, and economic evaluation; and well-tested dissemination will allow violence prevention to become increasingly effective so that, indeed, by the turn of the 22nd century there may be cause for reflection on how dramatically violence was reduced in the 21st century.

REFERENCES

Ards, S. D., Myers, S. L., Jr., Chung, C., Malkis, A., & Hagerty, B. (2003). Decomposing Black–White differences in child maltreatment. *Child Maltreatment, 8,* 112–121.

Armstrong, K. A. (1983). Economic analysis of a child abuse and neglect treatment program. *Child Welfare, 62,* 3–13.

Brooten, D., Kumar, S., Brown, L. P., Butts, P., Finkler, S. A., Bakewell-Sachs, S., et al. (1986). A randomized clinical trial of early hospital discharge and home follow-up of very-low-birth-weight infants. *New England Journal of Medicine, 315,* 934–939.

Centers for Disease Control and Prevention. (2000, October 27). Building data systems for monitoring and responding to violence against women: Recommendations from a workshop. *Morbidity and Mortality Weekly Report, 49*(RR11), 1–18.

Centers for Disease Control and Prevention. (2004). *Assessing health risk behaviors among young people: Youth risk behavior surveillance system 2004.* Atlanta, GA: National Center for Chronic Disease Prevention and Health Promotion.

Chaffin, M. (2004). Is it time to rethink Healthy Start/Healthy Families? *Child Abuse & Neglect, 28,* 589–595.

Corso, P. S., & Lutzker, J. (in press). Commentary: The need for economic evaluation in child maltreatment prevention research. *Child Abuse & Neglect.*

Daro, D. (1988). *Confronting child abuse research for effective program design.* New York: Free Press.

Dobson, D., & Cook, T. J. (1980). Avoiding Type III error in program evaluation: Results from a field experiment. *Evaluation and Program Planning, 3,* 269–276.

Drake, B., & Zuravin, S. (1998). Bias in child maltreatment reporting: Revisiting the myth of classlessness. *American Journal of Orthopsychiatry, 68,* 295–304.

Edwards, V. J., Anda, R. F., Felitti, V. J., & Dube, S. R. (2004) Adverse childhood experiences and health-related quality of life as an adult. In K. A. Kendall-Tackett (Ed.), *Health consequences of abuse in the family: A clinical guide for evidence-based practice* (pp. 81–94). Washington, DC: American Psychological Association.

Filene, J. H., Lutzker, J. R., Hecht, D., & Silovsky, J. (2005). Project SafeCare: Issues in replicating an ecobehavioral model of child maltreatment prevention. In K. Kendall-Tackett & S. Giacomoni (Eds.), *Child victimization* (pp. 18-1–18-18). New York: Civic Research Institute.

Finkelstein, E., & Corso, P. (2003). Cost-of-illness analyses for policy making: A cautionary tale of use and misuse. *Expert Review of Pharmacoeconomics and Outcomes Research, 3,* 367–369.

Flay, B. R. (1986). Efficacy and effectiveness trials (and other phases of research) in the development of health promotion programs. *Preventive Medicine, 15,* 451–474.

Fromm, S. (2001). *Total estimated cost of child abuse and neglect in the United States: Statistical evidence.* Chicago: Prevent Child Abuse America.

Garbarino, J. (1989). The incidence and prevalence of child maltreatment. In L. Ohlin & M. Tonry (Eds.), *Family violence* (pp. 219–262). Chicago: University of Chicago Press.

Glasgow, R. E., Lichtenstein, E., & Marcus, A. C. (2003). Why don't we see more translation of health promotion research to practice? Rethinking the efficacy-to-effectiveness transition. *Public Health Matters, 93,* 1261–1267.

Haddix, A. C., Teutsch, S. M., & Corso, P. S. (Eds.). (2003). *Prevention effectiveness: A guide to decision analysis and economic evaluation.* New York: Oxford University Press.

Hampton, R. L., & Newberger, E. H. (1989). Child abuse incidence and reporting by hospitals: The significance of severity, race and class. *American Journal of Public Health, 75,* 56–60.

Hansen, D. J., Warner-Rogers, J. E., & Hecht, D. B. (1998). Effectiveness of individualized behavioral intervention for maltreating families. In J. R. Lutzker (Ed.), *Handbook of child abuse research and treatment* (pp. 133–158). New York: Plenum Press.

Health Services Research. (2000). *Health care costs associated with violence in Pennsylvania.* Camp Hill, PA: Highmark.

Hodgson, T., & Meiners, M. (1982). Cost-of-illness methodology: A guide to current practices and procedures. *Health Society, 60,* 429–462.

Ingram, E. M. (2004). Expert panel recommendations on elder mistreatment using a public health framework. *Journal of Elder Abuse and Neglect, 15,* 45–65.

Irazuzta, J. E., McJunkin, J. E., Danadian, K., Arnold, F., & Zhang, J. (1997). Outcome and cost of child abuse. *Child Abuse & Neglect, 21,* 751–757.

Joint State Government Commission. (1995). *The cost of juvenile violence in Pennsylvania.* Harrisburg: General Assembly of the Commonwealth of Pennsylvania.

Karoly, L. A., Greenwood, P. N., Everingham, S. S., Hoube, J., Kilburn, M. R., Rydell, C. P., et al. (1998). *Investing in our children: What we know and don't know about the costs and benefits of early childhood interventions.* Santa Monica, CA: Rand.

Miller, T. R., Cohen, M. A., & Wiersema, B. (1996). *Victim costs and consequences: A new look.* Washington, DC: U.S. Department of Justice, National Institute of Justice.

National Center for Injury Prevention and Control. (2003). *Costs of intimate partner violence against women in the United States.* Atlanta, GA: Centers for Disease Control and Prevention.

Olds, D. L., Henderson, C. R., Jr., Phelps, C., Kitzman, H., & Hanks, C. (1993). Effects of prenatal and infancy nurse home visitation on government spending. *Medical Care, 31,* 155–174.

Owens, D. K. (2002). Analytic tools for public health decision making. *Medical Decision Making, 22*(5), S3–S10.

Poling, A., & Fuqua, R. W. (Eds.). (1986). *Research methods in applied behavior analysis: Issues and advances.* New York: Plenum Press.

Rice, D. P. (1967). Estimating the cost-of-illness. *American Journal of Public Health, 57,* 424–440.

Rice, D. P., Hodgson, T., & Kopstein, A. (1985). Economic cost-of-illness: Replication and update. *Healthcare Financing Review, 7,* 61–68.

Rossi, P. H., Lipsey, M. W., & Freeman, H. E. (2003). *Evaluation: A systematic approach.* Newbury Park, CA: Sage.

Rovi, S., Chen, P., & Johnson, M. S. (2004). The economic burden of hospitalizations associated with child abuse and neglect. *American Journal of Public Health, 94,* 586–590.

Saltzman, L. E., Fanslow, J. L., McMahon, P. M., & Shelley, G. A. (1999). *Intimate partner violence surveillance: Uniform definitions and recommended data elements.* Atlanta, GA: Centers for Disease Control and Prevention, National Center for Injury Prevention and Control.

Saltzman, L. E., Fanslow, J. L., McMahon, P. M., & Shelley, G. A. (2002). *Intimate partner violence surveillance: Uniform definitions and recommended data elements.* Atlanta, GA: Centers for Disease Control and Prevention, National Center for Injury Prevention and Control.

Shadish, W. R., Jr., Cook, T. D., & Leviton, L. C. (1991). *Foundations of program evaluation: Theories of practice*. Newbury Park, CA: Sage.

Thompson, M. P., Arias, I., Basile, K. C., & Desai, S. (2002). The association between childhood physical and sexual victimization and health problems in adulthood in a nationally representative sample of women. *Journal of Interpersonal Violence, 17*, 1115–1129.

AUTHOR INDEX

Numbers in italics refer to listings in the references.

Bugental, D. B., 59, 64
Buka, S. L., 51, 66
Bulik, C. M., 31, 44
Bunney, W. E., 227, 234
Burdick, N., 80, 90
Burgess, P., 229, 235
Burgos, G., 235
Burian-Fitzgerald, M., 153, 161
Burns, B. J., 228, 236
Burr, M., 126, 142
Burt, M. R., 205, 208
Busch, A. L., 258
Butchart, A., 152, 162
Butler, J., 269, 278
Buttell, F. P., 185, 189
Butts, P., 294
Buyske, S., 103, 124
Bybee, D. I., 180, 190, 196, 200, 206, 207, 208, 211

Cado, S., 35, 45
Cahn, T., 187, 191
Cain, D., 199, 210
Caine, E. D., 232
Calam, R., 34, 41
Calhoun, L. G., 221, 236
California Department of Education, 135, 141
Campbell, J. C., 201, 208, 210
Cantor, D., 126, 142
Caralis, P. V., 196, 208
Card, J., 52, 65
Cardarelli, A. P., 34, 43
Carlson, B. E., 247, 255
Carlson, V., 76, 89
Carlton, R. P., 258
Carr, J., 202, 208
Carrillo, J. E., 259, 276
Cartwright, N., 157, 161
Casas, J. F., 151, 161
Cascardi, M., 250, 254
Caspi, A., 99, 103, 104, 109, 118, 120, 121, 187, 189, 221, 235
Cassavia, E., 40
Catalano, R. F., 103, 106, 115, 118, 119, 126, 129, 131, 137, 139, 141, 143, 144, 271, 276
Cavanaugh, K., 197, 209
Center for the Study and Prevention of Violence, 276

Centers for Disease Control and Prevention, 4, 8, 9, 14, 97, 116, 135, 141, 178, 180, 182, 184, 189, 218, 223, 227, 231, 268, 276, 282, 294
Cerdá, M., 152, 162
Chaffin, M., 25, 28, 29, 39, 41, 50, 51, 53, 54, 59, 60, 64, 67, 285, 294
Chalk, R., 239, 255
Chamgers, M., 153, 165
Chapman, D. P., 35, 42
Charach, A., 159, 161
Chasan-Taber, L., 61, 64
Chaudry, N., 130, 141
Chen, H., 14
Chen, P., 289, 296
Chen, T., 220, 231
Chen, X., 84, 90
Cheyne, B., 43
Chiappetta, L., 220, 231
Child Abuse Prevention and Treatment Act, as amended, 42 U.S.C. §5101 et seq., 11, 14
Chung, C., 281, 294
Chung, I. J., 102, 105, 106, 109, 116
Cicchetti, D., 31, 46, 71, 75, 76, 82–84, 89, 110, 120, 122, 123, 227, 233
Clark, C., 72, 90
Clark, D., 220, 231
Clark, S. J., 205, 208
Clayton, S. L., 59, 67
Clements, M., 250, 256
Clifford, R. M., 86, 90
Clingempeel, W. G., 114, 118
Cohen, J. A., 35, 41
Cohen, M. A., 289, 296
Cohen, P., 14, 26, 41
Cohn, A. C., 58, 64
Coie, J. D., 101–103, 105, 107, 115, 116, 150, 164
Coker, A. L., 183, 189
Cole, P., 199, 210
Cole, R. E., 66, 121
Colenda, C. C., 234
Colloton, M., 47
Conduct Problems Prevention Research Group, 130, 131, 137, 139, 140, 141
Connelly, C. D., 29, 41
Conroy, J., 163
Conte, J. R., 33, 41

Dube, S. R., 26, 35, *42*, 248, *258*, 280, *295*
Duberstein, P. R., *232*
Dubowitz, H., 26, *42*
Duggan, A. K., 59, *64*
Dumas, J. E., 138, *142*
Dumka, L. E., 272, *278*
Dunford, F. W., 204, 206, *209*
D'Unger, A. V., 99, *116*
During, S. M., 52, *63*
Durkheim, E., 220, *232*
Dutton, D. G., 184–187, *189*, *190*
Dutton, M. A., 201, *209*, 241, *255*
Duys, D., 151, *164*
Dykman, R. A., 30, *40*
Dziuba-Leatherman, J., 24, 28, *43*, 49–50, 61, *64*

Earls, F., 111, *122*
Eccles, A., 57, *66*
Eckenrode, J. J., 66, 76, 89, *121*
Eckhardt, C. L., 187, *190*
Eddy, J. M., 131, *142*
Edelson, G. A., 35, *43*
Edgar, M., 52, *66*
Edleson, J. L., 51, *64*, 110, *117*, 197, 199, 203–205, *209*, *210*, *212*, 240, *255*
Edwards, T., *118*
Edwards, V. J., *42*, *232*, 280, *295*
Egeland, B., 24, 25, 27, *43*
Eggert, L. L., 224, 225, *232*, *236*
Egolf, B. P., 31, *44*
Ehrensaft, M. K., 9, *14*, 185, *190*
Ehrhardt, K. E., 81, *89*
Eisenstadt, T. H., 53, *64*, *66*
El-Bayoumi, G., 201, *209*
Ellerson, P. C., *64*
Elliott, A., *117*
Elliott, D. M., 9, *14*
Elliott, D. S., 100, 101, 105, 111, 112, 113, *121*, 136, *144*, *117*, *124*, 125, 126, 130, 137, *142*
Ellis, M., 131, *144*
Embry, D. D., 131, *142*
English, D. J., 25, *45*
Ennett, G., *96*
Ensminger, M., 101, *121*
Entwisle, D., 75, *89*
Epstein, D., 197, *209*

Erickson, M. F., 24, 25, 27, *43*
Eriksson, A., 224, *234*
Eron, L. D., 99, *118*
Esbensen, F., 105, *118*
Espelage, D. L., 36, 38, *41*, *43*, 132, *141*
Espinosa, M., 52, *65*
Espiritu, R., 105, *118*
Everett Jones, S., *122*
Everingham, S. S., *296*
Everson, M. D., 35, *43*
Eyberg, S., 53, *64*, *66*
Eyeson-Annan, M. L., 219, *231*

Faccia, K., 137, *141*
Fagan, A., 113, *121*, 136, *144*
Fagan, J. A., 185, 187, *190*
Famularo, R., 30, *43*
Fanshel, D., 52, *67*
Fanslow, J. L., 173, *193*, 282, *296*
Fantuzzo, J. F., *90*
Fantuzzo, J. W., 72–73, 76, 78–85, 89–90, *91*
Faragher, E. B., 227, *231*
Farnworth, M., 110, *123*
Farrell, A. D., 127, 129, 132, 133, 136–139, *142–144*
Farrington, D. P., 98–100, 102–104, 107–110, 112, 113, 115, *117*, *118*, 120, *122*, *123*, 126, 144, 152, *162*
Favazza, A., *143*
Feder, L., 204, 206, *209*
Fein, R., 153, *165*
Feldbau-Kohn, S., 186, *193*, 247, *258*
Feldberg, C., 229, *231*
Feldman, R. S., 31, *46*
Felitti, V. J., 26, 35, *42*, 220, *232*, 248, *258*, 280, *295*
Felner, R. D., 126, 132, 134, *143*
Fenton, T., 30, *43*
Fergusson, D. M., 33, *43*, 115, *117*, 226, *232*
Fernandez, Y. M., 56, *66*
Ferris, J. A. J., *236*
Fetrow, R. A., 131, *142*
Fiedler, J., 180, *192*
Figueredo, A. J., 247, *256*
Filene, J. H., 288, *295*
Fine, D. N., 131, *143*
Finkelhor, D., 24, 28, 29, 33–35, *40*, *41*, *43*, *44*, *46*, 49–51, 60–61, *64–65*

Graham-Bermann, S. A., 110, *119*
Green, A. R., 259, *276*
Green, L. F., 81, *90*
Greenberg, M. T., 157, *161*
Greene, B. F., 29, *45*, 242, *256*
Greenfield, D. B., 72, *90*
Greenwald, E., 35, *45*
Greenwood, P. N., *296*
Griffin, M., 129, *144*
Griffith, E. H., 219, *233*
Grills, A. E., 37, *44*
Grossman, D. C., 130, *143*
Gruber, K. J., 153, *161*
Grunbaum, J. A., 125, *143*, 152, *161*
Grundy, J. F., 52, *67*
Grusec, J. E., 30, *44*
Gu, K., *143*
Guarrera, J., *45*
Guerra, N. G., 100, 105, *122*, *124*, 127,
    129, 137, *143*, *145*
Guevremont, D. C., 52, *63*
Guze, S. B., 219, *233*

Haapala, D. A., 26, *40*
Haddix, A. C., 289, *295*
Hage, S. M., 267, *277*
Hagen, C. A., 126, *142*
Hagerty, B., 281, *294*
Hahn, R. A., 114, *117*
Haileyesus, T., 9, *14*
Halsey, S., *47*
Hamberger, L. K., 187, *190*, 240, 241,
    243, *255*
Hamburg, B., 125, *142*
Hamby, S. L., 29, *46*, 246, *258*
Hammer, M., 31, *46*
Hammond, W. R., 132, *143*
Hampton, G., 80, 81, *90*
Hampton, R. L., 185, 188, *190*, 281, *295*
Hampton, V., 85, *89*
Hangaduambo, S., 151, *164*
Hanks, C., 291, *296*
Hansen, D. J., 30, 33, *44*, *45*, 113, *121*,
    136, *144*, 285, *295*
Hansen, K. V., 187, *190*
Hanson, K. W., 228, *233*
Hanson, R. K., 55, 57, *65*
Hantman, I., 126, *142*
Harachi, T. W., *118*
Harding, K., 59, *64*

Harkell, G., 197, *208*
Harms, T., 86, *90*
Harrington, H., 104, *121*
Harris, A. J. R., *65*
Harris, E. C., 219, *233*
Harris, K. M., *235*
Harrop, J. W., 188, *190*
Hart, B. J., 20, *22*, 205, *210*
Hartley, C. C., 51, *65*
Hasbrouck, L., 264, *278*
Hastings, J. E., 187, *190*
Haugaard, J., *67*
Hausman, A., 134, *143*
Hawker, D. S., 153, *162*
Hawkins, D. L., 159, *162*
Hawkins, J. D., 99, 102, 103, 106, 113,
    115, *116*, *118*, *119*, 126, 129,
    131, 139, *141*, *143*, *144*, *161*,
    271, *276*
Hay, D. F., 101, 102, *120*
Hay Group, 228, *233*
Haywood, Y., 201, *209*
Health Services Research, 289, *295*
Healy, D., *232*
Heath, J. L., *143*
Hecht, D. B., 285, 288, *295*
Heflin, A., 32, 36, *42*
Henderson, C. R., Jr., 66, *121*, 291, *296*
Henggeler, S. W., 55, *64*, 114, *118*, 272,
    276, *277*
Henke, R. R., 84, *90*
Hennen, J., 226, *236*
Henriques, G., 226, *233*
Henry, B., 103, *118*
Henry, D. B., 139, *144*
Herbert, P., *232*
Hernandez, P., *277*
Herrenkohl, E. C., 31, *44*
Herrenkohl, R. C., 31, *44*
Herrenkohl, T. I., 103, 108, *118*, *119*
Herrmann, J. H., *232*
Hersen, M., 32, *42*, *46*
Heyman, R. E., 28, *41*, 51, *67*, 185–187,
    190, *193*, 247, *258*
Heyne, D., *44*
Hildyard, K. L., 27, *44*
Hill, C. L., 272, *278*
Hill, K. G., 102, 106, *115*, *116*, *118*
Hill, R., 53, *64*
Hinshaw, S. P., 227, *233*
Hipwell, A. E., 115, *118*

McPherson, W. B., 30, *40*
McRae, B., 35, *41*
McReynolds, L., *163*
McWayne, C., 81, *90*
Mederos, F., 240, *254*
Mednick, S. A., 103, *122*
Meiners, M., 289, *295*
Melbin, A., 199, *210*
Melikian, M., 225, *232*
Mellsop, G. W., 219, *231*
Meltzer, H. Y., 226, *234*
Menard, A., 199, *210*
Menard, S., 105, *117*
Mendler, A. N., 156, *161*
Mercy, J. A., 3, *14*, 114, *117*, 152, *162*, 175, *192*, 273, *277*
Metropolitan Area Child Study Research Group, 136, 139, 140, *144*
Meyer, A. L., 127, 129, 132, 133, 136–139, *142–144*, 269, *277*
Meyer, S. L., 187, *192*
Meyers, J. E. B., 32, *45*
Meyers, R., *90*
Michel, K., 229, *234*
Mickus, M., *234*
Middleton, K. A., *258*
Mihalic, S. F., 113, 114, *121*, 136, 138, *144*, 154, *163*, 272, *277*
Miller, A. K., 31, 37, 40, *42*, *161*
Miller, E. N., 32, *42*, 251, *255*
Miller, L. S., 127, 137, *145*
Miller, T. R., 289, *296*
Miller-Johnson, S., 107, *116*
Miller-Perrin, C., 25–27, *45*
Mills, R., 30, *44*
Milne, B. J., 104, *121*
Milner, J. S., 30, *42*, *45*
Minnesota Department of Health, 180, *192*
Mitchell, A. J., 226, *234*
Mitchell, M. E., 221, *236*
Mitchell, M. S., 245, *257*
Mittelman, M. S., *63*
Modestin, J., 227, *234*
Modzeleski, W., 153, *165*
Moffitt, T. E., 99, 100, 103, 104, 109, 110, *118*, 120, *121*, 134, *144*, 187, *189*
Mohr, W., 72–73, *90*
Molnar, B. E., 51, *66*

Moore, D. W., 29, *46*
Morenoff, J. D., 111, 112, *121*, *122*
Moriarty, A. E., 222, *234*
Moritz, G. M., *231*
Moro, P. E., 56, *66*
Morris, P., 71, *89*
Morrison, D. M., *118*, *143*
Morrissey-Kane, E., *277*
Mulder, R. T., 224, *231*
Mullen, P. E., 33, *43*, *44*
Mullins, M. J., 30, *42*
Mulsant, B. H., *231*
Multisite Violence Prevention Project, 133, 139, 140, *144*, *145*, 156, *163*, 269, *277*
Mulvey, E. P., 103, *116*
Murphy, A., 201, *210*
Murphy, C. M., 187, *192*
Murphy, L. B., 222, *234*
Murphy, S. L., 97, *119*, 218, *233*
Murphy, W. D., 63, *65*
Murray, N., 159, *163*
Murtaya, N., 205, *207*
Musialowski, R., 196, *208*
Myers, L. J., *277*
Myers, S. L., Jr., 281, *294*
Myerson, N., *44*
Mytton, J. A., 155, *163*

Nagin, D. S., 99, 102, 103, 104, *116*, *121*
Nansel, T. R., 36–38, *45*, 151, *163*
Nation, M., 260, 264, *277*
National Association of School Psychologists, 147, *163*
National Center for Children in Poverty, 70, *90*
National Center for Health Statistics, *234*
National Center for Injury Prevention and Control, 9, *14*, 115, *121*, *296*
National Council of Juvenile and Family Court Judges, 199, *210*
National Institute for Occupational Safety and Health, 220, *234*
National Institute of Child Health and Human Development, Early Child Care Research Network, 77, *90*

National Institute of Mental Health, 70, 73, *91*
National Research Council, 111, *121,* 196, 203, 206, 207, *210*
Naumann, P., 201, *210*
Neckerman, H. J., *143*
Neidig, P. H., 250, *256*
Nelson, C., 57, *66*
Nelson, S., 133, *142*
Neutel, C. I., 226, *234*
Newberger, E. H., 39, *45*, 247, *256*, 281, *295*
Newcomb, K., 53, *64, 66*
Newman, D. A., 149, 157, 158, *163*
Newman, T. B., 226, *234*
Newman-Carlson, D., 155, 157, *162*
Newton, J. E. O., 30, *40*
Newton, P. J., *208*
Nichols, E., 261, *277*
Nixon, J., 197, *208*
Noonan, M., *161*
Noonan, N., *143*
Nordenberg, D., *232*
Norris, F. H., 197, *207*
Northup, W., 127, *144*
Nurius, P. S., 52, *66*

Oakes, J., 111, *121*
O'Brien, K., 248, *255*
O'Brien, M. U., *161*
O'Donnell, J., *118, 143*
O'Hara, N., *64*
O'Keefe, M., 246, 247, *256*
Oklahoma State Department of Health, 180, *192*
Olafsson, R. F., 148, *164*
Olds, D. L., 58, 59, *66*, 114, *121, 291, 296*
Oldsmith, S. K., 227, *234*
O'Leary, K. D., 174, 185–187, *189, 190, 192*, 240, 241, 245, 246, 248, 250, 251, *256, 257*
O'Leary, S. G., 243, 245, 246, 249, *257, 258*
Ollendick, T. H., 37, *44*
Olson, J. J., 139, *141*
Olweus, D., 36–38, *45*, 99, *121*, 133, *145*, 149, 150, 154, 158, *163*
O'Moore, M., 153, *163*
Ondersma, S. J., 50, *67*

Oregon Department of Human Services, 180, *192*
Orpinas, P., 148, 149, 152, 155–157, 159, *162, 163*
Ortega, R., 155, *164*
Ostrom, M., 223, 224, *231, 234*
Overpeck, M., *45, 163*
Owens, D. K., 289, *296*

Pagelow, M. D., 186, 188, *192*
Paikoff, R. L., 266, *278*
Paine, M. L., 33, *45*
Painter, S., 184, *190*
Pape, K. T., 184, *189*
Parcel, G. S., *162*
Parsons, B. V., 52, *63*
Path, M. R. C., *236*
Patten, S. B., 226, *234*
Patterson, C. J., 110, *116*
Patterson, G. R., 30, *45*, 104, 107, *116, 122*
Paymar, M., 204, *210*
Pearson-Clarke, T., 114, *117*
Pedersen, P. B., 261, *277*
Peled, E., 197, 199, *210*
Pellegrini, A. D., 38, *45*, 150, *164*
Pellmar, T. C., 227, *234*
Pence, E., 204, *210*, 241, 243, *257*
Penn, C. E., 187, *193*
Penn, D. L., 227, 228, *232*
Pepler, D. J., 149, 159, *160–162*
Perkins, R., 224, *236*
Perlick, D. A., *235*
Perper, J. A., *231*
Perrin, R. D., 25–27, *45*
Perry, D. G., 38, *44*, 150, *164*
Perry, L. C., 150, *164*
Perry, M. A., 82, *90*
Perryman, D., 202, *208*
Pescosolido, B. A., 228, *235*
Peter, K., *42, 161*
Peters, S. D., 33, *47*
Petersen, A., 132, *142*
Peterson, P. L., *115*
Peterson, R. D., 111, *122*
Petrona, L., 180, *192*
Pettit, G. S., 31, *42, 116, 119*
Phelps, C., 291, *296*
Phillips, D. A., 69, *91*

Rossman, B. B., 51, 67
Roth, C., *231*
Roth, J. A., 111, *122*
Rothery, M. A., 197, 198, *212*
Rouleau, J. L., *63*
Rovi, S., 289, *296*
Roy, A., 219, *235*
Ruan, W. J., *45, 163*
Ruddy, S. A., 37, 40, *42*
Runtz, M., 35, *41*
Runyan, D. K., 29, 46, 35, *43*
Runyon, M. K., 31–32, *46*
Rushe, R., *191*
Rutter, M., 221, 222, *235*
Rutz, W., 225, *235*
Ryan, E. E., 32, *46*
Ryan, J. A. M., 129, *141*, 271, *276*
Rydell, C. P., *296*

Sackeim, H. A., 226, *235*
Salkever, D. S., *64*
Salmivalli, C., 149, *164*
Saltzman, L. E., 173, 177, 183, 188, 189, *193*, 282, *296*
Salzer Burks, V., *116*
Salzinger, S., 26, 31, *41*, *46*
Samios, M., 174, *189*
Samples, F., 127, 130, 134, 137, 140, *141, 145*
Sampson, R. J., 111, 112, *117, 121, 122*
Sanderson, M., *189*
Sandler, J., 52, *68*
Sarason, B. R., 222, *235*
Sarason, R. G., 222, *235*
Sarvela, P. D., 151, *164*
Saunders, D., 204, *211*
Sauzier, M., 34, *43*
Schechter, S., 195, 197, *211*, 240, *257*
Scheidt, P., *45, 163*
Schewe, P., 197, *208*
Schmidt, F. L., 140, *144*
Schneider, B. H., 151, *164*
Schneider, E. C., 228, *231*
Schneider, E. M., 201, *211*
Schneiderman, N., 175, *193*
Schneiger, A., 133, *142*
Schock, M. D., 203, *209*
Schulberg, H. C., *231*
Schulte, M. M., 205, *208*

Schultz, L. H., 130, *145*
Schumacher, J. A., 186, *193*, 247, 248, *257, 258*
Schwartz, D., 150, *164*
Schwartz, H. A., 245, *256*
Schwarzenbach, F. A., 227, *234*
Schweers, J., *231*
Scott, C., 97, *119*, 218, *233*
Sedlak, A. J., 24, 28, 29, 33, 39, *46*, 70, *91*, 197, *211*
Sedlar, G., 30, *44*
Sekino, Y., 81, *90*
Seligman, M. E. P., 222, *235, 260, 278*
Selman, R. L., 130, *145*
Senchak, M., 187, *191*
Seracini, A. M., 108–110, *124*
Serna, P., *234*
Seto, M. C., *65*
Seybolt, D., *277*
Shadish, W. R., Jr., 285, *297*
Shannon, H. S., *66*
Shapiro, S., *232*
Sharp, S., 155, *164*
Shelley, G. A., 173, *193*, 282, *296*
Shepard, M., 206, *211*
Sheridan, D. J., 201, *211*
Sherrod, L. R., 72, *91*
Shields, A., 110, *122*
Shim, M., *143*
Shipman, K. L., 51, *67*
Shonkoff, J. P., 69, *91*
Shriver, T. P., 222, *236*
Siegel, B. R., 242, *255*
Sigel, I. E., 73, *91*
Silovsky, J., 64, 288, *295*
Silva, P. A., 99, 103, *118, 121*, 187, *189*
Silver, H. K., 6, *14*, 174, *191*
Silverman, F. N., 6, *14*, 174, *191*
Silvernail, D. L., 153, *164*
Simon, B., 221, *230*
Simon, T. R., 36, 38, *41, 43*, 152, *161*
Simons-Morton, B., *163*
Simons-Morton, S., *45*
Sirey, J. A., 228, *235*
Sitzman, R., 35, *41*
Sjostrom, L., 149, *164*
Skinner, M. L., 107, *116*
Skopek, M. A., 224, *236*
Slaby, R. G., 105, *122*
Slack, K. S., 26, *46*

SUBJECT INDEX

317

CPA treatment interventions, *continued*
    group parenting classes/support, 52
    multisystemic therapy, 54–55
    parent–child interaction therapy, 53–54
    Project 12-Ways/Project SafeCare, 54
CPPRG (Conduct Problems Prevention Research Group), 137
CPS. *See* Child protective services
Crime surveys, 181
Criminality, family, 109
Criminal justice system, 50
Criminal legal-focused interventions, 201–203
CRISP (Computer Retrieval of Information for Scientific Projects), 244
Cross-cutting issues, 213–215, 293
CSA. *See* Child sexual abuse
CSA treatment interventions, 55–57
    CBSOS, 56
    effectiveness of, 57
    surgical/pharmacological, 56–57
CUA. *See* Cost-utility analysis
Culhane, Dennis, 87
Cultural competence, 265–267
Cultural relevance, 264–265
Culture, 10, 72–73, 259–276
    and battered women's shelters, 198
    and batterer intervention programs, 205
    complexity of, 261–262
    definition of, 261
    issues related to, 292–293
Culture-centered research, 267
Culture in violence prevention
    and APA's multicultural guidelines, 266–270
    conceptualizing/operationalizing, 262–263
    and cultural competence, 265–266
    and cultural relevance, 264–265
    importance of, 261–262
    and social epidemiology/ecology, 270–271
Cyproterone acetate, 56–57

Dating violence, 134, 242
Death(s)
    from suicide, 9, 217, 218
    from violence, 3

Decision-making responsibilities, 187
"Deep structure modifications," 269
Denmark, 152
Denver Youth Survey, 100, 106
Depression
    and child physical abuse, 29, 30
    and peer abuse, 153
    in sex offenders, 57
    and suicide, 219, 221
Developmental stage of target population, 127, 128
Diagnostic and Statistical Manual of Mental Disorders, 245
Disruptive behavior disorder, 103
Dissemination of findings, 176, 288
Divalproex, 226
Division of Veterans' Affairs (DVA), 230
Division of Violence Prevention (of NCIPC), 4, 177, 268
DOJ. *See* U.S. Department of Justice
Domestic violence, 12, 173
Duluth program, 241
Dunedin (New Zealand) Multidisciplinary Health and Development Study, 103–104
DVA (Division of Veterans' Affairs), 230

Early child-care experiences, 78–79
Early childhood educational experiences, 77
Early Childhood Environment Rating Scale—Revised Edition (ECERS–R), 86
ECERS–R (Early Childhood Environment Rating Scale—Revised Edition), 86
Ecological models
    of child abuse, 242
    of development/prevention, 271
Economic evaluation, 288–292
ECT. *See* Electroconvulsive therapy
Educational neglect, 25
Effectiveness, 287–288
Efficacy, 287–288
Elder abuse, 293–294
Elderly, suicide and, 227, 229
Electroconvulsive therapy (ECT), 225, 226

Elementary schools
    bullying in, 152
    violence prevention programs in,
        130–132
Emic norms, 265
Emotional abuse, 180
Emotional neglect, 25
Endangerment (term), 28
England, 152
Epidemiologic Catchment Area survey,
    25, 28
Errors, 286–287
Estrogens, 56
Ethnicity, neglect related to, 26
Ethnic minority communities, 10
    health disparities in, 259–260
    and neglect, 29
Etic norms, 265
Etiology, 282–284
Evaluation studies, 137–139, 176,
    284–286
Evolve, 205
Expulsion, school, 112

Failure to thrive, 25
Family, youth violence and, 108–110
Family Connections, 53
Family management, poor, 108
Family management training, 131
Family-of-origin factors, 247–248
    and child physical abuse, 29
    and neglect, 26
Family preservation and reunification
        models, 53
Family Resource Room, 133
Family surveys, 181–182
Family therapy (FT), 54
Family violence, 242
Fast Track, 131–132
Federal Bureau of Investigation, 7, 181
Females
    aggressive, 241–243
    and peer abuse, 37–38
Feminist theory, 185–186, 240–241, 250
Fidelity, 286–287
Fights on school property, 152
Finland, 153
Firearm legislation, 224
First response teams (for battered
        women), 202–203

Fluoxetine, 57
Food and Drug Administration, 226
Formal child care, 78
Formative research, 285
Friendships, 38, 153
FT (family therapy), 54
Funding, lack of, 244–245

Gangs, 106, 266, 267
Gatekeeper training, 225
Gender (of perpetrator)
    bullying behavior, 151
    and child physical abuse, 29, 50
    and child sexual abuse, 50
    and family-of-origin factors, 248
    and peer abuse, 36–38
    and youth crime, 100–101
Gender (of victim)
    and child physical abuse, 29, 50
    and child sexual abuse, 33, 50
    from IPV, 173–174, 180
    and suicide, 218–219
General attributional style, 30–31
Germany, 152
Good Behavior Game, 158
Gossiping, 150
GREAT Schools and Family Program,
        133–134
Greenland, 152
Grid model for classifying school-based
        youth violence prevention,
        126–130
Grooming, 33
"Guidelines on Multicultural Education,
        Training, Research, Practice, and
        Organizational Change for
        Psychologists" (APA), 266–270
Guns, suicide and, 224

Handbook of Child Abuse Research and
        Treatment (Lutzker), 239
Handguns, 224
Harm (term), 28
Harm reduction, 61–62
Hawaii Healthy Start, 58, 59
Head Start, 79–84
Health care settings
    and intimate partner violence, 201
    and suicide prevention, 228–229

Healthy Families America, 58, 59
Healthy People 2010 campaign, 244,
  260
Healthy Start Program, 58, 59
Helplessness, 222
High schools
  bullying in, 152
  violence prevention programs in,
    134–135
Hispanics
  and child physical abuse, 29
  homicide among, 263
  and neglect, 26
Homebuilders, 53
Home visitation, 58–60, 114
Homicides
  intimate-partner committed, 181
  in schools, 125
  in U.S., 97
Hospitalization for suicidal behavior,
  226–227
Housing programs, transitional, 199
Hyperactivity, 103–104

Imitation, suicide, 223
Immigrant women, 198
Implementation of interventions, 176
Indicated interventions, 13, 113, 114,
  127, 128, 250
Individual interventions, 130
Informal child care, 78
Informed consent document, 243
Injuries
  from intimate partner violence, 174,
    180, 182–183
  from violence, 3
Injury Research Agenda (NCIPC), 9
Institute of Medicine (IOM), 229, 230
Integration of child and partner abuse
    agendas, 174, 239–254
  conditional probabilities of child and
    partner aggression as evidence
    for, 246–247
  co-occurrence of child and partner
    abuse as evidence for, 245–246
  evidence supporting, 245–249
  lack of funding as barrier to,
    244–245
  legal reporting requirements as
    barriers to, 243

model differences as barriers to,
  240–243
preventive implications of, 249–253
reasons for independence of fields,
  240–245
theoretical conceptualizations of risk
  markers as evidence for, 247–249
Intention, 153
Intervention(s), 49–63
  child abuse prevention. *See* Child
    abuse prevention
  culturally-appropriate, 268
  definition of, 12–13
  future of, 62–63
  integrating child-/partner-abuse,
    249–253
  intimate-partner. *See* IPV
    interventions
  multiple domains of influence
    incorporated in, 113
  need for better, 136–137
  need for better evaluations of,
    137–139
  suicide. *See* Suicide prevention
  targets/intensity of, 113
  timing of, 112–113
  treatment, 51–57
Intimate partner violence (IPV), 3,
  169–171
  and child abuse. *See* Integration of
    child and partner abuse agendas
  complexity of problem, 179
  conditional probabilities of child
    abuse and, 246–247
  co-occurrence of child abuse and,
    245–246
  and culture, 263
  data regarding, 4, 8, 174
  definitions of, 12, 173–174
  etiology of, 184–188
  interpersonal factors of, 187
  intrapersonal factors of, 186–187
  laws requiring action on, 243
  models of, 240–242
  physical, 182–183
  psychological, 183–184
  and public health, 174–176
  rates of, 180
  sensitive nature of, 178–179
  sexual, 169, 183
  sociocultural factors of, 188

School Transitional Environment
Project, 134
Seattle Social Development Project, 113,
131
Second Step Program, 130
Security cameras, 134
Security measures, 134–135
Selective interventions, 13, 113
Selective prevention approach, 114
Selective programs, 127, 128
Selective serotonin reuptake inhibitors
(SSRIs), 226–227
Self-agency, 267
Self-directed violence, 9
Self-esteem, 153
Self-inflicted injuries, 4
Separatist phenomenon, 239–240
Sertraline, 57
Seville, 155
Sex offenders, 34, 56
Sexual abuse prevention, 60–62
Sexual assault, 169
Sexual bullying, 149, 150
Sexual intimate partner violence, 183
Sheffield Project, 155
Shelter programs (for battered women),
197–198
Smart Talk, 132
SOAR (Suicide Options Awareness and
Relief), 225
Social–cognitive deficits, 105, 107
Social epidemiology, 270–271
Social isolation, 150, 188, 283–284
Social learning model, 30
Social rejection, 107
Social system levels, 127–129
Socioeconomic status, 282–283
and child physical abuse, 28–29, 70
and intimate partner violence, 188
and neglect, 26
South Carolina, 275
SSRIs. *See* Selective serotonin reuptake
inhibitors
Stigma
and intimate partner violence,
178–179
and suicide treatment, 227–228
Stigma reduction, 72–73
STOP IT NOW!, 61
Student education about bullying,
158–159

Students for Peace, 152
Substance abuse
and child–partner abuse link,
248–249
and child physical abuse, 29
parental, 109
and suicide, 220, 228
Substance Abuse and Mental Health
Services Administration
(SAMHSA), 230
Suffolk County (New York), 246
Suicidal behaviors, 9, 226
Suicidal ideation, 153
Suicidal thoughts, 229
Suicide, 217–230
and barriers to treatment, 227–229
biological factors in, 219
and culture, 263
data regarding, 9
definition of, 12
epidemiology of, 217–219
interventions for, 222–227
number of reports of, 4
protective factors against, 220–222
psychological/psychiatric, 219–220
risk factors for, 219–220
Suicide Ideation Questionnaire, 224
Suicide Options Awareness and Relief
(SOAR), 225
Suicide prevention, 9, 213–214, 222–227
indicated, 225–227
integrated, 227
research about, 10, 11
selective, 224–225
universal, 223–224
Suicide Prevention Programs for Rural
American Indian Communities,
227
Supervision
and bullying, 158
and youth violence, 108–109
Support groups, 197–198
Support networks
and neglect, 27
and peer abuse, 38
"Surface structure modifications," 269
Surgical interventions for sex offenders, 56
Surveillance, 281–282
of intimate partner violence,
177–184
public health, 175–176

developmental pathways leading to,
98–102
implications for prevention of,
112–114
number of reports of, 4
predictors of, 102–112

Youth violence prevention
implications for, 112–114
research about, 10–11
school-based, 7–8, 125–141
YRBS. *See* Youth Risk Behavior Survey
YV. *See* Youth violence

ABOUT THE EDITOR

John R. Lutzker, PhD, received his degree from the University of Kansas. He is currently executive director of the Marcus Institute, Atlanta, Georgia; he previously served as distinguished consultant and chief, Prevention Development and Evaluation Branch of the Division of Violence Prevention, National Center for Injury Prevention and Control, Centers for Disease Control and Prevention, Atlanta, Georgia. He was the Florence and Louis Ross Distinguished Professor and chair of the Department of Psychology and director of graduate training in behavioral psychology at the University of Judaism in Bel Air, California (1988–2001) and also served as acting provost of the university. He is also an adjunct professor of applied behavioral science at the University of Kansas and was president of Behavior Change Associates, Agoura Hills, California.

Dr. Lutzker has published over 120 professional articles and chapters and has presented over 350 professional papers. He is a fellow of the American Psychological Association (Divisions 25, 33, 37, 53) and is a clinical fellow of the Behavior Therapy and Research Society. He is a past editor of *The Behavior Therapist* and the *APA Division 25 Recorder*. He has been associate editor of *Education and Treatment of Children* and is currently on the editorial boards of the *Journal of Family Violence*, the *Journal of Behavior Therapy and Experimental Psychiatry*, *Child and Family Behavior Therapy*, and *Behavioral Interventions*. Dr. Lutzker was coauthor of *Behavior Change, Ecobehavioral Family Interventions in Developmental Disabilities*, and *Reducing Child Maltreatment: A Guidebook for Parent Services*. He was editor of the *Handbook of Child Abuse Research and Treatment*. His current major research interests are intervention and prevention of child maltreatment and other forms of violence. He is a recipient of the James M. Gaudin Outstanding Research Award from the Georgia Professional Society on the Abuse of Children and the Alumni Distinguished Achievement Award from the University of Kansas.